Attribution in International Law and Arbitration

Attribution in International Law and Arbitration

CARLO DE STEFANO

OXFORD
UNIVERSITY PRESS

OXFORD
UNIVERSITY PRESS

Great Clarendon Street, Oxford, OX2 6DP,
United Kingdom

Oxford University Press is a department of the University of Oxford.
It furthers the University's objective of excellence in research, scholarship,
and education by publishing worldwide. Oxford is a registered trade mark of
Oxford University Press in the UK and in certain other countries

First Edition published in 2020

Impression: 1

Published in the United States of America by Oxford University Press
198 Madison Avenue, New York, NY 10016, United States of America

British Library Cataloguing in Publication Data
Data available

Library of Congress Control Number: 2019949145

ISBN 978–0–19–884464–8

Printed and bound by
CPI Group (UK) Ltd, Croydon, CR0 4YY

Preface

This book aims to clarify, critically discuss, and propose solutions for the application of international rules of attribution of conduct to States under public international law in general and, more specifically, under international investment law. The issue is that of the applicability of the principles of 'attribution' to States of acts that are in breach of their obligations under international custom or international treaties, with a focus on their commitments pertaining to the treatment of foreign investors under International Investment Agreements (IIAs), mostly bilateral investment treaties (BITs), and their application by arbitral tribunals. Of special interest and the object of extensive debate within this context is the responsibility of States when the alleged breach has been committed not by the State itself through its organs, but by entities which have separate legal personality under domestic law, which, nevertheless, may engage the responsibility of the State under international law, such as State-owned enterprises (SOEs). Other significant issues that are dealt with in this monograph pertain to the treatment of *de jure* organs having independent juristic personality, such as regulatory authorities, the thresholds of State control on *de facto* organs and individuals, and, in the realm of international investment law, the applicability of treaty clauses on the observance of contractual obligations (*umbrella clauses*) to SOEs.

The book addresses the relevant issues in a systematic way, approaching them first in general terms on the basis of the Draft Articles on Responsibility of States for Internationally Wrongful Acts (ARSIWA) on attribution, finalized by the International Law Commission (ILC) in 2001, and proceeding thereafter to the specifics of international investment law, based on an accurate examination of the law, practice, and case law, with full knowledge and consideration of the academic debate. To this extent, the book convincingly submits that the general principles on attribution are fully applicable within international investment law, which is not a closed system governed by different principles, and that tribunals have to apply them as they generally do. Finally, the connection suggested by the Author between the international rules of attribution of conduct and the law of State immunity shows his ability to propose clear and even original solutions to the complex problems that this issue raises. Based on its original approach and exhaustiveness, the book fills a gap in the academic literature, especially by assessing recent case law in investment treaty claims and placing relevant decisions in the context of prior scholarly debates and decided cases. It is definitely suggested reading as a single reference book on the rules of attribution of conduct to States in public international law and international investment arbitration.

I am especially pleased to sign the preface to this outstanding work because the Author, Carlo de Stefano, was a graduate, in 2016, of the Ph.D. in International Law and Economics of Bocconi University, Milan, which I launched in 1990 and have directed for many years. Dr de Stefano joins a cohort of graduates of this specialized interdisciplinary doctoral programme who have succeeded in academia, notably through publications such as the present volume, international organizations, diplomacy, law firms, and NGOs.

Giorgio Sacerdoti

Acknowledgements

I address the most grateful acknowledgement to those who have supported me in the realization of this book with their scientific advice and moral encouragement.

A special tribute is rendered to Professor Giorgio Sacerdoti, my mentor and supervisor of my doctoral dissertation, which formed the basis of this monograph. In addition, I am grateful to Professor Paola Gaeta and Professor Zachary Douglas, who kindly agreed to complete the PhD thesis committee.

This book would not have been possible without extensive research and consultation, mainly conducted at the Lilian Goldman Law Library of the Yale Law School, at the Kathryn and Shelby Cullom Davis Library of the Graduate Institute for International and Development Studies of Geneva, and at the Library of the Max Planck Institute Luxembourg for International, European, and Regulatory Procedural Law. To this extent, I thank Professor W Michael Reisman, Professor Zachary Douglas, and Professor Hélène Ruiz Fabri, respectively, who have generously offered me the opportunity to visit their academic institutions.

Carlo de Stefano

Contents

Table of Cases

EARLY ARBITRAL CASES

DIPLOMATIC NOTES

PERMANENT COURT OF INTERNATIONAL JUSTICE

INTERNATIONAL COURT OF JUSTICE

IRAN-US CLAIMS TRIBUNAL

INTERNATIONAL CRIMINAL TRIBUNAL FOR THE FORMER YUGOSLAVIA

EUROPEAN COURT OF HUMAN RIGHTS

WORLD TRADE ORGANIZATION DISPUTE SETTLEMENT SYSTEM

INTERNATIONAL INVESTMENT ARBITRATION

INTERNATIONAL COMMERCIAL ARBITRATION

DOMESTIC COURTS

Australia

Austria

Belgium

France

Germany

Italy

Netherlands

Pakistan

United Kingdom

United States

Table of Legislation

League of Nations and United Nations Documents

LEAGUE OF NATIONS

UNITED NATIONS

Projects of Codification of Learned Societies and Academic Institutions

INSTITUTE OF INTERNATIONAL LAW

HARVARD LAW SCHOOL

List of Abbreviations

ALC	Congo Liberation Army
ARSIWA	Draft Articles on Responsibility of States for Internationally Wrongful Acts
BIT	bilateral investment treaty
DRC	Democratic Republic of the Congo
ECT	Energy Charter Treaty
ECtHR	European Court of Human Rights
FDI	foreign direct investment
FET	fair and equitable treatment
FRY	Federal Republic of Yugoslavia
ICC	International Chamber of Commerce
ICJ	International Court of Justice
ICSID	International Centre for Settlement of Investment Disputes
ICTY	International Criminal Tribunal for the Former Yugoslavia
IIA	international investment agreement
ILC	International Law Commission
ISDS	investor–State dispute settlement
ITLOS	International Tribunal of the Law of the Sea
JVA	Joint Venture Agreement
LCIA	London Court of International Arbitration
MLC	Congo Liberation Movement
NAFTA	North American Free Trade Agreement
PCA	Permanent Court of Arbitration
PCIJ	Permanent Court of International Justice
PMC	Private Military Company
PPP	Public–Private Partnership
SCC	Stockholm Chamber of Commerce
SOE	State-owned enterprise
UCLAs	Unilaterally Controlled Latino Assets
UNCITRAL	United Nations Commission of International Trade Law
UNCLOS	United Nations Convention on the Law of the Sea
UNCSI	United Nations Convention on Jurisdictional Immunities of States and Their Property
VCCR	Vienna Convention on Consular Relations
VCDR	Vienna Convention on Diplomatic Relations
WTO	World Trade Organization

Introduction

A Study on Attribution

If a trader is always a trader, a State remains a State

Lord Wilberforce
I Congreso del Partido
[1983] 1 AC 244

This treatise proceeds from a comprehensive observation and verification of the persistent role of States as traditional sources of *authority*, which may ultimately be defined as their prerogative to unilaterally, but legitimately, compel the behaviour of natural and legal persons.[1] This dimension of legitimacy distinguishes the authority of the State from the *power* exercised by human beings and other economic and social organizations.[2] This authority justifies the character of States as being 'full' subjects of international law ('the State remains the central building block of the international legal order').[3] Hence, the scholarly interest in a study devoted to the elucidation of the international rules of *attribution*, which is the set of tests and principles allowing the identification of such conduct of the State being susceptible to trigger its international responsibility. On one side, an abstract concept of 'State' inevitably orients the interpreter in the application of the rules of attribution. On the other side, the idea of 'State' itself is influenced by the functioning of attribution, which ultimately qualifies given acts or omissions as being attributable or not to the sovereign. Accordingly, the illustration of the international rules of attribution presumes a constructivist coil, where the law is but an element of a broader scenario informed by sociopolitical, historical, and economic factors.[4]

[1] Joseph E Stiglitz et al, *The Economic Role of the State* (Arnold Heertje ed, Basil Blackwell in association with Bank Insinger de Beaufort NV 1989) 21.

[2] W Michael Reisman, *Nullity and Revision. The Review and Enforcement of International Judgments and Awards* (Yale University Press 1971) 4–6.

[3] Christian Tomuschat, 'In the Twilight Zones of the State' in Isabelle Buffard, James Crawford, Alain Pellet, and Stephan Wittich (eds), *International Law Between Universalism and Fragmentation. Festschrift in Honour of Gerhard Hafner* (Martinus Nijhoff Publishers 2008) 479.

[4] Wolfgang G Friedmann, 'The Growth of State Control over the Individual, and its Effect upon the Rules of International State Responsibility' (1938) 19 British Year Book of International Law 118; Wolfgang G Friedmann, 'Some Impacts of Social Organization on International Law' (1956) 50 American Journal of International Law 475, 481: 'No theoretical distinction can provide certainty. It can only provide guidance for individual decisions.'; Wolfgang G Friedmann, *The Changing Structure of International Law* (Stevens & Sons 1964) 341 et seq.

Attribution in International Law and Arbitration. Carlo de Stefano, Oxford University Press (2020).

DOI: 10.1093/law-oso/9780198844648.001.0001

Nevertheless, the definition of 'the State according to international law' (*'l'Etat selon le droit international'*)[5] is central in order to understand the contemporary world order, which—notwithstanding recent phenomena of administrative decentralization, functional externalization of nationwide public services, and privatization of public undertakings, which pursue the policy of subsidiarity[6]—continues to be governed in essence by the (international) public law tenets elaborated in connection with the liberal revolutions of the XVIII century.[7] In particular, the principles of the institutional, territorial, and functional unity of the State and of the irresponsibility of the sovereign for the conduct of 'private' individuals still remain as fundamental pillars of the law of State responsibility for international delinquencies, notwithstanding 'transition from the "night-watchman" state to one actively moulding the economic and social life of the nation'.[8] This relative 'immobility' of the architectural structure of the international legal order should not be considered as an element of backwardness of international law (or '*statolâtrie*').[9] On the contrary, the 'classic' rules of State responsibility for internationally wrongful acts represent an effective instrument to foster the accountability of sovereigns in their cross-border relationships, which should not be undermined and diminished by the transformation of the political and economic systems at the national and transnational level (at least in the absence of an effective equivalent alternative for legal redress). At the same time, the unprecedented evolution of the international society provides the international jurist with a challenge in ensuring the answerability of States in relation to the entirety of *their* conduct, which is identified upon application of the international rules of attribution. While certain cases may appear to be crystal-clear with regard to the issue of attribution (for instance,

[5] Mathias Forteau, 'L'État selon le droit international: une figure à géométrie variable?' (2007) 111 Revue Générale de Droit International Public 737.

[6] Rosalyn Higgins, 'The Concept of "The State": Variable Geometry and Dualist Perceptions' in Laurence Boisson de Chazournes and Vera Gowlland-Debbas (eds), *The International Legal System in Quest of Equity and Universality. Liber Amicorum Georges Abi-Saab* (Martinus Nijhoff Publishers 2001) 547; Martti Koskenniemi, 'The Future of Statehood' (1991) 32 Harvard International Law Journal 397; Christoph H Schreuer, 'The Waning of the Sovereign State: Towards a New Paradigm for International Law?' (1993) 4 European Journal of International Law 447, 450; Anne van Aaken, 'Blurring Boundaries between Sovereign Acts and Commercial Activities: A Functional View on Regulatory Immunity and Immunity from Execution' in Anne Peters, Evelyne Lagrange, Stefan Oeter, and Christian Tomuschat (eds), *Immunities in the Age of Global Constitutionalism* (Brill 2015) 131; Joel P Trachtman, 'L'Etat, C'est Nous: Sovereignty, Economic Integration and Subsidiarity' (1992) 33 Harvard International Law Journal 459, 462; Sébastien Miroudot and Alexandros Ragoussis, 'Actors in the International Investment Scenario: Objectives, Performance and Advantages of Affiliates of State-Owned Enterprises and Sovereign Wealth Funds' in Roberto Echandi and Pierre Sauvé (eds), *Prospects in International Investment Law and Policy: World Trade Forum* (Cambridge University Press 2013) 51; Pier Angelo Toninelli, 'The Rise and Fall of Public Enterprise. The Framework' in Pier Angelo Toninelli (ed), *The Rise and Fall of State-Owned Enterprise in the Western World* (Cambridge University Press 2000) 3.

[7] See Benjamin Constant, *De la liberté des Anciens comparée à celle des Modernes* (Athénée Royal de Paris, 1819).

[8] Wolfgang G Friedmann, *Law in a Changing Society* (2nd edn, Stevens & Sons 1972) 475.

[9] Hélène Ruiz Fabri, 'Genèse et disparition de l'État à l'époque contemporaine' (1992) 38 Annuaire Français de Droit International 153.

the physical apprehension of an alien by police forces), other cases may beget more reasoned analysis as to the conclusion of a given conduct as being an 'act of the State' (for instance, the issue by regulatory bodies of guidelines or codes of conduct to the private sector). Thus, the international rules of attribution assist the interpreter in the normative operation to *bridge* given acts and omissions to the person of the State, whereas 'sensory' skills may fail to capture the circumstance of the sovereign being involved. Accordingly, the tests of attribution under customary international law disclose a normative synopsis of the various manifestations of the phenomenology of State authority, with a view to ensuring effective enforcement of the international regime of State responsibility.

It might be questioned whether a (new) study on attribution issues in international law and arbitration may be helpful to the international community and scholarship, or just represents a 'tedious' doctrinal exercise.[10] Scholars have already provided answers to this question. Starke's seminal article on attributability in international delinquencies justified its focus on terminological issues for the sake of a more scientific application of attribution doctrines:

> The main point intended to be made is simply that a knowledge of the doctrine of imputability clarifies both the rules and the terminology, and leads to greater exactness in their application.[11]

Gordon Christenson has emphasized the role of attribution by adapting his contribution to the dichotomy, on the one side, and the interaction, on the other, between 'primary' and 'secondary' rules of international law:

> Not much is new in the rules of who acts on behalf of a State as outlined by writers and codified in drafts. The commentary on various draft articles on attribution is wearisome and seems mechanical if not doctrinaire. Indeed, the remarkable acquiescence by nations in those rules suggests plodding dullness, lack of either novelty or controversy. Far more exciting are the substantive norms that make up the core of State Responsibility. When viewed as part of a comprehensive process, however, the principles of attribution assume broad theoretical importance, for they are the connection between a wide range of international obligations and conduct by those whose actions constitute acts of the State. A State is responsible to other States to ensure that its conduct meets these obligations. It is essential,

[10] Gordon A Christenson, 'Attributing Conduct to the State: Is Anything New?' (1990) 84 American Society of International Law Proceedings 51. To the contrary, see the recent book by Csaba Kovács, *Attribution in International Investment Law* (Kluwer Law International 2018).

[11] J G Starke, 'Imputability in International Delinquencies' (1938) 19 British Year Book of International Law 104.

> then, if States are to be held accountable for wrongful conduct, that the international community define what action properly is attributable to them.[12]

The present study wishes to continue the previous doctrinal efforts to explain the nature and functioning of attribution rules with the awareness that scholarly elucidation is still demanded. This book investigates the application of attributability rules in public international law disputes, including the practice of early arbitrations, the Permanent Court of International Justice (PCIJ), the International Court of Justice (ICJ), the Iran–US Claims Tribunal, the International Criminal Tribunal for the Former Yugoslavia (ICTY), investor–State arbitration, and the World Trade Organization (WTO) dispute settlement system. This means that the practice of other international courts and tribunals that is relied on (as to the attribution of conduct to a State) by the International Law Commission (ILC) in its Commentaries to the Draft Articles on Responsibility of States for Internationally Wrongful Acts (ARSIWA)[13] is not scrutinized in this study. Critical problems are still outstanding in relation to the attribution of the acts or omissions of 'independent' State organs exercising functions of a regulatory or administrative nature (such as central banks and independent authorities), the definition of *governmental authority* for the purposes of attribution of conduct of parastatal entities, and the determination of the thresholds of State 'control' either on de facto organs or on 'private' individuals.[14] With regard to investment arbitration, it is relevant to clarify the operation of the dialectics between *lex generalis* (customary international law) and *lex specialis* (international investment treaties) in relation to attribution issues. In particular, it will be determined to what extent international investment agreements (IIAs) and tribunals deviate or may deviate from customary international law rules of attributability.[15] One of the central tenets of this treatise is the emphasis on the logical, technical, and 'objective' features of the international rules of attribution of acts and omissions to States. This peculiar nature is held to justify their pedagogic role and influence in the treatment of the 'State' (as comprising its organs, instrumentalities, and, in certain cases, even 'private' individuals) so as to ensure consistent resolutions of attribution issues by the adjudicators of international law.

[12] Gordon A Christenson, 'The Doctrine of Attribution in State Responsibility' in Richard B Lillich (ed), *International Law of State Responsibility for Injuries to Aliens* (University Press of Virginia 1983) 321.

[13] Draft Articles on Responsibility of States for Internationally Wrongful Acts (ARSIWA), Annex to A/RES/56/83, 12 December 2001.

[14] See Chapter II.

[15] See Chapter III.

I
The Meaning of Attribution

1. Notion

'[I]mputability ... is one of the most delicate aspects of the entire theory of responsibility.'[1] As corporate entities, States do not possess physical personification as such,[2] but 'can act only by and through their agents and representatives', namely such natural or juridical persons acting *on their behalf*.[3] The body of rules of attribution (or attributability) functions as a legal *bridge* (a *link*) between the State and the conduct potentially liable to trigger its international responsibility, so as to complete the physiologic—not the normative—gap between the acts and omissions of State 'agents' and the State itself. Therefore, attribution stands as a basic and indispensable constituent element of the law of responsibility of States for internationally wrongful acts.[4] Attribution represents the subjective element for the

[1] *Military and Paramilitary Activities in and against Nicaragua (Nicaragua v United States of America)*, Merits, Separate Opinion of Judge Ago, 27 June 1986, para 19, ICJ Reports 1986, 181, 190.

[2] Hans Kelsen, *(The) Pure Theory of Law* (2nd edn, University of California Press 1960, translated 1967) 290–312; Dionisio Anzilotti, *Corso di diritto internazionale, Volume Primo: Introduzione – Teorie generali* (3rd edn, Athenaeum 1928) 418; Mario Marinoni, *La responsabilità degli stati per gli atti dei loro rappresentanti secondo il diritto internazionale* (Athenaeum 1913) 33; Tomaso Perassi, *Lezioni di diritto internazionale, Parte Prima* (Edizioni Italiane 1942) 97; Theodor Meron, 'International Responsibility of States for Unauthorized Acts of Their Officials' (1957) 33 British Year Book of International Law 85, 86: 'Imputability, which is the attribution of an act of an official to the State, is necessitated by the fact that all acts are those of individuals, while the international consequences of such acts—at least according to traditional international law—are imposed on the State which is the subject of rights and obligations.'; Luigi Condorelli and Claus Kress, 'The Rules of Attribution: General Considerations' in James Crawford, Alain Pellet, and Simon Olleson (eds), *The Law of International Responsibility* (Oxford University Press 2010) 237; Ian Brownlie, 'State Responsibility and the International Court of Justice' in Malgosia Fitzmaurice and Dan Sarooshi (eds), *Issues of State Responsibility before International Judicial Institutions* (Hart Publishing 2004) 11, 12; Christian Tomuschat, 'Attribution of International Responsibility: Direction and Control' in Malcolm Evans and Panos Koutrakos (eds), *The International Responsibility of the European Union: European and International Perspectives* (Hart Publishing 2013) 7.

[3] *German Settlers in Poland*, Advisory Opinion No 6, 10 September 1923, PCIJ Series B No 6, 22.

[4] Dionisio Anzilotti, *Corso di diritto internazionale, Volume Primo: Introduzione – Teorie generali* (3rd edn, Athenaeum 1928) 418; C F Amerasinghe, 'Imputability in the Law of State Responsibility for Injuries to Aliens' (1966) 22 Revue Égyptienne de Droit International 91, 96; James Crawford, *State Responsibility. The General Part* (Cambridge University Press 2013) 113; David D Caron, 'The Basis of Responsibility: Attribution and Other Trans-substantive Rules of State Responsibility' in Richard B Lillich and Daniel B Magraw (eds), *The Iran–United States Claims Tribunal: Its Contribution to the Law of State Responsibility* (Transnational Publishers, Inc 1998) 109, 110, 127–28: 'The rules of attribution are thus a set of trans-substantive rules that delineate one of the potential boundaries of State responsibility. The rules seek to define when the act complained of should be regarded as an act of the State.'; Luigi Condorelli, 'L'imputation à l'État d'un fait internationalement illicite: solutions classiques

Attribution in International Law and Arbitration. Carlo de Stefano, Oxford University Press (2020).

DOI: 10.1093/law-oso/9780198844648.001.0001

configuration of State responsibility.[5] At the same time, it does not represent a state of mind or, more precisely, a psychological element, such as negligence or malice.[6] Nor is it to be assimilated to principles governing the link of causation between an act of an agent of the State and a given injury.[7] It rather consists in a variety of tests, whose operative result is the bestowing of given acts upon the person of the State. In this respect, the subjective element may be interpreted as meaning the 'personal' element or as comprising the subjective side of the act of the State.

As provided by ARSIWA Article 2, attribution is a requisite (or pre-requisite) for the application of the regime of State responsibility for internationally wrongful acts:

et nouvelles tendances' (1984) 189 Recueil des Cours 9, 24; Claus Kress, 'L'organe de facto en droit international public' (2001) 105 Revue Générale de Droit International Public 93, 95; Rosalyn Higgins, 'Issues of State Responsibility before the International Court of Justice' in Malgosia Fitzmaurice and Dan Sarooshi (eds), *Issues of State Responsibility before International Judicial Institutions* (Hart Publishing 2004) 1, 2; Mathias Forteau, 'L'État selon le droit international: une figure à géométrie variable?' (2007) 111 Revue Générale de Droit International Public 737, 738; Rüdiger Wolfrum, 'State Responsibility for Private Actors: an Old Problem of Renewed Relevance' in Maurizio Ragazzi (ed), *International Responsibility Today. Essays in Memory of Oscar Schachter* (Martinus Nijhoff Publishers 2005) 423, 424; Jörn Griebel and Milan Plücken, 'New Developments Regarding the Rules of Attribution? The International Court of Justice's Decision in *Bosnia v. Serbia*' (2008) 21 Leiden Journal of International Law 601, 602–03.

[5] Pierre-Marie Dupuy, 'Quarante ans de codification du droit de la responsabilité internationale des États: un bilan' (2003) 107 Revue Génerale de Droit International Public 305, 316–19.

[6] Gaetano Arangio-Ruiz, 'State Fault and the Forms and Degrees of International Responsibility: Questions of Attribution and Relevance' in *Le droit international au service de la paix, de la justice et du développement. Mélanges Michel Virally* (Éditions A Pedone 1991) 25; Hazel Fox, 'The International Court of Justice's Treatment of Acts of the State and in Particular the Attribution of Acts of Individuals to the State' in Nisuke Ando, Edward McWhinney, and Rüdiger Wolfrum (eds), *Liber Amicorum Judge Shigeru Oda*, vol 1 (Kluwer Law International 2002) 147, 155–56: 'The conclusion must be that even when an organ acts, the attribution of its act depends on the proof of knowledge and consent on the part of the State, the precise nature of these elements being largely determined by the content of the primary obligation.'

[7] Dionisio Anzilotti, *Corso di diritto internazionale, Volume Primo: Introduzione – Teorie generali* (3rd edn, Athenaeum 1928) 228: '*L'imputazione giuridica si distingue così nettamente dal rapporto di causalità; un fatto è giuridicamente proprio di un soggetto, non perché prodotto o voluto da questo, nel senso che tali parole avrebbero nella fisiologia o nella psicologia, ma perché la norma glielo attribuisce.*' A certain hesitation on this specific point is found in Ian Brownlie, *System of the Law of Nations. State Responsibility. Part I* (Clarendon Press 1983) 133, who refers to 'imputability' as a 'causal connection between the corporate entity of the state and the harm done'; Hildebrando Accioly, 'Principes généraux de la responsabilité internationale d'après la doctrine et la jurisprudence' (1959) 96 Recueil des Cours 349, 358: '*Il s'agit ici de la situation connue comme lien de causalité, qui établit un rapport direct, de cause à effet, entre le dommage réel et l'acte illicite, ou plutôt entre le manquement à une obligation et l'Etat.*' See also League of Nations, Committee of Experts for the Progressive Codification of International Law, Second Session, 12–29 January 1926, Annex to Questionnaire No 4, 'Responsibility of States for Damage Done in Their Territories to the Person or Property of Foreigners', Report of the Sub-Committee (Mr Gustavo Guerrero, Rapporteur), Conclusions, para 3, League of Nations publication, V.Legal, 1926.V.3, document C.46.M.23.1926.V and League of Nations publication, V.Legal, 1926.V.11, document C.96.M.47.1926.V, (1926) 20 American Journal of International Law Special Supplement 176, 201–02: 'A State is responsible for damage incurred by a foreigner attributable to an act contrary to international law or to the omission of an act which the State was bound under international law to perform.'

Article 2
Elements of an internationally wrongful act of a State

There is an internationally wrongful act of a State when conduct consisting of an action or omission:

(a) is attributable to the State under international law; and

(b) constitutes a breach of an international obligation of the State.[8]

The structure of the internationally wrongful act as comprising a subjective (attribution) and an objective (breach of an international obligation) element is firmly rooted in customary international law following early arbitral practice and decisions of the Permanent Court of International Justice. Thus, the Mexico–US General Claims Commission deliberated in the case of the *Dickson Car Wheels*:

> Under international law, apart from any convention, in order that a State may incur responsibility it is necessary that an unlawful international act be imputed to it, that is, that there exist a violation of a duty imposed by an international juridical standard.[9]

[8] Draft Articles on Responsibility of States for Internationally Wrongful Acts, with commentaries (ARSIWA Commentaries), in Report of the International Law Commission on the Work of its Fifty-Third Session, 23 April, 1 June, 2 July, and 10 August 2001, document A/56/10, Yearbook of the International Law Commission, 2001, Volume II (Part Two), 34, document A/CN.4/SER.A/2001/Add.1 (Part 2). cf Dionisio Anzilotti, *Corso di diritto internazionale, Volume Primo: Introduzione – Teorie generali* (3rd edn, Athenaeum 1928) 418: '*Perché si abbia un fatto illecito internazionale occorre dunque. A) Che si tratti di un comportamento di uno Stato, ossia imputabile ad uno Stato; B) che il comportamento sia diverso da quello imposto dalla norma*.' It is evident that *damage* is not per se an indefeasable constitutive element of an internationally wrongful act. cf Brigitte Stern, 'Et si on utilisait la notion de préjudice juridique? Retour sur une notion délaissée à l'occasion de la fin des travaux de la C.D.I. sur la responsabilité des États' (2001) 47 Annuaire Français de Droit International 3. This is clearly spelt out in the investment case of *Total SA v The Argentine Republic*, ICSID Case No ARB/04/01, Decision on Objections to Jurisdiction, 25 August 2006, para 89, fn 51: 'A basic issue in the present dispute is whether Argentina has committed an internationally wrongful act, that is whether it has breached the international obligations contained in the BIT by conduct attributable to it. As held by the I.L.C. these two conditions are sufficient to establish such a wrongful act giving rise to international responsibility. Having caused damage is not an additional requirement, except if the content of the primary obligation breached has an object or implies an obligation not to cause damages.' See also James Crawford, First report on State Responsibility, by Mr James Crawford, Special Rapporteur, 24 April, 1, 5, 11, and 26 May, 22 and 24 July, 12 August 1998, para 112 et seq, document A/CN.4/490 and Add. 1-7, Yearbook of the International Law Commission, 1998, Volume II (Part One), 1, 28, document A/CN.4/SER.A/1998/Add.1(Part 1): 'the question whether damage is a prerequisite for a breach becomes a matter to be determined by the relevant primary rule. It may be that many primary rules do contain a requirement of damage, however defined. Some certainly do. But there is no warrant for the suggestion that this is necessarily the case, that it is an a priori requirement.'

[9] *Dickson Car Wheel Company (USA) v United Mexican States* (July 1931) 4 RIAA 669, 678; *Claim of the Salvador Commercial Company ('El Triunfo Company')* (8 May 1902) 15 RIAA 455, 477; *Eastern Steamship Lines, Inc (United States) v Germany (War-Risk Insurance Premium Claim)* (11 March 1924) 2 RIAA 71.

Even more precisely, the PCIJ formulated the threshold rule in the *Phosphates in Morocco* case:

> This act being attributable to the State and described as contrary to the treaty right of another State, international responsibility would be established immediately as between the two States.[10]

In point of legal theory, the rules of attribution embody a section of the law of State responsibility whose application is *preliminary*[11] to the other categories of norms (for instance, the existence of circumstances excluding wrongfulness, remedies, countermeasures, dispute settlement, and other rules pertaining to the *mise en oeuvre* of State responsibility).[12] Once the subjective element has been ascertained, it shall be coupled with the objective element, which entails the existence of the violation of a substantive obligation of international law incumbent upon the State.[13] Based on the distinction between 'primary' and 'secondary' rules, which is at the basis of the 'Ago revolution' that allowed the long-standing *impasse* in the process of codification of the law of State responsibility to be overcome,[14] principles

[10] *Phosphates in Morocco*, Judgment, 14 June 1938, PCIJ Series A/B No 74, 10, 22.

[11] ICTY, Appeals Chamber, *Tadić*, IT-94-1-A, Judgement, 15 July 1999, 41, para 104.

[12] J G Starke, 'Imputability in International Delinquencies' (1938) 19 British Year Book of International Law 104, 106: 'Responsibility only begins where imputability ends.'; Gordon A Christenson, 'The Doctrine of Attribution in State Responsibility' in Richard B Lillich (ed), *International Law of State Responsibility for Injuries to Aliens* (University Press of Virginia 1983) 321, 324.

[13] Hints of a reversed logical sequence are also found in the international legal scholarship. For instance, Theodor Meron seems to consider the objective element as having a prior consideration to the prongs of attributability. cf Theodor Meron, 'International Responsibility of States for Unauthorized Acts of Their Officials' (1957) 33 British Year Book of International Law 85, 86.

[14] Roberto Ago, First Report on State Responsibility, by Mr Roberto Ago, Special Rapporteur, 'Review of previous work on codification of the topic of the international responsibility of States', 7 May 1969 and 20 January 1970, paras 2–5, 65, 89, document A/CN.4/217 and ADD.1, Yearbook of the International Law Commission, 1969, Volume II, 125, 126–27, 135–36, 138–39, document A/CN.4/SER.A/1969/Add.1: 'Nevertheless, as a result of the exceptional difficulties inherent in the subject, the uncertainties with which it has always been fraught, and the divergences of opinion and interests in the matter, previous codification efforts have not proved successful, their resumption having been postponed until a more propitious moment. On the strong recommendation of the General Assembly of the United Nations, the International Law Commission has now decided to make a fresh attempt in that direction, with the firm intention of overcoming the obstacles and of ultimately succeeding in the task, so far unaccomplished, of preparing a draft codification for submission to States. [. . .] The continued confusion of State responsibility with other topics was undoubtedly one of the reasons which prevented it from becoming ripe for codification.' The expression 'Ago revolution' is borrowed from Alain Pellet, 'The ILC's Articles on State Responsibility for Internationally Wrongful Acts and Related Texts' in James Crawford, Alain Pellet, and Simon Olleson (eds), *The Law of International Responsibility* (Oxford University Press 2010) 75, 76–77. The *manifesto* of the 'Ago revolution' had already been revealed, at the latest, in Roberto Ago, Report by Mr Roberto Ago, Chairman of the Sub-Committee on State Responsibility (Approved by the Sub-Committee), 16 January 1963, document A/CN.4/152, Yearbook of the International Law Commission, 1963, Volume II, 187, 251, document A/CN.4/SER.A/1963/ADD.1: 'In my opinion, the first step must be to define the general theory of responsibility. That theory exists. Its application in practice has yielded uneven results; it has proved more fruitful and effective in certain fields of international relations than in others. But that is no reason for denying that it exists or that certain principles have a general scope transcending the particular case of responsibility to which they are applied. State responsibility should therefore be considered as a whole.' For a concise illustration of the distinction between 'primary' and 'secondary' rules of State responsibility, see James

of attribution are included within the latter.[15] On closer inspection, attributability rules are vested with a function that renders them more peculiar than the other secondary rules, in that they provide for criteria based on structural, technical, mechanical, and logical (ie 'objective') elements. This is the twofold nature of attribution rules: they are classified as 'subjective' while at the same time being based on objective features (for instance, the institutional status of State organs, the functional empowerment of the governmental authority of an entity formally separated from the State machinery, or a factual link of a person with a State organ). Therefore, attribution rules may be also described as 'trans-substantive' rules or rules that are preliminary to the application of the other secondary rules and, *a fortiori*, of the applicable primary rules of international law.[16]

The terminological binomial attribution–attributability is generally preferred to imputation–imputability,[17] as confirmed by the choice adopted in ARSIWA for the title of the second chapter of Part One.[18] Indeed, the term 'imputation' has yielded a certain degree of confusion with the concept of a psychological element, which, as mentioned above, is unknown to the mechanism of attribution, while

Crawford, First report on State Responsibility, by Mr James Crawford, Special Rapporteur, 24 April, 1, 5, 11, and 26 May, 22 and 24 July, 12 August 1998, para 12 et seq, document A/CN.4/490 and Add. 1-7, Yearbook of the International Law Commission, 1998, Volume II (Part One), 1, 6, document A/CN.4/SER.A/1998/Add.1(Part 1).

[15] Jean Combacau and Denis Alland, '"Primary" and "Secondary" Rules in the Law of State Responsibility: Categorizing International Obligations' (1985) 16 Netherlands Yearbook of International Law 81. Contra Giorgio Gaja, 'Primary and Secondary Rules in the International Law on State Responsibility' (2014) 97 Rivista di Diritto Internazionale 981, 989. For a critique of the 'myth' of secondary rules, cf Paul Reuter, 'Trois observations sur la codification de la responsabilité internationale des États pour fait illicite' in *Le droit international au service de la paix, de la justice et du développement. Mélanges Michel Virally* (Éditions A Pedone 1991) 389, 395–96.

[16] David D Caron, 'The Basis of Responsibility: Attribution and Other Trans-substantive Rules of State Responsibility' in Richard B Lillich and Daniel B Magraw (eds), *The Iran-United States Claims Tribunal: Its Contribution to the Law of State Responsibility* (Transnational Publishers, Inc 1998) 109, 110; David D Caron, 'The ILC Articles on State Responsibility: the Paradoxical Relationship Between Form and Authority' (2002) 96 American Journal of International Law 857, 871.

[17] The term 'imputability' is largely used by J G Starke, 'Imputability in International Delinquencies' (1938) 19 British Year Book of International Law 104; Dionisio Anzilotti, *Corso di diritto internazionale, Volume Primo: Introduzione – Teorie generali* (3rd edn, Athenaeum 1928) 418; Theodor Meron, 'International Responsibility of States for Unauthorized Acts of Their Officials' (1957) 33 British Year Book of International Law 85; C F Amerasinghe, 'Imputability in the Law of State Responsibility for Injuries to Aliens' (1966) 22 Revue Égyptienne de Droit International 91; Ian Brownlie, 'State Responsibility and the International Court of Justice' in Malgosia Fitzmaurice and Dan Sarooshi (eds), *Issues of State Responsibility before International Judicial Institutions* (Hart Publishing 2004) 11, 16. Indeed, 'imputability' had been the term predominantly used in the previous phase of the codification of the law of State responsibility (cf Roberto Ago, Report by Mr Roberto Ago, Chairman of the Sub-Committee on State Responsibility (Approved by the Sub-Committee), 16 January 1963, document A/CN.4/152, Yearbook of the International Law Commission, 1963, Volume II, 187, 253, document A/CN.4/SER.A/1963/ADD.1) and by the ICJ in seminal cases such as *Hostages* and *Nicaragua*. See *United States Diplomatic and Consular Staff in Tehran (United States of America v Iran)*, Judgment, 24 May 1980, ICJ Reports 1980, 3, 29; *Military and Paramilitary Activities in and against Nicaragua (Nicaragua v United States of America)*, Merits, Judgment, 27 June 1986, ICJ Reports 1986, 14.

[18] ARSIWA Commentaries (n 8) 38.

possibly being enshrined within the analysis of the existence of an internationally wrongful act (where dictated by the applicable primary norm).[19] In addition, 'imputation' has been considered to suggest resort to a legal fiction, which the drafters of ARSIWA definitely wished to avoid.[20] Nevertheless (and inevitably so), the terminology should not engender substantial implications, since a fictional character is integral to the rules of attribution.[21] Attribution is a normative technique, governed by international law, which is exactly designed to transfer a given conduct from a natural or juridical person to the person of the State (*Zurechnung*).[22] It definitely entails a fictitious mechanism based on the structure of the State (a fiction itself) as corporate entity.[23] However, the term *attribution* may suggest more

[19] Roberto Ago, Third Report on State Responsibility, by Mr Roberto Ago, Special Rapporteur, 'The internationally wrongful act of the State, source of international responsibility', 5 March, 7 April, 28 April, and 18 May 1971, para 50, document A/CN.4/246 and Add.1-3, Yearbook of the International Law Commission, 1971, Volume II (Part One), 199, 214, document A/CN.4/SER.A/1971/Add.1 (Part 1): 'the Commission was particularly anxious to avoid the ambiguities inherent in notions which can evoke very different ideas because of their meaning in certain municipal criminal law systems. It is for that reason that at the end of the discussion of the second report on State responsibility at the twenty-second session, the Commission concluded, at the suggestion of some of its members that it would be better for it to avoid using the expressions "imputability" and "imputation" and that when speaking in its own name it would be better for it to use the term "attribution" to indicate the simple fact of attaching to the State a given action or omission. That conclusion is reflected in this report.'

[20] International Law Commission, Statement of the Chairman of the Drafting Committee, Mr Bruno Simma, 13 August 1998, 6.

[21] C F Amerasinghe, 'Imputability in the Law of State Responsibility for Injuries to Aliens' (1966) 22 Revue Égyptienne de Droit International 91, 92: 'imputation is the result of an intellectual operation'; Claus Kress, 'L'organe de facto en droit international public' (2001) 105 Revue Générale de Droit International Public 93, 95, fn 2; Mathias Forteau, 'L'Ètat selon le droit international: une figure à géométrie variable?' (2007) 111 Revue Générale de Droit International Public 737, 738: '*Mais si ce qui peut être attribué à l'Etat en droit international varie en fonction de la règle internationale que l'on entend mettre en œuvre, ne s'en déduit-il pas que l'opération d'attribution est d'ordre normatif en droit international, par conséquent que l'Etat est nécessairement construit par celui-ci?*'

[22] Dionisio Anzilotti, *Corso di diritto internazionale, Volume Primo: Introduzione - Teorie generali* (3rd edn, Athenaeum 1928) 228, 418: '*Caratteristica dell'imputazione giuridica è di essere un puro effetto della norma; una volizione, un atto sono imputabili a un dato subietto soltanto perché la norma lo stabilisce*'; Wilhelm Wengler, *Völkerrecht*, Bd 1 (Springer Verlag 1964) 33; Roberto Ago, 'Le délit international' (1939) 68 Recueil des Cours 415, 450: '*Cette imputation dont on parle ici, cette Zurechnung, comme disent les Allemands, n'est évidemment pas un lien créé par la nature: elle est le résultat d'une opération logique effectuée par une règle de droit, donc un lien juridique.*'; Constantin Th Eustathiades, 'Les sujets du droit international et la responsabilité internationale: nouvelles tendances' (1953) 84 Recueil des Cours 397, 479: '*On sait que l'imputation est une opération logique accomplie par un système de droit, en vertu de laquelle en présence d'une certaine situation on crée un lien juridique entre un sujet donné et un tort ou fait illicite.*'; James Crawford, *State Responsibility. The General Part* (Cambridge University Press 2013) 113–14.

[23] Gaetano Arangio-Ruiz, 'State Fault and the Forms and Degrees of International Responsibility: Questions of Attribution and Relevance' in *Le droit international au service de la paix, de la justice et du développement. Mélanges Michel Virally* (Éditions A Pedone 1991) 25. See Gaetano Arangio-Ruiz, Second Report on State Responsibility, by Mr Gaetano Arangio-Ruiz, Special Rapporteur, 9 and 22 June 1989, para 173, document A/CN.4/425 and Add.l, Yearbook of the International Law Commission, 1989, Volume II (Part One), 1, 51, document A/CN.4/SER.A/1989/Add. 1 (Part 1): 'Attribution does not really seem to be an operation carried out by legal rules, notably by national or international law—or not in the same sense, surely, in which the qualification of an act as wrongful and the "imputation" of responsibility are legal operations.' See also the more recent essay by Gaetano Arangio-Ruiz, 'State Responsibility Revisited: The Factual Nature of the Attribution of Conduct to the State' (2017) 100 (Supplement to Issue No. 1) Rivista di Diritto Internazionale 1.

objective features, which is more consistent with the twofold nature of such rules, as described above.

2. Primacy of International Law

Although ARSIWA Article 3 establishes a principle of primacy of international law, vis-à-vis municipal law, with regard to the 'characterization of an act of a State as internationally wrongful',[24] the same concept may nevertheless be adapted to the rules concerning the subjective element of the internationally wrongful act, as inferred from the provision of ARSIWA Article 4.2: '[a]n organ includes any person or entity which has that status in accordance with the internal law of the State.'[25] This is a clear indication that attribution is an independent and autonomous normative process in relationship to domestic law, the latter representing an important, but not decisive, factor for a determination of attributability. As Starke has remarked:

> It is always to be remembered that the imputation of liability results from rules of international law operating in an autonomous manner, and depends only in an indirect and secondary degree on municipal law. ... Consequently imputability for the purpose of state responsibility depends directly on rules of international law operating of their own force.[26]

[24] See Harvard Law School (Manley O Hudson, Director), 'Research in International Law (Nationality, Responsibility of States, Territorial Waters). Drafts of Conventions Prepared in Anticipation of the First Conference on the Codification of International Law, The Hague, 1930', 1 April 1929, Part II, 'Responsibility of States' (Edwin M Borchard, Rapporteur), Article 2, (1929) 23 Special Number Supplement American Journal of International Law 133: 'The responsibility of a state is determined by international law or treaty, anything in its national law, in the decisions of its national courts, or in its agreements with aliens, to the contrary notwithstanding.'; Harvard Law School, Draft Convention on the International Responsibility of States for Injuries to (the Economic Interests of) Aliens (Louis B Sohn and R R Baxter, Rapporteurs), Article 2 (*Primacy of International Law*), (1961) 55 American Journal of International Law 545: '1. The responsibility of a State under Article 1 is to be determined according to this Convention and international law, by application of the sources and subsidiary means set forth in paragraph 1 of Article 38 of the Statute of the International Court of Justice. 2. A State cannot avoid international responsibility by invoking its municipal law.'

[25] ARSIWA Commentaries (n 8) 36, 42.

[26] J G Starke, 'Imputability in International Delinquencies' (1938) 19 British Year Book of International Law 104, 105–06; Theodor Meron, 'International Responsibility of States for Unauthorized Acts of Their Officials' (1957) 33 British Year Book of International Law 85, 87, 88: '*Imputability is an independent process of international law*'; C F Amerasinghe, 'Imputability in the Law of State Responsibility for Injuries to Aliens' (1966) 22 Revue Égyptienne de Droit International 91, 96; Roberto Ago, 'Le délit international' (1939) 68 Recueil des Cours 415, 461: '*L'imputation, comme toute opération juridique, ne peut avoir lieu dans un ordre juridique donné que par l'effet des règles du même ordre*'; Brigitte Stern, 'The Elements of an Internationally Wrongful Act' in James Crawford, Alain Pellet, and Simon Olleson (eds), *The Law of International Responsibility* (Oxford University Press 2010) 193, 201: 'on the one hand, there must be conduct which is *attributable* to a State, and on the other hand, that conduct must be *wrongful*. These two conditions are naturally determined by the international legal order, and by the international legal order alone.'; James Crawford, Thomas Grant, and Francesco Messineo, 'Towards An International Law of Responsibility: Early Doctrine' in Laurence Boisson de Chazournes and Marcelo Kohen (eds),

On one side, States exercise the highest degree of freedom in the organization of their internal structure. On the other side, the international law of attributability of internationally wrongful acts follows its own criteria, not to be understood in isolation from municipal practices. This consideration elucidates the possibility of divergence between the norms of attributability of conduct to the State under municipal and international law.

3. Customary Status of the Rules of Attribution in the Articles on Responsibility of States for Internationally Wrongful Acts

ARSIWA do not have the form and binding scope of an international treaty.[27] At the culmination of the works of codification of the law of State responsibility for internationally wrongful acts, the ILC decided to recommend to the General Assembly to 'take note' of ARSIWA, whereas the possibility of convening an international conference with a view to concluding an international convention on the topic of State responsibility was reserved for 'a later stage, in the light of the importance of the topic'.[28] This is revealed by the choice to maintain the denomination of 'articles', rather than 'convention', notwithstanding the adoption of a treaty-like form.[29] Indeed, on 12 December 2001, the General Assembly resolved:

> *The General Assembly,*
>
> ...
>
> 3. *Takes note* of the articles on responsibility of States for internationally wrongful acts, presented by the International Law Commission, the text of which

International Law and the Quest for its Implementation. Liber Amicorum Vera Gowlland-Debbas (Brill 2010) 377, 396–97 (emphasizing the contribution of Heinrich Triepel and Dionisio Anzilotti on the principle of primacy of international law with regard to the issue of attribution).

---

[27] James Crawford, *The International Law Commission's Articles on State Responsibility. Introduction, Text and Commentaries* (Cambridge University Press 2002) 58–60; James Crawford, Jacqueline Peel, and Simon Olleson, 'The ILC's Articles on Responsibility of States for Internationally Wrongful Acts: Completion of the Second Reading' (2001) 12 European Journal of International Law 963, 969; James Crawford, 'The ILC's Articles on Responsibility of States for Internationally Wrongful Acts: A Retrospect' (2002) 96 American Journal of International Law 874, 889–90; Bruno Simma, 'The Work of the International Law Commission and its Fifty-Third Session (2001)' (2002) 71 Nordic Journal of International Law 123, 136–37; Christian J Tams, 'All's Well that Ends Well: Comments on the ILC's Articles on State Responsibility' (2002) 62 Zeitschrift für Ausländisches Öffentliches Recht und Völkerrecht 759, 768–70; James Crawford and Simon Olleson, 'The Continuing Debate on a UN Convention on State Responsibility' (2005) 54 International & Comparative Law Quarterly 959.

[28] A/RES/56/83, 12 December 2001. See Shabtai Rosenne, 'State Responsibility – *Festina Lente*' in Shabtai Rosenne, *Essays on International Law and Practice* (Martinus Nijhoff Publishers 2007) 533, 535–37.

[29] Karl Zemanek, 'Appropriate Instruments for Codification. Reflections on the ILC Draft on State Responsibility' in *Studi di diritto internazionale in onore di Gaetano Arangio-Ruiz*, vol II (Editoriale Scientifica 2004) 897.

> is annexed to the present resolution, and commends them to the attention of Governments without prejudice to the question of their future adoption or other appropriate action;[30]

The General Assembly periodically commended ARSIWA to the attention of Governments 'without prejudice to the question of their future adoption or other appropriate action'[31] and acknowledged their importance[32] or continued to acknowledge their importance and usefulness.[33]

Whether the entirety of ARSIWA correspond to the content of customary international law, namely to concepts of common currency in international law that reflect 'what actually happens in the life of international society',[34] and is, therefore, binding to the international community is controverted.[35] Accordingly, James Crawford has stated:

> The fact that the Articles have been so widely used does not mean that they necessarily constitute general international law. An adjudicator must always consider the relationship between each of the ILC Articles and general international law. One of the things that the Commission learned about codification at a very early stage is that it is impossible to write down any proposition of international law without engaging in an act of creation. Questions will arise as to the precise formulation of the rule, even if there is no doubt about it in principle. It is equally

[30] A/RES/56/83, 12 December 2001. See also General Assembly Official Records (GAOR), Fifty-Sixth Session, 12 December 2001, A/56/PV.85, at 3: 'the General Assembly would welcome the conclusion of the work of the International Law Commission on this topic and the adoption by the Commission of draft articles and a detailed commentary. The Assembly would also take note of the articles on responsibility of States for internationally wrongful acts and commend them to the attention of Governments without prejudice to the question of their future adoption or other appropriate action.' As to the divergent positions of States regarding the 'adoption' of ARSIWA, see the discussion within the Sixth Committee of the General Assembly, Seventy-First Session, Summary Record of the 31st meeting, 4 November 2016, document A/C.6/71/SR.31.

[31] A/RES/59/35, 2 December 2004; A/RES/62/61, 6 December 2007; A/RES/65/19, 6 December 2010; A/RES/68/104, 16 December 2013; A/RES/71/133, 13 December 2016.

[32] A/RES/65/19, 6 December 2010.

[33] A/RES/68/104, 16 December 2013; A/RES/71/133, 13 December 2016.

[34] Report of the International Law Commission on the Work of its Twenty-Fifth Session, 7 May–13 July 1973, document A/9010/REV.1, Yearbook of the International Law Commission, 1973, Volume II, 161, 190, para 11, document A/CN.4/SER. A/1973/Add. 1.

[35] See, *ex multis*, Helmut Philipp Aust, 'Through the Prism of Diversity: the Articles on State Responsibility in the Light of the ILC Fragmentation Report' (2006) 49 German Yearbook of International Law 165, 171; Stephan Wittich, 'The International Law Commission's Articles on the Responsibility of States for Internationally Wrongful Acts Adopted on Second Reading' (2002) 15 Leiden Journal of International Law 891, 917; Christine Chinkin, 'A Critique of the Public/Private Dimension' (1999) 10 European Journal of International Law 387; Ian Brownlie, 'State Responsibility and the International Court of Justice' in Malgosia Fitzmaurice and Dan Sarooshi (eds), *Issues of State Responsibility before International Judicial Institutions* (Hart Publishing 2004) 11, 12, referring to *Gabčikovo-Nagymaros Project (Hungary v Slovakia)*, Judgment, 25 September 1997, ICJ Reports 1997, 7; James Crawford, 'The International Court of Justice and the Law of State Responsibility' in Christian J Tams and James Sloan, *The Development of International Law by the International Court of Justice* (Oxford University Press 2013) 85.

difficult to segregate a rule into those parts which constitute a declaration of the existing law and those that do not. The two relate to each other in subtle ways.[36]

The ICJ has significantly relied, in its decisions, upon the draft articles provisionally adopted from 1973 to 1996 and upon the draft articles adopted on first reading in 1996 and ARSIWA, and has established the customary character of the rules of attribution codified therein.[37] Notably, this applies to the rules provided by ARSIWA Articles 4 (conduct of organs of a State), 5 (conduct of persons or entities exercising elements of governmental authority), 7 (excess of authority or contravention of instructions), and 8 (conduct directed or controlled by a State). A close reading of the *travaux préparatoires* of ARSIWA shows that the rules of attributability did not cause serious divergences within the codification process. This holds true even in relation to the works of the unsuccessful 1930 Hague Conference for the Codification of International Law,[38] and may be affirmed with regard to the works of the ILC under the chairmanship of Roberto Ago, at the latest.[39]

[36] James Crawford, 'Investment Arbitration and the ILC Articles on State Responsibility' (2010) 25 ICSID Review – Foreign Investment Law Journal 127, 128. See also David D Caron, 'The ILC Articles on State Responsibility: the Paradoxical Relationship Between Form and Authority' (2002) 96 American Journal of International Law 857, 867–68: 'To my surprise, I found that the Tribunal did not assess the articles but, instead, tended to accept them as given.'

[37] See *United States Diplomatic and Consular Staff in Tehran (United States of America v Iran)*, Judgment, 24 May 1980, ICJ Reports 1980, 3; *Military and Paramilitary Activities in and against Nicaragua (Nicaragua v United States of America)*, Merits, Judgment, 27 June 1986, ICJ Reports 1986, 14; *Differences Relating to Immunity from Legal Process of a Special-Rapporteur of the Commission of Human Rights*, Advisory Opinion, 29 April 1999, ICJ Reports 1999, 62; *Armed Activities in the Territory of the Congo (DRC v Uganda)*, Judgment, 19 December 2005, ICJ Reports 2005, 168; *Application of the Convention on the Prevention and Punishment of the Crime of Genocide (Bosnia and Herzegovina v Serbia and Montenegro)*, Judgment, 26 February 2007, ICJ Reports 2007, 43. Outside the jurisdiction of the ICJ, cf ICTY, Appeals Chamber, *Tadić*, IT-94-1-A, Judgement, 15 July 1999.

[38] Roberto Ago, First Report on State Responsibility, by Mr Roberto Ago, Special Rapporteur, 'Review of previous work on codification of the topic of the international responsibility of States', 7 May 1969 and 20 January 1970, para 39, document A/CN.4/217 and ADD.1, Yearbook of the International Law Commission, 1969, Volume II, 125, 132, document A/CN.4/SER.A/1969/Add.1: 'Serious divergences [at the 1930 Hague Conference for the Codification of International Law] appeared, however, which related less to the principles concerning responsibility as such than to the substantive principles governing the treatment of foreigners, the two questions being closely connected in the draft under consideration.' The Third Committee of the Hague Conference for the Codification of International Law never explicitly contemplated a distinction between primary and secondary norms, the codification undertaking being particularly focused on the substantive rules on reparation by States for the injuries inflicted to aliens in their territory. However, the majority of the articles proposed by the Third Committee established rules that were later classified as ones of 'attribution' (Articles 1, 6, 7, 9, 10). This is an important pointer that, even at the time of the Codification Conference, there was unequivocal consensus in the community of nations as to the codification of attributability rules, also by virtue of a plethora of arbitral case law that already clarified their fundamental tenets. See Third Committee of the Conference for the Codification of International Law, The Hague, 13 March–12 April 1930, Text of Articles on Responsibility of States for Damage Done in Their Territory to the Person or Property of Foreigners, League of Nations publication, V.Legal, 1930.V.7, document C.228.M.115.1930.V, (1930) 24 Special Supplement American Journal of International Law 188.

[39] Roberto Ago, Third Report on State Responsibility, by Mr Roberto Ago, Special Rapporteur, 'The internationally wrongful act of the State, source of international responsibility', 5 March, 7 April, 28 April, and 18 May 1971, para 16, document A/CN.4/246 and Add.1-3, Yearbook of the International

In international legal scholarship, the recognition of the customary status of the attribution rules codified in ARSIWA is broadly accepted,[40] even though minority positions to the contrary are recorded.[41] Out of the decisions of international courts, tribunals, and other bodies that have been compiled every three years by the Secretary-General at the request of the General Assembly, the relative majority pertain to the application of Chapter II of Part One of ARSIWA (Articles 4 to 11).[42]

The prospective adoption or non-adoption of ARSIWA in the form of an international treaty would not affect the conclusion that the rules of attributability established therein codify customary international law. ARSIWA's rules on attribution of conduct to a State stand as the most authoritative statement of customary international law on the topic (*ratio scripta*), also noting that in the field of international responsibility in general 'informal sources are still dominating'.[43] Such a conclusion is consistent with a warranted rationalist posture rather than a strictly voluntarist approach to international law making.[44]

Law Commission, 1971, Volume II (Part One), 199, 201-202, document A/CN.4/SER.A/1971/Add.1 (Part 1).

---

[40] *Ex multis*, Alain Pellet, 'Remarques sur la jurisprudence récente de la C.I.J. dans le domaine de la responsabilité internationale' in Marcelo Kohen, Robert Kolb, and Djacoba Liva Tehindrazanarivelo (eds), *Perspective of International Law in the 21st Century. Liber Amicorum Professor Christian Dominicé* (Martinus Nijhoff Publishers 2012) 321, 322, 332; James Crawford, 'Investment Arbitration and the ILC Articles on State Responsibility' (2010) 25 ICSID Review – Foreign Investment Law Journal 127, 133; Rosalyn Higgins, 'The Concept of "The State": Variable Geometry and Dualist Perceptions' in Laurence Boisson de Chazournes and Vera Gowlland-Debbas (eds), *The International Legal System in Quest of Equity and Universality. Liber Amicorum Georges Abi-Saab* (Martinus Nijhoff Publishers 2001) 547, 559; Pierre-Marie Dupuy, 'Quarante ans de codification du droit de la responsabilité internationale des États: un bilan' (2003) 107 Revue Génerale de Droit International Public 305, 316; Maurizio Arcari, 'Le juge et la codification du droit de la responsabilité: quelques remarques concernant l'application judiciaire des articles de la CDI sur la responsabilité de l'État pour fait internationalement illicite' in Nerina Boschiero et al (eds), *International Courts and the Development of International Law: Essays in Honour of Tullio Treves* (TMC Asser Press 2013) 19, 21.

[41] Gregory Townsend, 'State Responsibility for Acts of De Facto Agents' (1997) 14 Arizona Journal of International & Comparative Law 635.

[42] Report of the Secretary-General, 'Responsibility of States for internationally wrongful acts. Compilation of decisions of international jurisdictions and other international organs', document A/62/62 (1 February 2007), document A/62/62/Add.1 (17 April 2007), document A/65/76 (30 April 2010), document A/68/72 (30 April 2013), document A/71/80 (21 April 2016). The compilation of 2010 showed that, out of 182 references, 59 specifically concerned the attribution of an internationally wrongful act to a State. See Maurizio Arcari, 'Le juge et la codification du droit de la responsabilité: quelques remarques concernant l'application judiciaire des articles de la CDI sur la responsabilité de l'État pour fait internationalement illicite' in Nerina Boschiero et al (eds), *International Courts and the Development of International Law: Essays in Honour of Tullio Treves* (TMC Asser Press 2013) 19, 20–22, fn 9.

[43] Christian Tomuschat, 'Attribution of International Responsibility: Direction and Control' in Malcolm Evans and Panos Koutrakos (eds), *The International Responsibility of the European Union: European and International Perspectives* (Hart Publishing 2013) 7, 12.

[44] Roberto Ago, 'Nouvelles réflexions sur la codification du droit international' (1988) 92 Revue Générale du Droit International Public 539, 540, 573.

4. 'Act of the State' and *Act of State*

The set of international rules of attribution operates to determine what conduct may be qualified as an 'act of the State under international law', an expression adopted by Roberto Ago in his capacity as Special Rapporteur for the topic of State responsibility.[45] Attribution doctrines are to be clearly distinguished from the *act of State* doctrine applied by common law courts. The latter doctrine represents a rule of decision that pertains to the merits of proceedings and prevents a domestic court from sitting in judgment on the validity of an official act of a foreign State executed within its jurisdiction.[46] While attribution (as well as sovereign immunity) rules derive from customary international law, the *act of State* doctrine is based on 'constitutional underpinnings',[47] appearing as an expression of the municipal principle of separation of powers applied in international relations.[48] On one hand, the *act of State* doctrine proceeds from domestic law and commands a national judge to defer to a foreign sovereignty. On the other hand, attribution operates in the context of an international dispute, as being a requisite for the imposition of international responsibility to a sovereign.

5. Attribution and Jurisdiction

'Questions of attribution, a chapter of international responsibility, are logically distinct from issues of jurisdiction.'[49] As to the jurisdiction of a domestic court, the

[45] This concept is clearly elucidated in *Eastern Steamship Lines, Inc (United States) v Germany (War-Risk Insurance Premium Claim)*, 11 March 1924, 7 RIAA 71, 73.

[46] *Underhill v Hernandez*, 168 US 250, 18 S Ct 83 (1897); *Ricaud v American Metal Co*, 246 US 304 (1917); *Luther v Sagor* [1921] 3 KB 532; *Bernstein v NV Nederlandsche-Amerikaansche Stoomvaart-Maatschappij*, 210 F2d 375 (1954); *Banco Nacional de Cuba v Sabbatino*, 376 US 398, 84 S Ct 923 (1964); *Alfred Dunhill of London, Inc v Republic of Cuba et al*, 425 US 682, 96 S Ct 1854 (1976); *Kirkpatrick and C, Inc et al v Environmental Tectonics Corp, International*, 493 US 400, 110 S Ct 701 (1990).

[47] *Banco Nacional de Cuba v Sabbatino*, 376 US 398, 423 (1964).

[48] Howard Thayer Kingsbury, 'The "Act of State" Doctrine' (1910) 4 American Journal of International Law 359; George Grenville Phillimore, 'Immunité des Ètats au point de vue de la juridiction ou de l'exécution forcée' (1925) 8 Recueil des Cours 413, 436; E C S Wade, 'Act of State in English Law: Its Relation with International Law' (1934) 15 British Year Book of International Law 98; F A Mann, 'The Sacrosanctity of Foreign Acts of State' (1943) 59 Law Quarterly Review 42; Richard A Falk, *The Role of Domestic Court in the International Legal Order* (Syracuse University Press 1964) 139; Martin Domke, 'Act of State: Sabbatino in the Courts and in Congress' (1964) 3 Columbia Journal of Transnational Law 99; Michael Singer, 'The Act of State Doctrine of the United Kingdom: An Analysis with Comparisons to United States Practice' (1981) 75 American Journal of International Law 283; Thomas H Hill, 'Sovereign Immunity and Act of the State Doctrine. Theory and Policy in the United States' (1982) 46 Rabels Zeitschrift für Ausländisches und Internationales Privatrecht 118, 123; Hazel Fox, 'Reexamining the Act of State Doctrine: An Integrated Conflicts Analysis' (1992) 33 Harvard International Law Journal 521; Harold H Koh, 'International Business Transactions in United States Courts' (1996) 261 Recueil des Cours 9, 77.

[49] Christian Tomuschat, 'Attribution of International Responsibility: Direction and Control' in Malcolm Evans and Panos Koutrakos (eds), *The International Responsibility of the European Union: European and International Perspectives* (Hart Publishing 2013) 7, 33.

criteria embodied within the rules for the application of the doctrine of sovereign immunity are distinct from the prongs of attribution for the purposes of international responsibility for internationally wrongful acts.[50] However, a convergence between two such normative regimes is not only found in international law, but is also desirable from a policy viewpoint.[51] As to the jurisdiction of an international court or tribunal, attributability does not stand as a jurisdictional issue affecting its power to adjudicate a given dispute. Instead, attribution represents a question of merits consisting in the establishment of a requisite for the finding of international responsibility of a State. This notwithstanding, it is open to States to qualify issues of attribution as of (international) jurisdiction. This appears to be the choice adopted by the US and Iran in the Algiers Accords of 19 January 1981 to establish the jurisdiction of the Iran–US Claims Tribunal pursuant to the Claims Settlement Declaration Article VII(3)–(4).[52]

6. Attribution and Immunity

Sovereign immunity and attribution are different legal aspects of the same sociopolitical requirement to refer certain conduct to the person of the State as actor in a dimension of internationality, both contributing to define the State '*selon le droit international*'.[53] The international law of State immunity operates in the context of proceedings between a foreign sovereign and a natural or juridical person pending before a national judge, requiring the latter to refrain from the adjudication of certain, though not all, disputes (*restrictive* theory of State immunity).[54]

[50] David D Caron, 'The Basis of Responsibility: Attribution and Other Trans-substantive Rules of State Responsibility' in Richard B Lillich and Daniel B Magraw (eds), *The Iran-United States Claims Tribunal: Its Contribution to the Law of State Responsibility* (Transnational Publishers, Inc 1998) 109, 164.

[51] See section 6 of this chapter, section 4.2 of Chapter II, and section 4.2.2 of Chapter III.

[52] Declaration of the Government of the Democratic and Popular Republic of Algeria Concerning the Settlement of Claims by the Government of the United States of America and the Government of the Islamic Republic of Iran (Claims Settlement Declaration), 19 January 1981, 1 IRAN-US CTR 11-12 (1981-1982):

Article VII
For the purposes of this Agreement:

[...]

3. 'Iran' means the Government of Iran, any political subdivision of Iran, and any agency, instrumentality, or entity controlled by the Government of Iran or any political subdivision thereof.
4. The 'United States' means the Government of the United States, any political subdivision of the United States, and any agency, instrumentality or entity controlled by the Government of the United States or any political subdivision thereof.

[53] Mathias Forteau, 'L'État selon le droit international: une figure à géométrie variable?' (2007) 111 Revue Générale de Droit International Public 737, 752–54.

[54] For a doctrinal review, cf Dionisio Anzilotti, 'L'esenzione degli stati stranieri dalla giurisdizione (Saggio di critica e di ricostruzione)' (1910) 5 Rivista di Diritto Internazionale 477; André Weiss,

The international law of attribution dictates the criteria to qualify given conduct as attributable to the State in the context of public international law disputes.[55] Accordingly, they serve markedly different purposes:

> The restrictive theory of sovereign immunity does not constitute a limit on the international responsibility of States, but rather a limit on the municipal immunity of States for certain activities. The restrictive theory of immunity serves to make available certain municipal court remedies, not to alter the international responsibility of the State.[56]

'Compétence ou incompétence des tribunaux a l'égard des États étrangers' (1923) 1 Recueil des Cours 521; George Grenville Phillimore, 'Immunité des Ètats au point de vue de la juridiction ou de l'exécution forcée' (1925) 8 Recueil des Cours 413; Charles Fairman, 'Some Disputed Applications of the Principle of State Immunity' (1928) 22 American Journal of International Law 566; Gerald G Fitzmaurice, 'State Immunity from Proceedings in Foreign Courts' (1933) 14 British Year Book of International Law 101; Eleonor W Allen, *The Position of Foreign States Before National Courts, Chiefly in Continental Europe* (The Macmillan Company 1933); Gaetano Morelli, 'Limiti dell'ordinamento statuale e limiti della giurisdizione' (1933) 25 Rivista di Diritto Internazionale 382; Jean-Paulin Niboyet, 'Les immunités des États étrangers engagés dans des transactions privées' (1936) 43 Revue Générale de Droit International Public 525; Charles Carabiber, 'De quelques aspects nouveaux de l'immunité de juridiction des Ètats' (1938) 33 Revue Critique de Droit International 369; Charles Rousseau, 'Compétence des tribunaux internes à l'égard des États étrangers' (1939) 46 Revue Générale de Droit International Public 427; Rolando Quadri, *La giurisdizione sugli Stati stranieri* (Giuffrè 1941); J E S Fawcett, 'Legal Aspects of State Trading' (1948) 25 British Year Book of International Law 34; Jean-Paulin Niboyet, 'Immunité de juridiction et incompétence d'attribution' (1950) 39 Revue Critique de Droit International Privé 139; Hersch Lauterpacht, 'The Problem of Jurisdictional Immunities of Foreign States' (1951) 28 British Year Book of International Law 220; Charles Freyria, 'Les limites de l'immunité de juridiction et d'exécution des États étrangers' (1951) 40 Revue Critique de Droit International Privé 207; Jean-Flavien Lalive, 'L'immunité de juridiction des Etats et des organisations internationales' (1953) 84 Recueil des Cours 205; Louis Cavaré, 'L'immunité de juridiction des États étrangers' (1954) 58 Revue Générale de Droit International Public 177; N C H Dunbar, 'Controversial Aspects of Sovereign Immunity in the Case Law of Some States' (1971) 132 Recueil des Cours 197; Riccardo Luzzatto, *Stati stranieri e giurisdizione nazionale* (Giuffré 1972); Sompong Sucharitkul, 'Immunities of Foreign States Before National Authorities' (1976) 149 Recueil des Cours 87; Leo J Bouchez, 'The Nature and Scope of State Immunity from Jurisdiction and Execution' (1979) 10 Netherlands Yearbook of International Law 1; Ian Sinclair, 'The Law of Sovereign Immunity. Recent Developments' (1980) 167 Recueil des Cours 113; James Crawford, 'Execution of Judgments and Foreign Immunity' (1981) 75 American Journal of International Law 820; James Crawford, 'International Law and Foreign Sovereigns: Distinguishing Immune Transactions' (1983) 54 British Year Book of International Law 75; Peter D Troboff, 'Foreign State Immunity: Emerging Consensus on Principles' (1986) 200 Recueil des Cours 235; Christoph H Schreuer, *State Immunity: Some Recent Developments* (Cambridge University Press 1988) 69–70; Joe Verhoeven (ed), *Le droit international des immunités: contestation ou consolidation?* (Larcier 2004); Natalino Ronzitti and Gabriella Venturini, *Le immunità giurisdizionali degli Stati e degli altri enti internazionali* (CEDAM 2008); Sally El Sawah, *Les immunités des États et des organisations internationales. Immunités et procès équitable* (Larcier 2012); Anne Peters, Evelyne Lagrange, Stefan Oeter, and Christian Tomuschat (eds), *Immunities in the Age of Global Constitutionalism* (Brill 2015); Hazel Fox and Philippa Webb, *The Law of State Immunity* (3rd edn revised and updated, Oxford University Press 2013) 25 et seq.

---

[55] Dionisio Anzilotti, 'La responsabilité internationale des États a raison des dommages soufferts par des étrangers' (1906) 13 Revue Générale de Droit International Public 5, 13.

[56] David D Caron, 'The Basis of Responsibility: Attribution and Other Trans-substantive Rules of State Responsibility' in Richard B Lillich and Daniel B Magraw (eds), *The Iran-United States Claims Tribunal: Its Contribution to the Law of State Responsibility* (Transnational Publishers, Inc 1998) 109, 164.

Nevertheless, it pays to emphasize the overlap and convergence of criteria adopted within the application of the law of State immunity before the municipal judge and the international rules of attribution resorted to by international judges and arbitrators.[57] Indeed, the attribution of conduct to the State logically represents a preliminary determination to a domestic court's decision whether to grant or deny to a sovereign the exemption from suit. Thus, it appears that both the law of State immunity and the international rules of attribution concur as to the operation to *bridge* the conduct of State organs and instrumentalities to the sovereign. What ultimately differs is not the attributability of an act to the State, but the applicability of an exception to immunity associated with that act.

The distinction between immunity and attribution issues had already been acknowledged in the early arbitral practice. In the case of the *Zafiro*, the British–American Mixed Claims Commission observed:

> We have no difficulty in distinguishing those cases from the one before us. The *Exchange* [[58]] case had to do with the immunity of warships in foreign ports. So also the other cases first cited have to do with claims to immunity from process while in foreign ports. That is quite a different question from the one before us, which is not one of what immunity the *Zafiro* might have claimed in Hong Kong, but of what responsibility attaches to the United States for her action, in Manila Bay, where and while she was acting as a supply ship for Admiral Dewey's squadron, in the naval operations he was then and there conducting, and was under his orders through a naval officer put on board to carry them out.[59]

The comparison between the law of sovereign immunity and the law of attribution is apposite only in case of activities undertaken by State organs pursuant to ARSIWA Article 4 and 'persons' pursuant to ARSIWA Article 5. Instead, as discussed below, the conduct of 'private' individuals pursuant to ARSIWA Article 8 does not require any official capacity or exercise of governmental authority for the purposes of attribution.[60] Therefore, their activities do not regularly offer any commonality in scope as a possible ground for application of the doctrine of sovereign immunity, which under its restrictive tenets only covers the acts of the State that embody an exercise of its sovereignty (*acta jure imperii*), unless otherwise waived (for instance, by way of express or implied consent).[61] This reveals a constant

[57] Emmanuel Gaillard, 'Effectivité des sentences arbitrales: immunité des Etats et autonomie des personnes morales dépendant d'eux' in Isabelle Pingel-Lenuzza (ed), *Droit des immunités et exigences du procès équitable. Actes du colloque du 30 avril 2004* (Éditions A Pedone 2004) 119, 124.

[58] *The Schooner Exchange v McFaddon et al*, 11 US 116 (1812).

[59] *D Earnshaw and Others (Great Britain) v United States (Zafiro case)*, 30 November 1925, 6 RIAA 160, 162.

[60] See section 5.3 of Chapter II.

[61] Carlo de Stefano, 'Arbitration Agreements as Waivers to Sovereign Immunity' (2014) 30 Arbitration International 59.

problem in the functioning of the rule of State immunity, which displays a combination of *ratione materiae* and *ratione personae* elements.[62] Nevertheless, the United Nations Convention on Jurisdictional Immunities of States and Their Property of 2 December 2004 (UNCSI), which has not yet entered into force, clearly endorses a *ratione materiae* (functional) approach to the law of State immunity.[63] Indeed, a State activity is held to be either governmental or commercial on the basis of its nature and, only on a subsidiary ground, of its purpose.[64] In general, UNCSI proceeds from the cardinal assumption that 'jurisdictional immunities of States and their property are generally accepted as a principle of customary international law', as clarified by the Preamble of the Convention.[65] The denial of immunity is conceived as an exception to the general rule, on the basis of a catalogue of enumerated justifications—generally *ratione materiae*—that are provided by the Convention ('list method').[66]

6.1 State Organs

Pursuant to UNCSI Article 2.1(b)(i), (ii), and (iv), the mantle of sovereign immunity may cover the 'State and its various organs', 'constituent units of a federal State or political subdivisions of the State, which are entitled to perform acts in the exercise of sovereign authority, and are acting in that capacity', and 'representatives of the State acting in that capacity'. Immunity from jurisdiction is attracted by *acta jure imperii* (in exercise of sovereign authority), while a municipal judge

[62] Gerald G Fitzmaurice, 'State Immunity from Proceedings in Foreign Courts' (1933) 14 British Year Book of International Law 101, 121: 'The truth is that a sovereign State does not cease to be a sovereign State because it performs acts which a private citizen might perform.' Lord Wilberforce observed in *I Congreso del Partido* [1983] 1 AC 244: 'If a trader is always a trader, a State remains a State.'

[63] United Nations Convention on Jurisdictional Immunities of States and Their Property (UNCSI), Annex to A/RES/59/38, 2 December 2004. See David P Stewart, 'The UN Convention on Jurisdictional Immunities of States and Their Property' (2005) 99 American Journal of International Law 194; Gerhard Hafner and Ulrike Köhler, 'The United Nations Convention on Jurisdictional Immunities of States and Their Property' (2004) 35 Netherlands Yearbook of International Law 3; Gerhard Hafner and Leonore Lange, 'La Convention des Nations Unies sur les immunités juridictionnelles des Etats et de leurs biens' (2004) 50 Annuaire Français de Droit International 45; Isabelle Pingel-Lenuzza, 'Observations sur la convention du 17 janvier 2005 sur les immunités juridictionnelles des Etats et de leurs biens' (2005) 122 Journal du Droit International (Clunet) 1045.

[64] UNCSI Article 2.2.

[65] UNCSI Preamble.

[66] The same legislative framework is adopted in the US Foreign Sovereign Immunities Act 1976, 28 USC §§ 1602–1611 and in the UK State Immunity Act 1978, *The Public General Acts* (HM Stationery Office 1978), Part I, Chapter 33, 715. See also Singapore State Immunity Act 1979, Pakistan State Immunity Ordinance 1981, South Africa Foreign State Immunities Act 1981, Canadian State Immunity Act 1982, Malawi Immunities and Privileges Act 1984, Australian Foreign State Immunities Act 1985. cf the relevant texts in the Codification Division of the Office of Legal Affairs of the Secretariat of the United Nations, *Materials on Jurisdictional Immunity of States and Their Property*, United Nations Legislative Series, Book 20, 1982, document ST/LEG/SER.B/20 (Sales No E/F.81.V.10); Andrew Dickinson, Rae Lindsay, and James P Loonam, *State Immunity. Selected Materials and Commentary* (Oxford University Press 2004).

can ordinarily adjudicate State commercial acts. The requirement to act in sovereign (governmental) capacity seems to exclude from the cover of immunity such conducts not falling, even incidentally, in the scope of the office or authority of the organ. Such conducts may embody acts of a private or personal nature (similarly to purely private acts not attributable to the State pursuant to the *ultra vires* rule under ARSIWA Article 7).

Immunity may comprehensively cover the conduct of all powers exercising a State function, such as the legislative, the executive, the judiciary, or other authority of a regulatory or administrative nature. Accordingly, the meaning of 'State' encompasses all the various organs of government, however designated, such as monarchs or heads of State, heads of government, ministries, departments, and offices (to the inclusion of subordinate officials), as well as diplomatic missions and consular posts.[67] Moreover, the application of the regime of sovereign immunity is not affected by the adoption of a particular form of State or government.[68] The circumstance of a given administrative authority as having separate legal personality under domestic law does not preclude its qualification as *de jure* State organ, as such possibly benefiting from the exemption from suit or seizure before foreign courts.[69]

Constituent units and political subdivisions are demanded to fulfil the dual requirement of being entitled to perform acts in the exercise of sovereign authority and of acting in that capacity (entitlement and actual performance).[70] Similar to the logic of the international rules of attribution, the threshold rationale is that the internal delegation of sovereignty between the central and the peripheral levels of government is, as a general practice, irrelevant for the purposes of sovereign immunity. Accordingly, courts have traditionally granted immunity to acts in the exercise of governmental authority undertaken by federated states,[71]

[67] Draft Articles on Jurisdictional Immunities of States and Their Property, with commentaries, in Report of the International Law Commission on the Work of its Forty-Third Session, 29 April–19 July 1991, document A/46/10, Yearbook of the International Law Commission, 1991, Volume II (Part Two), 13, 14, 15–16, document A/CN.4/SER.A/1991/Add.1 (Part 2).

[68] Austrian Supreme Court, 10 May 1950, *Dralle v Republic of Czechoslovakia*, Case No 41, 17 ILR 155; *Kingdom of Norway v Federal Sugar Refining Co*, 286 F. 188 (1923); *Kahan v Pakistan Federation* [1951] 2 KB 1003 (CA). See André Weiss, 'Compétence ou incompétence des tribunaux a l'égard des Etats étrangers' (1923) 1 Recueil des Cours 521, 526; Sompong Sucharitkul, 'Immunities of Foreign States Before National Authorities' (1976) 149 Recueil des Cours 93, 99.

[69] *La Générale des Carrières et des Mines v FG Hemisphere Associates LLC*, 17 July 2012, Privy Council Appeal No 6/2011 [2012] UKPC 27 (Judicial Committee of the Privy Council), para 16: 'But an organ of the state may under certain circumstances have legal personality.'; *R (on the application of Alamieyeseigha) v Crown Prosecution Service* [2005] EWCH 2704; *Mackenzie-Kennedy v Air Council* [1927] LR 2 KB 517.

[70] UNCSI Article 2.1(b)(ii).

[71] Cour d'Appel de Bruxelles, 22 November 1907, *Feldman v Etat de Bahia*, Pasicrisie Belge, 1908-II-55, (1932) 26 Supplement to the American Journal of International Law 484; Cour d'Appel de Colmar, 1928, *Etat de Céara v Dorr et al*, Dalloz Périodique, 1933-I-196; *Sullivan v State of Sao Paulo*, 36 F.Supp. 503 (1941), 10 Annual Digest of Public International Law Cases (1941-1942), Case No 50, 178; Tribunale di Firenze, 1906, *Somigli v Stato di San Paolo nel Brasile*, (1907) 2 Rivista di Diritto Internazionale 379-380; Cour d'Appel de Bruxelles, 1891, *De Bock v Etat indépendant du Congo*,

municipalities,[72] and other territorial entities, to the inclusion of overseas territories.[73]

ARSIWA Article 4 holds as attributable both *acta jure imperii* and *acta jure gestionis* executed by all categories of State organs.[74] As David Caron has remarked:

> If, for example, a Ministry of Defense were to enter into a contract for the purchase of goods and later repudiate the contract, then it seems clear that Ministry may be subject to suit in given municipal courts depending on the terms of the contract and the nature of the transaction, and that the State of which the Ministry is an organ may be internationally responsible for the repudiation.[75]

This concept has been stated in the case of *Noble Ventures v Romania* by an international investment tribunal established under the aegis of the International Centre for Settlement of Investment Disputes (ICSID):

> The distinction plays an important role in the field of sovereign immunity when one comes to the question of whether a State can claim immunity before the courts of another State. However, in the context of responsibility, it is difficult to see why commercial acts, so called acta iure gestionis, should by definition not be attributable while governmental acts, so call acta iure imperii, should be attributable. The ILC draft does not maintain or support such a distinction.[76]

Pasicrisie Belge, 1891-II-419, 420. Contra, Tribunal de grand instance de Paris, 15 January 1969, *Neger v Land de Hesse*, (1970) 59 Revue Critique de Droit International Privé 99–101.

---

[72] Cour de Cassation, Chambre des requêtes, 1 July 1895, *Ville de Genève v Consorts de Civry*, Sirey 1896-I-225, (1894) 21 Journal du Droit International Privé (Clunet) 1032. See Jean-Paulin Niboyet, 'Immunité de juridiction et incompétence d'attribution' (1950) 39 Revue Critique de Droit International Privé 139, 147; Charles Rousseau, 'Compétence des tribunaux internes à l'égard des Etats étrangers', (1939) 46 Revue Générale de Droit International Public 427; Louis Cavaré, 'L'immunité de juridiction des États étrangers' (1954) 25 Revue Générale de Droit International Public 202; C J Hamson, 'Immunity of Foreign States: The Practice of the French Courts' (1950) 27 British Year Book of International Law 321.

[73] *Van Heyningen v Netherlands Indies Government* [1948] QWN 22, 15 Annual Digest of International Law Cases, Case No 43, 138 (per Judge Philipps of the Supreme Court of Queensland).

[74] Luigi Condorelli, 'L'imputation à l'État d'un fait internationalement illicite: solutions classiques et nouvelles tendances' (1984) 189 Recueil des Cours 9, 74: '*En conclusion, il nous semble justifié d'affirmer qu'en matière d'imputation à l'Etat des comportements de ses organes il n'y a aucune distinction à faire entre les comportements par lesquels s'exercent les prérogatives de la puissance publique et les autres: tous sont attribuables à l'Etat, le fait qu'ils constituent ou non une infraction dépendant du contenu des normes internationales en jeu.*'

[75] David D Caron, 'The Basis of Responsibility: Attribution and Other Trans-substantive Rules of State Responsibility' in Richard B Lillich and Daniel B Magraw (eds), *The Iran-United States Claims Tribunal: Its Contribution to the Law of State Responsibility* (Transnational Publishers, Inc 1998) 109, 164.

[76] *Noble Ventures, Inc v Romania*, ICSID Case No ARB/01/11, Award, 12 October 2005, para 82.

It may be submitted that the *noyau dur* of international disputes arises out of breaches of international law based on *acta jure imperii* (for instance, the unlawful use of force by one State against another State). Thus, from a descriptive perspective, a final finding of State responsibility is usually adjudicated in relation to attributable acts that would be immune from jurisdiction before the national judge.[77] Nevertheless, States, as Parties to international treaties, are at liberty to contract international obligations arising out of contractual breaches triggered through *acta jure gestionis* undertaken by State organs.[78] This may be the case of a State organ producing transboundary pollution to the detriment of neighbouring States. Instead, this is not the case of an 'umbrella clause' inserted in international investment agreements (clause of observance of obligations or undertakings, *clause de couverture*).[79] Indeed, the umbrella clause (similar to an 'elevator') grants an investor the possibility of filing a contract claim before an international investment tribunal, but it does not ultimately transform the law applicable to the cause of action from domestic to international.

In conclusion, all the acts of State organs that are immune from jurisdiction (*acta jure imperii*) are attributable to the State. Not all the acts attributable to the State (*acta jure imperii* and *acta jure gestionis*) are immune from jurisdiction. It is therefore established that the number of actions of State organs that are attributable to the State under public international law is normatively larger than the number of actions of State organs that are immune from jurisdiction before a domestic judge.

6.2 State Instrumentalities

UNCSI Article 2.1(b)(iii) also grants immunity to 'agencies or instrumentalities of the State or other entities, to the extent that they are entitled to perform and are actually performing acts in the exercise of sovereign authority of the State'. At the same time, UNCSI Article 10.3 underlines that immunity does not apply to 'a State enterprise or other entity established by a State which has an independent legal personality' in relation to its activities *jure privatorum*. The terms 'agencies' and 'instrumentalities' are used in UNCSI Article 2.1(b)(iii) as being interchangeably

[77] *Impregilo SpA v Islamic Republic of Pakistan*, ICSID Case No ARB/03/3, Decision on Jurisdiction, 22 April 2005, para 260: 'Only the State in the exercise of its sovereign authority ("puissance publique"), and not as a contracting party, may breach the obligations assumed under the BIT.'; *Bayindir Insaat Turizm Ticaret Ve Sanayi AS v Islamic Republic of Pakistan*, ICSID Case No ARB/03/29, Decision on Jurisdiction, 14 November 2005, para 83: 'When an investor invokes a breach of a BIT by the host State (not itself party to the investment contract), the alleged treaty violation is by definition an act of "puissance publique".'

[78] Luigi Condorelli, 'L'imputation à l'État d'un fait internationalement illicite: solutions classiques et nouvelles tendances' (1984) 189 Recueil des Cours 9, 145; Christine Chinkin, 'A Critique of the Public/Private Dimension' (1999) 10 European Journal of International Law 387, 392.

[79] See section 2.2 of Chapter III.

equivalent.[80] In addition, the drafters of the Convention inserted the reference to 'other entities' in order to cover 'private' persons exceptionally endowed with governmental authority, such as commercial banks entrusted by the State to grant import and export licences.[81]

Both State organs and instrumentalities benefit from immunity according to the same criteria, namely in connection to their *acta jure imperii* only.[82] Instead, the international law of attribution provides different tests for State organs and State instrumentalities. The core of the functional test enshrined in ARSIWA Article 5 is the finding of the exercise of elements of governmental authority by the 'State entity' in the particular instance in question. This functional test of attribution should be consistent with the nature test dictated by the law of State immunity to define governmental vis-à-vis commercial acts.[83] This necessitates that—differently from the set theory analysis undertaken for State organs—the number of actions of 'State entities' that are attributable to the State under ARSIWA Article 5 is normatively equal to the number of actions of 'State entities' that are immune from jurisdiction

[80] See also *Krajina v Tass Agency* [1949] 2 All ER 274 (CA); *Compañía Mercantil Argentina v United States Shipping Board* [1924] All ER 186 (CA); *Baccus SRL v Servicio National del Trigo* [1957] 1 QB 438 (CA).

[81] Draft Articles on Jurisdictional Immunities of States and Their Property, with commentaries, in Report of the International Law Commission on the Work of its Forty-Third Session, 29 April–19 July 1991, document A/46/10, Yearbook of the International Law Commission, 1991, Volume II (Part Two), 13, 17, document A/CN.4/SER.A/1991/Add.1 (Part 2). See also Catherine Kessedjan and Christoph H Schreuer, 'Le projet d'articles de la Commission du Droit International sur les immunités des Etats' (1992) 96 Revue Générale de Droit International Public 299, 321.

[82] Sompong Sucharitkul, *State Immunities and Trading Activities in International Law* (Stevens & Sons 1959) 104, 112–13; Christoph H Schreuer, *State Immunity: Some Recent Developments* (Cambridge University Press 1988) 92 et seq; Jean-Flavien Lalive, 'Contracts Between a State or a State Agency and a Foreign Company' (1964) 13 International & Comparative Law Quarterly 987; Paul Lagarde, 'Une notion ambivalente: l'"émanation" de l'Etat nationalisant' in *Droits et libertés à la fin du XXe siècle – Etudes offertes à Claude-Albert Colliard* (Éditions A Pedone 1984) 539; Fouad A M Riad, 'L'entreprise publique ou semi-publique en droit international privé' (1963) 108 Recueil des Cours 561; Karl-Heinz Böckstiegel, *Arbitration and State Enterprises. A Survey on the National and International State of Law and Practice* (Kluwer Law and Taxation Publishers 1984) 14, 34; K W Wedderburn, 'Sovereign Immunity of Foreign Public Corporations' (1957) 6 International & Comparative Law Quarterly 290; P J Kincaid, 'Sovereign Immunity of Foreign State-Owned Corporations' (1976) 10 Journal of World Trade Law 110.

[83] James Crawford, *State Responsibility. The General Part* (Cambridge University Press 2013) 130. See, in particular, Harvard Law School, Draft Convention on the International Responsibility of States for Injuries to (the Economic Interests of) Aliens (Louis B Sohn and R R Baxter, Rapporteurs), Article 17(2), (1961) 55 American Journal of International Law 545:

Article 17
(Levels of Government)

[...]

2. The terms 'organ of a State', 'agency of a State', 'official of a State', and 'employee of a State', as used in this Convention, do not include any organ, agency, official, or employee of any enterprise normally considered as commercial which is owned in whole or in part by a State or one of the entities referred to in paragraph 1 if such enterprise is, under the law of such State, a separate juristic person with respect to which the State neither accords immunity in its own courts nor claims immunity in foreign courts.

before a domestic judge. In this respect, coordination between the national and the international judiciary is of threshold importance in order to avoid jurisdictional lacunae that can frustrate the effectiveness of the right to legal redress of aliens against sovereigns.[84] As noted by Gordon Christenson:

> if immunity follows, the acts are attributable. A State cannot have it both ways. It cannot escape responsibility by claiming non-State action on the one hand while maintaining sovereign immunity on the other.[85]

To this extent, an overlap of liability under international and domestic law is applicable in relation to the conduct of State organs, in that their *acta jure gestionis* may be both attributable under ARSIWA Article 4 and non-immune from jurisdiction. Instead, the conduct of State instrumentalities is either attributable under ARSIWA Article 5 and immune from adjudication (*acta jure imperii*), or it is non-attributable under ARSIWA Article 5 and subject to domestic jurisdiction (*acta jure gestionis*). Accordingly, States should not overlook the legal implications of the use of the defence of immunity of their parastatals before municipal judges, since this very argument may be resorted to against them (*non venire contra factum proprium*) before an international jurisdiction to support a finding of empowerment to exercise elements of governmental authority.[86]

The foregoing analysis pertains to the treatment of State instrumentalities or parastatals for the purposes of attribution of conduct under ARSIWA Article 5. In addition, their acts *jure gestionis* may also be attributable pursuant to ARSIWA Article 8 based on the test of instructions, or direction or control, by a State organ. At the same time, those acts are not covered by State immunity in domestic court proceedings, since they are not undertaken in the exercise of sovereign or governmental authority.

7. Plan of the Study

This chapter has provided a definition of 'attribution' for the purposes of State responsibility for internationally wrongful acts and has emphasized the preliminary operation of rules of attributability in contrast to other secondary rules of

[84] Michel Cosnard, *La soumission des États aux tribunaux internes. Face à la théorie des immunités des États* (Éditions A Pedone 1996) 226.

[85] Gordon A Christenson, 'The Doctrine of Attribution in State Responsibility' in Richard B Lillich (ed), *International Law of State Responsibility for Injuries to Aliens* (University Press of Virginia 1983) 321, 330.

[86] As to early arbitral practice, see *Dickson Car Wheel Company (USA) v United Mexican States*, July 1931, 4 RIAA 669, 685. As to the practice of the Iran–US Claims Tribunal, see *SeaCo, Inc v The Islamic Republic of Iran, The Iranian Meat Organization, Iran Express Lines, and Star Line Co*, 11 IRAN-US CTR 210, 215 (1986-II).

international law. In addition, it has discussed the threshold principle of the supremacy of international law in order to elucidate the autonomous dimension of attribution issues in international law vis-à-vis municipal law. Last, it has offered an attempt at distinction between issues of attribution, on the one hand, and issues of jurisdiction and of State immunity, on the other.

Hereinafter, this treatise proceeds as follows. Chapter II illustrates the application of attribution rules in public international law, which have now been codified by ARSIWA. Accordingly, it explains the tests for attributability of the conduct of State organs (*de jure* and *de facto*) pursuant to ARSIWA Article 4, 'State entities' pursuant to ARSIWA Article 5, and individuals pursuant to ARSIWA Article 8. The rule of attribution of acts *ultra vires* pursuant to ARSIWA Article 7 is also analysed, which applies to the conduct of State organs and 'State entities', but not of 'private' individuals. Chapter III elucidates the application of attribution rules by international investment tribunals. This chapter is similar in structure to Chapter II, which is a consequence of the proximity of international investment law to public international law with regard to the topic of attribution of conduct to a Party to the applicable treaty. In addition, the treatise of attribution issues in investor–State dispute settlement (ISDS) requires further critical discussion, chiefly on the dialectics between *lex generalis* (customary international law) and *lex specialis* (international investment law), and on the distinction between treaty claims and contract claims for the purposes of the operation of umbrella clauses. Finally, the Conclusion provides more general reflections on the role and function of international principles and rules of attribution for the treatment of State organs, State instrumentalities, and 'private' individuals.

II
Attribution in Public International Law

1. State Organs

1.1 Notion

'According to a well-established rule of international law, the conduct of any organ of a state must be regarded as an act of that state. This rule, which is of a customary character, ...'[1] The ICJ addressed, with these words in the *Cumaraswamy affaire*, the canonical rule of attribution to the State of the acts and omissions of its organs, which has been codified by ARSIWA Article 4:

Article 4
Conduct of organs of a State

1. The conduct of any State organ shall be considered an act of that State under international law, whether the organ exercises legislative, executive, judicial or any other functions, whatever position it holds in the organization of the State, and whatever its character as an organ of the central Government or of a territorial unit of the State.
2. An organ includes any person or entity which has that status in accordance with the internal law of the State.[2]

The principle of attributability of the conduct of State organs may even appear to be tautological or the result of a circular line of reasoning: it is self-explanatory that a State is to be held liable for the acts of the 'persons' making up its machinery.[3] However, correlated problems of qualification and categorization have frequently arisen in international law practice. Hence, the function of ARSIWA Article 4 is to encompass all the varieties of such persons capable of engaging the international responsibility of a State on the basis of their institutional link with its apparatus.

[1] *Differences Relating to Immunity from Legal Process of a Special-Rapporteur of the Commission of Human Rights*, Advisory Opinion, 29 April 1999, ICJ Reports 1999, 62, 87; *Armed Activities in the Territory of the Congo (DRC v Uganda)*, Judgment, 19 December 2005, ICJ Reports 2005, 168, 242; *Application of the Convention on the Prevention and Punishment of the Crime of Genocide (Bosnia and Herzegovina v Serbia and Montenegro)*, Judgment, 26 February 2007, para 385, ICJ Reports 2007, 43, 202.

[2] ARSIWA Commentaries 40.

[3] Gordon A Christenson, 'Attributing Acts of Omission to the State' (1990–1991) 12 Michigan Journal of International Law 312, 333.

Attribution in International Law and Arbitration. Carlo de Stefano, Oxford University Press (2020).

DOI: 10.1093/law-oso/9780198844648.001.0001

Notwithstanding the marked degree of detail in relation to the various ramifications of public powers (to the inclusion of the sub-national level of government), from the standpoint of international law State organs should not to be categorized in an overly technical manner by reference to the definitions and status of internal law. What is relevant is the exercise of some power or authority as an expression of the government of a State, irrespective of formality and internal allocation of powers and competences ('*quelle que soit l'autorité de l'Etat dont elle procède*').[4] Indeed, in early arbitral practice, a plethora of generic references is found to State 'authorities',[5] 'agents',[6] and 'officials' or 'officers',[7] the latter being more often ascribed to the executive branch. The concept of 'organ' has eventually been preferred in the course of the process of codification of the law of State responsibility, since it indicates the mechanism of (organic) 'identification' (*agency*) exactly between a particular person and the person of the State, which is at the heart of the canonical rule of attribution. This is the proper meaning of the expression 'acting on behalf of the State', which was central in the doctrinal exercise undertaken by Roberto Ago in the codification process.

The forms of State or government of a given country are mere elements of the factual context, which is taken into consideration for the qualification of a person as being an organ for the purposes of attribution under international law.[8] Even

[4] Institut de Droit International, 'Responsabilité internationale des Etats à raison des dommages causés sur leur territoire à la personne et aux biens des étrangers' (Leo Strisower, Rapporteur), Résolution du 1 septembre 1927, Session de Lausanne, (1927) 33(III) Annuaire de l'Institut de Droit International 330-335, Article I(1).

[5] *Alabama Claims of the United States of America against Great Britain*, 14 September 1872, 29 RIAA 125, 131; *Underhill Cases*, 1903-1905, 9 RIAA 155-161; *Affaire relative à l'acquisition de la nationalité polonaise (Allemagne contre Pologne)*, 10 July 1924, 1 RIAA 401; *Owner of the Sarah B Putnam (United States) v Great Britain*, 6 November 1925, 6 RIAA 156-157; *La Masica Case (Great Britain, Honduras)*, 7 December 1916, 11 RIAA 549, 554; *Union Bridge Company (United States) v Great Britain*, 8 January 1924, 6 RIAA 138, 142; *Laura M B Janes et al (USA) v United Mexican States*, 16 November 1925, 4 RIAA 82; *Francisco Mallén (United Mexican States) v USA*, 27 April 1927, 4 RIAA 173, 178; *J J Boyd (USA) v United Mexican States*, 12 October 1928, 4 RIAA 380; *William E Chapman (USA) v United Mexican States*, 24 October 1930, 4 RIAA 632.

[6] *Administrative Decision No II*, 1 November 1923, 7 RIAA 23, 24; *Poggioli case (of a general nature)*, 1903, 10 RIAA 669, 673; *Miliani Case (of a general nature)*, 1903, 10 RIAA 584, 587; *Claims of Charles Oberlander and Barbara M Messenger against the Government of Mexico (United States of America/Mexico)*, 19 November 1897, 29 RIAA 327; *Queirolo*, 30 September 1901, 15 RIAA 407; *Don Juan B Sanguinetti*, 30 September 1901, 15 RIAA 403–04; *Don Jeronimo Sessarego*, 30 September 1901, 15 RIAA 400–01; *Don Luis Chiessa*, 30 September 1901, 15 RIAA 399–400; *Don Pablo Vercelli*, 30 September 1901, 15 RIAA 406–07; *Don José Miglia*, 30 September 1901, 15 RIAA 411–12; *Don Lorenzo Roggero*, 30 September 1901, 15 RIAA 408, 409; *Lehigh Valley Railroad Company, Agency of Canadian Car and Foundry Company, Limited, and Various Underwriters (United States) v Germany (Sabotage Cases)*, 16 October 1930, 8 RIAA 84, 86. See L H Woolsey, 'The Arbitration of the Sabotage Claims Against Germany' (1939) 33 American Journal of International Law 737.

[7] *Claim of Finnish shipowners against Great Britain in respect of the use of certain Finnish vessels during the war (Finland, Great Britain)*, 9 May 1934, 3 RIAA 1479, 1501; *Metzger Case*, 1903, 10 RIAA 417; *Union Bridge Company (United States) v Great Britain*, 8 January 1924, 6 RIAA 138; *H G Venable (USA) v United Mexican States*, 8 July 1927, 4 RIAA 219; *Maal Case*, 1903, 10 RIAA 730, 733; *Owners, Officers and Men of the Wanderer (Gr Br) v United States*, 9 December 1921, 6 RIAA 68; *Hayden's*, in Moore, III (GPO 1898) 2995.

[8] Ian Brownlie, *System of the Law of Nations. State Responsibility. Part I* (Clarendon Press 1983) 133, 136, 150.

the domestic constitutional principle of the separation of powers has no particular standing, at least for the sake of attribution.[9] In early arbitrations, cases are found of 'mixed' organs exercising the role of security forces, as well as judicial functions.[10] Thus, the inclusion of a given organ into a specific branch of government may be addressed as a 'matter of internal organization and local fashion'[11] that is relevant as a question of fact.[12]

The status of State organ, although representing a strong prima facie case for the attribution of an internationally wrongful act, does not necessarily entail attributability of conduct to the State it belongs to. This is the case of State organs put at the disposal of another State, regulated by ARSIWA Article 6.[13] Indeed, their conduct results in being attributed to the receiving State in so far as it constituted an exercise of 'elements of the governmental authority'.[14]

1.2 Role of Domestic Law

As mentioned in the previous chapter, ARSIWA Article 4.2 represents a corollary of the principle of supremacy of international law.[15] Indeed, the qualification of a person as State organ under international law is not dependent upon the status of organ according to internal law. This rule represents a major change with respect to the text of the draft articles adopted on first reading, where the status of organ under the internal law of its State constituted a required element of the attribution rule.[16] The term 'includes' does not entail a mechanism of *renvoi* such

[9] As to the relevance of the principle of the separation of powers for other purposes, see Zachary Douglas, 'International Responsibility for Domestic Adjudication: Denial of Justice Deconstructed' (2014) 63 International and Comparative Law Quarterly 867, 876.

[10] *Laura M B Janes et al (USA) v United Mexican States*, 16 November 1925, 4 RIAA 82 ('police magistrate').

[11] Ian Brownlie, *System of the Law of Nations. State Responsibility. Part I* (Clarendon Press 1983) 142.

[12] Luigi Condorelli, 'L'imputation à l'État d'un fait internationalement illicite: solutions classiques et nouvelles tendances' (1984) 189 Recueil des Cours 9, 63. '*Dans cette logique, l'emprise de l'organisation étatique sur ces entités ou leur "étiquetage" constituent certes des indices sérieux d'imputabilité (étant donné que normalement tous ceux à qui l'on confie des fonctions publiques sont soumis à un régime centralisé de surveillance et de contrôle), mais somme toute des indices secondaires: ce qui explique qu'on ne se soucie pas ici d'analyser quand, par quels moyens et sous quelles formes cette emprise est réalisée.*'

[13] ARSIWA Commentaries 43–44.

[14] *Affaire Chevreau (France contre Royaume-Uni)*, 9 June 1931, 2 RIAA 1113.

[15] See Chapter I, section 2.

[16] 'Draft Articles on State Responsibility' in Report of the International Law Commission on the Work of its Twenty-Seventh Session, 5 May–25 July 1975, document A/10010/Rev.1, Yearbook of the International Law Commission, 1975, Volume II, 47, 51, 60, document A/CN.4/SER.A/1975/Add.l:

Article 5
Attribution to the State of the conducts of its organs

For the purposes of the present articles, conduct of any State organ having that status under the internal law of that State shall be considered as an act of the State concerned under international law, provided that organ was acting in that capacity in the case in question.

as that operating in private international law.[17] This means that the status of organ 'in accordance with the internal law of the State' is not automatically received by and incorporated into international law. As already submitted, attribution to the State of the acts of its organ as a subjective element of the internationally wrongful act is normatively governed by international law only.[18] Hence, international law may qualify a person as an organ of a State, notwithstanding the absence of official status under municipal law of that State. There are two competing instances in this respect. On one hand, international law acknowledges the maximum degree of liberty of sovereign States as to their internal organization (*self-organization*).[19] On the other hand, it dictates a principle of (institutional) unity and continuity of the State, so that matters of internal machinery do not become grounds for the circumvention of rules concerning attributability of internationally wrongful acts.[20] However, the ritual status of organ pursuant to domestic law is not to be regarded as irrelevant. On the contrary, it usually represents the prior—and almost always sufficient—step for the determination of the status of organ *under international law*. The autonomous definition of State organ established by international law intervenes on a supplementary and residual basis in exceptional cases where a person—not having the official status of organ (or receiving an incorrect classification) according to internal law—acts *in fact* on behalf of the State.[21] Thus, ARSIWA Article 4.2 embodies the ground for the legal foundation of the doctrine of the *de*

[17] Mathias Forteau, 'L'État selon le droit international: une figure à géométrie variable?' (2007) 111 Revue Générale de Droit International Public 737. See also Roberto Ago, Third Report on State Responsibility, by Mr Roberto Ago, Special Rapporteur, 'The internationally wrongful act of the State, source of international responsibility', 5 March, 7 April, 28 April, and 18 May 1971, para 117, document A/CN.4/246 and Add.1-3, Yearbook of the International Law Commission, 1971, Volume II (Part One), 237, document A/CN.4/SER.A/1971/Add.1 (Part 1): 'The State machinery is always a fact for the international legal system; its structures are not "received" into that system and do not acquire the character of legal structures in it, even if international law takes them into consideration for its own purposes. One must not be misled by the use of the term "referral" ("renvoi") which is sometimes used to describe this phenomenon.'

[18] Roberto Ago, 'Le délit international' (1939) 68 Recueil des Cours 415, 465: '*En un mot: c'est exclusivement dans l'ordre juridique interne que l'organe de l'État a la qualité juridique d'organe; du point de vue de l'ordre international, cette qualité d'organe n'est considérée que comme une condition de fait nécessaire pour pouvoir examiner sa conduite et apprécier comme une conduite juridique de l'État.*'

[19] Luigi Condorelli, 'L'imputation à l'État d'un fait internationalement illicite: solutions classiques et nouvelles tendances' (1984) 189 Recueil des Cours 9, 62; Alwyn V Freeman, *The International Responsibility of States for Denial of Justice* (Longmans, Greenman and Company 1938) 23.

[20] *Aguilar-Amory and Royal Bank of Canada claims (Great Britain v Costa Rica) (Tinoco case)*, 18 October 1923, 1 RIAA 369, 378.

[21] International Law Commission, Statement of the Chairman of the Drafting Committee, Mr Bruno Simma, 13 August 1998, 6. On this point, cf Paolo Palchetti, 'Comportamento di organi di fatto e illecito internazionale nel progetto di articoli sulla responsabilità internazionale degli Stati' in Marina Spinedi, Alessandra Gianelli, and Maria Luisa Alaimo (eds), *La codificazione della responsabilità internazionale degli Stati alla prova dei fatti: problemi e spunti di riflessione* (Giuffrè 2006) 3, 6; Christine Chinkin, 'A Critique of the Public/Private Dimension' (1999) 10 European Journal of International Law 387, 388.

facto organ, which has only rather recently received a conclusive systematization within the international rules of attribution.[22]

1.3 Functions of the Central Government

1.3.1 Legislative

The acts of the legislative branch are usually considered to be attributable, as well as decrees of a normative character emanated by the executive.[23] The principle is firmly rooted throughout the history of codification of responsibility of States for internationally wrongful acts,[24] in legal scholarship,[25] and in early arbitral case law.[26] Statutes or laws of expropriation or confiscation infringing international law constitute traditional examples of attributable acts.[27] The conduct of the legislature may also be represented by an omission, namely failure to incorporate given rules in municipal legislation that are required by treaty obligations.

It has been pointed out that statutory law as such is not sufficient to actually engender State responsibility:

> *A notre avis, l'activité normative abstraite, la simple adoption d'une loi, quoique contraire au droit international, n'implique pas en soi la responsabilité de l'Etat.*[28]

[22] See section 3 of this chapter. Reference is clearly made to *Application of the Convention on the Prevention and Punishment of the Crime of Genocide (Bosnia and Herzegovina v Serbia and Montenegro)*, Judgment, 26 February 2007, ICJ Reports 2007, 43.

[23] *Certain German Interests in Polish Upper Silesia*, Judgment No 7, 25 May 1926, PCIJ Series A No 7, 3, 18-19, 23 (Polish law of 14th July 1920 concerning the transfer of the rights of the German Treasury and of members of reigning German Houses to the Treasury of the State of Poland); *Claim of the Salvador Commercial Company ("El Triunfo Company")*, 8 May 1902, 15 RIAA 467.

[24] Institut de Droit International, 'Responsabilité internationale des Etats à raison des dommages causés sur leur territoire à la personne et aux biens des étrangers' (Leo Strisower, Rapporteur), Résolution du 1 septembre 1927, Session de Lausanne, (1927) 33(III) Annuaire de l'Institut de Droit International 330-335, Article I(1); League of Nations, Committee of Experts for the Progressive Codification of International Law, Preparatory Committee of the Conference for the Codification of International Law (The Hague, 1930), Bases of Discussions, No 2, League of Nations publication, V. Legal, 1929.V.3, document C.75.M.69.1929.V, (1930) 24 Special Supplement American Journal of International Law 3; Francisco V García Amador, 'Draft on international responsibility of the State for injuries caused in its territory to the person or property of aliens', Article 2, Annex to International responsibility: Third report by F. V. García Amador, Special Rapporteur, 'Responsibility of the State for Injuries Caused in its Territory to the Person or Property of Aliens. Part II: The International Claim', 2 January 1958, document A/CN A/111, Yearbook of the International Law Commission, 1958, Volume II, 47, 71, document A/CN.4/SER.A/1958/Add.l.

[25] C F Amerasinghe, 'Imputability in the Law of State Responsibility for Injuries to Aliens' (1966) 22 Revue Égyptienne de Droit International 91, 98; Ian Brownlie, *System of the Law of Nations. State Responsibility. Part I* (Clarendon Press 1983) 135, 142.

[26] *Affaire de l'impôt sur les bénéfices de guerre (France contre Espagne)*, 15 June 1922, 1 RIAA 302; *Norwegian Shipowners' Claims (Norway v USA)*, 13 October 1922, 1 RIAA 307, 309.

[27] *German Settlers in Poland*, Advisory Opinion No 6, 10 September 1923, PCIJ Series B No 6, 22; *The Factory at Chorzów*, Judgement No 13, Merits, 13 September 1928, PCIJ Series A No 17, 2.

[28] Benedetto Conforti, 'La Cour constitutionnelle italienne et le droits de l'homme méconnus sur le plan international' (2015) 119 Revue Générale de Droit International Public 353, 357. The function of a constitutional court is to be assimilated to the legislative power, rather than to the judiciary.

This appears to be a reflection connected to the operation of the applicable primary rule, namely that abstract legislative activity might not beget as such an international wrongful act. Although not exclusively related to the functioning of the attribution rule, this can explain the requirement, illustrated in legal scholarship, of some act of the executive or of the judiciary giving effect to legislation.[29] This situation had already been addressed in early arbitration practice:

> [O]rdinarily and in this case, claim for expropriation of property arises when possession of owner is interfered with (actual confiscation), and not when legislation is passed which makes later deprivation of possession possible.[30]

1.3.2 Executive

The most comprehensive category of attributable acts undoubtedly pertains to the executive branch, which embodies 'the most direct manifestation of state power'.[31] The ICJ has established the international responsibility of the State based on the conduct of its executive and administrative machinery.[32] In early arbitral cases and in the practice of the Iran–US Tribunal, the same rule is applied with regard to acts and omissions of heads of State and government,[33] ministries,[34]

[29] James Crawford, *State Responsibility. The General Part* (Cambridge University Press 2013) 120–21; Dionisio Anzilotti, *Corso di diritto internazionale, Volume Primo: Introduzione—Teorie generali* (3rd edn, Athenaeum 1928) 426.

[30] *Mariposa Development Company and Others (United States) v Panama*, 27 June 1933, 6 RIAA 338.

[31] James Crawford, *State Responsibility. The General Part* (Cambridge University Press 2013) 119. Conventional examples are governmental orders to enforce or prevent a given conduct, or decrees of seizure, confiscation, or expropriation. See *Armstrong Cork Company Case—Decision No 18*, 22 October 1953, 14 RIAA 159; *Martini Case (of a general nature)*, 1903, 10 RIAA 644-9; *Différend concernant l'interprétation de l'article 79, par 6, lettre C, du Traité de Paix (Biens italiens en Tunisie—Échange de lettres du 2 février 1951)—Décisions nos 136, 171 et 196*, 25 June 1952, 6 July 1954 and 7 December 1955, 13 RIAA 389.

[32] *Elettronica Sicula SpA (ELSI) (United States of America v Italy)*, Judgment, 20 July 1989, ICJ Reports 1989, 15, 33; *Avena and Other Mexican Nationals (Mexico v United States of America)*, Judgment, 31 March 2004, ICJ Reports 2004, 12, 19; *LaGrand (Germany v United States of America)*, Judgment, 27 June 2001, ICJ Reports 2001, 466, 475, 499.

[33] *Orinoco Steamship Company Case*, 1903–1905, 9 RIAA 180; *Jarvis Case*, 1903–1905, 9 RIAA 208; *Turnbull, Manoa Company (Limited), and Orinoco Company (Limited) Cases*, 1903–1905, 9 RIAA 261; *Kummerow, Otto Redler and Co, Fulda, Fischbach, and Friedericy Cases*, 1903, 10 RIAA 369; *Aguilar-Amory and Royal Bank of Canada claims (Great Britain v Costa Rica) (Tinoco case)*, 18 October 1923, 1 RIAA 369.

[34] *Questech, Inc v The Ministry of National Defence of the Islamic Republic of Iran*, Case No 59, 20 September 1985, Award No 191-59-1, 9 IRAN-US CTR 107 (1985-II); *McCollough & Company, Inc v The Ministry of Post, Telegraph and Telephone, The National Iranian Oil Company and Bank Markazi*, Case No 89, 22 April 1986, Award No 225-89-3, 11 IRAN-US CTR 3, 6 (1986-II); *American Bell International, Inc v The Islamic Republic of Iran, The Ministry of Defense of the Islamic Republic of Iran, The Ministry of Post, Telegraph and Telephone of the Islamic Republic of Iran, and The Telecommunications Company of Iran*, Case No 48, 19 September 1986, Award No 255-48-3, 12 IRAN-US CTR 170, 174 (1986-III); *Otis Elevator Company v The Islamic Republic of Iran, and Bank Mellat (formerly Foreign Trade Bank of Iran)*, Case No 284, 29 April 1987, Award No 304-284-2, 14 IRAN-US CTR 283, 292 (1987-I); *Kaysons International Corporation v The Government of the Islamic Republic of Iran, The Ministry of Industries and Mines, The Alborz Investment Corporation, The Tolid Daru Company, The Payegozar, The Pakhs Alborz Company, and The KBC Company*, Case No 367, 28 June 1993, Award No

agencies,[35] or the government in its entirety.[36] The rules of attribution in ARSIWA do not assume a given form of government (for instance, parliamentary or presidential republic, constitutional monarchy, theocratic State, etc). To this extent, customary rules of attribution have been applied in connection with political and constitutional organs resulting from non-Western forms of government and not being characterized by the principle of separation of powers, as in the case of the Iranian Revolutionary Council.[37] As mentioned above, the categorization of an organ as belonging to a given State 'function' (legislative, executive, judicial, or other) is not per se a threshold determination for the purposes of attributing acts or omissions to the State. However, in the case of controversial qualifications, the conduct is generally absorbed into the category of acts of the executive, based on some exercise of 'governmental authority' (legitimate use of the public force, chiefly). Seconding Ian Brownlie's spectrum of State agents belonging to the executive/administrative power, it is possible to cite the following examples: ministers, (senior) police officials,[38] diplomatic (and consular) agents,[39] fishery protection officers, customs officials, 'and many others of higher or lower rank in the state service'.[40]

548-367-2, 29 IRAN-US CTR 222, 227 (1993); *Unidyne Corporation v The Islamic Republic of Iran acting by and through The Navy of the Islamic Republic of Iran*, Case No 368, 9 March 1994, Decision No DEC 122-368-3, 30 IRAN-US CTR 19 (1994); *State University of New York College of Environmental Science and Forestry v Ministry of Culture and Higher Education, and The Islamic Republic of Iran*, Case No B-71, 16 December 1986, Award No 277-B71-2, 13 IRAN-US CTR 277 (1986-IV); *Iowa State University of Science and Technology v Ministry of Culture and Higher Education, and The Islamic Republic of Iran*, Case No B-72, 16 December 1986, Award No 276-B72-2, 13 IRAN-US CTR 271 (1986-IV).

---

[35] *International Technical Products Corporation and ITP Export Corporation, its wholly-owned subsidiary, v The Government of the Islamic Republic of Iran and its agencies, The Islamic Republic Iranian Air Force and the Ministry of National Defense, acting for the Civil Aviation Organization*, Case No 302, 24 October 1985, Award No 196-302-3, 9 IRAN-US CTR 206, 238 (1985-II); *Tippetts, Abbett, McCarthy, Stratton v TAMS-AFFA Consulting Engineers of Iran, The Government of the Islamic Republic or Iran, Civil Aviation Organization, Plan and Budget Organization, Iranian Air Force, Ministry of Defence, Bank Melli, Bank Sakhteman, Mercantile Bank of Iran and Holland*, Case No 7, 22 June 1984, Award No 141-7-2, 6 IRAN-US CTR 219, 221 (1984-II).

[36] *Flexi-Van Leasing, Inc v The Government of the Islamic Republic of Iran*, Case No 36, 11 October 1986, Award No 259-36-1, 12 IRAN-US CTR 335, 348-351 (1986-III); *Arthur Young & Company v The Islamic Republic of Iran, Telecommunications Company of Iran, Social Security Organization of Iran*, Case No 484, 30 November 1987, Award No 338-484-1, 17 IRAN-US CTR 245, 257 (1987-IV); *James M Saghi, Michael R Saghi, Allan J Saghi v The Islamic Republic of Iran*, Case No 298, 22 January 1993, Award No 544-298-2, 29 IRAN-US CTR 20, 23 (1992).

[37] *Tippetts, Abbett, McCarthy, Stratton v TAMS-AFFA Consulting Engineers of Iran, The Government of the Islamic Republic or Iran, Civil Aviation Organization, Plan and Budget Organization, Iranian Air Force, Ministry of Defence, Bank Melli, Bank Sakhteman, Mercantile Bank of Iran and Holland*, Case No 7, 22 June 1984, Award No 141-7-2, 6 IRAN-US CTR 219, 226-226 (1984-II); *Charles P Stewart v The Islamic Republic of Iran*, Case No 12458, 9 February 1990, Award No 468-12458-2, 24 IRAN-US CTR 116, 119 (1990-I).

[38] *Don Jacinto Gadino*, 30 September 1901, 15 RIAA 414–16; *Gust Adams (United States) v Panama*, 21 June 1933, 6 RIAA 321, 322; *Cecelia Dexter Baldwin, Administratrix of the Estate of Harry D Baldwin, and Others (United States) v Panama*, 26 June 1933, 6 RIAA 328, 329; *In the matter of the death of James Pugh (Great Britain, Panama)*, 6 July 1933, 3 RIAA 1439; *Différend Dame Mossé—Décisions nos 144 et 157*, 17 January and 6 October 1953, 13 RIAA 486, 490. See also *Affaire Mantovani*, 17 March 1965, in Charles Rousseau, 'Chronique des faits internationaux' (July-September 1965) 69 Revue Générale de Droit International Public 835.

[39] *Asphalt Company Case (on merits)*, 1903, 9 RIAA 389.

[40] Ian Brownlie, *System of the Law of Nations. State Responsibility. Part I* (Clarendon Press 1983) 138–39.

It is apposite to delve more precisely into the conduct of armed forces.[41] The acts of official land,[42] sea,[43] and air[44] forces are attributable to their State, as far as their military operations are concerned,[45] but also in relation to their potential exercise of civil and political functions.[46] The status of armed forces requires a higher standard of prudence (due diligence) in their discipline and control, in the discharge of their functions.[47] In early arbitral practice, numerous references are found to the requirement that troops belonging to army corps of belligerent forces be regular, defined, and determined with precision.[48] The distinction between regular and irregular troops has relevance for the purposes of attribution. Indeed, irregulars may not be classified as *de jure* organs, without prejudice to a finding of *de facto* agency. Instead, the status of auxiliary corps, even though controversial, should be ascribed to the category of official organs.

A threshold question is whether attributability may rest upon the conduct of ordinary soldiers (those who have been enlisted), irrespective of their acts occurring under the control, in the presence, and under the direct command of their chiefs.[49]

41 Alwyn V Freeman, *Responsibility of States for Unlawful Acts of their Armed Forces* (A W Sijthoff 1957).

42 *Ex multis, Military and Paramilitary Activities in and against Nicaragua (Nicaragua v United States of America)*, Merits, Judgment, 27 June 1986, ICJ Reports 1986, 14; *Armed Activities in the Territory of the Congo (DRC v Uganda)*, Judgment, 19 December 2005, ICJ Reports 2005, 168; *Application of the Convention on the Prevention and Punishment of the Crime of Genocide (Bosnia and Herzegovina v Serbia and Montenegro)*, Judgment, 26 February 2007, ICJ Reports 2007, 43.

43 *Opinion in the Lusitania Cases*, 1 November 1923, 7 RIAA 32; *D Earnshaw and Others (Great Britain) v United States (Zafiro case)*, 30 November 1925, 6 RIAA 160, 165; *José Marîia Vásquez Díaz, Assignee of Pablo Elías Velásquez (Panama) v US*, 27 June 1933, 6 RIAA 341; *Owners, Officers and Men of the Wanderer (Gr Br) v United States*, 9 December 1921, 6 RIAA 68. As to the Iran–US Claims Tribunal, see *Unidyne Corporation v The Islamic Republic of Iran acting by and through The Navy of the Islamic Republic of Iran*, Case No 368, 9 March 1994, Decision No DEC 122-368-3, para 9, 30 IRAN-US CTR 19 (1994).

44 *Intrend International, Inc v The Imperial Iranian Air Force, The Islamic Republic of Iran and The Provisionary Revolutionary Government of Iran*, Case No 220, 27 July 1983, Award No 59-220-2, 3 IRAN-US CTR 110 (1983-II).

45 *Poggioli Case (of a general nature)*, 1903, 10 RIAA 669, 670; *Dona Clara Lanatta, veuve de Campodonico*, 30 September 1901, 15 RIAA 416–17; *La Masica Case (Great Britain, Honduras)*, 7 December 1916, 11 RIAA 549, 554; *Paula Mendel and Others (United States) v Germany*, 13 August 1926, 7 RIAA 372; *Cornelia J Pringle, et al, (Santa Isabel Claims) (USA) v United Mexican States*, 26 April 1926, 4 RIAA 783; *Teodoro García and M A Garza (United Mexican States) v United States of America*, 3 December 1926, 4 RIAA 119; *Dunbar & Belknap*, in Moore, III (GPO 1898) 2998; *Glenn*, 1868, in Moore, III (GPO 1898) 3138. The rule is not only found in early cases, but also in diplomatic notes. See *Affaire Vracaritch*, in Charles Rousseau, 'Chronique des faits internationaux' (April–June 1962) 66 Revue Générale de Droit International Public 376–78.

46 *Star and Herald*, in Moore, VI (GPO 1906) 775; *Irene Roberts Case*, 1903–1905, 9 RIAA 204–08; *Island of Palmas case (Netherlands, USA)*, 4 April 1928, 2 RIAA 829, 836.

47 Ian Brownlie, *System of the Law of Nations. State Responsibility. Part I* (Clarendon Press 1983) 140.

48 *Don Juan B Sanguinetti*, 30 September 1901, 15 RIAA 4034; *Don Jeronimo Sessarego*, 30 September 1901, 15 RIAA 4001; *Don Aquilino Capalleti*, 30 September 1901, 15 RIAA 4389; *Don Ricardo Castiglione*, 30 September 1901, 15 RIAA 41718; *Don Pablo Vercelli*, 30 September 1901, 15 RIAA 406–07; *Don Evangelista Machiavello and Don Francisco Olivari*, 30 September 1901, 15 RIAA 439, 440; *Don Lorenzo Roggero*, 30 September 1901, 15 RIAA 408, 409; *Cecelia Dexter Baldwin, Administratrix of the Estate of Harry D Baldwin, and Others (United States) v Panama*, 26 June 1933, 6 RIAA 328, 330.

49 *Eis, et al (US v USSR)*, United States, Foreign Claims Settlement Commission, 2 March 1959, 30 ILR 116; *Don Ricardo Castiglione*, 30 September 1901, 15 RIAA 417–18: '*en présence de leurs chefs*'; *Don*

This issue was addressed in the early case of the *Zafiro*.[50] The Zafiro was a British merchant vessel that had been purchased by the US navy and registered as a vessel of the US merchant navy in order to discharge the function of collier and supply ship. Accordingly, its original crew, made up of British officers and Chinese sailors, was enrolled in the American merchant service. The status of the vessel appears to be that of an auxiliary corp. While the vessel was anchored in Manila Bay, the crew was granted shore leave and abandoned itself to acts of looting, pillage, and destruction in the surrounding neighbourhoods. The Commission required a test of command and (effective) control by the State with respect to the navy personnel, in order to attribute the latter's conduct to the former.[51] At the same time, a State may be held liable for lack of due diligence ('want of supervision') for having left its militaries off-duty in given circumstances.[52] The crew of the Zafiro had clearly committed some purely private acts out of actual or apparent office. It is questionable whether the high threshold of command and control equally applies in the case of delinquencies executed by armed forces *ultra vires*. In this respect, the strict test of command and control is superseded by the applicability of the rule of attribution of *ultra vires* acts and omissions of State organs (or persons or entities pursuant to ARSIWA Article 5).[53] A similar line of argument may be resorted to with regard to *de facto* organs.[54] The absence of an official and formal institutional

José Miglia, 30 September 1901, 15 RIAA 411–12: '*soumises au commandement de leurs chefs*'; *Irene Roberts Case*, 1903–1905, 9 RIAA 204–08; *Crossman Case (interlocutory)*, 1903, 9 RIAA 356, 357: 'In the present case it does not appear confirmed in any way that the troops obeyed superior orders, nor that the nearest military authorities could have avoided the damages done.'; *J M Henriquez Case*, 1903, 10 RIAA 727, 728: 'There is no proof that the injuries done to the building were in consequence of, or as an incident to, the occupancy of said building as a place of rendezvous under official orders, but it has more the appearance of reckless and undirected action of ungoverned soldiery.', *D Earnshaw and Others (Great Britain) v United States (Zafiro case)*, 30 November 1925, 6 RIAA 160, 163: 'But it is not necessary that an officer be on the very spot'; *Ruden*, in Moore, II (GPO 1898) 1653-1655; *Terry and Angus*, 31 March 1847, in Moore, III (GPO 1898) 2993. See also *Louis B Gordon (USA) v United Mexican States*, Dissenting Opinion of Commissioner Nielsen, 8 October 1930, 4 RIAA 586, 591.

[50] *D Earnshaw and Others (Great Britain) v United States (Zafiro case)*, 30 November 1925, 6 RIAA 160.

[51] *D Earnshaw and Others (Great Britain) v United States (Zafiro case)*, 30 November 1925, 6 RIAA 160, 163–64: 'We have next to inquire whether at the time of the looting in question the Chinese crew were under discipline and officered so as to make the United States responsible, ... It is well settled that we must distinguish between soldiers or sailors under the command of officers, on the one hand, and, on the other hand, bodies of straggling and marauding soldiers not under the command of an officer, or marauding sailors not under command or control of officers. ... In the case before us, we think the officers were not actually present at the houses when the looting was done. ... we feel that there was no effective control of the Chinese crew at the time when the real damage took place.'

[52] *D Earnshaw and Others (Great Britain) v United States (Zafiro case)*, 30 November 1925, 6 RIAA 160, 164–65: 'we cannot agree that letting this Chinese crew go ashore uncontrolled at the time and place in question was like allowing shore leave to sailors in a policed port where social order is maintained by the ordinary agencies of government.'

[53] *Don Francisco Grocce*, 30 September 1901, 15 RIAA 448–49: '*et que, même en admettant que les soldats qui ont commis de pareils actes ne se trouvaient actuellement sous les ordres d'aucun officier, on ne saurait laisser impuni un fait qui mérite un châtiment.*'

[54] See section 3 of this chapter.

link would realistically demand a marked degree of control (equivalent to the one between the military commanders and their subordinates) from *de jure* to *de facto* organs. But, once a finding of *de facto* agency has been established, the regime for the attribution of conduct of State organs has to be applied in its entirety, to the inclusion of the *ultra vires* rule and the attributability of *acta jure gestionis* performed in an official capacity.

1.3.3 Judiciary

The attributability of the acts of a judicial power is a rule of common currency in customary international law.[55] The attribution of conduct operates equally in relation to acts performed by public officials in charge of ancillary functions to the judiciary, as seen in the case of co-ownership trustees (*syndics*), liquidators, and sequestrators appointed by decree by the Italian government for the administration of enemy property seized in time of war.[56] However, it had been repeatedly submitted in earlier times that the independence of the judiciary from the executive power should have prevented attribution to the State. The issue was resolved by Dionisio Anzilotti in favour of attributability to the State of the conduct of judges, as a corollary of the irrelevance of the principle of the separation of powers at the international level for the purposes of attribution.[57] The concept was elucidated in the case of the *Biens italiens en Tunisie*:

> *Si, dans certaines sentences arbitrales du XXe siècle, on trouve exprimée l'opinion que l'indépendance des tribunaux, conforme au principe de la division des pouvoirs généralement reconnu dans les pays civilisés, exclut la responsabilité internationale de l'Etat du fait des actes du pouvoir judiciaire contraires au droit, cette théorie semble aujourd'hui universellement et justement répudiée par la doctrine et la jurisprudence internationales. La sentence rendue par l'autorité judiciaire est une*

[55] *Elettronica Sicula SpA (ELSI) (United States of America v Italy)*, Judgment, 20 July 1989, ICJ Reports 1989, 15, 36; *Avena and Other Mexican Nationals (Mexico v United States of America)*, Judgment, 31 March 2004, ICJ Reports 2004, 12, 27; *Differences Relating to Immunity from Legal Process of a Special-Rapporteur of the Commission of Human Rights*, Advisory Opinion, 29 April 1999, ICJ Reports 1999, 62. As to early case law, see *H G Venable (USA) v United Mexican States*, 8 July 1927, 4 RIAA 219; *Francisco Mallén (United Mexican States) v USA*, 27 April 1927, 4 RIAA 173; *William T Way (USA) v United Mexican States*, 18 October 1928, 4 RIAA 391, 400; *Ethel Morton (USA) v United Mexican States*, 2 April 1929, 4 RIAA 428; *B E Chattin (United States) v United Mexican States*, 23 July 1927, 4 RIAA 282; *Clyde Dyches (USA) v United Mexican States*, 9 April 1929, 4 RIAA 458.

[56] *Différend Société Verdol—Décisions nos 20 et 34*, 5 April and 16 November 1949, 13 RIAA 94, 96; *Différend Joseph Ousset—Décisions nos 93 et 170*, 14 April 1951 and 5 July 1954, 13 RIAA 252; *Currie Case—Decision No 21*, 13 March 1954, 14 RIAA 21–27.

[57] Dionisio Anzilotti, *Corso di diritto internazionale, Volume Primo: Introduzione—Teorie generali* (3rd edn, Athenaeum 1928) 427: '*L'indipendenza del potere giudiziario è un principio di diritto costituzionale, che ha di mira i rapporti tra questo e gli altri poteri dello Stato: di fronte agli Stati esteri, invece, vi è lo Stato subietto del diritto internazionale, cioè lo Stato nella sua unità, non i singoli poteri dello Stato.*'; Dionisio Anzilotti, 'La responsabilité internationale des États a raison des dommages soufferts par des étrangers' (1906) 13 Revue Générale de Droit International Public 285, 296–98; Eduardo Jiménez de Aréchaga, 'International Law in the Past Third of a Century' (1978-I) 159 Recueil des Cours 1, 278: 'the judgment given by a judicial authority emanates from an organ of the State in just the same

émanation d'un organe de l'Etat, tout comme la loi promulguée par l'autorité législative, ou la décision prise par l'autorité executive.[58]

The responsibility of States for internationally wrongful acts on the basis of the attribution of acts or omissions of the judiciary is historically related to two categories of primary norms: on one side, the set of substantive obligations, a violation of which may give rise to a denial of justice; on the other side, immunity rules.

The denial of justice in international law has received various definitions in the legal literature.[59] It is based on a finding of a State judge's wilful departure from the rule of law in a fashion of arbitrariness and unfairness that results in being outrageous and intolerable to an international common sense of juridical and even societal propriety.[60] In early arbitral practice, a denial of justice broadly encompassed cases of unlawful detention, failure to investigate and to collect evidence, failure to apprehend or punish, lack of due process, summary executions, and lack of care in custody.[61] If brought to abstraction, the State duties underlying the entirety of such instances may be categorized under the concept of due diligence obligations.

way as a law promulgated by the legislature or a decision taken by the executive.'; Djamchid Momtaz, 'Attribution of Conduct to the State: State Organs and Entities Empowered to Exercise Elements of Governmental Authority' in James Crawford, Alain Pellet, and Simon Olleson (eds), *The Law of International Responsibility* (Oxford University Press 2010) 237, 239–40.

---

[58] *Différend concernant l'interprétation de l'article 79, par 6, lettre C, du Traité de Paix (Biens italiens en Tunisie—Échange de lettres du 2 février 1951)—Décisions nos 136, 171 et 196*, 25 June 1952, 6 July 1954 and 7 December 1955, 13 RIAA 389, 438.

[59] Edwin M Borchard, *The Diplomatic Protection of Citizens Abroad or The Law of International Claims* (The Banks Law Publishing Co 1915) 81: the municipal judge's decision should be 'grossly unfair and notoriously unjust'; Clyde Eagleton, 'Denial of Justice in International Law' (1928) 22 American Journal of International Law 538; Dionisio Anzilotti, 'La Responsabilité Internationale des États a Raison des Dommages Soufferts par des Étrangers' (1906) 13 Revue Générale de Droit International Public 5, 21; Alwyn Freeman, *The International Responsibility of States for Denial of Justice* (Longmans, Greenman and Company 1938) 40; Constantin T Eustathiades, *La Responsabilité Internationale de l'État pour les Actes des Organes Judiciaires et le Problème du Déni de Justice en Droit International*, Tome II (Éditions A Pedone 1936) 424; Jan Paulsson, *Denial of Justice in International Law* (Cambridge University Press 2005) 57.

[60] *Elettronica Sicula SpA (ELSI) (United States of America v Italy)*, Judgment, 20 July 1989, ICJ Reports 1989, 15, 76: 'It is a wilful disregard of due process of law, an act which shocks, or at least surprises, a sense of juridical propriety', referring to *Asylum (Colombia v Peru)*, Judgment, 20 November 1950, ICJ Reports 1950, 266, 284.

[61] *Jesús Navarro Tribolet, et al, Next of Kin of Robert Tribolet, Deceased (USA) v United Mexican States*, 8 October 1930, 4 RIAA 598, 600; *Francisco Quintanilla (United Mexican States) v United States of America*, 16 November 1926, 4 RIAA 101–04; *Davy Case (on merits)*, 1903, 9 RIAA 467; *J W and N L Swinney (USA) v United Mexican States*, 16 November 1926, 4 RIAA 98; *Margaret Roper (USA) v United Mexican States*, 4 April 1927, 4 RIAA 145, 147–48; *Alexander St J Corrie (USA) v United Mexican States*, 5 March 1929, 4 RIAA 416, 417; *Gust Adams (United States) v Panama*, 21 June 1933, 6 RIAA 321, 323; *Cecelia Dexter Baldwin, Administratrix of the Estate of Harry D Baldwin, and Others (United States) v Panama*, 26 June 1933, 6 RIAA 328, 331–33; *Salome Lerma Vda De Galvan (United Mexican States) v USA*, 21 July 1927, 4 RIAA 273; *George Adams Kennedy (USA) v United Mexican States*, 6 May 1927, 4 RIAA 194; *George David Richards (USA) v United Mexican States*, 23 July 1927, 4 RIAA 275, 276; *Louis B Gordon (USA) v United Mexican States*, 8 October 1930, 4 RIAA 586, 590, where a denial of justice was not established: 'it cannot be said decision amounts to an outrage, or that it is rendered in bad faith,

Mixed Claims Commissions not only interpreted the doctrine of denial of justice liberally, but also—in line with various projects of codification[62]—applied it to arbitrary conduct by the executive powers, although this was generally connected to the activities of the local judges, as in episodes of arrest and subsequent detention, refusal to issue documents, or failure to bring to trial (denial of *access* to justice).[63]

A State's obligation to grant immunity from legal process is particularly incumbent on their judges.[64] Public international law provides for various categories of immunity, which can be ordered in three groupings: State immunity from jurisdiction and execution, immunities of international organizations, and diplomatic immunities. Pursuant to Article 6.1 of the United Nations Convention on Jurisdictional Immunities of States and Their Property (UNCSI), a national judge

or shows a wilful neglect of duty or insufficiency of governmental action so far short of international standards as to constitute a denial of justice.'

[62] Francisco V García Amador, 'Draft on international responsibility of the State for injuries caused in its territory to the person or property of aliens', Article 4.2, Annex to International responsibility: Third report by F. V. Garcia Amador, Special Rapporteur, 'Responsibility of the State for Injuries Caused in its Territory to the Person or Property of Aliens. Part II: The International Claim', 2 January 1958, document A/CN A/111, Yearbook of the International Law Commission, 1958, Volume II, 47, 71, document A/CN.4/SER.A/1958/Add.l.

[63] *Jesús Navarro Tribolet, et al, Next of Kin of Robert Tribolet, Deceased (USA) v United Mexican States*, 8 October 1930, 4 RIAA 598, 600; *Francisco Quintanilla (United Mexican States) v United States of America*, 16 November 1926, 4 RIAA 101–04; *Claims of Charles Oberlander and Barbara M Messenger against the Government of Mexico (United States of America/Mexico)*, 19 November 1897, 29 RIAA 327, 335; *Laura M B Janes et al (USA) v United Mexican States*, 16 November 1925, 4 RIAA 82, 86, 88: 'Denial of justice, in its broader sense, may cover even acts of the executive and the legislative; in cases of improper governmental action of this type, a nation is never held to be liable for anything else than the damage caused by what the executive or the legislative committed or omitted itself. In cases of denial of justice in its narrower sense, Governments again are held responsible exclusively for what they commit or omit themselves. Only in the event of one type of denial of justice, the present one, a State would be liable not for what it committed or omitted itself, but for what an individual did' (Mexican police magistrate); *Teodoro García and M A Garza (United Mexican States) v United States of America*, 3 December 1926, 4 RIAA 119; *Charles S Stephens and Bowman Stephens (USA) v United Mexican States*, 15 July 1927, 4 RIAA 265–68; *Francisco Mallén (United Mexican States) v USA*, 27 April 1927, 4 RIAA 173, 178; *F R West (USA) v United Mexican States*, 21 July 1927, 4 RIAA 270, 272; *Louise O Canahl (USA) v United Mexican States*, 15 October 1928, 4 RIAA 389; *Glenn*, 1868, in Moore, III (GPO 1898) 3138; *The Interoceanic Railway of Mexico (Acapulco to Veracruz) (Ltd), and the Mexican Eastern Railway Company (Ltd), and the Mexican Southern Railway (Ltd) (Great Britain) v United Mexican States*, 18 June 1931, 5 RIAA 178, 185: 'The Commission deem that these examples, which could be supplemented by many others, show that non-judicial authorities also can be guilty of a denial or undue delay of justice, and if it could, in the case now before them, be shown that such authorities had been guilty of that international delinquency, they would not hesitate to declare themselves competent ...'; *Laura M B Janes et al (USA) v United Mexican States*, 16 November 1925, 4 RIAA 82, 86, 88: 'Denial of justice, in its broader sense, may cover even acts of the executive and the legislative.'

[64] *Jurisdictional Immunities of the State (Germany v Italy: Greece intervening)*, Judgment, 3 February 2012, ICJ Reports 2012, 99; *Differences Relating to Immunity from Legal Process of a Special-Rapporteur of the Commission of Human Rights*, Advisory Opinion, 29 April 1999, ICJ Reports 1999, 62, 88; *Arrest Warrant of 11 April 2000 (Democratic Republic of Congo v Belgium)*, Judgment, 14 February 2002, ICJ Reports 2002, 3, 22; *Certain Questions of Mutual Assistance in Criminal Matters (Djibouti v France)*, Judgment, 4 June 2008, para 196, ICJ Reports 2008, 177, 244.

is obliged to raise questions of State immunity *in limine litis* and even *proprio motu*, in the absence of a party's motion to this extent.[65] Accordingly, a court's failure to grant immunity or immunities is definitely attributable to the State and may result in a finding of international responsibility, provided that the substantive criteria dictated by the relevant rules of exemption from suit have been misapplied.[66] For instance, the Italian Constitutional Court has famously decided that the ICJ judgment in the case of *Jurisdictional Immunities of the State* not be applicable and enforceable within the Italian jurisdiction.[67] The function of a constitutional judge is to be assimilated to the legislative power, rather than to the judiciary.[68] Accordingly, decisions of a constitutional court do not ordinarily entail as such the breach of the applicable international obligation of the State. However, said breach may later occur on the basis of the application by ordinary judges of the principle of law encapsulated by the constitutional court.[69]

1.3.4 'Any Other Functions': Central Banks and Independent Authorities

In line with the purpose of encompassing all the varieties of persons that can engage the international responsibility of the State, ARSIWA Article 4 provides for an open-ended catalogue of powers, not only consisting of the legislative, executive, and judicial branches, but also comprising 'any other functions'. This 'catch-all' proviso certainly includes the acts and omissions of central banks, independent authorities, or administrative agencies entrusted with regulatory and administrative functions. These are clearly State 'organs', but their qualification as persons or entities empowered by the law to exercise elements of the governmental authority (for instance, parastatals) is recorded in the scholarly debate.[70] An authoritative suggestion is to resolve the taxonomy issue by finding he precise relationship of the 'entity' concerned with the government on a rather casuistic basis.[71]

[65] UNCSI Article 6.1:

Article 6
Modalities for giving effect to State immunity

1. A State shall give effect to State immunity under article 5 by refraining from exercising jurisdiction in a proceeding before its courts against another State and to that end shall ensure that its courts determine on their own initiative that the immunity of that other State under article 5 is respected.

[66] *Jurisdictional Immunities of the State (Germany v Italy: Greece intervening)*, Judgment, 3 February 2012, ICJ Reports 2012, 99.

[67] Corte Costituzionale, Judgment No 238, 22 October 2014, (2015) 109 American Journal of International Law 400, note Riccardo Pavoni.

[68] See section 1.3.1 in this chapter.

[69] Benedetto Conforti, 'La Cour constitutionnelle italienne et le droits de l'homme méconnus sur le plan international' (2015) 119 Revue Générale de Droit International Public 353.

[70] Jane Chalmers, 'State Responsibility for Acts of Parastatals Organized in Corporate Form' (1990) 84 American Society of International Law Proceedings 60.

[71] James Crawford, *State Responsibility. The General Part* (Cambridge University Press 2013) 128.

Investor–State arbitration provides relevant practice establishing that the circumstance of a public entity benefiting from separate juristic personality under domestic law does not preclude a finding of *de jure* organ.[72] The distinction between the legal personality of public and of private law appears to be vested with threshold importance. The former would attract a 'public body' into the 'official' boundaries of the State as *de jure* organ.[73] On the contrary, the latter is usually a prerequisite for the operation of the attribution rule under ARSIWA Article 5 as to State instrumentalities ('State entities'), or under ARSIWA Article 8 as to 'private' individuals.[74]

1.4 Territorial Units of the State

The principle of (territorial) unity of the State dictates that from the standpoint of international law the forms of State and administration are legally irrelevant for the purposes of attribution.[75] The delegation of governmental powers and authority from the State (primary level) to sub-state territorial entities (secondary level) does not exempt the central government from attribution of the acts of the organs of the peripheral level.[76] This normative mechanism is preserved irrespective of the independence accorded to local autonomies by constitutional or statutory law or of the effective control of the State on its political subdivisions.[77] The rule has been formulated by the PCIJ in the *Upper Silesia* case:

[72] See *Eureko BV v Republic of Poland*, Ad Hoc Arbitration, Partial Award, 19 August 2005, para 120; *Toto Costruzioni Generali SpA v The Republic of Lebanon*, ICSID Case No ARB/07/12, Decision on Jurisdiction, 11 September 2009, para 46, 56: 'Moreover, the CDR acts as an agent of the State.'

[73] See Chapter III, section 3.1.

[74] See sections 4.3 and 5.3.2 of this chapter and Chapter III, section 4 and 5.3.

[75] Christian Tomuschat, 'Attribution of International Responsibility: Direction and Control' in Malcolm Evans and Panos Koutrakos (eds), *The International Responsibility of the European Union: European and International Perspectives* (Hart Publishing 2013) 7, 11; André JJ de Hoogh, 'Articles 4 and 8 of the 2001 ILC Articles on State Responsibility, the *Tadić* Case and Attribution of Acts of Bosnian Serb Authorities to the Federal Republic of Yugoslavia' (2001) 72 British Year Book of International Law 255, 265.

[76] Institut de Droit International, 'Responsabilité internationale des Etats à raison des dommages causés sur leur territoire à la personne et aux biens des étrangers' (Leo Strisower, Rapporteur), Résolution du 1 septembre 1927, Session de Lausanne, (1927) 33(III) Annuaire de l'Institut de Droit International 330-335, Article II: '*L'Etat est responsable du fait des collectivités qui exercent sur son territoire des fonctions publiques*'; Harvard Law School (Manley O Hudson, Director), 'Research in International Law (Nationality, Responsibility of States, Territorial Waters). Drafts of Conventions Prepared in Anticipation of the First Conference on the Codification of International Law, The Hague, 1930', 1 April 1929, Part II, 'Responsibility of States' (Edwin M Borchard, Rapporteur), Article 3, (1929) 23 Special Number Supplement American Journal of International Law 133.

[77] *Estate of Hyacinthe Pellat (France) v United Mexican States*, 7 June 1929, 5 RIAA 534, 536: '*le principe de la responsabilité internationale, souvent dite indirecte, d'un État fédéral pour tous les actes des États particuliers qui donnent lieu à des réclamations d'États étrangers. Cette responsabilité indirecte ne saurait être niée, pas même dans les cas où la Constitution fédérale dénierait au Gouvernement central le droit de contrôle sur les États particuliers, ou le droit d'exiger d'eux qu'ils conforment leur conduite aux*

> Again, communes, outside their own sphere of activity, also exercise functions as organs of the State itself; they are subject to the control of the State authorities as regards both the activities which are directly incumbent upon them and those which they undertake in virtue of powers delegated by the State. An essential and necessary bond therefore unites the commune and the State of which it forms part;[78]

Accordingly, the principle is readily applied to constituent States of federal States,[79] autonomous regions,[80] autonomous territories,[81] overseas provinces,[82] territories under military occupation,[83] counties,[84] municipalities,[85] mayors of a municipality,[86] and municipal police.[87] Likewise, the same rule was adapted in earlier times to colonies,[88] protectorates,[89] and capitulations.[90]

prescriptions du droit international.' But see *Montijo*, 25 July 1875, in Moore, II (GPO 1898) 1421, 1441, which posits the question why all taxpayers of a federation should be affected by the delinquencies of one of its constituent units.

---

[78] *Certain German Interests in Polish Upper Silesia*, Judgment No 7, 25 May 1926, PCIJ Series A No 7, 3, 75.

[79] *Montijo*, 25 July 1875, in Moore, II (GPO 1898) 1421, 1440; *Eliza (US v Peru)*, 27 November 1867, in Albert de La Pradelle and Nikolaos Politis, *Recueil des Sentences Arbitrales*, II, 1856–1872 (Éditions A Pedone 1923) 271, 277: '*les États particuliers ne sont, vis-à-vis des États étrangers, que des organes de l'État fédéral*'; *Tunstall*, 1878, in Moore, VI (GPO 1906) 662; *Cases of Amelia de Brissot, Ralph Rawdon, Joseph Stackpole and Narcisa de Hammer v Venezuela (the steamer* Apure *case)*, 1885, 29 RIAA 240, 256: 'The ultimate responsibility of Venezuela for these wrongs is in nowise dependent upon her form of government; or the domestic distribution of her powers. For redress of injuries done her citizens, the United States must look to Venezuela, and not to any of her political subdivisions.'; *Estate of Hyacinthe Pellat (France) v United Mexican States*, 7 June 1929, 5 RIAA 534, 535; *Jesús Navarro Tribolet, et al, Next of Kin of Robert Tribolet, Deceased (USA) v United Mexican States*, 8 October 1930, 4 RIAA 598, 600; *Irene Roberts Case*, 1903–1905, 9 RIAA 204–08; *Francisco Mallén (United Mexican States) v USA*, 27 April 1927, 4 RIAA 173, 181; *William T Way (USA) v United Mexican States*, 18 October 1928, 4 RIAA 391; *Salome Lerma Vda De Galvan (United Mexican States) v USA*, 21 July 1927, 4 RIAA 273.

[80] *Différend Héritiers de SAR Mgr le Duc de Guise*, Decisions Nos 43, 87, 107 and 162, 3 April, 18 December 1950, 15 September 1951, and 20 November 1953, 13 RIAA 150.

[81] *Star and Herald*, in Moore, VI (GPO 1906) 775.

[82] *Island of Palmas case (Netherlands, USA)*, 4 April 1928, 2 RIAA 829, 836.

[83] *Legal Consequences for States of the Continued Presence of South Africa in Namibia (South West Africa) notwithstanding Security Council Resolution 276 (1970)*, Advisory Opinion, 21 June 1971, para 118, ICJ Reports 1971, 16, 54: 'Physical control of a territory, and not sovereignty or legitimacy of title, is the basis of State liability for acts affecting other States.'

[84] *Davy Case (on merits)*, 1903, 9 RIAA 467.

[85] *Pieri Dominique and Co Case*, 14 August 1905, 10 RIAA 139.

[86] *Elettronica Sicula SpA (ELSI) (United States of America v Italy)*, Judgment, 20 July 1989, ICJ Reports 1989, 15, 32.

[87] *J W and N L Swinney (USA) v United Mexican States*, 16 November 1926, 4 RIAA 98.

[88] *Union Bridge Company (United States) v Great Britain*, 8 January 1924, 6 RIAA 138; *Paula Mendel and Others (United States) v Germany*, 13 August 1926, 7 RIAA 372; *Responsabilité de l'Allemagne à raison des dommages causés dans les colonies portugaises du sud de l'Afrique (sentence sur le principe de la responsabilité) (Portugal contre Allemagne)*, 31 July 1928, 2 RIAA 1011, 1013.

[89] *Cayuga Indians (Great Britain) v United States*, 22 January 1926, 6 RIAA 173.

[90] *Affaire des biens britanniques au Maroc espagnol (Espagne contre Royaume-Uni) (Spanish Zone of Morocco)*, 1 May 1925, 2 RIAA 615, 649.

1.5 Minor Officials

The proviso 'whatever position it holds in the organization of the State' is meant to render as attributable to the State the acts of *every* officer making up the machinery of the State, irrespective of its hierarchic ranking. The provision undoubtedly refers to the old question of the responsibility of States for acts of minor (subordinate, 'petty') officials, which is nevertheless firmly established in international law.[91] As affirmed in the *Moses* case:

> An officer or person in authority represents pro tanto his government, which in an international sense is the aggregate of all officers and men in authority.[92]

Accordingly, the international responsibility of States may be triggered on the basis of the acts and omissions of lower officials, since they participate in the same exercise of authority as their superiors. Indeed, they are supposed to enforce their policies. However, such a rule of attributability has not always received unanimous consensus in early arbitral cases and projects of codification.[93] For instance, Mixed Claims Commissions have formerly recognized attributability only on the basis of the conduct of the organs that are responsible for a State's foreign policy and external relations.[94] As already submitted, the principle of (institutional) unity of the State dictates attribution of the conduct of every agent of the State. Early arbitral practice indeed already offered a plethora of cases, where the acts and omissions of 'petty' officials had been definitely attributed to their State, be such conduct

[91] Clyde Eagleton, *The Responsibility of States in International Law* (New York University Press 1928) 45–49; Jean-Pierre Quéneudec, *La responsabilité internationale de l'État pour les fautes personnelles de ses agents* (LGDJ 1966) 55–68; Alwyn V Freeman, *Responsibility of States for Unlawful Acts of their Armed Forces* (A W Sijthoff 1957) 23; David D Caron, 'The Basis of Responsibility: Attribution and Other Trans-substantive Rules of State Responsibility' in Richard B Lillich and Daniel B Magraw (eds), *The Iran-United States Claims Tribunal: Its Contribution to the Law of State Responsibility* (Transnational Publishers, Inc 1998) 109, 130; Hazel Fox, 'The International Court of Justice's Treatment of Acts of the State and in Particular the Attribution of Acts of Individuals to the State' in Nisuke Ando, Edward McWhinney, and Rüdiger Wolfrum (eds), *Liber Amicorum Judge Shigeru Oda*, vol 1 (Kluwer Law International 2002) 147, 158; Ian Brownlie, 'State Responsibility and the International Court of Justice' in Malgosia Fitzmaurice and Dan Sarooshi (eds), *Issues of State Responsibility before International Judicial Institutions* (Hart Publishing 2004) 11, 12; Ian Brownlie, *System of the Law of Nations. State Responsibility. Part I* (Clarendon Press 1983) 135: 'In any case an administration is for legal purposes to be seen as integral and thus as a system of government. A minor official acting on behalf of the government is by definition a person whose acts and omissions are subject to the control of the state by way of command and authority.'

[92] *Moses*, in Moore, III (GPO 1898) 3127, 3129. See also *Maal Case*, 1903, X RIAA 730: 'the acts of their subordinates in the line of their authority, however odious their acts may be, the Government must stand sponsor for.'

[93] See Harvard Law School (Manley O Hudson, Director), 'Research in International Law (Nationality, Responsibility of States, Territorial Waters). Drafts of Conventions Prepared in Anticipation of the First Conference on the Codification of International Law, The Hague, 1930', 1 April 1929, Part II, 'Responsibility of States' (Edwin M Borchard, Rapporteur), Article 7(a)-(b), (1929) 23 Special Number Supplement American Journal of International Law 133.

[94] *Bensley*, 1844, in Moore, III (GPO 1898) 3016.

an expression of the executive power (a local custom authority,[95] port captain,[96] Mexican *mayor* and *capitán primero*,[97] sheriff,[98] local police,[99] deputy constable,[100] jail keeper[101]) or of judicial functions (judge of first instance,[102] district court,[103] Venezuelan *jefe civil*,[104] rural judge,[105] bankruptcy court,[106] mixed court of first instance,[107] a Mexican *alcalde*,[108] an *administrateur-séquestre*[109]). In other instances, attributability was eventually recognized not really on the basis of the acts of subordinate employees, but upon resort to the doctrine of vicarious liability of the State on the basis of the conduct of chief officers. References have been variously addressed to the rules of obedience and *respondeat superior*,[110] as well as to various doctrines of State 'fault' (*culpa in eligendo, in custodiendo, in instruendo, in vigilando*).[111] The abandonment of theses doctrines is consistent with the *Gestalt* of ARSIWA Article 4 (institutional unity of the State), which renders attributable to the State the acts of minor officials *themselves*, without any requirement to resort to a different act or omission of a superior organ (*direct responsibility*).[112]

[95] *Lewis*, in Moore, III (GPO 1898) 3019, 3020; *Only Son*, 1854, in Moore, IV (GPO 1898) 3404; *Owner of the Sarah B Putnam (United States) v Great Britain*, 6 November 1925, 6 RIAA 156, 157; *Pieri Dominique and Co Case*, 14 August 1905, 10 RIAA 139; *Lacaze*, 19 March 1864, in Albert de La Pradelle and Nikolaos Politis, *Recueil des Sentences Arbitrales*, II, 1856–1872 (Éditions A Pedone 1923) 290, 293; *Case of the Whale Ship "Canada" (United States v Brazil)*, 11 July 1870, in Moore, II (GPO 1898) 1733, 1742–1744.

[96] *William Lee*, in Moore, IV (GPO 1898) 3405–07.

[97] *Estate of Jean-Baptiste Caire (France) v United Mexican States*, 7 June 1929, 5 RIAA 516.

[98] *Francisco Quintanilla (United Mexican States) v United States of America*, 16 November 1926, 4 RIAA 101–04; *Francisco Mallén (United Mexican States) v USA*, 27 April 1927, 4 RIAA 173, 181.

[99] *J W and N L Swinney (USA) v United Mexican States*, 16 November 1926, 4 RIAA 98; *Margaret Roper (USA) v United Mexican States*, 4 April 1927, 4 RIAA 145, 147; *Alexander St J Corrie (USA) v United Mexican States*, 5 March 1929, 4 RIAA 416, 417.

[100] *Francisco Mallén (United Mexican States) v USA*, 27 April 1927, 4 RIAA 173, 175.

[101] *Gertrude Parker Massey (USA) v United Mexican States*, 15 April 1927, 4 RIAA 155, 157.

[102] *Elettronica Sicula SpA (ELSI) (United States of America v Italy)*, Judgment, 20 July 1989, ICJ Reports 1989, 15, 36.

[103] *LaGrand (Germany v United States of America)*, Judgment, 27 June 2001, ICJ Reports 2001, 466, 477.

[104] *Davy Case (on merits)*, 1903, 9 RIAA 467.

[105] *J W and N L Swinney (USA) v United Mexican States*, 16 November 1926, 4 RIAA 98; *Margaret Roper (USA) v United Mexican States*, 4 April 1927, 4 RIAA 145, 147–48.

[106] *H G Venable (USA) v United Mexican States*, 8 July 1927, 4 RIAA 219.

[107] *George David Richards (USA) v United Mexican States*, 23 July 1927, 4 RIAA 275, 276.

[108] *William T Way (USA) v United Mexican States*, 18 October 1928, 4 RIAA 391; *Donoughho* in Moore, III (1898) 3012, 3014.

[109] *Différend concernant l'interprétation de l'article 79, par 6, lettre C, du Traité de Paix (Biens italiens en Tunisie—Échange de lettres du 2 février 1951)—Décisions nos 136, 171 et 196*, 25 June 1952, 6 July 1954 and 7 December 1955, 13 RIAA 389, 432.

[110] *The Lottie May Incident (Great Britain, Honduras)*, 18 April 1899, 15 RIAA 23, 30.

[111] *Différend concernant l'interprétation de l'article 79, par 6, lettre C, du Traité de Paix (Biens italiens en Tunisie—Échange de lettres du 2 février 1951)—Décisions nos 136, 171 et 196*, 25 June 1952, 6 July 1954, and 7 December 1955, 13 RIAA 389, 432; *Différend Joseph Ousset—Décisions nos 93 et 170*, 14 April 1951 and 5 July 1954, 13 RIAA 252, 265.

[112] Gordon A Christenson, 'The Doctrine of Attribution in State Responsibility' in Richard B Lillich (ed), *International Law of State Responsibility for Injuries to Aliens* (University Press of Virginia 1983) 321, 326; Gordon A Christenson, 'Attributing Acts of Omission to the State' (1990–1991) 12 Michigan Journal of International Law 312, 335; Theodor Meron, 'International Responsibility of States for Unauthorized Acts of Their Officials' (1957) 33 British Year Book of International Law 85, 98; C F Amerasinghe, 'Imputability in the Law of State Responsibility for Injuries to Aliens' (1966) 22 Revue Égyptienne de Droit International 91, 95.

Finally, it is worth mentioning that the rule of irresponsibility of States for the acts of their subordinate officials has been traditionally corroborated by reference to the rule of exhaustion of local remedies. This especially pertains to judicial decisions. Notably, an alien should appeal unsatisfactory judgments before a higher judge in the same jurisdiction and, in turn, to a supreme court. Accordingly, the issue of attributability of conduct of lower judges would not even arise in practice. However, the rule of exhaustion of local remedies is a requirement for admissibility of a claim of diplomatic protection, and does not concern attributability proper. Seemingly, the argument gained importance when the international scholarship did not doctrinally distinguish between primary and secondary rules, attribution rules then standing as a mere appendix to the law of diplomatic protection for injuries to aliens.[113]

2. Attribution of *Ultra Vires* Conduct

> Both national and international law contemplate cases in which the body corporate or politic may be bound, as to third parties, by an *ultra vires* act of an agent.[114]

The issue of the responsibility for unauthorized acts of State organs has been frequently interlocked with the above discussed problem of the responsibility for the conduct of subordinate officials. A distinction between the two questions is required. The *ultra vires* rule is designed to attribute to the State the conduct of organs (either of a higher or lower level) executed in excess of authority or in contravention of instructions, provided that the organ was acting in its official capacity, on the basis of a principle of (institutional) unity and continuity, as well as of accountability of the State.[115] Instead, the rule of attribution of acts of minor officials pertains to the possibility of categorizing subordinate agents as 'State organs' for the purposes of a finding of international responsibility. Obviously, the *ultra vires* rule applies to every organ of the State, to the inclusion of minor officials. Both

[113] See the analysis in Roberto Ago, Third Report on State Responsibility, by Mr Roberto Ago, Special Rapporteur, 'The internationally wrongful act of the State, source of international responsibility', 5 March, 7 April, 28 April, and 18 May 1971, para 152, document A/CN.4/246 and Add.1-3, Yearbook of the International Law Commission, 1971, Volume II (Part One), 250, document A/CN.4/SER.A/1971/Add.1 (Part 1).

[114] *Certain Expenses of the United Nations (Article 17, paragraph 2 of the Charter)*, Advisory Opinion, 20 July 1962, ICJ Reports 1962, 151, 168.

[115] David D Caron, 'The Basis of Responsibility: Attribution and Other Trans-substantive Rules of State Responsibility' in Richard B Lillich and Daniel B Magraw (eds), *The Iran-United States Claims Tribunal: Its Contribution to the Law of State Responsibility* (Transnational Publishers, Inc 1998) 109, 141.

rules provide for the direct attributability of conduct to States, to the abandonment of any theory of vicarious responsibility or fault doctrine.[116]

The rule of attribution of *ultra vires* acts of organs unquestionably reflects customary international law,[117] as being codified by ARSIWA Article 7:

> ***Article 7***
> ***Excess of authority or contravention of instructions***
>
> The conduct of an organ of a State or of a person or entity empowered to exercise elements of the governmental authority shall be considered an act of the State under international law if the organ, person or entity acts in that capacity, even if it exceeds its authority or contravenes instructions.

The *ultra vires* rule provided by customary international law is independent in its scope and application with regard to the existence of *ultra vires* rules in national jurisdictions governing the liability of States vis-à-vis their nationals.[118] The content of the international rule may well diverge from the national rule applicable to

[116] Dionisio Anzilotti, 'La responsabilité internationale des États a raison des dommages soufferts par des étrangers' (1906) 13 Revue Générale de Droit International Public 285, 287–88, 292; Theodor Meron, 'International Responsibility of States for Unauthorized Acts of Their Officials' (1957) 33 British Year Book of International Law 85, 103–04. *Contra*, Edwin M Borchard, '"Responsibility of States" at the Hague Codification Conference' (1930) 24 American Journal of International Law 517, 530.

[117] *Armed Activities in the Territory of the Congo (DRC v Uganda)*, 19 December 2005, paras 213–14, 243, ICJ Reports 2005, 168, 242, 251; *Sea-Land Service, Inc v The Islamic Republic of Iran, Ports and Shipping Organization of Iran*, Case No 33, 20 June 1984, Award No 135-33-1, 6 IRAN-US CTR 149, 202 (1984-II): 'a State is responsible for acts of its officials—whether authorized, unauthorized, or even contrary to specific governmental instructions.' But in early cases the *ultra vires* rule was not firmly established. See *Star and Herald*, in Moore, VI (GPO 1906) 775, 780: 'no government is responsible for the acts of its agents or subalterns which are not in perfect accord with the faculties conferred upon them by law or the instructions which the government itself may have given them'; *William Yeaton*, in Moore, III (GPO 1898) 2944, 2947; *Claims of Charles Oberlander and Barbara M Messenger against the Government of Mexico (United States of America/Mexico)*, 19 November 1897, 29 RIAA 327, 335.

[118] *Contra*, Harvard Law School (Manley O Hudson, Director), 'Research in International Law (Nationality, Responsibility of States, Territorial Waters). Drafts of Conventions Prepared in Anticipation of the First Conference on the Codification of International Law, The Hague, 1930', 1 April 1929, Part II, 'Responsibility of States' (Edwin M Borchard, Rapporteur), Article 7(a), (1929) 23 Special Number Supplement American Journal of International Law 133: 'A state is responsible if an injury to an alien results from the wrongful act or omission of one of its higher authorities within the scope of the office or function of such authority, if the local remedies have been exhausted without adequate redress.'; League of Nations, Committee of Experts for the Progressive Codification of International Law, Second Session, 12–29 January 1926, Annex to Questionnaire No 4, 'Responsibility of States for Damage Done in Their Territories to the Person or Property of Foreigners', Report of the Sub-Committee (Mr Gustavo Guerrero, Rapporteur), Conclusions, para 4, League of Nations publication, V.Legal, 1926.V.3, document C.46.M.23.1926.V and League of Nations publication, V.Legal, 1926.V.11, document C.96.M.47.1926.V, (1926) 20 American Journal of International Law Special Supplement 176, 187–88, 201–02: 'If the act of the official is accomplished outside the scope of his competence, that is to say, if he has exceeded his powers, we are then confronted with an act which, juridically speaking, is not an act of the State. It may be illegal, but, from the point of view of international law, the offence cannot be imputed to the State.'

the same agent at issue.[119] This is but an application of the principle of supremacy of international law.[120]

Although 'excess of authority' and 'contravention of instructions' represent two distinct prongs, nevertheless they result in the delimitation of the boundaries of the *agency* of a State organ. This boundary is generally set by the nature of the functions entrusted to an organ and may additionally be circumscribed in relation to a specific act by the instructions of a superior organ. The international *ultra vires* rule prescribes attributability 'even if' the State official exceeded or abused its powers, or acted contrary or opposite to directives.[121] The justification for the adoption of this solution by international law rests on a policy for security in international relations. Since a State cannot predict and prevent the entirety of the acts (including bona fide errors in judgment)[122] of their organs (acting either within or outside their authority), a risk theory turns out to be appropriate in order to protect the other members of the international community from the consequences that may derive from the States' freedom of internal self-organization.[123]

Customary international law, as codified by ARSIWA Article 7, also requires that a State organ 'acts in that capacity', namely in its official capacity.[124] This appears to be rather logical: in order to be exceeded, an actual or (at least) apparent 'authority' must be in place. As a consequence, the *ultra vires* acts shall not be executed by the organ manifestly outside its scope of authority and general competence (outside the 'regular agencies of government').[125] In this respect, the acts relating to the organ's office (*actes de fonction*) should be performed under cover, colour (or even

[119] *Lacaze*, 19 March 1864, in Albert de La Pradelle and Nikolaos Politis, *Recueil des Sentences Arbitrales*, II, 1856–1872 (Éditions A Pedone 1923) 290, 302: '*L'acte fait par le fonctionnaire en dehors de sa compétence ou au mépris des lois qui règlent ses attributions n'est pas, il est vrai, au regard du droit interne, un acte de l'État, mais au point de vue international il en a tous les caractères intrinsèques.*'

[120] See Pierre-Marie Dupuy, 'Relations Between the International Law of Responsibility and Responsibility in Municipal Law' in James Crawford, Alain Pellet, and Simon Olleson (eds), *The Law of International Responsibility* (Oxford University Press 2010) 173, 176.

[121] See especially the case of *Thomas H Youmans (USA) v United Mexican States*, 23 November 1926, 4 RIAA 110, 115: 'acts of ten soldiers and one officer of the State of Michoacân, who, after having been ordered by the highest official in the locality to protect American citizens, instead of carrying out orders given them acted in violation of them in consequence of which the Americans were killed.'

[122] *Lacaze*, 19 March 1864, in Albert de La Pradelle and Nikolaos Politis, *Recueil des Sentences Arbitrales*, II, 1856–1872 (Éditions A Pedone 1923) 290, 302. '*Mais une distinction a fini par s'établir entre les fautes de service et les fautes grossières des autorités: l'État répond des premières, comme d'un risque de ses services publics; il laisse les secondes à la charge de leurs auteurs*'; *Owners, Officers and Men of the Wanderer (Gr Br) v United States*, 9 December 1921, 6 RIAA 68, 74.

[123] Dionisio Anzilotti, *Corso di diritto internazionale, Volume Primo: Introduzione—Teorie generali* (3rd edn, Athenaeum 1928) 420; Dionisio Anzilotti, 'La responsabilité internationale des États a raison des dommages soufferts par des étrangers' (1906) 13 Revue Générale de Droit International Public 285, 289; Charles de Visscher, 'La responsabilité internationale des États' in *Bibliotheca Visseriana*, vol II (Brill 1924) 89, 92; Ian Brownlie, *System of the Law of Nations. State Responsibility. Part I* (Clarendon Press 1983) 145: 'The rule accords generally with a regime of objective responsibility.'

[124] *Claim of the Salvador Commercial Company ('El Triunfo Company')*, 8 May 1902, 15 RIAA 455, 477.

[125] Ian Brownlie, *System of the Law of Nations. State Responsibility. Part I* (Clarendon Press 1983) 142.

claim) of authority.[126] The circumstance of an organ actually using the means put at its disposal by virtue of its office and duties ('*en se servant des moyens mis, à ce titre, à leur disposition*') is interpreted as sufficient ground for the operation of the *ultra vires* rule.[127] Purely private acts of organs are not attributable to the State, either executed in the exercise of their office or off-duty. In the former case, attribution does not intervene where the conduct at issue radically (and visibly) departs from the functions of the organ.[128] In the latter case, attribution never occurs, as far as the *ultra vires* rule is concerned.[129] A clear instance of a purely private act is recorded in the early case of *Bensley*:

> The detention of the boy appears to have been a wanton trespass committed by the governor, under no color of official proceedings, and without any connection with his official duties.[130]

[126] *Estate of Jean-Baptiste Caire (France) v United Mexican States*, 7 June 1929, 5 RIAA 516, 530: '*Mais pour pouvoir admettre cette responsabilité, dite objective, de l'Etat pour les actes commis par ses fonctionnaires ou organes en dehors des limites de leur compétence, il faut qu'ils aient agi au moins apparemment comme des fonctionnaires ou organes compétents, ou que, en agissant, ils aient usé de pouvoirs ou de moyens propres à leur qualité officielle.*'; *American Bible Society (US v Turkey)*, 1885, in Moore, VI (GPO 1906) 743: 'it is a rule of international law that sovereigns are not liable, in diplomatic procedure, for damages to a foreigner when arising from the misconduct of agents acting out of the range not only of their real but of their apparent authority.'; *Davy Case (on merits)*, 1903, 9 RIAA 467; *Owners of the Jessie, the Thomas F Bayard and the Pescawha (Great Britain) v United States*, 2 December 1921, 6 RIAA 57, 59: 'any Government is responsible to other Governments for errors, in judgment of its officials purporting to act within the scope of their duties and vested with power to enforce their demands.'; Court of Claims of the United States, No H-252, decided 7 December 1931, *Royal Holland Lloyd, a Corporation v The United States*, (1932) 26 American Journal of International Law 399, 410: 'any government is responsible to other nations for error in judgment of its officials purporting to act within the scope of their duties.'

[127] Institut de Droit International, 'Responsabilité internationale des Etats à raison des dommages causés sur leur territoire à la personne et aux biens des étrangers' (Leo Strisower, Rapporteur), Résolution du 1 septembre 1927, Session de Lausanne, (1927) 33(III) Annuaire de l'Institut de Droit International 330-335, Article I(3).

[128] *Estate of Jean-Baptiste Caire (France) v United Mexican States*, 7 June 1929, 5 RIAA 516, 531: '*l'Etat n'étant pas responsable dans le seul cas où l'acte n'a eu aucun rapport avec la fonction officielle et n'a été, en réalité, qu'un acte d'un particulier.*' See Francisco V García Amador, 'Draft on international responsibility of the State for injuries caused in its territory to the person or property of aliens', Article 3.3, Annex to International responsibility: Third report by F. V. Garcia Amador, Special Rapporteur, 'Responsibility of the State for Injuries Caused in its Territory to the Person or Property of Aliens. Part II: The International Claim', 2 January 1958, document A/CN A/111, Yearbook of the International Law Commission, 1958, Volume II, 47, 71, document A/CN.4/SER.A/1958/Add.l: 'the international responsibility of the State shall not be involved if the lack of competence was so apparent that the alien should have been aware of it and could, in consequence, have avoided the injury.'

[129] *Alexander St J Corrie (USA) v United Mexican States*, 5 March 1929, 4 RIAA 416, 417; *Ethel Morton (USA) v United Mexican States*, 2 April 1929, 4 RIAA 428; *Louis B Gordon (USA) v United Mexican States*, 8 October 1930, 4 RIAA 586, 588: 'The principle is that the personal acts of officials not within the scope of their authority do not entail responsibility upon a State'; *Teodoro García and M A Garza (United Mexican States) v United States of America*, 3 December 1926, 4 RIAA 119, 126: 'There is no question with regard to the rule of international law that a nation is responsible for acts of soldiers which are not acts of malice committed in their private capacity.'

[130] *Bensley*, 1844, in Moore, III (GPO 1898) 3016, 3018. See also *Stanley M Parker v Mexico* in Moore, III (GPO 1898) 2996; *Carlock's* in Moore, III (GPO 1898) 2996; *Jeannaud* in Moore, III (GPO 1898) 3000, 3001.

The *ultra vires* rule applies to both State organs and persons or entities pursuant to ARSIWA Article 5. The case law on attribution of *ultra vires* acts of (statutory organs of) parastatal entities is definitely more exiguous. An example is found in the *Yeager* case with regard to the State-owned company Iran Air, where the act of bribery of an employee of said company was aptly qualified as a purely private act, and as such not subject to the *ultra vires* rule of ARSIWA Article 7.[131] As discussed in the following chapter, investor–State arbitration provides more cases on the attribution of *ultra vires* acts of persons pursuant to ARSIWA Article 5.[132]

3. *De Facto* Organs

The rule of attribution to the State of the conduct of its *de facto* organs has historically been developed through the case law of the Mixed Claims Commissions,[133] the ICJ,[134] the Iran–US Claims Tribunal,[135] and the International Criminal Tribunal for the Former Yugoslavia (ICTY).[136] After decades of judicial elaboration, this norm has found its codification in the provision of ARSIWA Article 4.2:[137] '[a]n organ includes any person or entity which has that status in accordance with the internal law of the State.' The rationale behind this rule is to prevent States from escaping international responsibility by having non-agents carry out acts that the State cannot lawfully perform from the viewpoint of international legality and, consequently, from objecting that such persons actually participating in governmental functions are not classified as State organs under national legislation.[138] As the ARSIWA Commentaries state: 'a State cannot avoid responsibility for the conduct of a body which does in truth act as one of its organs merely by denying it that status under its own law. This result is achieved by the use of the word "includes" in

[131] *Kenneth P Yeager v The Islamic Republic of Iran*, Case No 10199, 2 November 1987, Award No 324-10199-1, 17 IRAN-US CTR 92, 111 (1987-IV): 'There is no indication in this case that the Iran Air agent was acting for any other reason than personal profit, or that he had passed on the payment to Iran Air. He evidently did not act on behalf or in the interest of Iran Air. The Tribunal finds, therefore, that this agent acted in a private capacity and not in his official capacity as an organ of Iran Air.'

[132] See Chapter III, section 3.3.

[133] *Charles S Stephens and Bowman Stephens (USA) v United Mexican States*, 15 July 1927, 4 RIAA 265.

[134] *Military and Paramilitary Activities in and against Nicaragua (Nicaragua v United States of America)*, Merits, Judgment, 27 June 1986, paras 109–15, ICJ Reports 1986, 14, 62–5; *Application of the Convention on the Prevention and Punishment of the Crime of Genocide (Bosnia and Herzegovina v Serbia and Montenegro)*, Judgment, 26 February 2007, paras 390–95, ICJ Reports 2007, 43, 204–06.

[135] *Kenneth P Yeager v The Islamic Republic of Iran*, Case No 10199, 2 November 1987, Award No 324-10199-1, 17 IRAN-US CTR 92, 102 (1987-IV).

[136] ICTY, Appeals Chamber, *Tadić*, IT-94-1-A, Judgement, 15 July 1999, 33-72, paras 80–162.

[137] See section 1.2 of Chapter I, and section 1.2 of this chapter.

[138] ICTY, Appeals Chamber, *Tadić*, IT-94-1-A, Judgement, 15 July 1999, 47–48, para 117; *Kenneth P Yeager v The Islamic Republic of Iran*, Case No 10199, 2 November 1987, para 45, Award No 324-10199-1, 17 IRAN-US CTR 92, 105 (1987-IV): 'Under international law Iran cannot, on the one hand, tolerate the exercise of governmental authority by revolutionary "Komitehs" or "Guards" and at the same time deny responsibility for wrongful acts committed by them.'

paragraph 2.'[139] The ICJ has emphasized that the spirit of the rule on *de facto* organs is to make 'reality ... prevail over appearances'.[140] Once a person or entity has been established as being a *de facto* agent, the regime of attributability of the conduct of State organs will apply in its entirety, including the *ultra vires* rule.[141]

Since one of the premises for a finding of *de facto* agency is the absence of the formal status of organ under domestic law, the rule hereby illustrated has been historically (and inextricably but incorrectly) developed in supposedly 'consubstantial' connection with the rule regarding attribution to the State of acts of private individuals, which is at present codified by ARSIWA Article 8.[142] Therefore, the doctrine of *de facto* organs has been mainly addressed at the realm of State responsibility for the acts of individuals, rather than in connection with the rule of attribution of the conduct of State organs, which proceeds from a theory of (public law) agency. This legal framework has historically engendered a considerable degree of confusion as to the possibility of providing a more distinct definition of *de facto* organ in international legal scholarship.[143] In point of legal terminology, *de facto* organs under ARSIWA Article 4.2—Article 8(a) on first reading—are persons not having the formal status of organ under internal law, but nonetheless acting in fact on behalf of the State (*agency*). Instead, private individuals under ARSIWA Article 8 are non-agents in fact acting on the instructions of, or under the direction or control of, the State.[144] While Article 8(a) of the draft articles adopted on first reading has traditionally been considered to be the predecessor of ARSIWA Article 8, this has not certainly contributed to an earlier doctrinal and normative final systematization of the rule on *de facto* organs.[145] The 'closure of the debate'

[139] ARSIWA Commentaries 36, 42.

[140] *Application of the Convention on the Prevention and Punishment of the Crime of Genocide (Bosnia and Herzegovina v Serbia and Montenegro)*, Judgment, 26 February 2007, para 291, ICJ Reports 2007, 43, 204.

[141] James Crawford, *State Responsibility. The General Part* (Cambridge University Press 2013) 126: 'Once such a relationship is proved, however, a de facto organ functions just like any other, and all acts it performs in the exercise of state authority are attributable to the state.'

[142] See section 5 of this chapter.

[143] Claus Kress, 'L'organe de facto en droit international public' (2001) 105 Revue Générale de Droit International Public 93, 96, 125; Frédéric Dopagne, 'La responsabilité de l'État du fait des particuliers: les causes d'imputation revisitées par les articles sur la responsabilité de l'État pour fait internationalement illicite' (2001) 34 Revue Belge du Droit International 492, 496; Gregory Townsend, 'State Responsibility for Acts of De Facto Agents' (1997) 14 Arizona Journal of International & Comparative Law 635, 641–42; Jörn Griebel and Milan Plücken, 'New Developments Regarding the Rules of Attribution? The International Court of Justice's Decision in *Bosnia v. Serbia*' (2008) 21 Leiden Journal of International Law 601, 608; Gordon A Christenson, 'Attributing Acts of Omission to the State' (1990–1991) 12 Michigan Journal of International Law 312, 333.

[144] See section 5.3 of this chapter.

[145] James Crawford, *State Responsibility. The General Part* (Cambridge University Press 2013) 126: 'the present work will use the term only in the context of ARSIWA Article 4, even though it was introduced by Special Rapporteur Ago with reference to the predecessor of ARSIWA Article 8.' However, Paolo Palchetti seems to exclude that the Ago's version engendered confusion. cf Paolo Palchetti, 'Comportamento di organi di fatto e illecito internazionale nel progetto di articoli sulla responsabilità internazionale degli Stati' in Marina Spinedi, Alessandra Gianelli, and Maria Luisa Alaimo (eds), *La codificazione della responsabilità internazionale degli Stati alla prova dei fatti: problemi e spunti di*

on this issue came with the *Bosnian Genocide* judgment, which finally anchored the doctrine of *de facto* organs to ARSIWA Article 4.[146] Hereinafter, an analysis of the relevant case law on the topic of *de facto* organs is provided. To this extent, a clarification is required, namely that *Nicaragua* and *Tadić* are denifitely part of this review of international judicial decisions. However, they will be addressed under the treatise on ARSIWA Article 8 in deferential conformity to the *sedes* attributed thereto by the ARSIWA Commentaries.

In the early case of *Stephens*, the Mexico–US General Claims Commission was confronted with the qualification of 'a sort of informal municipal guards organization', called '*defensas sociales*'. The Commission asserted:

> It is difficult to determine with precision the status of these guards as an irregular auxiliary of the army, the more so as they lacked both uniforms and insignia; but at any rate they were 'acting for' Mexico or for its political subdivisions.[147]

As mentioned above, auxiliary corps to the army should be ascribed into the category of *de jure* organs. However, in *Stephens* the guards were not formally registered, therefore not having a regular status. For this reason, *Stephens* may be regarded as one of the earliest cases covering *de facto* agents.[148]

The Iranian Revolutionary Committees (Komitehs) are one of the chief examples of *de facto* organs. During the Iranian Revolution, an unofficial system of government emerged in Iran in parallel to the official legislature, executive, and judiciary.[149] The Komitehs were local revolutionary committees, usually originating from 'neighbourhood committees', which served as local security forces empowered to arrest, confiscate property, and imprison. Only in May 1979 were they officially recognized as Revolutionary Guards, by which they also retained

riflessione (Giuffrè 2006) 3, 10: '*L'interprete avrebbe dovuto in primo luogo accertare se l'individuo agente avesse la qualità di organo in base al diritto interno o fosse comunque legato allo Stato da un rapporto formale di diritto interno. In assenza di un tale legame, si sarebbe dovuto verificare se tale individuo avesse in fatto agito per conto dello Stato ai sensi dell'art. 8 del Progetto.*'

146 *Application of the Convention on the Prevention and Punishment of the Crime of Genocide (Bosnia and Herzegovina v Serbia and Montenegro)*, Judgment, 26 February 2007, paras 390–95, ICJ Reports 2007, 43, 204–06. cf Paola Gaeta, 'Génocide d'Etat et responsabilité pénale individuelle' (2007) 111 Revue Général de Droit International Public 273.

147 *Charles S Stephens and Bowman Stephens (USA) v United Mexican States*, 15 July 1927, 4 RIAA 265, 267.

148 See Jérôme Reymond, *L'attribution de comportements d'organes* de facto *et d'agents de l'Etat en droit international. Etude sur la responsabilité internationale des Etats* (Schultess 2013) 134.

149 David D Caron, 'The Basis of Responsibility: Attribution and Other Trans-substantive Rules of State Responsibility' in Richard B Lillich and Daniel B Magraw (eds), *The Iran–United States Claims Tribunal: Its Contribution to the Law of State Responsibility* (Transnational Publishers, Inc 1998) 109, 141.

a permanent place in the State budget.[150] While the acts of the Revolutionary Guards after the official recognition clearly entail attribution as conduct of *de jure* organs,[151] the Iran–US Claims Tribunal was confronted with attribution to Iran of the acts of the Komitehs in the interim period between February and May 1979. In *Yeager*, the Tribunal held:

> While there is some doubt as to whether revolutionary 'Komitehs' or 'Guard' can be considered 'organs' of the Government of Iran, since they were not formally recognized during the period relevant to this Case, attributability of acts to the State is not limited to acts of organs formally recognized under internal law. Otherwise a State could avoid responsibility under international law merely by invoking its internal law. It is generally accepted in international law that a State is also responsible for acts of persons, if it is established that those persons were in fact acting on behalf of the State. See ILC-Draft Article 8(a).[152]

The ICJ rendered a definition of *de facto* organ in the *Nicaragua* case, where it basically established a test of (complete) dependence and (effective) control.[153] The ICTY in *Tadić* tried to 'overrule' *Nicaragua* by replacing its definition with a test of dependence and (overall) control, although limited to *organized* military and paramilitary groups.[154] Both cases will be discussed in detail below.[155] In conclusion,

[150] *Kenneth P Yeager v The Islamic Republic of Iran*, Case No 10199, 2 November 1987, Award No 324-10199-1, 17 IRAN-US CTR 92, 102 (1987-IV).

[151] *William L Pereira Associates, Iran v The Islamic Republic of Iran*, Case No 1, 17 March 1984, Award No 116-1-3, 5 IRAN-US CTR 198, 226–27 (1984-I): 'Under public international law the Government of the Islamic Republic of Iran must be deemed responsible for the actions of the Revolutionary Guards.'; *Sola Tiles, Inc v The Government of the Islamic Republic of Iran*, Case No 317, 22 April 1987, Award No 298-317-1, 14 IRAN-US CTR 223, 233 (1987-I): 'it is well settled that the Revolutionary Committees are among those organs whose acts are attributable to the Government of Iran, which is responsible for them as a matter of law.'

[152] *Kenneth P Yeager v The Islamic Republic of Iran*, Case No 10199, 2 November 1987, Award No 324-10199-1, 17 IRAN-US CTR 92, 103, para 42 (1987-IV). The jurisprudence *Yeager* has been consistently applied in subsequent cases. *Jimmie B Leach v The Islamic Republic of Iran*, Case No 12183, 6 October 1989, Award No 440-12183-1, 23 IRAN-US CTR 239 (1989-III); *Leonard and Mavis Daley v The Islamic Republic of Iran*, Case No 10514, 20 April 1988, Award No 360-10514-1, 18 IRAN-US CTR 232, 238 (1988-I); *Robert R Schott v Islamic Republic of Iran, Ministry of Mines and Industries of Iran, Ministry of Housing and Urban Development of Iran, Revolutionary Guard of Iran, Bank Markazi Iran*, Case No 268, 14 March 1990, Award No 474-268-1, Separate Opinion of Howard M Holtzmann, 24 IRAN-US CTR 203, 234 (1990-I); *Computer Sciences Corporation v The Government of the Islamic Republic of Iran, Ministry of Finance, Ministry of National Defence, Iran Aircraft Industries, Information Systems Iran, Bank Mellat, Bank Tejarat, the successors of the following entities: Imperial Iranian Air Force, Imperial Iranian Ground Force, Imperial Iranian Navy, Imperial Iranian Gendarmerie, Imperial Iranian National Police, The Supreme Commander's Staff*, Case No 65, 16 April 1986, Award No 221-65-1, 10 IRAN-US CTR 269, 303 (1986-I); *Houston Contracting Company v National Iranian Oil Company, National Iranian Gas Company, and The Islamic Republic of Iran*, Case No 173, 22 July 1988, Award No 378-173-3, 20 IRAN-US CTR 3, 123 (1988-III).

[153] *Military and Paramilitary Activities in and against Nicaragua (Nicaragua v United States of America)*, Merits, Judgment, 27 June 1986, paras 109–11, ICJ Reports 1986, 14, 62–65.

[154] ICTY, Appeals Chamber, *Tadić*, IT-94-1-A, Judgement, 15 July 1999, 62, 69, paras 145, 156.

[155] See section 5.3.4 of this chapter.

the *Bosnian Genocide* case intervened on the question and consacrated the category of *de facto* organs to be intended in its normative autonomy and not in connection with the rule for individuals acting in fact under the instructions, or direction or control, of the State.[156] Various jurists, notably in the Italian scholarship, 'anticipated' this achievement at the doctrinal level in a context of normative uncertainty, which had not yet been resolved by the adoption of ARSIWA on second reading.[157] The ICJ established the requirements of strict control, on one side,[158] and complete and total dependence, on the other side:[159]

> In such a case, it is appropriate to look beyond legal status alone, in order to grasp the reality of the relationship between the person taking action, and the State to which he is so closely attached as to appear to be nothing more than its agent: any other solution would allow States to escape their international responsibility by choosing to act through persons or entities whose supposed independence would be purely fictitious.[160]

Accordingly, the exceptional finding of *de facto* agency should be based on the absence of real autonomy of the person or group of persons vis-à-vis the State, so that they are ultimately established as representing a mere 'instrument' of the State.[161]

[156] *Application of the Convention on the Prevention and Punishment of the Crime of Genocide (Bosnia and Herzegovina v Serbia and Montenegro)*, Judgment, 26 February 2007, paras 390 et seq, ICJ Reports 2007, 43, 204.

[157] André JJ de Hoogh, 'Articles 4 and 8 of the 2001 ILC Articles on State Responsibility, the *Tadić* Case and Attribution of Acts of Bosnian Serb Authorities to the Federal Republic of Yugoslavia' (2001) 72 British Year Book of International Law 255, 268: 'It seems right therefore to reserve the phrase "*de facto* organ" for an organ considered as such by virtue of the supplementary role of international law under Article 4, paragraph 2.'; Paolo Palchetti, 'Comportamento di Organi di Fatto e Illecito Internazionale nel Progetto di Articoli sulla Responsabilità Internazionale degli Stati' in Marina Spinedi, Alessandra Gianelli, and Maria Luisa Alaimo (eds), *La Codificazione della Responsabilità Internazionale degli Stati alla Prova dei Fatti: Problemi e Spunti di Riflessione* (Giuffrè 2006) 3, 10; Paolo Palchetti, *L'Organo di Fatto dello Stato nell'Illecito Internazionale* (Giuffrè 2007) 30 et seq. However, it is appropriate to emphasize that Anzilotti already distinguished the category of *de facto* organs from the acts of private individuals, cf Dionisio Anzilotti, *Corso di diritto internazionale, Volume Primo: Introduzione—Teorie generali* (3rd edn, Athenaeum 1928) 431: '*Ciò che distingue questa categoria* [fatti di individui] *dalla precedente* [fatti di organi], *non è tanto la mancanza della qualità di organo dello Stato nell'autore, qualità, che, come si è visto, può mancare anche nei casi precedentemente esaminati, quanto il carattere oggettivo dei fatti stessi, che non si presentano esteriormente come un esercizio, legale o illegale, di attività statali e non ne rivestono le forme: in quelli l'autore, ne abbia o no il diritto poco importa, agisce* di fatto *come organo dello Stato; in questi no.*'

[158] *Application of the Convention on the Prevention and Punishment of the Crime of Genocide (Bosnia and Herzegovina v Serbia and Montenegro)*, Judgment, 26 February 2007, para 391, ICJ Reports 2007, 43, 204.

[159] *Application of the Convention on the Prevention and Punishment of the Crime of Genocide (Bosnia and Herzegovina v Serbia and Montenegro)*, Judgment, 26 February 2007, paras 392, 394, ICJ Reports 2007, 43, 205, 206.

[160] *Application of the Convention on the Prevention and Punishment of the Crime of Genocide (Bosnia and Herzegovina v Serbia and Montenegro)*, Judgment, 26 February 2007, para 392, ICJ Reports 2007, 43, 205.

[161] ibid.

However, it may not be affirmed that 'persons' pursuant to ARSIWA Article 8 do not retain their autonomy in carrying out their conduct, albeit under the instructions, direction, or control by organs of the State.

An overlap of normative criteria may be in place for a finding of *de facto* organs pursuant to ARSIWA Article 4 and persons or entities ('State entities') pursuant to ARSIWA Article 5, in so far as certain subjects, not having the formal or official status of State organs, 'exercise elements of the governmental authority'. For instance, in *Yeager* the Komitehs were found to execute customs, immigration, and security policies, which evidently embodies a manifestation of sovereign authority.[162] One of the decisive criteria in distinguishing the two categories rests upon the official empowerment 'by law' or by delegation of authority, which characterizes persons or entities under ARSIWA Article 5. The exceptional character of a finding of *de facto* agency would suggest that it can operate on a residual basis, only in so far as no element whatsoever of formality between a given person and the State has been established.

4. Persons or Entities Empowered by the Law of the State to Exercise Elements of the Governmental Authority

4.1 Notion

ARSIWA's mechanisms of attribution are not limited to the conduct of State organs, but also regulate acts and omissions of persons or entities empowered by the law to exercise 'elements of the governmental authority' (that is, 'State entities', including parastatal entities, State instrumentalities, State enterprises, and State-owned or State-controlled enterprises—SOEs/SCEs—in general). The rule is codified by ARSIWA Article 5:

> ***Article 5***
> ***Conduct of persons or entities exercising elements of governmental authority***
>
> The conduct of a person or entity which is not an organ of the State under article 4 but which is empowered by the law of that State to exercise elements of the governmental authority shall be considered an act of the State under international law, provided the person or entity is acting in that capacity in the particular instance.[163]

The demand for this rule emerged only at a rather advanced stage of the codification process, namely in Roberto Ago's Third Report on State Responsibility of 1971

[162] *Kenneth P Yeager v The Islamic Republic of Iran*, Case No 10199, 2 November 1987, Award No 324-10199-1, para 61, 17 IRAN-US CTR 92, 110 (1987-IV).

[163] ARSIWA Commentaries 43.

by reference to 'public institutions separate from the State'.[164] As explained in the ARSIWA Commentaries:

> The article is intended to take account of the increasingly common phenomenon of parastatal entities, which exercise elements of governmental authority in place of State organs, as well as situations where former State corporations have been privatized but retain certain public or regulatory functions.[165]

The scope of ARSIWA Article 5 comprehensively enshrines parastatal entities (an expression imported from Italian scholarship and practice,[166] and equivalent to the French '*émanations de l'État*'), either having a public law status or being privatized entities, or 'private' natural or juridical persons (for instance a stock exchange).[167] This is elucidated by the specific examples formulated in the ARSIWA Commentaries: 'private security firms contracted to act as prison guards', 'private or State-owned airlines exercising powers in relation to immigration control or quarantine', and 'railways companies granted with police powers'.[168]

Historically, the sociopolitical phenomenon of entities being legally separated by the State and its organs, but entrusted by the State itself to undertake functions of public interest, appeared in the XX century with the fascist 'government control' in Italy and the *New Deal* in the US.[169] These parastatals were characterized by a hybrid legal regime, a combination of public and private law.[170] The public side should have served to warrant the enforcement of the public policies, for which they were created (parastatals as State *instrumentalities*). The private side should have granted

[164] Roberto Ago, Third Report on State Responsibility, by Mr Roberto Ago, Special Rapporteur, 'The internationally wrongful act of the State, source of international responsibility', 5 March, 7 April, 28 April, and 18 May 1971, document A/CN.4/246 and Add.1-3, Yearbook of the International Law Commission, 1971, Volume II (Part One), 253–54, document A/CN.4/SER.A/1971/Add.1 (Part 1): 'public corporations and other public institutions which have their own legal personality and autonomy of administration and management, and are intended to provide a particular service or to perform specific functions.'

[165] ARSIWA Commentaries 43, para 1.

[166] Roberto Ago, Third Report on State Responsibility, by Mr Roberto Ago, Special Rapporteur, 'The internationally wrongful act of the State, source of international responsibility', 5 March, 7 April, 28 April, and 18 May 1971, para 164, document A/CN.4/246 and Add.1-3, Yearbook of the International Law Commission, 1971, Volume II (Part One), 199, 254, document A/CN.4/SER.A/1971/Add.1 (Part 1): '"para-State" institutions, i.e., institutions which possess an organization of their own and which, side by side with the State but separate from it, provide services and perform tasks of a public character.'

[167] James Crawford, *State Responsibility. The General Part* (Cambridge University Press 2013) 128.

[168] ARSIWA Commentaries 43, paras 2, 5.

[169] Pier Angelo Toninelli, 'The Rise and Fall of Public Enterprise. The Framework' in Pier Angelo Toninelli (ed), *The Rise and Fall of State-Owned Enterprise in the Western World* (Cambridge University Press 2000) 3, 14–21. It may also be submitted that such a sociopolitical phenomenon started long before the XX century with the Dutch East India Company (VOC) in the XVII century and other commercial instruments of colonialism in the XVIII and XIX century.

[170] Roberto Ago, Third Report on State Responsibility, by Mr Roberto Ago, Special Rapporteur, 'The internationally wrongful act of the State, source of international responsibility', 5 March, 7 April, 28 April, and 18 May 1971, para 164, document A/CN.4/246 and Add.1-3, Yearbook of the International

more efficiency, flexibility, and celerity in their attainment. Hence, the concept of 'a corporation clothed with the power of government but possessed of the flexibility and initiative of a private enterprise'.[171] In socialist economies, the chief example of parastatals is represented by State economic monopolies and trading agencies, either as a result of a nationalization or as a creation of the political power.[172] These economic and legal patterns were generally maintained after World War II, as in the case of the 'Partecipazioni Statali' (PPSS) in Italy, or installed from scratch in European countries or in the context of new socialist experiences.[173] While being redolent of the political power, parastatals formed by the State to discharge economic functions could compete on the market arena as every other business. Accordingly, they mainly execute *acta jure gestionis*. Paul de Visscher acknowledged the trend in the 1960s:

> *Nous voyons aujourd'hui se multiplier les personnes morales de droit public. Aux côtés de l'Etat et de ses subdivisions territoriales, nous voyons se constituer des établissements publics, des corporations publiques, des administrations personnalisées ou régies, et même des sociétés d'économie mixte sur lesquelles le pouvoir politique exerce un contrôle prépondérant. L'Etat, devenu commerçant et industriel, est contraint, pour des raisons de technique administrative et de bonne gestion, à se morceler lui-même en une poussière d'organismes publics ou semi publics, qui se voient tous dotés d'une personnalité juridique autonome.*[174]

After the collapse of the Soviet Union, the paradigm of direct intervention of the State into the economy was conceptually challenged, which prompted a season of privatization of State-owned companies. At the same time, the political idea of subsidiarity has spread, leading States to outsource their public functions, entrusting them to private 'autonomous' corporations.[175]

From the standpoint of the international law of attribution, it is not relevant whether the entity has public or private form, or whether it results from processes

Law Commission, 1971, Volume II (Part One), 199, 254, document A/CN.4/SER.A/1971/Add.1 (Part 1): 'subject, in their activities, to a legal regime sui generis, which may partake sometimes of public law and sometimes of private law, according to requirements.'

---

[171] Franklin D Roosevelt, Message to Congress Suggesting the Tennessee Valley Authority, 10 April 1933.

[172] A Stoupnitzky, *Statut international de l'U.R.S.S. État commerçant* (LGDJ 1936); John Quigley, *The Soviet Foreign Trade Monopoly. Institution and Laws* (Ohio State University Press 1974).

[173] Wolfgang G Friedmann, 'Public and Private Enterprise in Mixed Economies: Some Comparative Observations' in Wolfgang G Friedmann (ed), *Public and Private Enterprise in Mixed Economies* (Stevens & Sons 1974) 359, 365.

[174] Paul de Visscher, 'La Protection Diplomatique des Personnes Morales' (1961) 102 Recueil des Cours 395, 409.

[175] Anne van Aaken, 'Blurring Boundaries between Sovereign Acts and Commercial Activities: A Functional View on Regulatory Immunity and Immunity from Execution' in Anne Peters, Evelyne Lagrange, Stefan Oeter, and Christian Tomuschat (eds), *Immunities in the Age of Global Constitutionalism* (Brill 2015) 131.

of nationalization or privatization. It may be a 100% State-owned company or a privatized monopoly, where the State retains a *golden share*. What is decisive is a delegation of power by the State enabling such entities to exercise some governmental authority (*acta jure imperii*).[176] Although being legally separated, independent, and autonomous in their self-organization, such instrumentalities retain an undeniable proximity to and contact with the public sphere and they can and do participate in the exercise of governmental powers (*prerogatives de la puissance publique*) in given conditions.[177] The ambivalent character of parastatals has often been remarked upon at the scholarly level:

> There are certain other types of legal person, which are neither private legal persons nor simple organs of the state (according to the pertinent system of internal law) but which are public in terms of their provenance and function. They may be described as public corporations, 'parastatal entities', or 'quasi-public' legal persons.[178]

The Iran–US Claims Tribunal conveyed the same concept in the *Int'l Technical Products* case:

> Bank Tejarat is a government owned bank with a separate legal personality. Although in some respects it may be said to perform governmental functions, *i.e.*, to be a 'state organ', for the most part it appears to act in a private commercial capacity. One normally would assume that when acquiring real property Bank Tejarat acts in the latter role.[179]

The forms of State instrumentalities are extremely multifarious and diversified in the domestic practice of States. The ARSIWA Commentaries attempted to comprise them in the open formula of 'public corporations, semi-public entities, public agencies of various kinds and even, in special cases, private companies'.[180]

[176] *Dickson Car Wheel Company (USA) v United Mexican States*, Dissenting Opinion of Commissioner Nielsen, July 1931, 4 RIAA 669, 688: 'It is true that, when conduct on the part of persons concerned with the discharge of governmental functions results in a failure to meet obligations imposed by rules of international law, a nation must bear the responsibility.'

[177] Pierre-Marie Dupuy, 'Les émanations engagent-elles la responsabilité des Etats? Etude de droit international des investissements' (2006) EUI Working Paper LAW No 2006/7.

[178] Ian Brownlie, *System of the Law of Nations. State Responsibility. Part I* (Clarendon Press 1983) 162. See also Philippe Leboulanger, *Les contrats entre états et entreprises étrangères* (Economica 1985) 45.

[179] *International Technical Products Corporation and ITP Export Corporation, its wholly-owned subsidiary, v The Government of the Islamic Republic of Iran and its agencies, The Islamic Republic Iranian Air Force and the Ministry of National Defense, acting for the Civil Aviation Organization*, Case No 302, 24 October 1985, Award No 196-302-3, 9 IRAN-US CTR 206, 239 (1985-II).

[180] ARSIWA Commentaries 43, para 2. In the context of international economic disputes, see Luca Schicho, *State Entities in International Investment Law* (Nomos 2012) 70–81, who analyses: (i) State enterprises; (ii) regulatory and supervisory entities; (iii) infrastructure and development agencies;

4.2 Exercise of Elements of Governmental Authority: A Critique

Among the case law that has been perused for the purposes of this treatise, the ICJ practice on 'State entities' is not abundant.[181] Apart from a few early arbitration cases,[182] the bulk of case law on the subject has been rendered by the Iran–US Claims Tribunal and by international investment tribunals (in the context of the so-called 'investor–State dispute settlement' or ISDS), which will be discussed in the next chapter.[183] Far from representing a *lex specialis* on attribution issues, the jurisprudence of the Iran–US Claims Tribunal is particularly relevant for the evaluation of customary international law on the attribution of conduct of State-owned companies.[184] The Tribunal has rendered numerous decisions involving Iranian 'State entities' operating in strategic sectors, such as energy and commodities,[185] banking, securities and exchange controls,[186] public transportation, port

(iv) privatization agencies; (v) Public–Private Partnerships (PPPs), and; (vi) Sovereign Wealth Funds (SWFs).

---

[181] See *Military and Paramilitary Activities in and against Nicaragua (Nicaragua v United States of America)*, Merits, Judgment, 27 June 1986, ICJ Reports 1986, 14, 45.

[182] *H G Venable (USA) v United Mexican States*, 8 July 1927, 4 RIAA 219 (order of Superintendent of the National Railways of Mexico that locomotives not leave Mexico); *Dickson Car Wheel Company (USA) v United Mexican States*, July 1931, 4 RIAA 669. The Mexican government had majority ownership in the National Railways of Mexico and direct possession of the railway, at the same time being entitled by law to make requisitions of the lines. See also *Union Bridge Company (United States) v Great Britain*, 8 January 1924, 6 RIAA 138, 141 (act of the Storekeeper of the Cape Government Railways).

[183] See Chapter III, section 4.

[184] David D Caron, 'The Basis of Responsibility: Attribution and Other Trans-substantive Rules of State Responsibility' in Richard B Lillich and Daniel B Magraw (eds), *The Iran-United States Claims Tribunal: Its Contribution to the Law of State Responsibility* (Transnational Publishers, Inc 1998) 109, 126; Hans van Houtte and Barbara Concolino, 'The Iran-United States Claims Tribunal and its Contribution to International Law' in Geert De Baere and Jan Wouters (eds), *The Contribution of International and Supranational Courts to the Rule of Law* (Edward Elgar Publishing, Inc 2015) 303; Bernard Audit, 'Le Tribunal de Différends Irano-Américains (1981–1984)' (1985) 112 Journal du Droit International (Clunet) 791.

[185] *Dames and Moore v Iran*, Case No 54, 20 December 1983, Award No 97-54-3, 4 IRAN-US CTR 212, 218 (1983-III); *Oil Fields of Texas, Inc v Iran*, Case No 43, 8 October 1986, Award No 258-43-1, 12 IRAN-US CTR 308, 314 (1986-III); *Mobil Oil Iran, Inc v Iran*, Case No 74, 14 July 1987, Award No 311-74/76/81/150-3, 16 IRAN-US CTR 3, 18 (1987-III); *Houston Contracting Company v National Iranian Oil Company, National Iranian Gas Company, and The Islamic Republic of Iran*, Case No 173, 22 July 1988, Award No 378-173-3, 20 IRAN-US CTR 3, 123 (1988-III); *Phillips Petroleum Company Iran v The Islamic Republic of Iran, The National Iranian Oil Company*, Case No 39, 29 June 1989, Award No 425-39-2, 21 IRAN-US CTR 79, 112 (1988-III); *TME International, Inc v Iran*, Case No 357, 12 March 1990, Award No 473-357-1, 24 IRAN-US CTR 121 (1990-I); *Sedco, Inc v National Iranian Oil Company and The Islamic Republic of Iran*, Case No 129, 24 October 1985, Award No ITL 55-29-3, 9 IRAN-US CTR 248, 277 (1985-III); *United Painting Company, Inc v The Islamic Republic of Iran*, Case No 11286, 20 December 1989, Award No 458-11286-3, 23 IRAN-US CTR 351, 363 (1989-III); *Petrolane, Inc v Iran*, Case No 131, 14 August 1991, Award No 518-131-2, 27 IRAN-US CTR 64, 71 (1991-II).

[186] *Eastman Kodak Company v Iran*, Case No 12384, 11 November 1987, Award No 329-227/12384-3, 17 IRAN-US CTR 153, 163 (1987-IV); *United Painting Company, Inc v The Islamic Republic of Iran*, Case No 11286, 20 December 1989, Award No 458-11286-3, 23 IRAN-US CTR 351, 363 (1989-III).

and shipping,[187] industrial planning,[188] management of information systems,[189] healthcare,[190] and education.[191]

Whether 'public' institutions or parastatals operating within a 'non-western' social, political, and economic system, such as the one resulting from the Iranian revolution, may be legally captured by the rule of attribution of ARSIWA Article 5 in an effective way remains a markedly controversial issue.[192] The body of rules of attribution (and, hence, the international law of State responsibility) is based on a liberal conception of the State as governmental apparatus, not as society-community, and on a rather market-based model of the economic system.[193] It is doubtful, at most, whether ARSIWA Article 5 is an effective legal device to enhance accountability of States for the acts of their instrumentalities, especially in the context of rather undefined experiences of State-driven economies and, ultimately, of a non-western conception of the divide between public and private activities.[194]

[187] *Sea-Land Service, Inc v The Islamic Republic of Iran, Ports and Shipping Organization of Iran*, Case No 33, 20 June 1984, Award No 135-33-1, 6 IRAN-US CTR 149, 202 (1984-II).

[188] *Fedders Corporation v Loristan Refrigeration Industries, General Industrial Corporation, National Industries Organization of Iran, and The Islamic Republic of Iran*, Case No 250, Decision No DEC 51-250-3, 28 October 1986, 13 IRAN-US CTR 97, 98 (1986-IV); *Bechtel, Inc v Iran*, Case No 181, 4 March 1987, Award No 294-181-1, 14 IRAN-US CTR 149, 157 (1987-I).

[189] *Computer Sciences Corporation v The Government of the Islamic Republic of Iran, Ministry of Finance, Ministry of National Defence, Iran Aircraft Industries, Information Systems Iran, Bank Mellat, Bank Tejarat, the successors of the following entities: Imperial Iranian Air Force, Imperial Iranian Ground Force, Imperial Iranian Navy, Imperial Iranian Gendarmerie, Imperial Iranian National Police, The Supreme Commander's Staff*, Case No 65, 16 April 1986, Award No 221-65-1, 10 IRAN-US CTR 269, 278 (1986-I).

[190] *Dames and Moore v Iran*, Case No 54, 20 December 1983, Award No 97-54-3, 4 IRAN-US CTR 212, 218 (1983-III).

[191] *Kathryn Faye Hilt v Iran*, Case No 10427, 16 March 1988, Award No 354-10427-2, 18 IRAN-US CTR 154, 158 (1988-I).

[192] Pierre-Marie Dupuy, 'Attribution Issues in State Responsibility. Commentary' (1990) 84 American Society of International Law Proceedings 51, 72: 'there is a confusing use of a certain kind of legal ideology in the field of international economics litigation. At a time when the values of the free market and free enterprise are gaining ground all over the world, it is misleading to interpret the conduct of states, in particular in the Third World, with very liberal principles designed to protect individual property and private initiative in the industrialized countries. As Ms. Chalmers has shown, this attitude has led in several cases to precisely the opposite result. Thus, private investors have been deterred from taking initiative in countries that are able to successfully protect themselves behind the veil of the private corporate form.' See also David D Caron, 'The Basis of Responsibility: Attribution and Other Trans-substantive Rules of State Responsibility' in Richard B Lillich and Daniel B Magraw (eds), *The Iran-United States Claims Tribunal: Its Contribution to the Law of State Responsibility* (Transnational Publishers, Inc 1998) 109, 173.

[193] Christine Chinkin, 'A Critique of the Public/Private Dimension' (1999) 10 European Journal of International Law 387, 389–90. *Contra*, James Crawford, 'Revising the Draft Articles on State Responsibility' (1999) 10 European Journal of International Law 435, 438–40.

[194] *Phelps Dodge Corp and Overseas Private Investment Corp v The Islamic Republic of Iran*, Case No 99, 19 March 1986, Award No 217-99-2, Dissenting Opinion of Hamid Bahrami, 10 IRAN-US CTR 121, 143 (1986-I). In addition, in the totalitarian political experiences of a single party (a political party coincident with the State), it is rather the 'State' to be perceived as an instrument of the party. cf Roberto Ago, Third Report on State Responsibility, by Mr Roberto Ago, Special Rapporteur, 'The internationally wrongful act of the State, source of international responsibility', 5 March, 7 April, 28 April, and 18 May 1971, para 165, document A/CN.4/246 and Add.1-3, Yearbook of the International Law Commission, 1971, Volume II (Part One), 199, 254, document A/CN.4/SER.A/1971/Add.1(Part 1). See

A definition of governmental authority (*prerogatives de la puissance publique*) and capacity is not provided by ARSIWA. The ARSIWA Commentaries famously assert:

> Beyond a certain limit, what is regarded as 'governmental' depends on the particular society, its history and traditions. Of particular importance will be not just the content of the powers, but the way they are conferred on an entity, the purposes for which they are to be exercised and the extent to which the entity is accountable to government for their exercise. These are essentially questions of the application of a general standard to varied circumstances.[195]

Thus, 'the concept of "governmental authority", present in many of the articles concerned with attribution, is not only undefined but elusive when pursued'.[196]

The starting point for a more accurate and precise definition of the scope of operation of the rule of attribution pursuant to ARSIWA Article 5 is its proper nature. Differently from ARSIWA Article 4 (as to State organs), which discloses an *institutional* link (the judicial doctrine of *de facto* organs establishes an institutional link *ex post facto*), and Article 8 (as to private individuals), which discloses a *factual* link, Article 5 provides a *functional* test: attribution operates exclusively in relation to the conduct of 'State entities' in the exercise of governmental authority, based on previous empowerment by law to act 'in that capacity'. Hence, the target of the attribution rule is the specific act 'in the particular instance'. This calls into question the distinction between *acta jure imperii* and *acta jure gestionis*, elaborated in the context of the law of State immunity from jurisdiction. Pursuant to UNCSI Article 10, a State cannot invoke immunity from adjudication in proceedings before a domestic judge arising out of a commercial transaction with an alien. UNCSI Article 2.2 clarifies the use of the term 'commercial transaction':

> In determining whether a contract or transaction is a 'commercial transaction' under paragraph 1 (c), reference should be made primarily to the nature of the contract or transaction, but its purpose should also be taken into account if the parties to the contract or transaction have so agreed, or if, in the practice of the State of the forum, that purpose is relevant to determining the non-commercial character of the contract or transaction.

also Djamchid Momtaz, 'Attribution of Conduct to the State: State Organs and Entities Empowered to Exercise Elements of Governmental Authority' in James Crawford, Alain Pellet, and Simon Olleson (eds), *The Law of International Responsibility* (Oxford University Press 2010) 237, 244, who refers to the example of the Chinese Kuomintang's boycott of Japan in 1931–1932.

---

[195] ARSIWA Commentaries 43, para 6.

[196] David D Caron, 'The ILC Articles on State Responsibility: the Paradoxical Relationship Between Form and Authority' (2002) 96 American Journal of International Law 857, 861.

This definition reveals that the purpose test has a secondary role in comparison to the nature test. In addition, the purpose of the transaction or contract should not be taken into consideration according to the practice of the State Party to the dispute, but according to the practice of the forum State. By importing and adapting this principle into the realm of the law of attribution of acts of parastatals, it may be inferred that the State's purpose underlying the act of a 'State entity' should not be decisive. Consequently, the nature test has primary relevance for the purposes of attribution to the State of the conduct of parastatal entities.[197] According to this test, a governmental act is a conduct that a private person as such cannot perform.[198] As explained in the next chapter,[199] the test may be strengthened to comprise those acts that a private competitor in the market arena could not execute on a rational basis (principle of *competitive neutrality* of the State and SOEs).[200] Anne van Aaken has described competitive neutrality (or *competitive equality*) as 'a principle of international economic law enshrined in the principles of non-discrimination as the most-favored nation clause as well as national treatment clauses. Both are widely found in the WTO agreements, regional trade agreements and bilateral investment treaties. They were also part of the formerly concluded Treaties of Friendship, Commerce and Navigation.'[201] To this extent, the principle of competitive neutrality of SOEs may be considered as a corollary of

[197] Rosalyn Higgins, 'Certain Unresolved Aspects of the Law of State Immunity' (1982) 29 Netherlands International Law Review 265, 268–72; Christoph H Schreuer, *State Immunity: Some Recent Developments* (Cambridge University Press 1988) 69–70; James Crawford, 'International Law and Foreign Sovereigns: Distinguishing Immune Transactions' (1983) 54 British Year Book of International Law 75; M Sornarajah, 'Problems in Applying the Restrictive Theory of Sovereign Immunity' (1982) 31 International & Comparative Law Quarterly 661, 669; Leo J Bouchez, 'The Nature and Scope of State Immunity from Jurisdiction and Execution' (1979) 10 Netherlands Yearbook of International Law 1, 8, 16; Ignaz Seidl-Hohenveldern, 'L'immunité de juridiction et d'exécution des États et d'organisations internationales' in Institut des Hautes Etudes Internationales de Paris, *Cours et Travaux* (Éditions A Pedone 1981) 133; Rolando Quadri, *La giurisdizione sugli Stati stranieri* (Giuffrè 1941) 83–93; Hersch Lauterpacht, 'The Problem of Jurisdictional Immunities of Foreign States' (1951) 28 British Year Book of International Law 220, 220–26; J E S Fawcett, 'Legal Aspects of State Trading' (1948) 25 British Year Book of International Law 34, 34–36; Gamal M Badr, *State Immunity: An Analytical and Prognostic View* (Martinus Nijhoff Publishers 1984) 91, 96–97; Riccardo Luzzatto, 'La giurisdizione sugli Stati stranieri tra Convenzione di New York, norme internazionali generali e diritto interno' (2007) 23 Comunicazioni e Studi 1, 11–12.

[198] See Chapter III, section 4.2.2.

[199] ibid.

[200] 'Ensuring an Effective Legal and Regulatory Framework for State-Owned Enterprises' in *OECD Guidelines on Corporate Governance of State-Owned Enterprises* (OECD Publishing 2011), Chapter I: 'The legal and regulatory framework for state-owned enterprises should ensure a level-playing field in markets where state-owned enterprises and private sector companies compete in order to avoid market distortions'; Antonio Capobianco and Hans Christiansen, *Competitive Neutrality and State-Owned Enterprises: Challenges and Policy Options*, OECD Corporate Governance Working Papers, No 1 (OECD Publishing 2011).

[201] Anne van Aaken, 'Blurring Boundaries between Sovereign Acts and Commercial Activities: A Functional View on Regulatory Immunity and Immunity from Execution' in Anne Peters, Evelyne Lagrange, Stefan Oeter, and Christian Tomuschat (eds), *Immunities in the Age of Global Constitutionalism* (Brill 2015) 131, 173.

the general principle of non-discrimination and specifically of the national treatment rule, which is found in international trade and investment agreements.[202] Competitive neutrality considerations may be inserted in the context-based analysis of the nature test for the purposes of State immunity and attribution of conduct of parastatal entities.[203] As already submitted, the scope of acts of 'State entities' attributable to the State under ARSIWA Article 5 and the definition of State acts immune from the jurisdiction of domestic courts should be reciprocally consistent.[204]

A distinct, although related, attribution issue concerns the collusive interference of the State through its organs into a legal relationship between one of its instrumentalities and a foreigner. The Iran–US Claims Tribunal addressed this situation in *Int'l Technical Products*:

> In the present case the evidence does not suggest that Bank Tejarat when taking possession of the building acted on instructions of the Government or otherwise performed governmental functions. Therefore, even if it were found that the Bank came into possession of the building in an illegal manner, this would not automatically establish responsibility of the Government under international law. Rather it must be established additionally that some other government organ (acting in that capacity) through acts or omissions participated in the transfer of the property to Bank Tejarat, thereby depriving Claimants of their property in violation of international law.[205]

In this case, ARSIWA Article 4 does apply and renders attributable both *acta jure imperii* and *acta jure gestionis*, in so far as the State organ was acting in its official capacity, which means that the conduct in question should not be a purely private act of a personal nature (argument pursuant to ARSIWA Article 7).

[202] Jürgen Kurtz, *The WTO and International Investment Law: Converging Systems* (Cambridge University Press 2016) 79.

[203] cf Lord Wilberforce in *I Congreso del Partido* [1983] 1 AC 244, 278: 'The conclusion which emerges is that in considering, under the "restrictive" theory whether state immunity should be granted or not, the court must consider the whole context in which the claim against the state is made, with a view to deciding whether the relevant act(s) upon which the claim is based, should, in that context, be considered as fairly within an area of activity, trading or commercial, or otherwise of a private law character, in which the state has chosen to engage, or whether the relevant act(s) should be considered as having been done outside that area, and within the sphere of governmental or sovereign activity.'

[204] See Chapter I, section 6. cf James Crawford, *State Responsibility. The General Part* (Cambridge University Press 2013) 130: 'Application of these concepts to attribution under ARSIWA Article 5 is useful, and achieves consistency between these different areas of international law.'

[205] *International Technical Products Corporation and ITP Export Corporation, its wholly-owned subsidiary, v The Government of the Islamic Republic of Iran and its agencies, The Islamic Republic Iranian Air Force and the Ministry of National Defense, acting for the Civil Aviation Organization*, Case No 302, 24 October 1985, Award No 196-302-3, 9 IRAN-US CTR 206, 239 (1985-II).

4.3 Legal Criteria for the Identification of State Instrumentalities

The ARSIWA do not provide a static definition of 'State entities'. This is explained by the *functional* nature of the rule of attribution under ARSIWA Article 5 focusing on the exercise of governmental authority. However, a *structural* test is not to be neglected, since the basis for the operation of the functional test of attribution is the establishment of a given person to be a State instrumentality. Based on the scholarly attempts at definition, on one side,[206] and the available case law, notably of the Iran–US Claims Tribunal, on the other side,[207] it is possible to indicate a non-exhaustive list of symptoms of the status of 'State entity':

a) separate legal personality;
b) formation by the State;
c) performance of policies of public interest;
d) governmental oversight and supervision (accountability);
e) total, majority, or partial ownership–shareholding by the State;
f) ability to exercise authoritative powers by statute or bylaws;
g) appointment of directors by the government;
h) permanent place in the State budget;
i) waiver from ordinary accounting rules;
j) expedited customs treatment or waiver from customs regulation;
k) facilitated tax regime;
l) grant of loans by public banks at a lower interest rate;
m) direct or indirect subsidization from the government;
n) claim of jurisdictional immunity before domestic judges;
o) domestic regulatory immunity from competition and bankruptcy law.

In some cases, the Iran–US Claims Tribunal held that the recording of the *procès verbal* of the meeting of the parastatal's corporate organs, which was printed on paper bearing the official government emblem, pointed to the finding of governmental control.[208]

[206] *Ex multis*, Karl-Heinz Böckstiegel, *Arbitration and State Enterprises. A Survey on the National and International State of Law and Practice* (Kluwer Law and Taxation Publishers 1984) 14: '"State Enterprise" in this research project is understood to be any commercial enterprise predominantly owned or controlled by the state or by state institutions, with or without separate legal personality.'

[207] *Ex multis*, *Hyatt International Corporation, Hyatt Management, Inc, International Project System, Inc v The Government of the Islamic Republic of Iran, Bank Mellat (formerly known as Bank Omran), Alavi Foundation for the Oppressed, Iran Touring and Tourism Organization*, Case No 134, 17 September 1985, Award No ITL 54-134-1, 9 IRAN-US CTR 72, 88-97 (1985-II).

[208] *Economy Forms Corporation v Iran*, Case No 165, 14 June 1983, Award No 55-165-1, 3 IRAN-US CTR 42, 47 (1983-III); *Cal-Maine Foods, Inc v The Government of the Islamic Republic of Iran and Sherkat Seamourgh Company, Inc*, Case No 340, 31 May 1984, Award No 133-340-3, 6 IRAN-US CTR 52, 59 (1984-II); *Ultrasystems Incorporated v The Islamic Republic of Iran, Information Systems Iran*,

The establishment of whether a person or entity that is formally separate from the State can be ascribed to the category drawn by ARSIWA Article 5 represents an inductive process, which proceeds from an empirical and casuistic approach. The establishment of a single element or even a plurality of elements of the foregoing open list is not decisive per se. In *Schering*, the circumstance of the Workers' Council having being initiated by the Iranian State was not considered sufficient to hold it to be an entity controlled by the government, in the absence of proof of actual influence by the State on the life of the entity.[209] The repeated reliance of the Iran–US Claims Tribunal on the test of *governmental control* was dictated by the jurisdictional provisions contained in Article VII of the Claims Settlement Declaration, which required the respondent to be the government, any political subdivision, and *any agency, instrumentality, or entity controlled* by the government, or any political subdivision, either of Iran or the US.[210] The broad scope of application of the test could involve the entirety of the above listed circumstances. In *Foremost*, the Iran–US Claims Tribunal identified the main thresholds of its 'typologic' method:

> The two main indicators of government control of a corporation are the identity of its shareholders and the composition and behaviour of its board of directors.[211]

In general, the core of the finding of State instrumentality is a palpable degree of affiliation and mingling—either direct or indirect—between a government (or one of its ministries) and the entity, ranging from a markedly decisive influence to total management of the body.[212] Governmental control may be inferred from formal indicia, such as clauses in the charter of the entity or bylaws of the State-owned company (for instance the mandatory provision of a minister sitting in person as chairman or member of the board of directors or as president of the general assembly), as well as by practical elements pertaining to the undertaking of the activity of the entity (fiscal regime, customs treatment, financial facilitations). It

Case No 84, 4 March 1983, Award No 27-84-3, 2 IRAN-US CTR 100, 105 (1983-I); *Phelps Dodge Corp and Overseas Private Investment Corp v The Islamic Republic of Iran*, Case No 99, 19 March 1986, Award No 217-99-2, 10 IRAN-US CTR 121, 143 (1986-I).

---

209 *Schering Corporation v The Islamic Republic of Iran*, Case No 38, 13 April 1984, Award No 122-38-3, 5 IRAN-US CTR 361, 370 (1984-I). See also *Otis Elevator Company v The Islamic Republic of Iran, and Bank Mellat (formerly Foreign Trade Bank of Iran)*, Case No 284, 29 April 1987, Award No 304-284-2, 14 IRAN-US CTR 283, 293-295 (1987-I).

210 See Chapter I, section 1.5.

211 *Foremost Tehran, Inc v Iran*, Cases Nos 37 and 231, 10 April 1986, Award No 220-37/231-1, 10 IRAN-US CTR 228, 241-242 (1986-I).

212 *Dickson Car Wheel Company (USA) v United Mexican States*, Dissenting Opinion of Commissioner Nielsen, July 1931, 4 RIAA 669, 685: 'the Mexican Government was in complete control of the Railways and managed them as any department of the Government was managed.'

should be noted that the use of the corporate form is but one option for the creation of a parastatal entity. For instance, the case of the Foundation of the Oppressed ('Bonyad Mostazafan') involved a 'pious charity' created 'by the Revolution' for the purpose of management and utilization of the properties confiscated to the Pawlavi family, particularly for the supply of housing and other needs of the poor.[213]

4.4 Empowerment by Law

Not only should an instrumentality (be able to) exercise governmental authority, but such authority should be formally delegated to it. Under ARSIWA Article 5, the expression 'by law' refers to a specific legal instrument empowering an entity with sovereign functions 'rather than legality under the general law'.[214] The delegation of authority—expressly enumerating the applicable powers—may be found in the Constitution, statutory law, governmental decree, or in the establishing statute, company bylaws, or articles of association of the State entity.[215] In addition, the ARSIWA Commentaries clarify that the delegation of powers may be executed by public or private contract, in that it refers to 'private security firms ... contracted to act as prisons guards'.[216] This is a symbol of the public trend to outsource sovereign functions to private (profit-oriented) businesses.[217] Such processes of *ratione materiae* decentralization of governmental functions are justified upon grounds of efficiency, technical expertise, and the ability to operate swiftly in time of 'crisis' (for instance, wars or revolutionary upheavals).[218] However, contractual arrangements allow governments to deliberately avoid verification or scrutiny by parliamentary assemblies in relation to highly delicate and sensitive issues. Moreover, resort by the State to 'private contractors' in the sectors of immigration, health,

[213] *Hyatt International Corporation, Hyatt Management, Inc, International Project System, Inc v The Government of the Islamic Republic of Iran, Bank Mellat (formerly known as Bank Omran), Alavi Foundation for the Oppressed, Iran Touring and tourism Organization*, Case No 134, 17 September 1985, Award No ITL 54-134-1, 9 IRAN-US CTR 72, 91 (1985-II): 'The Foundation itself plays an investigative or prosecutorial role in the discovery and seizure of properties eligible for confiscation, and is empowered to call upon governmental agencies and institutions for aid in this pursuit'; *Foremost Tehran, Inc v Iran*, Cases Nos 37 and 231, 10 April 1986, Award No 220-37/231-1, 10 IRAN-US CTR 228, 240 (1986-I); *PepsiCo, Inc v Iran*, Case No 18, 11 October 1986, Award No 260-18-1, 13 IRAN-US CTR 3, 19 (1986-IV).

[214] James Crawford, *State Responsibility. The General Part* (Cambridge University Press 2013) 130–32.

[215] *Hyatt International Corporation, Hyatt Management, Inc, International Project System, Inc v The Government of the Islamic Republic of Iran, Bank Mellat (formerly known as Bank Omran), Alavi Foundation for the Oppressed, Iran Touring and tourism Organization*, Case No 134, 17 September 1985, Award No ITL 54-134-1, 9 IRAN-US CTR 72, 89 (1985-II).

[216] ARSIWA Commentaries 43, para 2.

[217] Christian Tomuschat, 'In the Twilight Zones of the State' in Isabelle Buffard, James Crawford, Alain Pellet, and Stephan Wittich (eds), *International Law between Universalism and Fragmentation. Festschrift in Honour of Gerhard Hafner* (Martinus Nijhoff Publishers 2008) 479, 494–96.

[218] Derek Jinks, 'State Responsibility for the Acts of Private Armed Groups' (2003) 4 Chicago Journal of International Law 83.

security, police, prison administration, and even military operation may relieve the sovereign from accountability towards the individuals that may be affected by such activities.[219] The chief example is that of Private Military Companies (PMCs), to the possible inclusion of proper 'mercenaries'.[220] Pursuant to ARSIWA Article 5, their activities of a private nature would not be attributable to the State. This is applicable to the majority of acts performed by PMCs: provision of IT services, logistic support, maintenance of weapons, intelligence services, training of military personnel, translation services, and even prison management. Only acts entailing the exercise of exclusive prerogatives of public power (*acta jure imperii*) are subject to attribution: military combat, security services (including prison guarding, and management of the hearings of prisoners), and the borderline case of escort services, which underlie some uses of force delegated by the State.[221]

Political, social, and economic processes of privatization and outsourcing may shift cases of attribution from ARSIWA Article 5 to Article 8 in a complementary fashion. In the case of private contractors not exercising governmental authority in the particular activity at issue, a contractual arrangement may be subsumed in the category of 'instructions' of the State demanded by ARSIWA Article 8 for the attribution to the State of conduct of private individuals.

5. Individuals

5.1 Notion

Pursuant to a universal rule of public international law, States are not responsible for the conduct of persons not having any sort of inclusion in their governmental machinery or not having been entrusted by the State to exercise governmental authority.[222] The rule of irresponsibility of governments for the acts of 'private' individuals (ἰδιώτης in Ancient Greece was said to be the man not taking care of the πόλις) is but a demonstration that international relations and international law are inspired by the concept of the State as (governmental) apparatus, comprehensive of its (official) authorities and

[219] Marina Spinedi, 'La Responsabilità dello Stato per Comportamenti di *Private Contractors*' in Marina Spinedi, Alessandra Gianelli, and Maria Luisa Alaimo (eds), *La Codificazione della Responsabilità Internazionale degli Stati alla Prova dei Fatti: Problemi e Spunti di Riflessione* (Giuffrè 2006) 67, 68–69.

[220] See University Centre for International Humanitarian Law, *Expert Meeting On Private Military Contractors: Status And State Responsibility For Their Actions*, Geneva, 29–30 August 2005.

[221] James Crawford, *State Responsibility. The General Part* (Cambridge University Press 2013) 130.

[222] Rüdiger Wolfrum, 'State Responsibility for Private Actors: an Old Problem of Renewed Relevance' in Maurizio Ragazzi (ed), *International Responsibility Today. Essays in Memory of Oscar Schachter* (Martinus Nijhoff Publishers 2005) 423, 424; Gordon A Christenson, 'Attributing Acts of Omission to the State' (1990–1991) 12 Michigan Journal of International Law 312, 322; N Okany and A Constantinides, 'State Delegation of Public Functions to Private Entities: a Basis for Attribution under the Rules of State Responsibility' in Kalliopi Koufa (ed), *State Responsibility and the Individual: 2003*

powers.[223] There are indeed some inconsistencies with the adoption of this framework by the law of international responsibility of States. Under customary international law, the constituent elements of statehood are a defined territory, a permanent population, and an effective government, plus capacity to enter into international relations with other States (independence).[224] The law of diplomatic protection 'romantically' imposes the requirement of a genuine connection between the State exercising a diplomatic espousal and the protected individual, thus emphasizing the political, economic, and cultural bond attached to a link of real and effective nationality.[225] When it turns to the international rules of attribution of conduct to the State for the sake of international responsibility for internationally wrongful acts, the prongs of territoriality and nationality drastically yield to a test of linkage (institutional, functional, or factual) between the State-government and given persons.[226] The concept of the State as community-society is rather neglected to this extent, which is a clear triumph of the ideology of political liberalism in the domain of international relations.[227]

The rule of irresponsibility of governments for the acts of private individuals has been firmly established in early arbitrations in notable relationship to conduct that occurs in the course of revolutionary upheavals, rebellions, mob violence, and civil

International Law Session (Sakkoulas Publications 2006) 327, 332; Olivier de Frouville, 'Attribution of Conduct to the State: Private Individuals' in James Crawford, Alain Pellet, and Simon Olleson (eds), *The Law of International Responsibility* (Oxford University Press 2010) 257, 261; Riccardo Monaco, 'La responsabilità internazionale dello Stato per fatti degli individui' (1939) 18 Rivista di Diritto Internazionale 3, 193, 216.

223 Benedetto Conforti, *Diritto internazionale* (9th edn, Editoriale Scientifica 2013) 12–13.

224 Montevideo Convention on the Rights and Duties of States, signed on 26 December 1933, entered into force on 26 December 1934, Article 1, 165 LNTS 19. cf James Crawford, 'The Criteria for Statehood in International Law' (1976–1977) 48 British Year Book of International Law 93.

225 *Nottebohm case (Liechtenstein v Guatemala)*, Second Phase, Judgment, 6 April 1955, ICJ Reports 1955, 4, 22–23: 'nationality is a legal bond having as its basis a social fact of attachment, a genuine connection of existence, interests and sentiments, together with the existence of reciprocal rights and duties.' See J Mervyn Jones, 'The Nottebohm Case' (1956) 5 International & Comparative Law Quarterly 230; Paul de Visscher, 'L'Affaire Nottebohm' (1956) 60 Revue Générale de Droit International Public 238; Suzanne Bastid, 'L'affaire Nottebohm devant la C.I.J.' (1956) 45 Revue Critique de Droit International Privé 607. For an interesting analysis of *Nottebohm*, see Robert D Sloane, 'Breaking the Genuine Link: The Contemporary International Legal Regulation of Nationality' (2009) 50 Harvard International Law Journal 1.

226 C F Amerasinghe, 'Imputability in the Law of State Responsibility for Injuries to Aliens' (1966) 22 Revue Égyptienne de Droit International 91, 92; Christine Chinkin, 'A Critique of the Public/Private Dimension' (1999) 10 European Journal of International Law 387, 395. See also James Crawford, First Report on State Responsibility, by Mr James Crawford, Special Rapporteur, 24 April, 1, 5, 11, and 26 May, 22 and 24 July, 12 August 1998, para 154, document A/CN.4/490 and Add. 1-7, Yearbook of the International Law Commission, 1998, Volume II (Part One), 1, 33, document A/CN.4/SER.A/1998/Add.1(Part 1).

227 Benjamin Constant, *De la liberté des Anciens comparée à celle des Modernes* (Athénée Royal de Paris, 1819).

strife.[228] In the *Sambiaggio* case, the Italy–Venezuela Mixed Claims Commission affirmed:

> Revolutionists are not the agents of government and a natural responsibility does not exist. Their acts are committed to destroy government and no one should be held responsible for the acts of an enemy attempting his life. The revolutionists (in this case) were beyond governmental control.[229]

This rule of law has been comprehensively applied to the generality of cases concerning the attributability of conduct of non-state actors.[230] Considering that early cases and doctrine did not yet envisage the category of 'State entities', from an historical and systematic viewpoint this rule is but an application of the rule of responsibility of States for the acts and omissions of their agents and representatives *only*:[231]

> It is well-established law that a state does not guarantee the person or property of a foreigner on its territory. It is liable only for its own delinquencies, which means, since the state itself is an abstraction, for such injurious acts or omissions of 'authorities' of the state, as international law, on principles of which the main outlines at least are well settled, attributes to the state itself; it is not liable for the acts of a private individual, who is not an 'authority' of the state.[232]

As a consequence, a *positive* formulation of the rule of attribution to the State of the conduct of private persons or groups of persons (at present codified in ARSIWA

228 Carlos Calvo, 'De la non-responsabilité des États à raison des pertes et dommages éprouvés par des étrangers en temps de troubles intérieurs ou de guerres civiles' (1869) 1 Revue de Droit International et de Legislation Comparée 417.

229 *Sambiaggio Case (of a general nature)*, 1903, 10 RIAA 499. See also, *Kummerow, Otto Redler and Co, Fulda, Fischbach, and Friedericy Cases*, 1903, 10 RIAA 369, 387: 'The Government is not liable to individuals for the damages which insurgents, revolutionists, or people in revolt, in whatever manner against the constituted authority may cause.'; *Affaire des biens britanniques au Maroc espagnol (Espagne contre Royaume-Uni) (Spanish Zone of Morocco)*, 1 May 1925, 2 RIAA 615, 642; *Home Frontier and Foreign Missionary Society of the United Brethren in Christ (United States) v Great Britain*, 18 December 1920, 6 RIAA 42, 44: 'A Government can not be held liable as the insurer of lives and property under the circumstances presented in this case'; *Annie Bella Graham Kidd (Great Britain) v United Mexican States*, 23 April 1931, 5 RIAA 142, 143–44.

230 *Affaire des biens britanniques au Maroc espagnol (Espagne contre Royaume-Uni) (Spanish Zone of Morocco)*, 1 May 1925, 2 RIAA 615, *affaires Menebhi* 709, *Ziat, Ben Kiran* 729; *Claim of Finnish shipowners against Great Britain in respect of the use of certain Finnish vessels during the war (Finland, Great Britain)*, 9 May 1934, 3 RIAA 1479, 1501: 'These acts must be committed by the respondent Government or its officials, since it has no direct responsibility under international law for the acts of private individuals.'; *Porter*, in Moore, III (GPO 1898) 2998.

231 *German Settlers in Poland*, Advisory Opinion No 6, 10 September, 1923, PCIJ Series B No 6, 22. See Francisco V García Amador, International Responsibility: Report by F V García Amador, Special Rapporteur, 20 January 1956, para 43, document A/CN.4/96, Yearbook of the International Law Commission, 1956, Volume II, 173, 181, document A/CN.4/SER.A/1956/Add.l.

232 J L Brierly, 'The Theory of Implied State Complicity in International Claims' (1928) 9 British Year Book of International Law 42.

Article 8) emerged rather recently in respect to the history of the codification of the law of State responsibility. Article 11.1 of the draft articles on State responsibility adopted on first reading still maintained a *negative* formulation of the provision ('Conduct of persons not acting on behalf of the State'),[233] in line with previous attempts at codification.[234] The current version of the rule rests upon a factual test, based on the two (alternative) prongs of State instructions, on one side, and State direction or control, on the other side.[235] Importantly, the attribution rule under ARSIWA Article 8 is still considered to be unique in character, susceptible as it is to restrictive, rather than extensive, interpretation.[236] The architecture of State responsibility appears to be framed by the policy to limit, to the maximum extent, the attributability of the conduct of private actors. However, this has not always been the case in the history of international relations. Before the analysis of the current status of customary international law on attributability of acts of private individuals, the following paragraph will describe the historical evolution of the rule and its connection with rules of a primary nature.

[233] 'Draft Articles on State responsibility' in Report of the International Law Commission on the Work of its Twenty-Seventh Session, 5 May–25 July 1975, document A/10010/Rev.1, Yearbook of the International Law Commission, 1975, Volume II, 47, 51, 60, document A/CN.4/SER.A/1975/Add.l:

Article 11

Conduct of persons not acting on behalf of the State

1. The conduct of a persons or a group of persons not acting on behalf of the State shall not be considered as an act of the State under international law.

...

See also James Crawford, First Report on State Responsibility, by Mr James Crawford, Special Rapporteur, 24 April, 1, 5, 11, and 26 May, 22 and 24 July, 12 August 1998, para 112 et seq, document A/CN.4/490 and Add. 1-7, Yearbook of the International Law Commission, 1998, Volume II (Part One), 1, 48, document A/CN.4/SER.A/1998/Add.1(Part 1).

[234] Institut de Droit International, 'Responsabilité internationale des Etats à raison des dommages causés sur leur territoire à la personne et aux biens des étrangers' (Leo Strisower, Rapporteur), Résolution du 1 septembre 1927, Session de Lausanne, (1927) 33(III) Annuaire de l'Institut de Droit International 330-335, Article III; League of Nations, Committee of Experts for the Progressive Codification of International Law, Second Session, 12–29 January 1926, Annex to Questionnaire No 4, 'Responsibility of States for Damage Done in Their Territories to the Person or Property of Foreigners', Report of the Sub-Committee (Mr Gustavo Guerrero, Rapporteur), Conclusions, paras 5 and 8, League of Nations publication, V.Legal, 1926.V.3, document C.46.M.23.1926.V and League of Nations publication, V.Legal, 1926.V.11, document C.96.M.47.1926.V, (1926) 20 Special Supplement American Journal of International Law 176, 202; Third Committee of the Conference for the Codification of International Law, The Hague, 13 March–12 April 1930, Text of Articles on Responsibility of States for Damage Done in Their Territory to the Person or Property of Foreigners, Article 10, League of Nations publication, V.Legal, 1930.V.7, document C.228.M.115.1930.V, (1930) 24 Special Supplement American Journal of International Law 188.

[235] See section 5.3 of this chapter.

[236] Paolo Palchetti, 'Comportamento di organi di fatto e illecito internazionale nel progetto di articoli sulla responsabilità internazionale degli Stati' in Marina Spinedi, Alessandra Gianelli, and Maria Luisa Alaimo (eds), *La codificazione della responsabilità internazionale degli Stati alla prova dei fatti: problemi e spunti di riflessione* (Giuffrè 2006) 3, 5.

5.2 Complicity, *Patientia*, *Receptus*, and Due Diligence

The principle of the accountability of States for international delinquencies perpetrated by members of their communities had received marked acceptance in previous centuries, which was significantly related to the feudal concept of 'collective responsibility' of Germanic origin. The apogee of the doctrine of State *complicity* is traditionally bestowed to Vattel, who proposed a strongly reinforced version thereof:[237]

> If a sovereign who has the power to see that his subjects act in a just and peaceable manner permits them to injure a foreign nation, either the State itself or its citizens, he does no less a wrong to that nation than if he injured it himself. . . . A sovereign who refuses to repair the evil done by one of his subjects, or to punish the criminal, or, finally, to deliver him up, makes himself in a way an accessory to the deed, and becomes responsible for it.[238]

Before Vattel, Grotius had also proposed a theory of State complicity.[239] However, he specifically distinguished the acts of individuals, on one hand, and the acts of the State (related to the former), on the other hand:

> Most authorities on this subject still adhere essentially to the view enunciated by Grotius, who rejected the notion of 'community liability' which was widely accepted in his day. In his opinion, the State could only be held responsible if its conduct with respect to the injurious act was inconsistent with its duties. The two most important and frequent forms of such conduct, according to Grotius, were *patientia* and *receptus*. The first of these two terms denotes the situation in which the State is aware of an individual's intention to perpetrate a wrongful act against a foreign State or sovereign, but fails to take the proper steps to thwart his designs; the second term denotes the situation in which the State receives an offender and, by refusing either to extradite or to punish him, assumes complicity in the offence. By such conduct, which constitutes tacit approval of the offence, the State tends to identify itself with the offender. And it is this tacit approval—and not the relationship between the individual and the community—which gives rise to the responsibility of the State. In other words, the responsibility of the State can only arise in such circumstances if its organs or officials have been guilty of an act or omission which in itself constitutes an international delinquency.[240]

[237] Emer de Vattel, *Le droit des gens, ou principes de la loi naturelle, appliqués à la conduit et aux affaires des nations et des souverains* (Londres 1758) Livre II, Chapitre VI, §§ 73–77.

[238] Translation from the original French of the 1758 edition by Charles G Fenwick, Washington, 1916.

[239] Hugo Grotius, *De Jure Belli ac Pacis Libri Tres. Libri II* (Amsterdam 1646) 366.

[240] Francisco V García Amador, International Responsibility: Second Report by F V García Amador, Special Rapporteur, 'Responsibility of The State For Injuries Caused in its Territory to the Person or Property of Aliens. Part I: Acts And Omissions', 15 February 1957, para 11, document A/CN.4/106,

García Amador and Ago categorize Grotius as an opponent of the doctrine of State complicity.[241] However, the conduct of both (*ex ante*) *patientia* and (*ex post*) *receptus* were susceptible to a broad and liberal interpretation, so that in fact numerous early cases, although complying with the principle formulated by Grotius, were rightly held to support a complicity theory attributing acts of private individuals to the State on a derivative and indirect basis.[242] The attribution of responsibility to the State operated on the fictitious ground of a tacit or implied complicity of the State vis-à-vis the culprits of injuries to aliens, which was inferred by distinct State conduct of (political) tolerance and approval, more or less stringently related to the facts of the dispute.[243] The final rejection of such doctrines of (either open or surreptitious) State complicity is found in the case law of the US–Mexico General Claims Commission, notably in the *Janes* case:

> The international delinquency in this case is one of its own specific type, separate from the private delinquency of the culprit. The culprit is liable for having killed or murdered an American national; the Government is liable for not having measured up to its duty of diligently prosecuting and properly punishing the offender. ... Even if the non-punishment were conceived as some kind of approval—which in the Commission's view is doubtful—still approving of a crime has never been deemed identical with being an accomplice to that crime; and even if nonpunishment of a murderer really amounted to complicity in the murder, still it is not permissible to treat this derivative and remote liability not as an attenuate form of responsibility, but as just as serious as if the Government had perpetrated the killing with its own hands.[244]

Yearbook of the International Law Commission, 1957, Volume II, 104, 123, document A/CN.4/SER.A/1957/Add.l.

---

[241] Roberto Ago, Fourth Report on State Responsibility, by Mr Roberto Ago, Special Rapporteur, 'The internationally wrongful act of the State, source of international responsibility', 30 June 1972 and 9 April 1973, para 139, document A/CN.4/264 and Add.l, Yearbook of the International Law Commission, 1972, Volume II, 71, 121, document A/CN.4/SER.A/1972/Add.1. But see Dionisio Anzilotti, 'La responsabilité internationale des États a raison des dommages soufferts par des étrangers' (1906) 13 Revue Générale de Droit International Public 5, 13: '*l'acte illicite, au point de vue du droit international, est en pareil cas, l'omission de l'Ètat et non pas l'action positive des individus; et l'Ètat est donc tenu pour son fai, mais non en qualité de complice des individus, comme on l'a dit si souvent depuis Grotius*.'

[242] *Bovallins and Hedlund cases*, 1903, 10 RIAA 768, 770: 'A State is responsible in damages committed by revolutionists where it subsequently appoints the participants and leaders of the revolution to office, thereby tacitly approving their conduct'; *Ruden*, in Moore, II (GPO 1898) 1653, 1655; *Cothesworth & Powell*, November 1875, in Moore, II (GPO 1898) 2050, 2082; *Cases of Amelia de Brissot, Ralph Rawdon, Joseph Stackpole, and Narcisa de Hammer v Venezuela (the steamer* Apure *case)*, 1885, 29 RIAA 240; *Poggioli case (of a general nature)*, 1903, 10 RIAA 669, 673: 'the Italian Commissioner insists that there was an implied responsibility on the part of the Government in these events, even if only a part of them were executed by its agents, because all were by them at least suggested or tolerated.'

[243] J L Brierly, 'The Theory of Implied State Complicity in International Claims' (1928) 9 British Year Book of International Law 42.

[244] *Laura M B Janes et al (USA) v United Mexican States*, 16 November 1925, 4 RIAA 82, 86–87; *Accord, Gertrude Parker Massey (USA) v United Mexican States*, 15 April 1927, 4 RIAA 155; *Owner of the*

More recently, the ICJ denied attribution based on 'complicity' in the *Hostages* case.[245] In this case, the ICJ considered as not attributable the acts of Iranian militants (students and other nationals), which consisted of the attack on the US Embassy in Tehran on 4 November 1979 and on the Consulates at Tabriz and Shiraz on the following day, and the seizure and detention of their personnel as hostages:

> No suggestion has been made that the militants, when they executed their attack on the Embassy, had any form of official status as recognized 'agents' or organs of the Iranian State. Their conduct in mounting the attack, overrunning the Embassy and seizing its inmates as hostages cannot, therefore, be regarded as imputable to that State on that basis. Their conduct might be considered as itself directly imputable to the Iranian State only if it were established that, in fact, on the occasion in question the militants acted on behalf on the State, having been charged by some competent organ of the Iranian State to carry out a specific operation. The information before the Court does not, however, suffice to establish with the requisite certainty the existence at that time of such a link between the militants and any competent organ of the State.[246]

Even various declarations of political approval and expressions of congratulations by the Ayatollah Khomeini were not interpreted as a demonstration of (actual) authorization from the State of Iran in relation to the attack on the US Embassy, held to be conduct of an 'initially independent and unofficial character'.[247]

Although States are relieved from the direct attribution of conduct of private individuals based on theories of complicity or endorsement (level of secondary rules), they are nevertheless subject to attribution of acts and omissions of their organs found in breach of the obligation to comply with a general standard of due diligence (level of primary rules). After the disappearance of the legal doctrine of implied State complicity, this legal reasoning has comprehensively replaced the former approach in the adjudication of equivalent cases, equally resulting in

Sarah B Putnam (United States) v Great Britain, 6 November 1925, 6 RIAA 156–57. See also the earlier *Glenn*, 1868, in Moore, III (GPO 1898) 3138; *Lenz*, 25 March 1899, in Moore, VI (GPO 1906) 794; *Renton*, in Moore, VI (GPO 1906) 794.

245 *United States Diplomatic and Consular Staff in Tehran (United States of America v Iran)*, Judgment, 24 May 1980, ICJ Reports 1980, 3.

246 *United States Diplomatic and Consular Staff in Tehran (United States of America v Iran)*, Judgment, 24 May 1980, ICJ Reports 1980, 3, 29. *Accord, Alfred LW Short v The Islamic Republic of Iran*, Case No 11135, 14 July 1987, Award No 312-11135-3, 16 IRAN-US CTR 76, 84-86 (1987-III); *Jack Rankin v The Islamic Republic of Iran*, Case No 10913, 3 November 1987, Award No 326-10913-2, 17 IRAN-US CTR 135, 141 (1987-IV).

247 *United States Diplomatic and Consular Staff in Tehran (United States of America v Iran)*, Judgment, 24 May 1980, ICJ Reports 1980, 3, 30.

a finding of State liability (from indirect or derivative responsibility based on a complicity argument to direct responsibility based on a failure to comply with due diligence standards). For instance, episodes of judicial pardon, condonation, and general amnesty would have earlier been considered as grounds for State complicity.[248] Afterwards, the same kind of conduct has been interpreted as representing a failure to punish.[249] Another example is the appointment of a culprit as a State official or dignitary, which was previously categorized as tacit complicity,[250] but later as a failure to protect.[251]

While the category of *patientia* (*ex ante* awareness or tolerance of mischiefs against foreigners) has been almost completely transferred into the realm of due diligence obligations (duty to prevent, chiefly), the category of *receptus* (*ex post* approval or ratification of acts of individuals) still retains standing in the domain of secondary rules of attribution.[252] Indeed, ARSIWA Article 11 provides for the acknowledgement and adoption by a State of *not otherwise attributable* conduct:

Article 11
Conduct acknowledged and adopted by a State as its own

> Conduct which is not attributable to a State under the preceding articles shall nevertheless be considered an act of that State under international law if and to the extent that the State acknowledges and adopts the conduct in question as its own.[253]

The most notable precedent for the application of the attribution rule of State acknowledgement and adoption of conduct *ex post facto* is the *Hostages* case.[254] Notwithstanding non-attributability of the acts of the Iranian militants attacking and occupying the US Embassy in Tehran, the ICJ nevertheless held that the endorsement by Iran—as embodied by the Ayatollah Khomeini's decree of 17 November 1979 and by a television interview of the minister of Foreign Affairs on 6 May 1980—had 'ratified' the militants' conduct, *transforming* (*ab initio*) their

[248] *Cothesworth & Powell*, November 1875, in Moore, II (GPO 1898) 2050, 2051.

[249] *Cornelia J Pringle, et al, (Santa Isabel Claims) (USA) v United Mexican States*, 26 April 1926, 4 RIAA 783; *Lettie Charlotte Denham and Frank Parlin Denham (United States) v Panama*, 22 May 1933, 6 RIAA 312–13; *F R West (USA) v United Mexican States*, 21 July 1927, 4 RIAA 270, 272.

[250] *Bovallins and Hedlund cases*, 1903, 10 RIAA 768, 770.

[251] *Francisco Mallén (United Mexican States) v USA*, 27 April 1927, 4 RIAA 173, 181.

[252] Frédéric Dopagne, 'La responsabilité de l'État du fait des particuliers: les causes d'imputation revisitées par les articles sur la responsabilité de l'État pour fait internationalement illicite' (2001) 34 Revue Belge du Droit International 492, 518: '*On ne peut cependant nier, nous semble-t-il, que le pas à franchir n'est pas énorme entre l'article 11 des articles et une certaine résurrection de la "complicité".*'

[253] ARSIWA Commentaries 52.

[254] *United States Diplomatic and Consular Staff in Tehran (United States of America v Iran)*, Judgment, 24 May 1980, ICJ Reports 1980, 3. The Commentaries also mention the *Affaire relative à la concession des phares de l'Empire ottoman (Lighthouses Arbitration) (France v Greece)*, 24 July 1956, 12 RIAA 155.

legal nature through the 'seal of official government approval'.[255] The ICJ deliberated that Iran's approval rendered the acts of the occupants as 'acts of that State' and that the authors of the attack 'had now become agents of the Iranian State'.[256] This language may be subject to understandable criticism. It is hardly possible to admit a retroactive agency relationship between the State and the private individuals subsequent to government's approval. Pursuant to the rule of acknowledgement and adoption of conduct, the direction (the 'arrow') of the mechanism of 'attribution' is exceptionally reversed: not from the conduct to the State (attribution of the act *to* the State), but rather from the State to the conduct (ratification *by* the State of the act). This rule appears to be rather strange compared to the functioning of the principle of attributability pursuant to ARSIWA Article 4 (*de jure* or *de facto* agency), which attracts significant consequences in the applicable regime, chiefly the operation of the *ultra vires* rule. In line with this argument, it is questionable whether ARSIWA Article 11 provides for a rule of attribution *at all*, rather than entailing different issues of opposability to States of their unilateral acts and declarations.[257] Another issue touches upon the form and extent of the acknowledgement and adoption. The ARSIWA Commentaries underline that it must be clear, equivocal, and also specific.[258] In this respect, the ARSIWA Commentaries allow the acknowledgement and adoption to take 'the form of words or conduct'.[259] Therefore, an implied ratification or endorsement remains a possible option provided by ARSIWA, which may appear reminiscent of the old theories of State complicity.

In the case of non-attributability of acts and omissions of private individuals, State responsibility can only be based upon some 'ultimate default' by State organs with regard to the 'objective conditions' embodied by the activities of private persons.[260] States are generally subject to due diligence obligations dictated by customary international law, as well as by treaty law.[261] These rules entail duties of care

[255] *United States Diplomatic and Consular Staff in Tehran (United States of America v Iran)*, Judgment, 24 May 1980, paras 73–74, ICJ Reports 1980, 3, 34–35.

[256] *United States Diplomatic and Consular Staff in Tehran (United States of America v Iran)*, Judgment, 24 May 1980, para 74, ICJ Reports 1980, 3, 35.

[257] Paolo Palchetti, 'Comportamento di organi di fatto e illecito internazionale nel progetto di articoli sulla responsabilità internazionale degli Stat' in Marina Spinedi, Alessandra Gianelli, and Maria Luisa Alaimo (eds), *La codificazione della responsabilità internazionale degli Stati alla prova dei fatti: problemi e spunti di riflessione* (Giuffrè 2006) 3, 24.

[258] ARSIWA Commentaries 52, paras 6, 8.

[259] ARSIWA Commentaries 52, para 8.

[260] Ian Brownlie, *System of the Law of Nations. State Responsibility. Part I* (Clarendon Press 1983) 159; Rüdiger Wolfrum, 'State Responsibility for Private Actors: an Old Problem of Renewed Relevance' in Maurizio Ragazzi (ed), *International Responsibility Today. Essays in Memory of Oscar Schachter* (Martinus Nijhoff Publishers 2005) 423, 424.

[261] *Alabama claims of the United States of America against Great Britain*, 14 September 1872, 29 RIAA 125, 127; *Sambiaggio Case (of a general nature)*, 1903, 10 RIAA 499, 502; *Affaire des biens britanniques au Maroc espagnol (Espagne contre Royaume-Uni) (Spanish Zone of Morocco)*, 1 May 1925, 2 RIAA 615, 645: '*il faut également reconnaître que l'État doit être considéré comme tenu à exercer une vigilance d'un ordre supérieur en vue de prévenir les délits commis, en violation de la discipline et de la loi militaires, par des personnes appartenant à l'armée. L'exigence de cette vigilance qualifiée n'est que le complément des*

and surveillance incumbent on the State, not only in relation to acts of revolutionaries, mob violence, or piracy, but also in relation to the conduct of every other private person, including corporate businesses, associations, trade unions, etc.[262] This universal principle has been consistently formulated by the Italy–Peru Mixed Claims Commission in relation to armed conflicts and civil strife:

> *Un principe de droit international veut que l'Etat soit responsable des violations du droit des gens commises par ses agents ou ceux d'un des partis belligérants, dans une guerre civile, lorsqu'il n'a pas été fait toutes les diligences nécessaires pour sauvegarder les intérêts neutres représentés par les étrangers dans leurs personnes et leurs biens.*[263]

The breach of due diligence should not necessarily be at the causal origin of the injury suffered by an alien, but should be sufficiently connected to it at a previous, contemporaneous, or subsequent phase.[264] Indeed, due diligence obligations enshrine a State's duty to prevent injuries and to protect aliens,[265] as well as to apprehend and adequately punish the authors of delinquencies against foreigners.[266]

pouvoirs du commandement et de la discipline de la hiérarchie militaire.'; *Walter A Noyes (United States) v Panama*, 22 May 1933, 6 RIAA 308, 309; *Trail Smelter Case (United States, Canada)*, 16 April 1938 and 11 March 1941, 3 RIAA 1905.

---

[262] Francisco V García-Amador, 'State Responsibility: Some New Problems' (1958) 94 Recueil des Cours 365, 404; Pierre-Marie Dupuy, 'Due Diligence in the International Law of State Responsibility' in *Legal Aspects of Transfrontier Pollution* (Organisation for Economic Co-operation and Development 1977) 369–79; Riccardo Pisillo Mazzeschi, 'The Due Diligence Rule and the Nature of the International Responsibility of States' (1992) 35 German Yearbook of International Law 9, 22; Riccardo Pisillo Mazzeschi, *'Due diligence' e responsabilità internazionale degli Stati* (Giuffrè 1989) 193, 224; Jan Arno Hessbruegge, 'The Historical Development of the Doctrines of Attribution and Due Diligence in International Law' (2003–2004) 36 New York University Journal of International Law and Politics 265; Gordon A Christenson, 'Attributing Acts of Omission to the State' (1990–1991) 12 Michigan Journal of International Law 312, 323.

[263] *Queirolo*, 30 September 1901, 15 RIAA 407, 408; *Don Juan B Sanguinetti*, 30 September 1901, 15 RIAA 403–04; *Don Jeronimo Sessarego*, 30 September 1901, 15 RIAA 400–01; *Don Jacinto Gadino*, 30 September 1901, 15 RIAA 414, 415. See also, as to the Italy–Venezuela Commission, *Sambiaggio Case (of a general nature)*, 1903, 10 RIAA 499, 512: 'The ordinary rule is that a government, like an individual, is only to be held responsible for the acts of its agents or for acts the responsibility for which is expressly assumed by it. To apply another doctrine, save under certain exceptional circumstances incident to the peculiar position occupied by a government toward those subject to its power, would be unnatural and illogical.'

[264] *Contra*, Institut de Droit International, 'Responsabilité internationale des Etats à raison des dommages causés sur leur territoire à la personne et aux biens des étrangers' (Leo Strisower, Rapporteur), Résolution du 1 septembre 1927, Session de Lausanne, (1927) 33(III) Annuaire de l'Institut de Droit International 330-335, Article III.

[265] As to early case law, see *Cornelia J Pringle, et al, (Santa Isabel Claims) (USA) v United Mexican States*, 26 April 1926, 4 RIAA 783. As to the Iran–US Claims Tribunal, see *Lillian Byrdine Grimm v The Government of the Islamic Republic of Iran*, Case No 71, 18 February 1983, Award No 25-71-1, 2 IRAN-US CTR 78 (1983-I).

[266] *George Adams Kennedy (USA) v United Mexican States*, 6 May 1927, 4 RIAA 194, 199; *Walter A Noyes (United States) v Panama*, 22 May 1933, 6 RIAA 308, 309.

Instead of covering artificial ways to link (municipally) wrongful 'private' acts to the State (such as theories of implied complicity or acquiescence), the focus of international law is whether the State has an independent obligation to prevent harm or to act affirmatively.[267] In this respect, the distinction between *direct* and *indirect* responsibility is definitely misleading, even though of moderate assistance to elucidate a legal phenomena, where the divide between primary and secondary rules fades. Indeed, the attribution mechanism here is necessarily intertwined with the applicability of a substantive (primary) rule of international law prescribing a standard of diligence. As a consequence, failure (by act or omission) to comply with such a standard is attributable per se to State organs (ARSIWA Article 4) or to State instrumentalities that may be entrusted with functions of surveillance, prevention, and punishment of delinquencies (ARSIWA Article 5):

> while the terminology of 'direct' and 'indirect' responsibility may express the intensity of involvement of the State in the situation, at each stage of the situation it may be said the State has 'directly' violated an international obligation. … It follows that to classify attributable acts of organs as producing direct state responsibility and attributable acts of other individuals as producing indirect state responsibility is a distinction without meaning, producing no difference.[268]

The due diligence principle found a solemn formulation by the ICJ in the *Corfu Channel* case, where the Court established the responsibility of Albania on the ground of:

> certain general and well-recognized principles, namely: elementary considerations of humanity, even more exacting in peace than in war; the principle of the freedom of maritime communication; and every State's obligation not to allow knowingly its territory to be used for acts contrary to the rights of other States.[269]

The *Corfu Channel* ruling—notably inspired by natural law tenets—attributes to States the omissive conduct of their organs in a very similar fashion to the early doctrine of *patientia*, re-elaborated at the level of primary rules as failure to take *appropriate steps* to prevent injuries to aliens. This means that, notwithstanding non-attributability of conduct of private individuals to the State, the very same

[267] Gordon A Christenson, 'The Doctrine of Attribution in State Responsibility' in Richard B Lillich (ed), *International Law of State Responsibility for Injuries to Aliens* (University Press of Virginia 1983) 321, 322.

[268] Hazel Fox, 'The International Court of Justice's Treatment of Acts of the State and in Particular the Attribution of Acts of Individuals to the State' in Nisuke Ando, Edward McWhinney, and Rüdiger Wolfrum (eds), *Liber Amicorum Judge Shigeru Oda*, vol 1 (Kluwer Law International 2002) 147, 152, 156.

[269] *Corfu Channel case*, Judgment, 9 April 1949, ICJ Reports 1949, 4, 22.

State is not 'free of any responsibility' arising in connection with the same conduct, as affirmed in *Hostages*.[270] In that case, the ICJ found the inaction of Iran as liable for breach of various substantive obligations deriving both from 'contractual' and 'general international law', namely due diligence duties and rules prescribed by the 1961 Vienna Convention on Diplomatic Relations (VCDR) and by the 1963 Vienna Convention on Consular Relations (VCCR).[271] Likewise, in the *Nicaragua* case, the ICJ found that the acts of the *contras* were not considered to be attributable to the US for lack of effective control,[272] but affirmed that the activities of the US 'in relation to the contras'[273] constituted a breach of the customary international law principles of the non-use or threat of force, and non-intervention in the internal affairs of another State.[274] In *Armed Activities*, the Court followed exactly the same reasoning. It held that, even though the activities of the Congo Liberation Movement (MLC) and Congo Liberation Army (ALC) could not be attributed to Uganda, Uganda's conduct of training and military support violated 'certain obligations of international law', substantiated as non-use of force, non-intervention, and non-violation of the sovereignty and territorial integrity of the Democratic Republic of the Congo (DRC).[275] The *Bosnian Genocide* case recently confirmed this legal scheme, by emphasizing the potential for States to contract primary norms prohibiting incitement, conspiracy, or complicity with non-state actors, for instance in relation to acts of genocide, terrorism, or intervention in the internal affairs of other States, as well as obligations to prevent in the domain of multifaceted sectors such as financial markets, air and maritime transportation, and public security issues (*duty to control*).[276] In all such cases, attribution generally proceeds from the

[270] *United States Diplomatic and Consular Staff in Tehran (United States of America v Iran)*, Judgment, 24 May 1980, para 61, ICJ Reports 1980, 3, 31.

[271] *United States Diplomatic and Consular Staff in Tehran (United States of America v Iran)*, Judgment, 24 May 1980, paras 62–68, ICJ Reports 1980, 3, 30–32.

[272] See section 5.3.4 of this chapter.

[273] *Military and Paramilitary Activities in and against Nicaragua (Nicaragua v United States of America)*, Merits, Judgment, 27 June 1986, para 228, ICJ Reports 1986, 14, 118: 'recruiting, training, arming, equipping, financing, supplying and otherwise encouraging, supporting, aiding, and directing military and paramilitary actions in and against Nicaragua.'

[274] *Military and Paramilitary Activities in and against Nicaragua (Nicaragua v United States of America)*, Merits, Judgment, 27 June 1986, ICJ Reports 1986, 14, 100, 147. Customary international law on non-use of force was also interpreted in light of General Assembly Resolution 2625 (XXV), 24 October 1970, 'Declaration on Principles of International Law concerning Friendly Relations and Co-operation among States in accordance with the Charter of the United Nations', A/8082.

[275] *Armed Activities in the Territory of the Congo (DRC v Uganda)*, Judgment, 19 December 2005, paras 161–64, ICJ Reports 2005, 168, 226–27.

[276] *Application of the Convention on the Prevention and Punishment of the Crime of Genocide (Bosnia and Herzegovina v Serbia and Montenegro)*, Judgment, 26 February 2007, para 430, ICJ Reports 2007, 43, 221: 'In this area the notion of "due diligence", which calls for an assessment in concreto, is of critical importance.' See also Summary of the Discussions in Various United Nations Organs and the Resulting Decisions: Working Paper Prepared by the Secretariat, 7 February 1964, document A/CN.4/165, Yearbook of the International Law Commission, 1964, Volume II, 125, 126, document A/CN.4/SER.A/1964/ADD.1; Proposals submitted to, and decisions of, various United Nations organs relating

rule governing the conduct of State organs (*de jure* or *de facto*), not from the rule of attributability of acts of private individuals to the State.[277]

5.3 Instructions, or Direction or Control

5.3.1 Scope

The foregoing analysis may assist the interpreter in understanding the structure and functioning of the rule of the attributability to the State of the conduct of individuals, currently codified by ARSIWA Article 8:

Article 8
Conduct directed or controlled by a State

> The conduct of a person or group of persons shall be considered an act of a State under international law if the person or group of persons is in fact acting on the instructions of, or under the direction or control of, that State in carrying out the conduct.

The rule is meant to cover instances of effective *private delegation* to undertake certain activities by a State to non-state actors, namely such persons or groups of persons not falling under the attribution mechanisms pertaining to the category of organs (*de jure* or *de facto*) pursuant to ARSIWA Article 4 or 'State entities' pursuant to ARSIWA Article 5.[278] As mentioned above,[279] the *positive* formulation of this rule represents a major advancement in comparison to Article 11 of the draft articles adopted on first reading, which propounded a mere *negative* formulation. ARSIWA Article 8 should also be read in historical continuity with Article 8(a) of the draft articles adopted on first reading, regulating the attribution of acts of *de facto* organs.[280] Indeed, the tests of (actual) instructions and (effective) control, which are currently employed in ARSIWA Article 8, were originally elaborated in

to the question of State responsibility: supplement prepared by the Secretariat to document A/CN.4/165, 28 February 1969, document A/CN.4/209, Yearbook of the International Law Commission, 1969, Volume II, 114, 117, document A/CN.4/SER. A/1969/Add.1: 'There was also agreement in principle that every State has the duty to refrain from involvement in civil strife and terrorist acts in another State. A number of the proposals submitted to the Committee would go further and require States not to tolerate, connive at, or acquiesce in, activities of a terrorist or subversive nature directed against another State.' See also, ICTY, Appeals Chamber, *Tadić*, IT-94-1-A, Separate Opinion of Judge Shahabuddeen, 15 July 1999, 150, 156, para 20: 'by deciding to use force through an entity, a state places itself under an obligation of due diligence to ensure that such use does not degenerate into such breaches, as it can.'

---

[277] *Application of the Convention on the Prevention and Punishment of the Crime of Genocide (Bosnia and Herzegovina v Serbia and Montenegro)*, Judgment, 26 February 2007, para 380, ICJ Reports 2007, 43, 200.

[278] James Crawford, *State Responsibility. The General Part* (Cambridge University Press 2013) 141.

[279] See section 5.1 of this chapter.

[280] Paolo Palchetti, 'Comportamento di organi di fatto e illecito internazionale nel progetto di articoli sulla responsabilità internazionale degli Stati' in Marina Spinedi, Alessandra Gianelli, and Maria Luisa

relation to the former Article 8(a). However, the rule of attribution of conduct of private individuals operates at present on the basis of a radically different mechanism in comparison to the attributability of acts of *de facto* agents pursuant to ARSIWA Article 4.2. This is testified by the elision of the phrase 'in fact acting on behalf of the State', which does not appear in the text of ARSIWA Article 8. Indeed, the attribution mechanism of ARSIWA Article 8 does not proceed from a concept of 'agency' as understood in public law (which is the case of ARSIWA Article 4 as to *de jure* or *de facto* organs), but rather from a private law concept of 'agency'.[281] This entails the absence of any exercise of elements of *official* (ARSIWA Article 4) or *governmental* (ARSIWA Article 5) authority whatsoever, but instead requires the existence of a *factual* link. It may even be questioned whether the conduct of non-state actors should be considered as 'acts of the State' proper, at least in Roberto Ago's terminology. It may be submitted that only the *effects* of the acts and omissions of the individuals are attributed to the State, rather than the conduct itself.

The point of departure of the attribution rule under ARSIWA Article 8 is the finding that State organs imparted instructions to or exercised direction or control over the activity of non-state actors.[282] The prongs of instructions and of direction or control are reciprocally alternative. However, in both cases their object and target shall be a specific conduct to be undertaken by individuals: '[t]he principle does not extend to conduct which was only incidentally or peripherally associated with an operation and which escaped from the State's direction or control.'[283] The Commentaries offer examples of individuals under ARSIWA Article 8, by referring to private persons or groups recruited or instigated to act as 'auxiliaries' or 'volunteers' while remaining outside the official structure of the State.[284] Such examples may engender confusion. Indeed, we have submitted that the category of *auxiliaries* is generally included in the status of State organs.[285] The term is used in conjunction with the example of 'volunteers'. Hence, the Commentaries might be held to use the two words in a synonymic fashion. Even in light of this interpretation, it should be underlined that *irregular* volunteers carrying out State functions are

Alaimo (eds), *La codificazione della responsabilità internazionale degli Stati alla prova dei fatti: problemi e spunti di riflessione* (Giuffrè 2006) 3, 7: '*In questo senso, la modifica introdotta in seconda lettura non sembra alterare i caratteri di fondo del criterio di attribuzione che era previsto all'art. 8, lett.* a).'

---

281 *Black's Law Dictionary* (9th edn, Thompson Reuters 2009): 'A fiduciary relationship created by express or implied contract or by law, in which one party (the *agent*) may act on behalf of another party (the *principal*) and bind that other party by words or actions.'

282 ARSIWA Commentaries 40, para 2: 'But the rule [ARSIWA Article 4] is nonetheless a point of departure. It defines the core cases of attribution, and it is a starting point for other cases. For example, under article 8 conduct which is authorized by the State, so as to be attributable to it, must have been authorized by an organ of the State, either directly or indirectly.'

283 ARSIWA Commentaries 47, paras 3, 7.

284 ARSIWA Commentaries 47, para 2.

285 *D Earnshaw and Others (Great Britain) v United States (Zafiro case)*, 30 November 1925, 6 RIAA 160. See section 1.3.2 of this chapter.

rather to be subsumed into the category of *de facto* organs. Accordingly, the kind of activities enshrined in ARSIWA Article 8 should be further investigated. The ARSIWA Commentaries state that 'it does not matter that the person or persons involved are private individuals nor whether their conduct involves "governmental activity" '.[286] 'Private individuals' may include State agents acting *jure privatorum* outside of their office, which further suggests that the undertaking of 'authoritative' acts by non-state actors is not a requirement contemplated by ARSIWA Article 8. Rather, it is submitted that ARSIWA Article 8 does not regularly cover activities performed in the exercise of authority.

5.3.2 State-Owned Enterprises

The practice of the Iran–US Claims Tribunal provides for numerous cases of attribution to the State of acts of 'private' State-owned or State-controlled enterprises.[287] Various criteria for the finding of State control overlap with the tests included in the typologic method employed for the structural identification of parastatals.[288] The decisive distinction between attributability under ARSIWA Articles 5 and 8 hinges on the exercise of elements of governmental authority (*prerogatives de la puissance publique)* by the entity in the particular instance at issue and formal empowerment by law of such an authority. This entails that—failing application of ARSIWA Article 5—attribution may be triggered on the basis of control pursuant to ARSIWA Article 8 in relation to the activities *jure gestionis* of 'State entities', including State-owned companies. Thus, the Iran–US Claims Tribunal repeatedly found the following factual findings as relevant indications of (effective) control: appointment by the government or public authorities of the managers of the company;[289] orders, directives, recommendations, or instructions by any

[286] ARSIWA Commentaries 47, para 2.

[287] See Chapter I, section 5.

[288] See section 4.3 of this chapter.

[289] *RayGo Warner Equipment Company v Star Line Iran Company*, Case No 17, 15 December 1982, 1 IRAN-US CTR 411, 413 (1982); *Kimberley-Clark Corporation v Bank Markazi Iran, Novzohour Paper Industries, Government of the Islamic Republic of Iran*, Case No 57, Award No 46-57-2, 25 May 1983, 2 IRAN-US CTR 334, 338 (1983-I); *Cal-Maine Foods, Inc v The Government of the Islamic Republic of Iran and Sherkat Seamourgh Company, Inc*, Case No 340, 31 May 1984, Award No 133-340-3, 6 IRAN-US CTR 52, 58-59 (1984-II); *Rexnord, Inc v The Islamic Republic of Iran, Tchacosh Company and Iran Siporex Industrial and Manufacturing Works, Limited*, Case No 132, 10 January 1983, Award No 21-132-3, 2 IRAN-US CTR 6 (1983-I); *Sedco, Inc v National Iranian Oil Company and The Islamic Republic of Iran*, Case No 129, 24 October 1985, Award No ITL 55-29-3, 9 IRAN-US CTR 248, 277 (1985-III); *SeaCo, Inc v The Islamic Republic of Iran, The Iranian Meat Organization, Iran Express Lines, and Star Line Co*, 11 IRAN-US CTR 210, 215 (1986-II); *McLaughlin Enterprises, Ltd v The Government of the Islamic Republic of Iran, Information System Iran*, Case No 289, 16 September 1986, Award No 253-289-1, 12 IRAN-US CTR 146, 149 (1986-III); *Emanuel Too v Greater Modesto Insurance Associates and The United States of America*, Case No 880, 29 December 1989, Award No 460-880-2, 23 IRAN-US CTR 378, 384 (1989-III); *Kaysons International Corporation v The Government of the Islamic Republic of Iran, The Ministry of Industries and Mines, The Alborz Investment Corporation, The Tolid Daru Company, The Payegozar, The Pakhs Alborz Company, and The KBC Company*, Case No 367, 28 June 1993, Award No 548-367-2, 29 IRAN-US CTR 222, 229 (1993).

governmental body;[290] and, a taking of or expropriation of the company itself by the Government.[291]

In *Eastman Kodak*, the Tribunal held that '[t]he concept of control, as used in commercial and international law, is far from being as clear and unequivocal a legal concept as one would desire'.[292] While State control over a company may also be indirect through another entity or parastatal,[293] majority ownership or shareholding is not per se a sufficient element for the purposes of attribution.[294] This appears to be a corollary of the principle of corporate separateness enshrined in domestic corporate law, which imposes markedly strict requirements for the application of the doctrine of 'piercing of the corporate veil.' The ICJ addressed this issue in the case of the *Barcelona Traction*.[295] The decision stands as one of the chief instances of transposition of legal institutions of municipal law into the realm of customary international law.[296] This is evident from the relevant extract of the decision:

> 56. ... the Court must here refer to municipal law. Forms of incorporation and their legal personality have sometimes not been employed for the sole purposes they were originally intended to serve; sometimes the corporate entity has been unable to protect the rights of those who entrusted their financial resources to it; thus inevitably there have arisen dangers of abuse, as in the case of many other

[290] *Schering Corporation v The Islamic Republic of Iran*, Case No 38, 13 April 1984, Award No 122-38-3, 5 IRAN-US CTR 361, 370 (1984-I).

[291] *Sedco, Inc v National Iranian Oil Company and The Islamic Republic of Iran*, Case No 129, 24 October 1985, Award No ITL 55-29-3, 9 IRAN-US CTR 248, 277 (1985-III).

[292] *Eastman Kodak Company v Iran*, Case No 12384, 11 November 1987, Award No 329-227/12384-3, 17 IRAN-US CTR 153, 166 (1987-IV).

[293] *Economy Forms Corporation v Iran*, Case No 165, 14 June 1983, Award No 55-165-1, 3 IRAN-US CTR 42, 47 (1983-III); *Ultrasystems Incorporated v The Islamic Republic of Iran, Information Systems Iran*, Case No 84, 4 March 1983, Award No 27-84-3, 2 IRAN-US CTR 100, 105 (1983-I); *Phelps Dodge Corp and Overseas Private Investment Corp v The Islamic Republic of Iran*, Case No 99, 19 March 1986, Award No 217-99-2, 10 IRAN-US CTR 121, 166–67 (1986-I).

[294] *PepsiCo, Inc v Iran*, Case No 18, 11 October 1986, Award No 260-18-1, 13 IRAN-US CTR 3, 21 (1986-IV); *Bechtel, Inc v Iran*, Case No 181, 4 March 1987, Award No 294-181-1, 14 IRAN-US CTR 149, 157 (1987-I). For the same position in international investment arbitration, see *Tulip Real Estate and Development Netherlands BV v Republic of Turkey*, ICSID Case No ARB/11/28, Award, 10 March 2014, para 289.

[295] *Barcelona Traction Light and Power Company, Limited (Belgium v Spain)*, Second Phase, Judgment, 5 February 1970, ICJ Reports 1970, 3. See Rosalyn Higgins, 'Aspects of the Case Concerning the Barcelona Traction, Light and Power Company, Ltd.' (1970–1971) 11 Virginia Journal of International Law 327; Richard B Lillich, 'The Rigidity of Barcelona' (1971) 65 American Journal of International Law 522; F A Mann, 'The Protection of Shareholders' Interests in the Light of the Barcelona Traction Case' (1973) 67 American Journal of International Law 259.

[296] Roberto Ago, Second Report on State Responsibility, by Mr Roberto Ago, Special Rapporteur, 'The origin of State responsibility', 20 April 1970, para 54, document A/CN.4/233, Yearbook of the International Law Commission, 1970, Volume II, 177, 195, document A/CN.4/SER.A/1970/Add.1: 'As writers have frequently pointed out, it is a mistake to attempt too direct a transposition into international law of ideas and concepts of municipal law which are very obviously linked with situations peculiar to municipal law.'

> institutions of law. Here, then, as elsewhere, the law, confronted with economic realities, has had to provide protective measures and remedies in the interests of those within the corporate entity as well as of those outside who have dealings with it: the law has recognized that the independent existence of the legal entity cannot be treated as an absolute. It is in this context that the process of 'lifting the corporate veil' or 'disregarding the legal entity' has been found justified and equitable in certain circumstances or for certain purposes. The wealth of practice already accumulated on the subject in municipal law indicates that the veil is lifted, for instance, to prevent the misuse of the privileges of legal personality, as in certain cases of fraud or malfeasance, to protect third persons such as a creditor or purchaser, or to prevent the evasion of legal requirements or of obligations.
>
> 57. Hence the lifting of the veil is more frequently employed from without, in the interest of those dealing with the corporate entity. However, it has also been operated from within, in the interest of—among others—the shareholders, but only in exceptional circumstances.
>
> 58. In accordance with the principle expounded above, the process of lifting the veil, being an exceptional one admitted by municipal law in respect of an institution of its own making, is equally admissible to play a similar role in international law. It follows that on the international plane also there may in principle be special circumstances which justify the lifting of the veil in the interest of shareholders.[297]

This section of the *Barcelona Traction* judgment is expressly referred to by the ILC in its Commentary to ARSIWA Article 8, where it states that:

> Questions arise with respect to the conduct of companies or enterprises which are State-owned and controlled. If such corporations act inconsistently with the international obligations of the State concerned the question arises whether such conduct is attributable to the State. In discussing this issue it is necessary to recall that international law acknowledges the general separateness of corporate entities at the national level, except in those cases where the 'corporate veil' is a mere device or a vehicle for fraud or evasion.[298]

It is questionable whether the attribution of SOEs' conduct to their establishing State under ARSIWA Article 8 should function on the basis of the restrictive requirements, such as the showing of fraud, set forth by the domestic law doctrines of 'veil piercing'. On the contrary, the establishment of effective control by the State through instructions and mandates to an SOE in relation to specific acts

[297] *Barcelona Traction Light and Power Company, Limited (Belgium v Spain)*, Second Phase, Judgment, 5 February 1970, paras 56–58, ICJ Reports 1970, 3, 38–39.

[298] ARSIWA Commentaries 48, para 6.

or omissions is sufficient for the purposes of attributability. Moreover, corporate separateness should be treated less orthodoxly in relation to governmental or public control as contrasted to ordinary private control.[299] This is due to various factors that may affect the sphere of public ownership, such as the undeniable proximity and political interference of the State with regard to the management of SOEs, the higher degree of solvency of the State, the more limited risk of the investment in a State-controlled company, competitive advantages of SOEs under domestic law (for instance, the exemption from bankruptcy rules, preferential tax treatment, and information asymmetries), and the unity of interests between the State and its SOEs.[300] These considerations may prompt the conclusion that the satisfaction of the tests expressly provided by ARSIWA Article 8 is also appropriate for the purposes of attribution of the conduct of SOEs to States.

5.3.3 Instructions

The prong of instructions to individuals embodies a concept of specific authorization or charge by State authorities to commit a particular act (*actual instructions*, borrowing Judge Ago's language in his Separate Opinion in *Nicaragua*).[301] ARSIWA Article 8 does not require formality, an oral communication 'in the field' being sufficient.[302] Instructions may be also incorporated within an agreement between a State and a private contractor, as in the case of PMCs.[303] Indeed, the large majority of the activities undertaken by private contractors is likely to be attributed to the State pursuant to ARSIWA Article 8, in the absence of exercise of governmental authority under ARSIWA Article 5. Such conduct may further entail State responsibility, provided that they give rise to a breach of an international obligation.

The ARSIWA Commentaries allow the possibility of attribution of conduct performed in contravention of State instructions or beyond the scope of the authorization, provided that the act in question maintains a certain affinity or relation with

[299] David D Caron, 'The Basis of Responsibility: Attribution and Other Trans-substantive Rules of State Responsibility' in Richard B Lillich and Daniel B Magraw (eds), *The Iran-United States Claims Tribunal: Its Contribution to the Law of State Responsibility* (Transnational Publishers, Inc 1998) 109, 173.

[300] See Chapter III, sections 4.2.2 and 5.4.

[301] *Military and Paramilitary Activities in and against Nicaragua (Nicaragua v United States of America)*, Merits, Separate Opinion of Judge Ago, 27 June 1986, para 19, ICJ Reports 1986, 181, 189; *Application of the Convention on the Prevention and Punishment of the Crime of Genocide (Bosnia and Herzegovina v Serbia and Montenegro)*, Judgment, 26 February 2007, para 400, ICJ Reports 2007, 43, 208: 'It must however be shown that this "effective control" was exercised, or that the State*'s instructions were given, in respect of each operation in which the alleged violations occurred, not generally in respect of the overall actions taken by the persons or groups of persons having committed the violations.*'

[302] James Crawford, *State Responsibility. The General Part* (Cambridge University Press 2013) 145.

[303] See section 4.4 of this chapter.

the mission entrusted to the individual.[304] In this respect, an analogy with the *ultra vires* rule pursuant to ARSIWA Article 7 is not particularly tenable, since attribution under ARSIWA Article 8 does not pertain to notions of authority or office.[305] This may rather be considered as an application of a principle of appearance, as in the private law of agency. In any event, the inapplicability of the test of State instructions does not prevent attributability based on direction or control, which is discussed in the following paragraph.

5.3.4 Direction or Control

Even though the ARSIWA Commentaries maintain the possibility of a disjunctive application of the prongs of direction (the power to head or guide a given situation) and control (the power to govern a given set of activities), the practice of international law does not embark in such a distinction and provides a single test that is illustrative of a unitary concept.[306] In the absence of a more detailed definition in ARSIWA, the effort to determine the degree, requirements, and thresholds of the test of 'direction and control' (with a more evident focus on 'control') has been mainly undertaken by the international judiciary. As mentioned above,[307] the tests for attribution to the State of acts of private individuals have been elaborated in conjunction with the development of the doctrine of *de facto* organs. This conundrum of judge-made norms is in part justified, in light of the former opinion that Article 8(a) adopted on first reading encompassed both *de facto* agents and 'private' individuals in the expression 'persons acting in fact on behalf of the State'. This overlap between distinct categories has created a considerable degree of normative uncertainty, in that the interpreter has had to disentangle a combination of non-homogenous elements corresponding to the different legal categories built by international tribunals. This situation persisted, even after the adoption of ARSIWA on second reading, until the *Bosnian Genocide* case, which has finally 'placed' the doctrine of *de facto* organs exclusively under the scope of ARSIWA Article 4 (more precisely, ARSIWA Article 4.2) and the rule of attribution of acts of private individuals under ARSIWA Article 8. There now follows an account of the historical evolution of the jurisprudence of international tribunals on the matter.

[304] ARSIWA Commentaries 48, para 8. For a more restrictive opinion on this point, see Rüdiger Wolfrum, 'State Responsibility for Private Actors: an Old Problem of Renewed Relevance' in Maurizio Ragazzi (ed), *International Responsibility Today. Essays in Memory of Oscar Schachter* (Martinus Nijhoff Publishers 2005) 423, 429.

[305] André JJ de Hoogh, 'Articles 4 and 8 of the 2001 ILC Articles on State Responsibility, the *Tadić* Case and Attribution of Acts of Bosnian Serb Authorities to the Federal Republic of Yugoslavia' (2001) 72 British Year Book of International Law 255, 281–82: 'some attention must be devoted to the absence of any relationship between Article 8 and Article 7.' But see Antonio Cassese, 'The *Nicaragua* and *Tadić* Tests Revisited in Light of the ICJ Judgement on Genocide in Bosnia' (2007) 18 European Journal of International Law 649, 654–55.

[306] ARSIWA Commentaries 48, para 7. See also James Crawford, *State Responsibility. The General Part* (Cambridge University Press 2013) 146.

[307] See sections 3 and 5.1 of this chapter.

In light of the above clarifications, this review will inevitably address issues of *de facto* agency in conjunction with the test required for a finding of State control over private individuals.

In *Nicaragua*, the ICJ was confronted with the issue of attributability to the US of the acts of the *contras*, a local force of civil unrest against the Sandinista government. The Court established (and the US admitted) extensive financial, logistic, and intelligence support to the *contras*, but could not establish that the latter had been created by the US, nor that all their operations 'at every stage of the conflict reflected strategy and tactics wholly devised by the United States', thereby distinguishing them from the so-called 'Unilaterally Controlled Latino Assets' (UCLAs), whose acts were subject to attribution.[308] Hence, the Court identified its *thema decidendum* in the following way:

> What the Court has to determine at this point is whether or not the relationship of the *contras* to the United States Government was so much one of dependence on the one side and control on the other that it would be right to equate the *contras*, for legal purposes, with an organ of the United States Government, or as acting on behalf of that Government.[309]

This language seems to suggest an attempt to apply two distinct prongs of attribution. The first (*dependence*) is based on the finding of a pervasive factual link between the State and certain formally independent persons or groups of persons in order to qualify the latter as *de facto* organs. The second (*control*) focuses on a factual relationship of 'subjection' of the same persons vis-à-vis a government. The test of 'control' advanced in *Nicaragua* represents an innovation in respect to *Hostages*, where the ICJ required a test of authorization by the State 'to carry out specific operations' (*actual instructions*).[310] This may also explain why the *Nicaragua* judgment did not cite *Hostages* as an applicable precedent, which was remarked upon by Judge Ago in his Separate Opinion in the same case.[311] To this extent, *Nicaragua* implicitly introduces a seminal distinction between 'instructions' and 'direction and control', which would later be embodied in the draft articles on second reading in order to codify the rule of attribution to a State of acts of 'private' individuals

[308] *Military and Paramilitary Activities in and against Nicaragua (Nicaragua v United States of America)*, Merits, Judgment, 27 June 1986, paras 106–08, ICJ Reports 1986, 14, 61. On UCLAs, see the Judgment at 45. Judge Ago, in his Separate Opinion, qualified UCLAs as 'persons or groups that, without strictly being agents or organs of that State, belong nevertheless to public entities empowered within its domestic legal order to exercise certain elements of the government authority', at 188.

[309] *Military and Paramilitary Activities in and against Nicaragua (Nicaragua v United States of America)*, Merits, Judgment, 27 June 1986, para 109, ICJ Reports 1986, 14, 62.

[310] *United States Diplomatic and Consular Staff in Tehran (United States of America v Iran)*, Judgment, 24 May 1980, ICJ Reports 1980, 3, 29–30.

[311] *Military and Paramilitary Activities in and against Nicaragua (Nicaragua v United States of America)*, Merits, Separate Opinion of Judge Ago, 27 June 1986, paras 16, 18, ICJ Reports 1986, 188, 190.

(ARSIWA Article 8). Nevertheless, in its reasoning, the ICJ seems to merge the criteria of dependence and control by emphasizing 'the potential for control inherent in the degree of the *contras*' dependence on aid', as such entailing an absence of actual or effective control (*contrôle effectif*).[312] This juxtaposition might suggest that the ICJ intended to apply a test of attributability of acts and omissions of *de facto* organs, not of private individuals, as corroborated by the Court's reliance on a test of absence of real autonomy of the *contras* vis-à-vis the government.[313] Therefore, paragraph 115 of *Nicaragua*, which has been interpreted as disclosing a test for attribution of the acts of private individuals, provides, instead, a test for *de facto* agency:

> The Court has taken the view (paragraph 110 above) that United States participation, even if preponderant or decisive, in the financing, organizing, training, supplying and equipping of the *contras*, the selection of its military or paramilitary targets, and the planning of the whole of its operation, is still insufficient in itself, on the basis of the evidence in the possession of the Court, for the purpose of attributing to the United States the acts committed by the *contras* in the course of their military or paramilitary operations in Nicaragua. All the forms of United States participation mentioned above, and even the general control by the respondent State over a force with a high degree of dependency on it, would not in themselves mean, without further evidence, that the United States directed or enforced the perpetration of the acts contrary to human rights and humanitarian law alleged by the applicant State. Such acts could well be committed by members of the *contras* without the control of the United States. For this conduct to give rise to legal responsibility of the United States, it would in principle have to be proved

[312] *Military and Paramilitary Activities in and against Nicaragua (Nicaragua v United States of America)*, Merits, Judgment, 27 June 1986, paras 109–11, ICJ Reports 1986, 14, 62: 'However, whether the United States Government at any stage devised the strategy and directed the tactics of the *contras* depends on the extent to which the United States made use of the potential for control inherent in that dependence. The Court already indicated that it has insufficient evidence to reach a finding on this point. ... In the view of the Court it is established that the *contra* force has, at least at one period been so dependent on the United States that it could not conduct its crucial or most significant military and paramilitary activities without the multi-faceted support of the United States. This finding is fundamental in the present case. Nevertheless, adequate direct proof that all or the great majority of *contra* activities during that period received this support has not been, and indeed probably could not be, advanced in every respect. It will suffice the Court to stress that a degree of control by the United States Government, as described above is inherent in the position in which the *contra* force finds itself in relation to that Government.'

[313] *Military and Paramilitary Activities in and against Nicaragua (Nicaragua v United States of America)*, Merits, Judgment, 27 June 1986, paras 114–15, ICJ Reports 1986, 14, 64–65. See ICTY, Appeals Chamber, *Tadić*, IT-94-1-A, Judgement, 15 July 1999, 45, para 112: 'Admittedly, in paragraph 115 of the Nicaragua judgement, where "effective control" is mentioned, it is unclear whether the Court is propounding "effective control" as an alternative test to that of "dependence and control" set out earlier in paragraph 109, or is instead spelling out the requirements of the same test. The Appeals Chamber believes that the latter is the correct interpretation.'

that that State had effective control of the military or paramilitary operations in the course of which the alleged violations were committed.[314]

In *Armed Activities*, the ICJ was required by the Democratic Republic of the Congo to declare the acts of the Congo Liberation Movement as attributable to the State of Uganda. Similar to the findings in *Nicaragua*, the Court did not find credible evidence to establish that Uganda created the MLC, although activities of training and military support were acknowledged by the respondent, and, consequently, could not ascertain a relationship of control between Uganda and those paramilitaries. The ICJ basically left unaffected the issue of the degree of control, thus affirming the precedent of *Nicaragua*:

> Accordingly, no issue arises in the present case as to whether the requisite tests are met for sufficiency of control of paramilitaries (see *Military and Paramilitary Activities in and against Nicaragua (Nicaragua* v. *United States of America), Merits, Judgment, I.C.J. Reports 1986*, pp. 62-65, paras. 109-115).[315]

The issue of control between States, on one side, and (the activities of) paramilitaries, on the other side, has also been adjudicated by the Trial Chamber and the Appeals Chamber of the ICTY in the *Tadić* case.[316] More precisely, the Trial Chamber presented the issue as one of applicability of Article 4 of the Fourth Geneva Convention (Convention relative to the Protection of Civilian Persons in Time of War), as referred by Article 2 of the Tribunal's Statute, in relation to the qualification of the victims of Tadić's atrocities as 'protected persons'.[317] Therefore, as a preliminary and antecedent question to this legal issue, the Trial Chamber had to define whether the armed conflict between the Republic of Bosnia and Herzegovina, on one side, and the Bosnian Serb forces (Republika Srpska and VRS), on the other side, was 'international' in character. This finding could be established only upon attribution of the acts and omissions of such entities to the

[314] *Military and Paramilitary Activities in and against Nicaragua (Nicaragua v United States of America)*, Merits, Judgment, 27 June 1986, para 115, ICJ Reports 1986, 14, 64–65.

[315] *Armed Activities in the Territory of the Congo (DRC v Uganda)*, Judgment, 19 December 2005, para 160, ICJ Reports 2005, 168, 226.

[316] ICTY, Trial Chamber, *Tadić*, Case No IT-94-1-T, Opinion and Judgment, 7 May 1997; ICTY, Appeals Chamber, *Tadić*, IT-94-1-A, Judgement, 15 July 1999, 124 ILR 61. See Marco Sassòli, 'La première décision de la chambre d'appel du Tribunal Pénal pour l'ex Yougoslavie: *Tadić* (Compétence)' (1996) 100 Révue Générale de Droit International Public 101.

[317] Convention (IV) relative to the Protection of Civilian Persons in Time of War, Geneva, 12 August 1949, 75 UNTS 287:

Article 4
Definition of Protected Persons

> Persons protected by the Convention are those who, at a given moment and in any manner whatsoever, find themselves, in case of a conflict or occupation, in the hands of a Party to the conflict or Occupying Power of which they are not nationals.

Federal Republic of Yugoslavia (FRY), as party to the conflict or Occupying Power. Hence, the Trial Chamber had to resort to principles of attribution under public international law ('as a rule of customary international law, the acts of persons, groups or organizations may be imputed to a State where they act as *de facto* organs or agents of that State').[318] The Chamber immediately clarified that rules of State responsibility were concerned only with regard to the issue of attributability, as referred to via Article 2 of the ICTY Statute and the Fourth Geneva Convention, the remaining issues being determined only under international humanitarian law.[319] Thus, the Tribunal deliberately intended to apply:

> general principles of international law relating to State responsibility for *de facto* organs or agents to the specific circumstance.[320]

The essence of the test for *de facto* agency was found to correspond to the threshold of *great dependence and* (effective) *control*, such as the one established in *Nicaragua*.[321] In the absence of sufficient evidence as to the exercise of real command and control, but rather in a situation of coordination,[322] the Trial Chamber concluded that the Republika Sprska and the VRS were 'mere allies, albeit highly dependent allies' of the FRY, thus denying attribution of the acts and omissions of the former to the latter.[323]

Presiding Judge McDonald dissented with the majority, which she believed to improperly import a test of effective control into the determination of whether victims of crimes against humanity can be considered to be protected persons.[324] On the contrary, she read *Nicaragua* as establishing two different and separate tests: one for *de facto* agents (dependence); another one for attribution to the State of acts of individuals (control).[325] This interpretation induced her to conclude that the requirement of effective control only affected the latter, while a test of dependence

[318] ICTY, Trial Chamber, *Tadić*, Case No IT-94-1-T, Opinion and Judgment, 7 May 1997, 204, para 584.

[319] ibid: 'Were the Trial Chamber to make this imputation it would not be concerned further with questions of State responsibility for those acts.'

[320] ibid 205, 207, para 585, 587.

[321] ibid 207, para 588.

[322] ibid 212, 215, 216, paras 600, 604, 605.

[323] ibid 216, para 606.

[324] ICTY, *Tadić*, Case No IT-94-1-T, Separate and Dissenting Opinion of Judge McDonald Regarding the Applicability of Article 2, 7 May 1997, 292–94. Nevertheless, Judge McDonald held that the effective control was supported by the evidence in the case before her.

[325] This is indeed an ambiguity of *Military and Paramilitary Activities in and against Nicaragua (Nicaragua v United States of America)*, Merits, Judgment, 27 June 1986, para 109, ICJ Reports 1986, 14, 62. Analytically, the reading of Judge McDonald is correct, as we also tried to show above. Nevertheless, the ICJ really elaborated a combined test of dependence and control for *de facto* organs. Although McDonald's analysis is apposite in principle, in fact the ICJ did not render criteria for the attribution of 'private' individuals requiring effective control.

was sufficient as to the former.[326] Interestingly, Judge McDonald delivered this judicial *dictum* (albeit as *obiter* in a dissenting opinion) on the degree of State control over the conduct of private individuals:

> State responsibility for the acts of individuals hinges on such [*effective*] control and it must therefore be established, but here that is not an issue. ... a close reading of *Nicaragua* leads me to conclude that the effective control standard supports a distinct and separate basis for the attribution of the conduct of non-agents to a State, and that it is not a necessary element for a finding of an agency relationship.[327]

Concerning the (*de facto*) agency test, the President emphasized the policies of international humanitarian law ('individual— as opposed to State—responsibility'), which she considered to be undermined by the approach adopted by the majority.[328] Indeed, the dissenting argument found that the test of dependence alone embodied a sufficient criteria for the purposes of attribution.

The Prosecutor appealed the judgment of the Trial Chamber, which prompted the appeal decision of 15 July 1999. The Appeals Chamber commenced its judicial reasoning from the Third Geneva Convention (Convention relative to the Treatment of Prisoners of War). Article 4A(2) of said Convention establishes a requirement of 'belonging to a party to the conflict' in order to qualify for the status of lawful combatants.[329] The ICTY interpreted this requirement to entail control, dependence, and allegiance, but first and foremost control,[330] or subjection to authority or control.[331] While asserting that such test of control was firmly established in international humanitarian law, the ICTY held that the latter should be supplemented by general international rules providing the criteria to qualify individuals as acting as *de facto* State organs:[332]

[326] ICTY, *Tadić*, Case No IT-94-1-T, Separate and Dissenting Opinion of Judge McDonald Regarding the Applicability of Article 2, 7 May 1997, 296, 288: '*the appropriate test of agency from Nicaragua is one of "dependency and control" and a showing of effective control is not required.*'

[327] ibid 298–99.

[328] ibid 297.

[329] Convention (III) relative to the Treatment of Prisoners of War, Geneva, 12 August 1949, 75 UNTS 135:

Article 4
Prisoners of War

A. Prisoners of war, in the sense of the present Convention, are persons belonging to one of the following categories, who have fallen into the power of the enemy:

...

(2) Members of other militias and members of other volunteer corps, including those of organized resistance movements, belonging to a Party to the conflict and operating in or outside their own territory, even if this territory is occupied ...

[330] ICTY, Appeals Chamber, *Tadić*, IT-94-1-A, Judgement, 15 July 1999, 38, paras 94–95.

[331] ibid 39, para 97.

[332] ibid 39, para 98.

> Consequently, it is necessary to examine the notion of control by a State over individuals, laid down in general international law, for the purpose of establishing whether those individuals may be regarded as acting as *de facto* State officials. This notion can be found in those general international rules on State responsibility which set out the legal criteria for attributing to a State acts performed by individuals not having the formal status of State officials.[333]

Contrary to the Prosecution's *pledoirie*, the Tribunal expressly held that the (preliminary) finding on *de facto* agency was governed by the same criteria under both public international law and international humanitarian law. Besides, while the Prosecution adopted the reading of *Nicaragua* proposed by Judge McDonald, the Appeals Chamber basically confirmed that in that case the ICJ rendered a test (or a set of tests) for *de facto* organs only.[334] Upon this finding, the ICTY intervened to 'overrule' the ICJ's determination (*Nicaragua*) on the degree of control required for *de facto* agency (effective control), perceived as unpersuasive and not consonant with the logic of the entire system of the international law of State responsibility, not only with the policies of international humanitarian law. Accordingly, the ICTY advanced an innovative survey of customary international law. On one hand, it held that between a State and unorganized groups of persons the link must be one of effective control in a context of specific instructions concerning the performance of the acts at issue.[335] On the other hand, the case of an 'organized and hierarchically structured group', such as a paramilitary group, should be distinguished, an *overall* control (*contrôle globale*) being sufficient for the purposes of attribution.[336] Such a prong of overall control comprises more than the mere provision of financial assistance or military equipment or training, but does not necessarily include the issue of specific orders by the State, or its direction on each individual operation.[337] *Tadić*'s determination on the attribution of acts of *de facto* organs based on dependence and (overall) control represents a marked departure from the applicable customary international law ('fragmentation through

[333] ibid 40, para 98. The expression 'individuals not having the formal status of State officials' should be interpreted as referring to persons being *de facto* agents, not to so-called 'private' individuals under ARSIWA Article 8. This remark is corroborated by the immediate reference to *Nicaragua* in the following paragraphs.

[334] ibid 43, para 107: 'The Appeals Chamber considers that the Prosecution's submissions are based on a misreading of the judgement of the International Court of Justice and a misapprehension of the doctrine of State responsibility on which that judgement is grounded.'

[335] ibid 48, para 118.

[336] ibid 49, para 120: 'One should distinguish the situation of individuals acting on behalf of a State without specific instructions, from that of individuals making up an organised and hierarchically structured group, such as a military unit or, in case of war or civil strife, armed bands of irregulars or rebels. Plainly, an organised group differs from an individual in that the former normally has a structure, a chain of command and a set of rules as well as the outward symbols of authority. Normally a member of the group does not act on his own but conforms to the standards prevailing in the group and is subject to the authority of the head of the group.'

[337] ibid 59, para 137.

conflicting interpretations of general law'),[338] which was consistently affirmed by the ICTY in subsequent cases (*Aleksovski*,[339] *Blaškić*,[340] *Mucić*,[341] *Naletilić and Martinović*,[342] *Kordić and Čerkez*,[343] *Delalić*).[344]

The issue of the degree of control required for *de facto* agents was again determined by the ICJ in the case of the *Bosnian Genocide*, which dealt with the same historical facts at the basis of the *Tadić* case.[345] This case has already been discussed with an emphasis on its 'loyalty' to *Nicaragua*, manifested by the ICJ establishing the requirements of strict control, on one side,[346] and complete and total dependence, on the other side, for a finding on *de facto* organs.[347] In this paragraph, the analysis will focus on the issue of attribution of acts of individuals on the basis of instructions, or direction, or control by the State pursuant to ARSIWA Article 8 ('a completely separate issue').[348] In this respect, the Court phrased its *thema decidendum* with the following language:

> What must be determined is whether FRY organs—incontestably having that status under the FRY's internal law—originated the genocide by issuing instructions to the perpetrators or exercising direction or control, and whether, as a result, the conduct of organs of the Respondent, having been the cause of the commission of acts in breach of its international obligations, constituted a violation of those obligations.[349]

The ICJ recalled *Nicaragua* by proposing a reasoning that is similar in structure (but not in its spirit) to the interpretation proposed by Judge McDonald in her dissenting opinion in *Tadić*. Indeed, the ICJ held that *Nicaragua* established two distinct tests: one for *de facto* agents, namely, complete dependence; another one for individuals, that is, effective control.[350] Remarkably, *Nicaragua* did not intend to

[338] Martii Koskenniemi, 'Fragmentation of International Law: Difficulties Arising from the Diversification and Expansion of International Law', Report of the Study Group of the International Law Commission, 13 April 2006, paras 49-52, document A/AC.4/L.682, 31–33.
[339] ICTY, Appeals Chamber, *Aleksovski*, Case No IT-95-14/I-A, Judgement, 24 March 2000.
[340] ICTY, Trial Chamber, *Blaskić*, Case No IT-95-14/T, Judgement, 3 March 2000.
[341] ICTY, Appeals Chamber, *Mucić et al "Čelebići Camp"*, Case No IT-96-21-A, Judgement, 20 February 2001.
[342] ICTY, Trial Chamber, *Naletilić and Martinović*, Case No IT-98-34-T, Judgement, 31 March 2003.
[343] ICTY, Appeals Chamber, *Kordić and Čerkez "Lašva Valley"*, Case No IT-95-14/2-A, Judgment, 17 December 2004.
[344] ICTY, Appeals Chamber, *Delalić*, Case No IT-96-21-A, Judgement, 20 February 2001.
[345] See section 3 of this chapter.
[346] *Application of the Convention on the Prevention and Punishment of the Crime of Genocide (Bosnia and Herzegovina v Serbia and Montenegro)*, Judgment, 26 February 2007, para 391, ICJ Reports 2007, 43, 204.
[347] ibid 43, 205, 206.
[348] ibid 207, para 397.
[349] ibid.
[350] ibid 208, para 400.

dictate a rule of attribution of acts of private individuals (non-agents), as currently enshrined in ARSIWA Article 8, but to establish a threshold of control (ie, effective control) to be applied within the test of 'dependence and control' for the attribution of acts and omissions of *de facto* agents. Therefore, in *Bosnian Genocide*, the ICJ, for the first time, qualified as *effective* the degree of State control required for attributability of acts of 'private' individuals, the only earlier precedent outside the ICJ's case law being the *obiter dictum* in the dissenting opinion of Judge McDonald in *Tadić*.[351] A conflict on this point of law with the ICTY Appeals Chambers has (or should have) never been at issue, since *Tadić* did not rule on persons under ARSIWA Article 8 (as instead submitted by the ICJ).[352] This clarification may assist in mitigating the 'conflict' between the two international judiciaries sitting in The Hague.[353]

5.3.5 Thresholds of State 'Control' on Individuals and *De Facto* Organs

The application of the test of effective State control for the sake of attribution under ARSIWA Article 8 is persuasive as against any laxer criteria, in that attribution to the State of acts or omissions of private individuals is to be maintained as exceptional, not really as a general rule. Hence, its operation can be triggered only upon restrictive prerequisites, such as the effectiveness of control or the actual character of instructions, as is consistent with the entire architecture and mind of the international law of State responsibility.[354] Hence, *Bosnian Genocide* stands as persuasive authority as to the survey of customary international law on this specific issue. The effective control test would also turn out to be sufficient to attribute the conduct of SOEs or parastatals to States. As discussed above,[355] in that context attributability intersects a different problem, since attribution to the State of the conduct *jure privatorum* of State-controlled companies ideally clashes with the traditional concept of corporate separateness and with the strict requirements for the application of the piercing of the corporate veil doctrines under municipal law.

[351] See *supra* within this section.

[352] *Application of the Convention on the Prevention and Punishment of the Crime of Genocide (Bosnia and Herzegovina v Serbia and Montenegro)*, Judgment, 26 February 2007, paras 402, 404–06, ICJ Reports 2007, 43, 209, 212.

[353] ibid 209, para 403: 'the Court observes that the ICTY was not called upon in the Tadić case, nor is it in general called upon, to rule on questions of State responsibility, since its jurisdiction is criminal and extends over persons only. . . . The situation is not the same for positions adopted by the ICTY on issues of general international law which do not lie within the specific purview of its jurisdiction and, moreover, the resolution of which is not always necessary for deciding the criminal cases before it.' See also *Military and Paramilitary Activities in and against Nicaragua (Nicaragua v United States of America)*, Merits, Judgment, 27 June 1986, para 116, ICJ Reports 1986, 14, 65: 'What the Court has to investigate is not the complaints relating to alleged violations of humanitarian law by the *contras*, regarded by Nicaragua as imputable to the United States, but rather unlawful acts for which the United States may be responsible directly in connection with the activities of the *contras*. The lawfulness or otherwise of such acts of the United States is a question different from the violations of humanitarian law of which the *contras* may or may not have been guilty.'

[354] See section 5.1 of this chapter.

[355] See section 5.3.2 of this chapter.

This conclusion as to ARSIWA Article 8 stands without prejudice to the applicability of a different test for *de facto* organs under ARSIWA Article 4. In *Tadić*, the ICTY advanced a test of overall control between the State and 'organized' groups (paramilitaries), leaving the requirement of effective control between a government and 'unorganized' groups unaffected. Other international courts also appear to favour laxer mechanisms of attribution to the State of the conduct of 'entities' that are, in one way or another, separate from its institutional system of command and control.[356] Notably, the ICTY, moved by the policy to condemn the perpetrators of international crimes, suggests to the international community and judiciary not to refuse or postpone the demand of a parallel finding of both international criminal responsibility of individuals and responsibility for internationally wrongful acts of such States that used the convicted individuals as their instruments:

> states may not evade responsibility towards other states when they, instead of acting through their own officials, use groups of individuals to undertake actions that are intended to damage, or in the event do damage, other states; if states so behave, they must answer for the actions of those individuals, even if such individuals have gone beyond their mandate or agreed upon tasks—lest the worst abuses should go unchecked.[357]

The ICTY's position that the finding of *de facto* agency should be undertaken upon application of the same criteria both in public international law (as a rule of attribution for the purposes of State responsibility for internationally wrongful acts) and international humanitarian law (as an antecedent question to establish the status of protected persons or lawful combatants) is methodologically correct.[358] Accordingly, the ICJ and specialized international courts may address the same legal issues and adjudicate them consistently to the benefit of the international legal system. Hence, the answer to the problem is not resorting to *lex specialis*, but rather engaging in a thorough study of the customary international law.[359] Therefore, a fair analysis of 'what actually happens in the life of international society' should

[356] ECtHR, *Loizidou v Turkey*, Judgment, Merits, 18 December 1996, para 56, 108 ILR 443.

[357] Antonio Cassese, 'The *Nicaragua* and *Tadić* Tests Revisited in Light of the ICJ Judgement on Genocide in Bosnia' (2007) 18 European Journal of International Law 649, 654.

[358] *Contra*, Theodor Meron, 'Classification of Armed Conflict in the Former Yugoslavia: Nicaragua's Fallout' (1998) 92 American Journal of International Law 236, 237, 239: 'even a quick perusal of international law literature would establish that imputability is not a test commonly used in judging whether a foreign intervention leads to the internationalization of the conflict and the applicability of those rules of international humanitarian law that govern armed conflicts of an international character.'; Katherine Del Mar 'The Requirement of 'Belonging' under International Humanitarian Law' (2010) 21 European Journal of International Law 105, 116–17.

[359] Antonio Cassese, 'The *Nicaragua* and *Tadić* Tests Revisited in Light of the ICJ Judgement on Genocide in Bosnia' (2007) 18 European Journal of International Law 649, 687.

be undertaken.[360] More accurately, it should be investigated whether the requirement of effective control has currently faded within the test for *de facto* agencies. As underlined above, the threshold of effective control has been explicitly demanded by the ICJ in *Nicaragua*, but has not been explicitly incorporated in *Bosnian Genocide* ('strict', it was written). Indeed, *Bosnian Genocide* expressly resorted to the effective control test in the radically different context of ARSIWA Article 8 as to the attributability of conduct of private individuals. The desuetude of the test of effective control by States on *de facto* organs propounded by *Nicaragua*[361] appears to be a viable argument for fostering the policies supported by the ICTY, although this also poses a risk to the preservation of the orderly functioning of the rules of attribution ('rules of engagement' of international responsibility) that are dictated by public international law for the security of international relations.

Tadić preferred not to embark in a complete *overruling* of the entire test of *de facto* agency, but rather *distinguished it*, based on the difference between organized and non-organized groups for the sake of attribution. This distinction turns out to be artificial and as such not really tenable as to the promotion of reform of customary international law on the attribution of the conduct of *de facto* organs. The ICTY's reasoning shifts the requirement of effectiveness from the control between States and 'organizations of persons' to the structure of such organizations. The circumstance of a chain of command and control inside a given entity (as entrusted to a 'head' or 'director') cannot affect the different issue of control between State organs and that very entity. In so deciding, the ICTY could even be interpreted as confirming the centrality of the test of 'effective control' in order to establish a *de facto* agency for all other cases of 'non-organized' groups. Instead, it seems more decisive to emphasize the desuetude of the prong of effective control for a finding of *de facto* organs. This argument may be advocated on the basis of the consistent indications rendered by specialized international tribunals and the eloquent silence (and different *sedes materiae* of the test of effective control) adopted by the ICJ in *Bosnian Genocide*.

6. Concluding Remarks

ARSIWA have ultimately provided a codification of customary international law as to the content and scope of the rules of attribution to the State of the conduct of State organs, State instrumentalities, and individuals, as a 'subjective' element for

[360] Report of the International Law Commission on the Work of its Twenty-Fifth Session, 7 May–13 July 1973, para 11, document A/9010/REV.1, Yearbook of the International Law Commission, 1973, Volume II, 161, 190, document A/CN.4/SER. A/1973/Add. 1.

[361] 'Effective control' was demanded in the *Zafiro* case as to the control between superior and subordinate *de jure* organs in the navy personnel. See *D Earnshaw and Others (Great Britain) v United States (Zafiro case)*, 30 November 1925, 6 RIAA 160.

the establishment of State responsibility for internationally wrongful acts. As was already emerging from the early practice of the Mixed Claims Commissions, the law of attribution has been systematically codified through the *travaux* of the ILC, notably under the guidance of Roberto Ago as special rapporteur for the topic of State responsibility. The rules of attribution were finally codified in ARSIWA and received further systematic scholarly attention and judicial analysis by the ICJ, especially in the *Bosnian Genocide* case (where the ICJ finally delimitated the scope of application of ARSIWA Article 4, as to *de facto* organs, and ARSIWA Article 8, as to 'private' individuals).[362] Indeed, a comprehensive examination of attribution issues turns out to be beneficial to understand the normative specificity and independence of each single test for attribution of acts and omissions to the sovereign. Moreover, a systematic understanding of the rules of attribution is relevant (and necessary) to foster their correct application in the realm of so-called 'self-contained' regimes, where an interaction with *lex specialis* issues may be in place, as will be discussed in the following chapter.

In this clearer context of evaluation and elucidation of the customary international rules of attribution, critical issues still persist. The bulk of controversy has hinged on the centrality of the legal test of control in relation to attribution issues in various respects:

a) Control within the State apparatus between superior and subordinate officials, for instance within the armed forces (ARSIWA Article 4.1);
b) State control for the purposes of a finding of *de facto* organ (ARSIWA Article 4.2);
c) State control for the purposes of a finding of the status of State instrumentality (ARSIWA Article 5);
d) State 'direction or control' on individuals (ARSIWA Article 8).

The key factor for the determination of the intensity of control between the State and a person or entity is the circumstance of the 'actor' having or not having separate juristic personality (especially of private law) vis-à-vis the State. This feature structurally distinguishes State organs ('*les organs de l'Etat, c'est l'Etat lui-même*') from 'State entities' and 'private' individuals.[363] The control of the State on its organs (*de jure* or *de facto*) should not necessarily be effective, which was sometimes established in early cases and scholarship. This is manifestly confirmed by the customary international rule of attribution of *ultra vires* conduct of State officials

[362] Alain Pellet, 'Remarques sur la jurisprudence récente de la C.I.J. dans le domaine de la responsabilité internationale' in Marcelo Kohen, Robert Kolb, and Djacoba Liva Tehindrazanarivelo (eds), *Perspective of International Law in the 21st Century. Liber Amicorum Professor Christian Dominicé* (Martinus Nijhoff Publishers 2012) 321.

[363] Pierre-Marie Dupuy, 'Les émanations engagent-elles la responsabilité des Etats? Etude de droit international des investissements' (2006) EUI Working Paper LAW No 2006/7, 5.

under ARSIWA Article 7, a corollary of the cardinal principles of primacy of international law, on the one hand, and of institutional unity and continuity of the State, on the other. The institutional link of the status of *organ* (even if established *ex post facto*) normatively supplements the absence of an official empowerment (authority or superior instructions) to undertake particular conduct. This principle should also receive full-fledged application in the case of *de facto* organs, which, once the establishment of *de facto* agency has been completed, are to be treated exactly as if they were *de jure* organs as to the relevant regime of attribution of conduct.

From the foregoing examination of the international law of attribution, it seems that the concept of *agency* applies with two different meanings. There is a 'public law' notion of agency, which operates for State organs (*de jure* and *de facto*), intended as persons acting *on behalf of* the State. This concept is described by a legal mechanism of institutional 'identification' of the State with its organs, so that their conduct is considered to be executed by the State itself. The 'public law' notion of agency is also found in connection with the conduct of State instrumentalities, but only in so far as they exercise governmental authority formally delegated by the State in the given instance in question. Indeed, customary international law does not provide for the category of *de facto* State instrumentalities for the purposes of attribution. There is also a 'private law' concept of agency, which operates for private individuals intended to be *non-agents* (pursuant to the public law notion of agency), similar to a legal mechanism of 'representation'. It is hardly tenable to hold that the acts of the private individuals constitute 'acts of the State' proper. It rather seems that the *effects* of the conduct of private individuals are exceptionally bestowed to the person of the State for the purposes of its international responsibility, on the ground of the restrictive prongs of instructions, or of direction or (effective) control. This elucidation, consistent with the ICJ's position in *Bosnian Genocide*, turns out to be relevant to understanding and justifying differences in the applicable regimes of attributability between the conduct of 'State actors', on one side, and 'non-state actors', on the other side.[364]

[364] Wolfgang G Friedmann, 'The Growth of State Control over the Individual, and its Effect upon the Rules of International State Responsibility' (1938) 19 British Year Book of International Law 118, 119, 144.

III
Attribution in International Investment Law

1. An Introduction to Attribution in International Investment Arbitration

This chapter aims to elucidate the resolution of problems of attribution of conduct to the State in the context of international investment arbitration ('investor–State dispute settlement' or ISDS).[1] International arbitration is an optional means of

[1] See specifically James Crawford, 'Investment Arbitration and the ILC Articles on State Responsibility' (2010) 25 ICSID Review—Foreign Investment Law Journal 127; Zachary Douglas, 'Other Specific Regimes of Responsibility: Investment Treaty Arbitration and ICSID' in James Crawford, Alain Pellet, and Simon Olleson (eds), *The Law of International Responsibility* (Oxford University Press 2010) 815; Yves Nouvel, 'Les entités paraétatiques dans la jurisprudence du CIRDI' in Charles Leben (ed), *Le Contentieux Arbitral Transnational Relatif à l'investissement. Nouveaux développements* (LGDJ 2006) 25; Pierre-Marie Dupuy, 'Les émanations engagent-elles la responsabilité des Etats? Etude de droit international des investissements' (2006) EUI Working Paper LAW No 2006/7; Jürgen Kurtz, 'The Paradoxical Treatment of the ILC Articles on State Responsibility in Investor-State Arbitration' (2010) 25 ICSID Review—Foreign Investment Law Journal 200; Kaj Hobér, 'State Responsibility and Attribution' in Peter Muchlinski, Federico Ortino, and Christoph Schreuer (eds), *The Oxford Handbook of International Investment Law* (Oxford University Press 2008) 550; Georgios Petrochilos, 'Attribution' in Katia Yannaca-Small (ed), *Arbitration under International Investment Agreements: A Guide to the Key Issues* (Oxford University Press 2010) 287; James Crawford and Paul Mertenskötter, 'The Use of the ILC's Attribution Rules in Investment Arbitration' in Meg N Kinnear, Geraldine R Fischer, Jara Mínguez Almeida, Luisa Fernanda Torres, and Mairée Uran Bidegain (eds), *Building International Investment Law. The First 50 Years of ICSID* (Kluwer Law International 2015) 27; Csaba Kovács, *Attribution in International Investment Law* (Kluwer Law International 2018); Nick Gallus, 'State Enterprises as Organs of the State and BIT Claims' (2006) 7 Journal of World Investment & Trade 761; Thomas W Wälde and Patricia K Wouters, 'State Responsibilty and the Energy Charter Treaty: the Rules Regarding State Enterprises, Entities, and Subnational Authorities' (1997) 2 Hofstra Law and Policy Symposium 117; Michael Feit, 'Responsibility of the State Under International Law for the Breach of Contract Committed by a State-Owned Entity' (2010) 28 Berkeley Journal of International Law 142; Michael Feit, 'Attribution and the Umbrella Clause: Is there a Way out of the Deadlock?' (2012) 21 Minnesota Journal of International Law 21; Srilal M Perera, 'State Responsibility: Ascertaining the Liability of States in Foreign Investment Disputes' (2005) 6 Journal of World Investment & Trade 499; Clifford Larsen, 'ICSID Jurisdiction: the Relationship of Contracting States to Sub-states Entities' in Norbert Horn (ed), *Arbitrating Foreign Investment Disputes* (Kluwer Law International 2004) 353; Abby Cohen Smutny, 'State Responsibility and Attribution: When is a State Responsible for the Acts of State Enterprises? *Emilio Agustín Maffezini v. The Kingdom of Spain*' in Todd Weiler (ed), *International Investment Law and Arbitration: Leading Cases from the ICSID, NAFTA, Bilateral Treaties and Customary International Law* (Cameron May 2005) 17; Albert Badia, 'Attribution of Conducts of State-Owned Enterprises Based on Control by the State' in Crina Baltag (ed), *ICSID Convention after 50 Years: Unsettled Issues* (Kluwer Law International 2016) 189; Albert Badia, *Piercing the Veil of State Enterprises in International Arbitration* (Kluwer Law International 2014); Emmanuel Gaillard and Jennifer Younan (eds), *State Entities in International Arbitration* (Juris Publishing, Inc 2008); Luca Schicho, *State Entities in International Investment Law* (Nomos 2012); Luca Schicho, 'Attribution and State Entities: Diverging Approaches

Attribution in International Law and Arbitration. Carlo de Stefano, Oxford University Press (2020).

DOI: 10.1093/law-oso/9780198844648.001.0001

dispute settlement, based on the Parties' will to arbitrate. Such consent may be contained in international investment agreements (IIAs) stipulated between States, investment contracts directly entered into by a State and an investor, or national investment statutes. The large majority of investment disputes are based on IIAs, notably bilateral investment treaties (BITs), as well as multilateral investment treaties.[2] The most popular forum for ISDS is the International Centre for Settlement of Investment Disputes (ICSID), headquartered in Washington, DC, and established by the Convention on the Settlement of Investment Disputes Between States and Nationals of Other States of 18 March 1965 (Washington Convention or ICSID Convention).[3] In addition, Parties are at liberty to elect a different forum and opt for the application of different arbitration rules, such as those administered under the auspices of the Permanent Court of Arbitration (PCA), the United Nations Commission of International Trade Law (UNCITRAL), the International Chamber of Commerce (ICC), the London Court of International Arbitration (LCIA), or the Stockholm Chamber of Commerce (SCC). When an arbitration clause is embodied in an IIA, no further consent to arbitrate is required from a Party, it being sufficient for the written consent of the investor of another Party to be contained in the request for arbitration filed before the elected forum (*arbitration without privity*).[4] Various images depicted by international investment law scholars convey the concept of the asymmetric nature of international investment arbitration having IIAs as its jurisdictional basis (treaty-based investment arbitration). This is the case in Zachary Douglas's idea of the hybrid foundations of investor–State arbitration, Anthea Roberts's reference to the Australian platypus discovered by the European colonizers in the XVIII century, and Andrea Bjorklund's metaphor of the marriage between public international law and international commercial arbitration.[5] The

in Investment Arbitration' (2011) 12 Journal of World Investment & Trade 283; Rudolf Dolzer and Christoph Schreuer, *Principles of International Investment Law* (2nd edn, Oxford University Press 2012) 216–27; Christoph Schreuer, with Loretta Malintoppi, August Reinisch, and Anthony Sinclair, *The ICSID Convention: A Commentary* (2nd edn, Cambridge University Press 2009) 151, paras 23–27.

[2] Examples of multilateral investment agreements are: Energy Charter Treaty (ECT) (Annex I of the Final Act of the European Energy Charter Conference), signed on 17 December 1994, 34 ILM 373; North American Free Trade Agreement (NAFTA), adopted 17 December 1992, entered into force 1 January 1994, 32 ILM 612; ASEAN Comprehensive Investment Agreement, signed at Cha-am, Thailand, on 26 February 2009, at http://www.asean.org/resources/publications/asean-publications/item/asean-comprehensive-investment-agreement; Dominican Republic–Central America–United States Free Trade Agreement (CAFTA-DR), signed on 5 August 2004, entered into force for all seven signatories on 1 January 2009, at https://ustr.gov/trade-agreements/free-trade-agreements/cafta-dr-dominican-republic-central-america-fta.

[3] Convention on the Settlement of Investment Disputes between States and Nationals of Other States (ICSID Convention), opened for signature at Washington on 18 March 1965, entered into force on 14 October 1966, 575 UNTS 159.

[4] Jan Paulsson, 'Arbitration Without Privity' (1995) 10 ICSID Review—Foreign Investment Law Journal 232, 233: 'By allowing direct recourse by private complainants with respect to such a wide range of issues, these treaties create a dramatic extension of arbitral jurisdiction in the international realm.'

[5] Zachary Douglas, 'The Hybrid Foundations of Investment Treaty Arbitration' (2003) 74 British Year Book of International Law 151; Anthea Roberts, 'Clash of Paradigms: Actors and Analogies Shaping the Investment Treaty System' (2013) 107 American Journal of International Law 45; Andrea K Bjorklund, 'The Emerging Civilization of Investment Arbitration' (2009) 113 Penn State Law Review 1269, 1272.

peculiar features of ISDS may lead scholars and observers to treat international investment arbitration as a realm apart from classic public international law disputes. This view emphasizes the procedural aspects of the structure of investment arbitration, but neglects the marked degree of affinity, not to mention identity, with the law applied by international investment tribunals and international courts. This chapter will comprehensively address the dialectics between customary international law and international investment law with regard to the resolution of issues of attribution by investor–State tribunals.

1.1 Customary International Law and 'Self-Contained' Regimes

The applicability of customary international law rules, including the international law of State responsibility, prospers in not only ICJ litigation but also the entire variety of cases filed before other international judicial or quasi-judicial bodies. These disputes include, inter alia, cases of international trade law within the WTO dispute settlement system, human rights litigation before the European Court of Human Rights (ECtHR), international humanitarian law cases before international criminal courts, maritime disputes before the International Tribunal of the Law of the Sea (ITLOS), or international investment litigation before investor–State arbitral tribunals. This list is based on certain assumptions. First, the application of the law of State responsibility does not necessarily assume a State-to-State contentious dimension.[6] While at the level of lawmaking the inter-state dimension persists, the beneficiaries of the rights created by international treaties may vary according to the will of the Parties.[7] Indeed, what is relevant is the State as holder of international obligations vis-à-vis another State or, where applicable, a non-state actor in case of a treaty for the benefit of third parties (*pacta in favorem tertii*).[8] This

[6] ARSIWA Article 33.2: 'This Part is without prejudice to any right, arising from the international responsibility of a State, which may accrue directly to any person or entity other than a State'. cf ARSIWA Commentaries 94. Accord, *Flemingo DutyFree Shop Private Limited v the Republic of Poland*, UNCITRAL, Award, 12 August 2016, para 420; *William Ralph Clayton, William Richard Clayton, Douglas Clayton, Daniel Clayton and Bilcon of Delaware Inc v Government of Canada*, UNCITRAL, PCA Case No 2009-04, 17 March 2015, para 307. Contra, *Wintershall Aktiengesellschaft v Argentine Republic*, ICSID Case No ARB/04/14, Award, 8 December 2008, para 113: 'The ILC's Articles on State Responsibility is a detailed and official study on the subject but it contains no rules and regulations of State Responsibility vis-à-vis non-State actors'.

[7] Mahnoush H Arsanjani and W Michael Reisman, 'Interpreting Treaties for the Benefit of Third Parties: The "Salvors' Doctrine" and the Use of Legislative History in Investment Treaties' (2010) 104 American Journal of International Law 597, 603.

[8] The beneficiary of an international investment treaty may even be a State-owned entity, or SOE, in relation to its activity *jure gestionis*. See *Ceskoslovenska Obchodni Banka, AS (CSOB) v The Slovak Republic*, ICSID Case No ARB/97/4, Decision on Jurisdiction, 24 May 1999, para 16; *CDC Group plc v Republic of Seychelles*, ICSID Case No ARB/02/14, Award, 17 December 2003, para 17; *Rumeli Telekom AS and Telsim Mobil Telekomunikasyon Hizmetleri AS v Republic of Kazakhstan*, ICSID Case No ARB/05/16, Award, 29 July 2008, paras 324–29; *Emilio Agustín Maffezini v The Kingdom of Spain*, ICSID Case No ARB/97/7, Decision on Jurisdiction, 25 January 2000, para 80; *Flughafen Zürich AG and Gestión e Ingeniería IDC SA v Bolivarian Republic of Venezuela*, ICSID Case No ARB/10/19, Laudo, 18

assumption remains unaffected by the application of the theory of either *direct* or *derivative* rights in order to categorize the investor's right to access international arbitration.[9] Second, and more generally, it should be emphasized that so-called 'self-contained' regimes (special subsystems of international law), including international investment law, are not impermeable as to the application of customary international law, irrespective of their 'regulatory thickness'.[10]

Upon elaboration of the reports on State responsibility by William Riphagen,[11] Bruno Simma doctrinally analysed the concept of self-contained regimes around three decades ago.[12] Notably, he endorsed the 'self-containment' regime (ie, resort to special secondary rules) for the sake of 'effectiveness of the primary rules concerned and ... orderly procedures and collective decisions'.[13] In a more recent

November 2014, paras 279–86; *Beijing Urban Construction Group Co Ltd v Republic of Yemen*, ICSID Case No ARB/14/30, Decision on Jurisdiction, 17 May 2017, paras 31 et seq.; *Masdar Solar & Wind Cooperatief UA v Kingdom of Spain*, ICSID Case No ARB/14/1, Award, 16 May 2018, paras 166–73. See Aaron Broches, 'The Convention on the Settlement of Investment Disputes Between States and Nationals of Other States' (1972-II) 136 Recueil des Cours 331, 340, 355: 'a mixed economy company or government-owned corporation should not be disqualified as a "national of another Contracting State" unless it is acting as an agent for the government or is discharging an essentially governmental function'.

---

9 Eric De Brabandere, *Investment Treaty Arbitration as Public International Law. Procedural Aspects and Implications* (Cambridge University Press 2014) 62.

10 *Ex multis*, James Bacchus, 'Not in Clinical Isolation' in Gabrielle Marceau (ed), *A History of Law and Lawyers in the GATT/WTO. The Development of the Rule of Law in the Multilateral Trading System* (Cambridge University Press 2015) 507, clearly referring to the Appellate Body Report, *United States—Standards for Reformulated and Conventional Gasoline (US—Gasoline)*, WT/DS2/AB/R, 29 April 1996, 17; Robert Howse, 'From Politics to Technocracy—and Back Again: The Fate of the Multilateral Trade Regime' (2002) 96 American Journal of International Law 94, 110; Giorgio Sacerdoti, 'The Application of BITs in Time of Economic Crisis: Limits to Their Coverage, Necessity and the Relevance of WTO Law' in Giorgio Sacerdoti et al, *General Interests of Host States in International Investment Law* (Cambridge University Press 2014) 3, 18–19; Maurizio Arcari, 'Le juge et la codification du droit de la responsabilité: quelques remarques concernant l'application judiciaire des articles de la CDI sur la responsabilité de l'État pour fait internationalement illicite' in Nerina Boschiero et al (eds), *International Courts and the Development of International Law: Essays in Honour of Tullio Treves* (TMC Asser Press 2013) 19, 25, 29: '*Tout en présentant des nuances et des implications différentes, les trois décisions considérées confirment l'inclination des juges internationaux vers une utilisation "systèmique" des articles de la CDI aux fins du traitement des problèmes qui se posent dans le contentieux de la responsabilité. Une telle approche contribuerait bien évidemment à renforcer la valeur de principe des règles codifiées dans le Projet.*'; James Crawford, 'The ILC's Articles on Responsibility of States for Internationally Wrongful Acts: A Retrospect' (2002) 96 American Journal of International Law 874, 880: 'In my view, there cannot be, at the international level, any truly self-contained regime, hermetically sealed against bad weather'.

11 Willem Riphagen, Third Report on State Responsibility, by Mr Willem Riphagen, Special Rapporteur, 'The content, forms and degrees of international responsibility (part 2 of the draft articles)', 12 March, 30 March, and 5 May 1982, document A/CN.4/354 and Add.1 and 2, Yearbook of the International Law Commission, 1982, Volume II (Part One), 22, document A/CN.4/SER.A/1982/Add.l (Part 1).

12 Bruno Simma, 'Self-contained Regimes' (1985) 16 Netherlands Yearbook of International Law 111, 117: 'the concept of a "self-contained regime" should not be used as a synonym of "subsystem", but be reserved to designate a certain category of subsystems, namely those embracing, in principle, a full (exhaustive and definite) set of secondary rules. A "self-contained regime" would then be a subsystem which is intended to exclude more or less totally the application of the general legal consequences of wrongful acts, in particular the application of the countermeasures normally at the disposal of an injured party. As has been stated above, the majority of subsystems do not live up to this definition which is, however, the only one in accord with the normal meaning of the words "self-contained"'.

13 Bruno Simma, 'Self-contained Regimes' (1985) 16 Netherlands Yearbook of International Law 111, 135.

contribution, Bruno Simma and Dirk Pulkowski have examined in depth the residual operation of general secondary rules in connection with the existence and effectiveness of special secondary rules, established by international treaties inter se, notably addressing the topic of the recourse to countermeasures.[14] Accordingly, special international rules, seemingly more suited to the demands of enforcement of a given normative sector, replace the application of customary international law in light of its disposable nature. This is but an application of the general principle of *lex specialis* for the resolution of antinomies (*lex specialis derogat legi generali*).[15] This principle is functional to the concept of the sovereign equality of States in their international relations (*superiorem non recognoscens*) and to the horizontal and flexible paradigm of international law, notably lawmaking.[16] In general, there is no rule of hierarchy or rigidity (*lex superior derogat legi inferiori*) in international norms, save for the operation of peremptory norms of *jus cogens*, which are overriding and non-disposableby the Parties.[17] However, in case of lacunae in a normative subsystem, a fallback to customary international law is rendered necessary to complete the gap that is left in the self-contained regime.[18] To this extent, the applicability of general international law is restored, as a consequence of the 'failure' of

[14] Bruno Simma and Dirk Pulkowski, 'Of Planets and the Universe: Self-contained Regimes in International Law' (2006) 17 European Journal of International Law 483, 485: 'As international law has evolved into an elaborate, but fragmented, structure, in which multiple regimes govern the legal consequences of breach, the conceptual distinction between general and special laws remains important for maintaining systemic cohesion. In principle, the special secondary rules of the regime will prevail. Yet, to the extent that such rules are inexistent or ineffective, the general rules on state responsibility will remain applicable. Sociological regime differentiation does not preclude normative compatibility with general international law.'; Bruno Simma and Dirk Pulkowski, '*Leges Speciales* and Self-contained Regimes' in James Crawford, Alain Pellet, and Simon Olleson (eds), *The Law of International Responsibility* (Oxford University Press 2010) 139.

[15] Joost Pauwelyn, *Conflict of Norms in Public International Law. How WTO Law Relates to Other Rules of International Law* (Cambridge University Press 2003) 387 et seq.

[16] Jean Combacau, 'Le droit international: bric-à-brac ou système?' (1986) 31 Archives de Philosophie du Droit 85, 88; Hélène Ruiz Fabri, 'Genèse et disparition de l'État à l'époque contemporaine' (1992) 38 Annuaire Français de Droit International 153, 163; Christoph H Schreuer, 'The Waning of the Sovereign State: Towards a New Paradigm for International Law?' (1993) 4 European Journal of International Law 447, 454.

[17] Vienna Convention on the Law of Treaties (VCLT), signed on 23 May 1969, entered into force on 27 January 1980, 1155 UNTS 331, Article 53. See Alfred Verdross, '*Jus Dispositivum* and *Jus Cogens* in International Law' (1966) 60 American Journal of International Law 55: 'the question is whether all norms of international law have the character of *jus dispositivum* or if there exist some norms having the character of *jus cogens* too, from which no derogation is permitted by an agreement *inter partes*.' cf Robert Kolb, 'La détermination du concept de "*jus cogens*"' (2014) 118 Revue Générale de Droit International Public 5; Andrea Bianchi, 'Gazing at the Crystal Ball (again): State Immunity and *Jus Cogens* beyond *Germany v Italy*' (2013) 4 Journal of International Dispute Settlement 457; Hélène Ruiz Fabri, 'Enhancing the Rhetoric of *Jus Cogens*' (2012) 23 European Journal of International Law 1049. For a doctrinal position in favour of the so-called 'normative hierarchic theory', see Antonio Cassese, *International Law* (2nd edn, Oxford University Press 2005) 205–08.

[18] Martii Koskenniemi, *Fragmentation of International Law: Difficulties Arising from the Diversification and Expansion of International Law*, Report of the Study Group of the International Law Commission, 13 April 2006, para 64, document A/AC.4/L.682, 38.

the self-contained regime.[19] This framework is certainly compatible with ARSIWA Article 55 (*Lex specialis*):

> These articles do not apply where and to the extent that the conditions for the existence of an internationally wrongful act or the content or implementation of the international responsibility of a state are governed by special rules of international law.[20]

While the ARSIWA Commentaries do not expressly address the question of regime failure, the ILC has since espoused a 'generalist' approach, allowing for a fall-back to general secondary rules. As Martii Koskenniemi has stated it in relation to the *travaux* of ARSIWA:

> It was, in other words, accepted that the articles had residual nature, and that special regimes of responsibility could be adopted by States.[21]

With regard to the application of secondary rules of customary international law, as codified by ARSIWA, in the realm of international economic litigation, a cautious caveat against generalist solutions is found in legal scholarship. In relation to international investment arbitration, James Crawford has submitted:

> The ILC Articles are residual articles and an adjudicator must first look at the treaty under review and see what it says on the subject. If the treaty (such as a BIT) covers the field of the issue at stake, the ILC Articles have no role to play.[22]

In a similar vein, David Caron favours the preservation of the effectiveness of stipulations inter se, which may be undermined by the arbitrators' reliance on general international law solutions:

[19] Bruno Simma and Dirk Pulkowski, 'Of Planets and the Universe: Self-contained Regimes in International Law' (2006) 17 European Journal of International Law 483, 509. For a critique of the dominant 'regime failure doctrine', see Lorenzo Gradoni, *Regime failure nel diritto internazionale* (CEDAM 2009) 42–45.

[20] ARSIWA Commentaries 140, para 1: 'A treaty may expressly provide for its relationship with other rules. Often, however, it will not do so and the question will then arise whether the specific provision is to coexist with or exclude the general rule that would otherwise apply.'

[21] Martii Koskenniemi, *Fragmentation of International Law: Difficulties Arising from the Diversification and Expansion of International Law*, Report of the Study Group of the International Law Commission, 13 April 2006, para 142, document A/AC.4/L.682, 76.

[22] James Crawford, 'Investment Arbitration and the ILC Articles on State Responsibility' (2010) 25 ICSID Review—Foreign Investment Law Journal 127, 131.

> By too great and casual a deference to the *lex generalis* of the ILC draft articles, arbitrators may unconsciously undo the *lex specialis* of the parties.[23]

The relationship between general and special secondary rules deserves further study, notably in order to elucidate the scope of the margin of deviation of party autonomy from customary international law. The view that *lex specialis* ousts customary international law completely and to any extent is not ultimately accurate. *Lex specialis* is contracted for the sake of enhanced legal certainty, stability of legal relationships, and diminished defeasibility of bilateral or multilateral legal obligations, in order to dictate a norm that is closer (with a character of subsidiarity) to the problem that the contracting Parties intend to regulate ('*il paroît qu'on l'a voulu plus fortement*').[24] In light of the increasing demand to 'internationalize' various and multifaceted aspects of human intercourse (from human rights violations to trade and investment matters), States have massively resorted to international agreements inter se to face and solve the issues, the complexity of which had challenged the operation of classic (but somehow 'underdeveloped') customary international law.[25] Depending on the rule concerned, treaties may dictate norms that are either consistent or at variance with customary international law. *Lex specialis* comes into play in the former case, while in the latter case it is rather the *lex posterior* that operates. As to *lex specialis*, a treaty may reproduce the content or may also provide for a deviation from—but not really an objection to—customary international law, in terms of specification and quantitative development of the law. Accordingly, treaty law may provide and specify cases of application of international rules, which are not expressed, though possibly implied, in international custom. In other words, such stipulations may derogate from customary international law (*praeter legem*) but cannot undermine its core or indefeasible content (*contra legem*). As a consequence, *lex specialis* entails a confirmation of the content of customary international law. Instead, when treaty law objects to a rule of international law, it has a function of *lex posterior* with an effect of abrogation *inter partes* (*lex posterior derogat legi priori*). When customary international law is challenged by repeated objections in States' practices (or contrary evaluations by international courts), there is a persuasive case in favour of its desuetude or disappearance.

In light of this distinction, it is appropriate to delve into the operation of *lex specialis* (defined as treaty law that reproduces or specifies customary international law) in order to elucidate its comprehensive relationship with customary international law. In the *Nicaragua* case, the ICJ held:

23 David D Caron, 'The ILC Articles on State Responsibility: the Paradoxical Relationship Between Form and Authority' (2002) 96 American Journal of International Law 857, 872.

24 Emer de Vattel, *Le droit des gens, ou principes de la loi naturelle, appliqués à la conduit et aux affaires des nations et des souverains* (Londres 1758) Livre II, Chapitre XVII, § 316.

25 Wolfgang G Friedmann, 'Some Impacts of Social Organization on International Law' (1956) 50 American Journal of International Law 475, 476–77.

> even if the customary norm and the treaty norm were to have exactly the same content, this would not be a reason for the Court to hold that the incorporation of the customary norm into treaty law must deprive the customary norm of its applicability as *distinct* from that of the treaty norm. The existence of identical rules in international treaty law and customary law has been clearly recognized by the Court in the *North Sea Continental Shelf* cases. ... More generally, there are no grounds for holding that when customary international law is comprised of rules identical to those of treaty law, the latter 'supervenes' the former, so that the customary international law has no further existence of its own.[26]

By the same force of logic, it can be stated that customary international law retains its distinct applicability and axiologic function in coexistence with a possible *lex specialis* dictating *praeter legem* norms.[27] In such a situation of 'regulatory competition' between *lex generalis* and *lex specialis*, the latter prevails over the former in so far as it can exhaustively govern given phenomena. Otherwise, the self-contained system might encounter a failure, thus opening a path to the applicability of international custom (*fallback*).[28] The North American Free Trade Agreement (NAFTA) investment case of *Archer Daniels v Mexico* seems to support this theoretical framework:

> The Tribunal finds that Section A of Chapter Eleven offers a form of *lex specialis* to supplement the under-developed standards of customary international law relating to the treatment of aliens and property. In addition, Chapter Eleven confers upon the investor a right of action under Section B—through arbitration—that the dispute will be decided in accordance with the standards of Section A. ... Chapter Eleven of the NAFTA constitutes *lex specialis* in respect of its express content, but customary international law continues to govern all matters not covered by Chapter Eleven. In the context of Chapter Eleven, customary international law—as codified in the ILC Articles—therefore operates in a residual way.[29]

[26] *Military and Paramilitary Activities in and against Nicaragua (Nicaragua v United States of America)*, Merits, Judgment, 27 June 1986, para 177, ICJ Reports 1986, 14, 94-95 (emphasis added), referring to *North Sea Continental Shelf (Federal Republic of Germany v Denmark; Federal Republic of Germany v The Netherlands)*, Judgment, 20 February 1969, para 63, ICJ Reports 1969, 3, 39.

[27] Bruno Simma, 'Self-contained Regimes' (1985) 16 Netherlands Yearbook of International Law 111, 116: 'a treaty may create a subsystem of international law with its own, express or implied, "secondary" rules tailored to its "primary" rules. This does not necessarily mean that the existence of the subsystem *permanently* excludes the application of any *general* rules of customary international law relating to the legal consequences of wrongful acts.'

[28] Martii Koskenniemi, *Fragmentation of International Law: Difficulties Arising from the Diversification and Expansion of International Law*, Report of the Study Group of the International Law Commission, 13 April 2006, para 152(4), document A/AC.4/L.682, 82.

[29] *Archer Daniels Midland Company and Tate & Lyle Ingredients Americas, Inc v The United Mexican States*, ICSID Case No ARB (AF)/04/5, Award, 21 November 2007, paras 116–19.

The ICSID system is also considered to be a self-contained regime, at least in the wide notion of the concept upheld by ARSIWA.[30] This suggestion notably has a procedural dimension, since the ICSID Convention does not dictate substantive standards of protection of foreign investment. Indeed, as established by ICSID Convention Article 54(1), '[e]ach Contracting State shall recognize an award rendered pursuant to this Convention as binding and enforce the pecuniary obligations imposed by that award within its territories as if it were a final judgment of a court in that State.' This means that ICSID awards do not require orthodox ordinary proceedings of recognition in order to be enforced.[31] To this extent, as far as recognition is concerned, it may be concluded that the ICSID system is procedurally self-contained and autonomous from the domestic law machinery, rather than detached from general international law. As a confirmation, ICSID Convention Article 64 provides for the jurisdiction of the ICJ on disputes between Contracting States concerning the interpretation or application of the Convention.[32] In practice, the rule has not been applied, but represents an indication of the non-isolation

[30] Charles Leben, 'La responsabilité internationale de l'Etat sur le fondement des traités de promotion et de protection des investissements' (2004) 50 Annuaire Français de Droit International 683, 694; Zachary Douglas, 'Other Specific Regimes of Responsibility: Investment Treaty Arbitration and ICSID' in James Crawford, Alain Pellet, and Simon Olleson (eds), *The Law of International Responsibility* (Oxford University Press 2010) 815, 820: 'ICSID is another such regime.' See generally Aaron Broches, 'The Convention on the Settlement of Investment Disputes Between States and Nationals of Other States' (1972-II) 136 Recueil des Cours 331; Giorgio Sacerdoti, 'La Convenzione di Washington del 1965 per la soluzione delle controversie tra Stati e nazionali di altri Stati in materia di investimenti' (1969) 5 Rivista di Diritto Internazionale Privato e Processuale 614; Giorgio Sacerdoti, 'La Convenzione di Washington del 1965: bilancio di un ventennio dell'ICSID' (1987) 23 Rivista di Diritto Internazionale Privato e Processuale 13; C F Amerasinghe, 'The Jurisdiction of the International Centre for the Settlement of Investment Disputes' (1979) 19 Indian Journal of International Law 166; Georges R Delaume, 'Enforcement of State Contract Awards: Jurisdictional Pitfalls and Remedies' (1993) 8 ICSID Review—Foreign Investment Law Journal 29; Georges R Delaume, 'ICSID Arbitration and the Courts' (1983) 77 American Journal of International Law 784; Mario Amadio, *Le contentieux international de l'investissement privé et la Convention de la Banque Mondial du 18 mars 1965* (LGDJ 1967); Paul C Szasz, 'A Practical Guide to the Convention on Settlement of Investment Disputes' (1968) 1 Cornell Journal of International Law 1.

[31] On the contrary, non-ICSID awards (LCIA, ICC, UNCITRAL, SCC, etc) do need ordinary *exequatur* by the domestic judge. The distinction is of threshold importance with regard to the application of the test of immunity from jurisdiction vis-à-vis immunity from execution. Recognition proceedings have an adjudicative nature and, accordingly, are subject to the rules of immunity from jurisdiction, where the applicable test hinges on the distinction between *acta jure imperii* and *acta jure gestionis*. Since investment disputes regularly involve the exercise by States of sovereign prerogatives, a national judge may refuse *exequatur* of a non-ICSID award on the ground of immunity from suit. See Federal Court of Justice of Germany, Case No III ZB 40/12, 30 January 2013, *Werner Schneider as liquidator of Walter Bau AG v The Kingdom of Thailand*, (2013) 38 Yearbook Commercial Arbitration 384.

[32] ICSID Convention Article 64:

> ***Article 64***
>
> Any dispute arising between Contracting States concerning the interpretation or application of this Convention which is not settled by negotiation shall be referred to the International Court of Justice by the application of any party to such dispute, unless the States concerned agree to another method of settlement.

of the ICSID system from public international law, including in relation to procedural issues.[33] As far as the application of both primary and secondary international rules is concerned, the proper law governing investment disputes is usually—as above mentioned—an IIA, whose provisions embody *leges speciales*. In addition, ICSID Convention Article 42(1) envisages the residual application of 'the law of the Contracting State party to the dispute (including its rules on the conflict of laws) and such rules of international law as may be applicable'. To this extent, the absence or the insufficiency of the determinations of the Parties (*regime failure*) allow for the residual application of customary international law, consistent with the pattern endorsed by the ILC.[34] Accordingly, the example of international investment law warrants the predominant opinion as to the dialectics between *lex generalis* and *lex specialis*.[35]

1.2 Attribution in International Investment Law

The rules of attribution embodied in ARSIWA are generally recognized and applied by ISDS tribunals as a codification of customary international law.[36] However, IIAs—as agreements inter se—may codify different tests of attributability of acts

[33] Zachary Douglas, 'Other Specific Regimes of Responsibility: Investment Treaty Arbitration and ICSID' in James Crawford, Alain Pellet, and Simon Olleson (eds), *The Law of International Responsibility* (Oxford University Press 2010) 815, 816–17.

[34] This was acknowledged in *Asian Agricultural Products Ltd (AAPL) v Republic of Sri Lanka*, ICSID Case No ARB/87/3, Final Award, 27 June 1990, para 21: 'Furthermore, it should be noted that the Bilateral Investment Treaty is not a self-contained closed legal system limited to provide for substantive material rules of direct applicability, but it has to be envisaged within a wider juridical context in which rule from other sources are integrated through implied incorporation methods, or by direct reference to certain supplementary rules, whether of international law character or of domestic law nature.'

[35] Bruno Simma and Dirk Pulkowski, 'Two Worlds, but not Apart: International Investment Law and General International Law' in Marc Bungenberg, Jörn Griebel, Stephan Hobe, and August Reinisch (eds), *International Investment Law* (CH Beck-Hart-Nomos 2015) 361.

[36] *Flemingo DutyFree Shop Private Limited v the Republic of Poland*, UNCITRAL, Award, 12 August 2016, para 349, 420; *Tulip Real Estate and Development Netherlands BV v Republic of Turkey*, ICSID Case No ARB/11/28, Award, 10 March 2014, para 281; *Antoine Abou Lahoud and Leila Bounafeh-Abou Lahoud v Democratic Republic of the Congo*, ICSID Case No ARB/10/4, Award, 7 February 2014, para 375; *Saipem SpA v People's Republic of Bangladesh*, ICSID Case No ARB/05/07, Decision on Jurisdiction and Recommendation on Provisional Measures, 21 March 2007, para 148; *Bayindir Insaat Turizm Ticaret Ve Sanayi AS v Islamic Republic of Pakistan*, ICSID Case No ARB/03/29, Award, 27 August 2009, para 113, fn 19; *Noble Ventures, Inc v Romania*, ICSID Case No ARB/01/11, Award, 12 October 2005, para 69; *Jan de Nul NV and Dredging International NV v Arab Republic of Egypt*, ICSID Case No ARB/04/13, Award, 6 November 2008, para 156; *Gustav F W Hamester GmbH & Co KG v Republic of Ghana*, ICSID Case No ARB/07/24, Award, 18 June 2010, para 171; *Sergei Paushok, CJSC Golden East Company and CJSC Vostokneftegaz Company v The Government of Mongolia*, UNCITRAL, Award on Jurisdiction and Liability, 28 April 2011, para 576; *Emilio Agustín Maffezini v The Kingdom of Spain*, ICSID Case No ARB/97/7, Decision on Jurisdiction, 25 January 2000, para 76. Accord, Christoph Schreuer, with Loretta Malintoppi, August Reinisch, and Anthony Sinclair, *The ICSID Convention: A Commentary* (2nd edn, Cambridge University Press 2009) 150, para 233. See also Martins Paparinskis, 'Investment Treaty Arbitration and the New Law of State Responsibility' (2013) 24 European Journal of International Law 617, 618, who recognizes 'the presumption of positivity' of ARSIWA.

and omissions to sovereigns and consequently bind arbitrators to their application. This possibility is expressly recognized by the ARSIWA Commentaries, which unequivocally affirm:

> Thus, a particular treaty might impose obligations on a State but define the 'State' for that purpose in a way which produces different consequences than would otherwise flow from the rules of attribution in chapter II.[37]

In the same vein, the ICJ has stated in *Bosnian Genocide* that '[t]he rules for attributing alleged internationally wrongful conduct to a State do not vary with the nature of the wrongful act in question in the absence of a clearly expressed lex specialis'.[38] Accordingly, a special provision should have, as an object, peculiar tests of attribution deviating from the customary rules. The residual character of attribution rules established by the international custom is specifically envisaged by both international scholars[39] and arbitrators.[40] In practice, however, IIAs are largely silent on attributability issues and, in the rare instances where they cover such issues, a meaningful deviation from customary international law is not acknowledged.

One instance of investment treaties' specific treatment of issues of attributability is represented by NAFTA Articles 1502(3)(a) (*Monopolies and State Enterprises*)[41]

[37] ARSIWA Commentaries 140, para 3.

[38] *Application of the Convention on the Prevention and Punishment of the Crime of Genocide (Bosnia and Herzegovina v Serbia and Montenegro)*, Judgment, 26 February 2007, para 408, ICJ Reports 2007, 43, 201.

[39] Luigi Condorelli, 'L'imputation à l'État d'un fait internationalement illicite: solutions classiques et nouvelles tendances' (1984) 189 Recueil des Cours 9, 117; Yves Nouvel, 'Les entités paraétatiques dans la jurisprudence du CIRDI' in Charles Leben (ed), *Le contentieux arbitral transnational relatif à l'investissement. Nouveaux développements* (LGDJ 2006) 25, 37: '*Ce principe général d'attribution peut toutefois être modifié par les règles spéciales propres au droit des investissements*'.

[40] *United Parcel Service of America Inc (UPS) v Government of Canada*, UNCITRAL, Award on the Merits, 24 May 2007, para 55; *Bayindir Insaat Turizm Ticaret Ve Sanayi AS v Islamic Republic of Pakistan*, ICSID Case No ARB/03/29, Award, 27 August 2009, para 130; *F-W Oil Interests, Inc v The Republic of Trinidad and Tobago*, ICSID Case No ARB/01/14, Award, 3 March 2006, para 206: 'That the substantive standards against which the Claimant puts forward its claims are those laid down in a specific treaty, not general international law, immediately opens up the possibility that particular standards of attributability may apply, as *lex specialis*, in substitute for or supplementation of the general rules of State responsibility—a possibility to which the ILC draws attention repeatedly in its draft Articles and the Commentaries (notably Article 55 & Commentary).'

[41] NAFTA Article 1502:

Monopolies and State Enterprises

...

3. Each Party shall ensure, through regulatory control, administrative supervision or the application of other measures, that any privately owned monopoly that it designates and any government monopoly that it maintains or designates:
   (a) acts in a manner that is not inconsistent with the Party's obligations under this Agreement wherever such a monopoly exercises any regulatory, administrative or other governmental authority that the Party has delegated to it in connection with the monopoly good or service, such as the power to grant import or export licenses, approve commercial transactions or impose quotas, fees or other charges;

and 1503(2)-(3) (*State Enterprises*).[42] These provisions were thoroughly analysed by a NAFTA tribunal in the case of *UPS v Canada*, established under the UNCITRAL Rules, which recognized them as completely displacing the operation of criteria of attribution under ARSIWA:

> Several features of these provisions read as a whole lead the Tribunal to the conclusion that the general residual law reflected in article 4 of the ILC text does not apply in the current circumstances. The special rules of law stated in chapters 11 and 15, in terms of the principle reflected in article 55 of the ILC text, 'govern' the situation and preclude the application of that law ... Accordingly, we conclude that actions of Canada Post are not in general actions of Canada which can be attributed to Canada as a 'Party' within the meaning of articles 1102 to 1105 or for that matter in articles 1502(3)(a) and 1503(2). Chapter 15 provides for a *lex specialis* regime in relation to the attribution of acts of monopolies and state enterprises, to the content of the obligations and to the method of implementation. It follows that the customary international law rules reflected in article 4 of the ILC text do not apply in this case. ... We again recall however that the proposition in article 5 of the ILC text (as in other provisions) has 'a residual character'

(b) except to comply with any terms of its designation that are not inconsistent with subparagraph (c) or (d), acts solely in accordance with commercial considerations in its purchase or sale of the monopoly good or service in the relevant market, including with regard to price, quality, availability, marketability, transportation and other terms and conditions of purchase or sale;
(c) provides non-discriminatory treatment to investments of investors, to goods and to service providers of another Party in its purchase or sale of the monopoly good or service in the relevant market; and
(d) does not use its monopoly position to engage, either directly or indirectly, including through its dealings with its parent, its subsidiary or other enterprise with common ownership, in anticompetitive practices in a non-monopolized market in its territory that adversely affect an investment of an investor of another Party, including through the discriminatory provision of the monopoly good or service, crosssubsidization or predatory conduct.

[42] NAFTA Article 1503:

State Enterprises

...

2. Each Party shall ensure, through regulatory control, administrative supervision or the application of other measures, that any state enterprise that it maintains or establishes acts in a manner that is not inconsistent with the Party's obligations under Chapters Eleven (Investment) and Fourteen (Financial Services) wherever such enterprise exercises any regulatory, administrative or other governmental authority that the Party has delegated to it, such as the power to expropriate, grant licenses, approve commercial transactions or impose quotas, fees or other charges.
3. Each Party shall ensure that any state enterprise that it maintains or establishes accords non-discriminatory treatment in the sale of its goods or services to investments in the Party's territory of investors of another Party.

> and does not apply to the extent that the conditions for the existence of an internationally wrongful act or the content or implementation of a State's international responsibility are governed by special rules of international law — the *lex specialis* principle (paragraph 55 above). For the reasons which we have just given in relation to the argument based on article 4, and in particular the careful structuring and drafting of chapters 11 and 15 and which we need not repeat, we find that this argument also fails, as a general proposition.[43]

This conclusion has been confirmed more recently by the *Mesa Power Group v Canada* tribunal, which was also constituted under the NAFTA:

> The NAFTA thus establishes a special regime which distinguishes between a NAFTA Party and its enterprises, specifies what control obligations the former has over the latter, and thus organises the NAFTA Party's responsibility for acts of its enterprises. This regime cannot be displaced by the ILC Articles, which, as mentioned above, are residual in nature. Indeed, if the ILC Articles were to apply, then the conduct of a state enterprise discriminating in the sale of its goods or services would be attributable to that NAFTA Party. This would mean that a NAFTA Chapter 11 tribunal would have to consider such conduct, although Article 1116(1) restricts its jurisdiction to claims of breach of Article 1503(2). As a result, the Tribunal concludes that Article 1503(2) constitutes a *lex specialis* that excludes the application of Article 5 of the ILC Articles.[44]

Also, in the case of *Al Tamimi v Oman*, an ICSID tribunal found that the rule on the attribution of conduct of State enterprises contained in Article 10.1.2 of the US–Oman Free Trade Agreement (2009) had the effect that ARSIWA Articles 5 and 8 were 'not directly applicable to the present case'.[45] The provision that the conduct of State enterprises entails the responsibility of their establishing State under the applicable IIA whenever they exercise 'any regulatory, administrative, or other governmental authority delegated to it by that Party' is often found in US investment treaty practice.[46] As a consequence, the interpretation provided by the *Al Tamimi v Oman* tribunal, rather in line with the *UPS v Canada* tribunal, is liable to limit the

[43] *United Parcel Service of America Inc (UPS) v Government of Canada*, UNCITRAL, Award on the Merits, 24 May 2007, paras 59, 62, 63. See James Crawford, 'Investment Arbitration and the ILC Articles on State Responsibility' (2010) 25 ICSID Review—Foreign Investment Law Journal 127, 131; Jürgen Kurtz, 'The Paradoxical Treatment of the ILC Articles on State Responsibility in Investor-State Arbitration' (2010) 25 ICSID Review—Foreign Investment Law Journal 200, 208–09.

[44] *Mesa Power Group, LLC v Government of Canada*, UNCITRAL, PCA Case No 2012-17, Award, 24 March 2016, para 362.

[45] *Adel A Hamadi Al Tamimi v Sultanate of Oman*, ICSID Case No ARB/11/33, Award, 3 November 2015, para 324.

[46] cf US Model BIT (2012), Article 2(2)(a). See US-Oman Free Trade Agreement (2009), Article 10.1.2 ('A Party's obligations under this Section shall apply to a state enterprise or other person when

accountability of States for the conduct of their State enterprises in a potentially large number of ISDS cases.[47]

The motive for such a firm exclusion from any application of customary international law may dwell in the parsimonious behaviour of certain arbitrators, appointed by virtue of a specific instrument of consent, as to the application of general international law. For example, in the NAFTA, the *lex specialis* and the international custom on attribution are not in a relationship of reciprocal inconsistency.[48] With regard to ARSIWA Article 4, NAFTA does not affect the rule of attribution to the State of the conduct of its organs. Moreover, it codifies additional primary obligations of the Parties, incumbent on their organs, which shall warrant observance of the treaty by government and private monopolies (*duty to ensure*). With regard to ARSIWA Article 5, NAFTA Articles 1502(3)(a) and 1503(2) do not diverge from the customary norm, by listing particular instances of parastatals exercising 'elements of the governmental authority'. As far as the operation of the attribution test for parastatal entities is concerned, the NAFTA does not modify the customary rules of attributability, but expressly specifies certain grounds for its application in a non-exhaustive way. With regard to ARSIWA Article 8, NAFTA Articles 1502(3) and 1503(2) do not render the conduct *jure gestionis* of private monopolies and State enterprises as automatically attributable to a Party, but instead create a primary obligation for State organs to surveil on the consistency of

it exercises any regulatory, administrative, or other governmental authority delegated to it by that Party'), applied in *Adel A Hamadi Al Tamimi v Sultanate of Oman*, ICSID Case No ARB/11/33, Award, 3 November 2015, paras 314–44; US-Ukraine BIT (1994), Article II(2)(b) ('Each Party shall ensure that any State enterprise that it maintains or establishes acts in a manner that is not inconsistent with the Party's obligations under this Treaty wherever such enterprise exercises any regulatory, administrative or other governmental authority that the Party has delegated to it, such as the power to expropriate, grant licenses, approve commercial transactions, or impose quotas, fees or other charges'), applied in *Bosh International, Inc and B&P Ltd Foreign Investments Enterprise v Ukraine*, ICSID Case No ARB/08/11, Award, 25 October 2012, para 179; US-Ecuador BIT (1993), Article II(2)(b) ('Each Party shall ensure that any state enterprise that it maintains or establishes acts in a manner that is not inconsistent with the Party's obligations under this Treaty wherever such enterprise exercises any regulatory, administrative or other governmental authority that the Party has delegated to it, such as the power to expropriate, grant licences, approve commercial transactions, or impose quotas, fees or other charges'), applied in *Ulysseas, Inc v The Republic of Ecuador*, UNCITRAL, Final Award, 12 June 2012, para 124 et seq.

[47] Carlo de Stefano, 'Adel A Hamadi Al Tamimi v Sultanate of Oman. Attributing to Sovereigns the Conduct of State-Owned Enterprises: Towards Circumvention of the Accountability of States under International Investment Law' (2017) 32(2) ICSID Review—Foreign Investment Law Journal 267, 273.

[48] Accord, *Windstream Energy LLC v Government of Canada*, PCA Case No 2013-22, para 233: 'Article 1503(2) of NAFTA makes it clear that the State parties to NAFTA are responsible for the conduct of State enterprises, but only to the extent that such enterprises are empowered to exercise governmental authority. This is consistent with Article 5 of the ILC Articles, which further specifies that "[t]he conduct of a person or entity which is not an organ of the State ... but which is empowered by the law of that State to exercise elements of the governmental authority shall be considered an act of the State under international law, provided the person or entity is acting in that capacity in the particular instance." In other words, the conduct of persons or entities such as State enterprises which are not formal organs of the State can only be attributable to the State if the person or entity in question is exercising governmental authority in the particular instance.'

their activities with the treaty. Accordingly, a NAFTA tribunal will primarily apply the provisions codified by the treaty, but the concept of a rigid preclusion of any use of customary international rules of attribution of conduct does not seem to be warranted.

Another instance of the 'codification' of rules of attributability is found in the Energy Charter Treaty (ECT) Articles 22 (*State and Privileged Enterprises*)[49] and 23 (*Observance by Sub-National Authorities*).[50] ECT Article 22 does not technically codify rules of attributability, but introduces a substantive obligation (primary rule) to ensure that State enterprises established by a Party conduct their undertakings consistently with the treaty, either acting *jure imperii* or *jure gestionis*.[51] In the first instance, attribution as such is governed by the functional test of ARSIWA Article 5. In the second instance, the attribution of conduct of State enterprises, as being assimilated to 'private' individuals, would not be in place unless instructions, direction, or control by a Party are established pursuant to ARSIWA Article 8. ECT Article 23(1) reproduces the customary principle of the territorial unity of the State for the purposes of attribution and additionally dictates the Parties' duty to surveil

[49] ECT Article 22:

State and Privileged Enterprises

(1) Each Contracting Party shall ensure that any state enterprise which it maintains or establishes shall conduct its activities in relation to the sale or provision of goods and services in its Area in a manner consistent with the Contracting Party's obligations under Part III of this Treaty.
(2) No Contracting Party shall encourage or require such a state enterprise to conduct its activities in its Area in a manner inconsistent with the Contracting Party's obligations under other provisions of this Treaty.
(3) Each Contracting Party shall ensure that if it establishes or maintains an entity and entrusts the entity with regulatory, administrative or other governmental authority, such entity shall exercise that authority in a manner consistent with the Contracting Party's obligations under this Treaty.
(4) No Contracting Party shall encourage or require any entity to which it grants exclusive or special privileges to conduct its activities in its Area in a manner inconsistent with the Contracting Party's obligations under this Treaty.
(5) For the purposes of this Article, 'entity' includes any enterprise, agency or other organization or individual.

[50] ECT Article 23:

Observance by Sub-National Authorities

(1) Each Contracting Party is fully responsible under this Treaty for the observance of all provisions of the Treaty, and shall take such reasonable measures as may be available to it to ensure such observance by regional and local governments and authorities within its Area.
(2) The dispute settlement provisions in Parts II, IV and V of this Treaty may be invoked in respect of measures affecting the observance of the Treaty by a Contracting Party which have been taken by regional or local governments or authorities within the Area of the Contracting Party.

[51] Thomas W Wälde and Patricia K Wouters, 'State Responsibilty and the Energy Charter Treaty: the Rules Regarding State Enterprises, Entities, and Subnational Authorities' (1997) 2 Hofstra Law and Policy Symposium 117, 131: 'The ECT extends the breadth of a state-party's liability by making the conduct of state enterprises and entities in the energy sector the responsibility of the contracting state.'

on the activities of sub-state levels of government, which may result in a breach of the treaty. In line with the above analysis of the relevant provisions of the NAFTA, the ECT does not seem to embody a *lex specialis* as to attribution issues, but rather codifies the substantive duties of performance and surveillance incumbent on the organs of the Parties.[52]

The foregoing review of IIAs empirically confirms the scarcity or near absence of *pacta inter se* with regard to attribution issues. Accordingly, in the overwhelming majority of investment disputes, issues of attribution are governed by customary international law only.[53] However, a scholarly question remains whether States should be at liberty to modify customary rules of attributability and to what extent, provided that they may legally do so. The ARSIWA Commentaries offer a couple of examples of *leges speciales* affecting issues of attributability, both outside the realm of international investment law. The first example is represented by Article 1.1 of the United Nations Convention against Torture and Other Cruel, Inhuman or Degrading Treatment or Punishment of 10 December 1984, which applies to torture committed 'by or at the instigation of or with the consent or acquiescence of a public official or other person acting in an official capacity'.[54] The ILC explains that '[t]his is probably narrower than the bases for attribution of conduct to the State in Part One, chapter II'. While Article 1.2 of the Convention against Torture preserves the operation of 'any international instrument or national legislation which does or may contain provisions of wider application', it may be observed that the test of 'instigation' of a public official may be embedded within the prong of actual instructions by a State organ pursuant to ARSIWA Article 8. In addition, *patientia* and *receptus* by State agents entail a *wider* basis of attributability vis-à-vis the customary tests, as extensively demonstrated in the previous chapter.[55] Such a wider basis of attribution is (also) understood in light of the high legal rank of the primary norms dictated by the Convention against Torture. The second example is embodied by 'federal clauses' excluding constituent subdivisions of a State from the coverage of a treaty, as in Article 34(b) of the UNESCO Convention for the Protection of the World Cultural and Natural Heritage of 16 November 1972:[56]

52 See *Nykomb Synergetics Technology Holding AB v The Republic of Latvia*, SCC, Arbitral Award, 16 December 2003, para 4.2.

53 *Noble Ventures, Inc v Romania*, ICSID Case No ARB/01/11, Award, 12 October 2005, para 69: 'As States are juridical persons, one always has to raise the question whether acts committed by natural persons who are allegedly in violation of international law are attributable to a State. The BIT does not provide any answer to this question. The rules of attribution can only be found in general international law which supplements the BIT in this respect.'

54 United Nations Convention against Torture and Other Cruel, Inhuman or Degrading Treatment or Punishment, adopted by General Assembly Resolution 39/46 of 10 December 1984, entered into force on 26 June 1987, 1465 UNTS 85. See ARSIWA Commentaries 140, para 3, fn 820.

55 See Chapter II, section 5.2.

56 UNESCO Convention for the Protection of the World Cultural and Natural Heritage, Paris, adopted on 16 November 1972, entered into force on 17 December 1975, 1037 UNTS 151. See ARSIWA Commentaries 140, para 3, fn 820.

Article 34

The following provisions shall apply to those States Parties to this Convention which have a federal or non-unitary constitutional system:

. . .

(b) with regard to the provisions of this Convention, the implementation of which comes under the legal jurisdiction of individual constituent States, countries, provinces or cantons that are not obliged by the constitutional system of the federation to take legislative measures, the federal government shall inform the competent authorities of such States, countries, provinces or cantons of the said provisions, with its recommendation for their adoption.

The problem of the insertion of 'federal clauses' in IIAs has gathered interest in relation to the new Indian Model BIT. One of its drafts, which was proposed in 2015, provided a definition of 'Government' as 'only the Central Government and State Governments in the case of India' (Article 1.3(i)).[57] This formulation was meant to exclude attribution to India of the conduct of municipalities or territorial units beneath the State level, which entailed a significant departure from the principle of the unity of the State, a pillar of the international law of State responsibility. The subsequent version of the 2015 Indian Model BIT adopted a markedly different legal technique to enforce the same policy. The exclusion of the measures of 'local governments' is no longer addressed under the definition of 'Government', but is qualified as a carve-out from the substantive coverage of the BIT (Article 2.4(i)).[58] This amendment is seemingly illustrative of the will of India not to treat the exclusion of the conduct of municipalities as formally pertaining to attribution rules (ie, secondary rules), but rather limiting the regulatory scope of the investment treaty. It remains to be seen how many States will accept this specific Indian policy through the conclusion of binding agreements.[59] To this extent, it is advisable for States not to pass *lex specialis* in such a way as to restrict (in form or substance) the customary scope of rules of attribution of acts and omissions, as will be expanded in the conclusion of this section.

The question of the margin of deviation of States from customary international law in relation to attribution issues has already received attention in the legal

[57] Grant Hanessian and Kabir Duggal, 'The 2015 Indian Model BIT: Is This Change the World Wishes to See?' (2015) 30 ICSID Review—Foreign Investment Law Journal 729.

[58] See Grant Hanessian and Kabir Duggal, 'The Final 2015 Indian Model BIT: Is This the Change the World Wishes to See?' (2017) 32 ICSID Review—Foreign Investment Law Journal 216. Article 1.7 of the final 2015 Indian Model BIT provides a non-exhaustive definition of 'local governments': '"local government" includes: (i) An urban local body, municipal corporation or village level government; or (ii) an enterprise owned or controlled by an urban local body, a municipal corporation or a village level government.'

[59] For an example, see India-Belarus BIT (2018), signed on 24 September 2018.

doctrine. In relation to parastatal entities under ARSIWA Article 5, it has been stated that an investment treaty may exclude attribution of conduct of a parastatal entity by virtue of a sectoral exclusion contained in a carve-out provision (for instance with regard to the oil and mines sector).[60] Upon a closer inspection, this example pertains to the issue of jurisdiction *ratione materiae* of an international investment tribunal, not to the merits question of attribution. With regard to the definition of 'investment' contained in the applicable instrument of consent to arbitration, States are at liberty to restrict the scope of the jurisdiction of an international arbitration tribunal,[61] while it is debated whether they can enlarge such a jurisdiction to cover mere commercial transactions falling outside the 'objective' definition of investment propounded by the *Salini v Morocco* tribunal, at least in the realm of ICSID arbitration.[62] In relation to attribution issues, it is submitted that the Parties may extend the coverage of attribution rules, so as to include conduct that would

[60] Yves Nouvel, 'Les entités paraétatiques dans la jurisprudence du CIRDI' in Charles Leben (ed), *Le contentieux arbitral transnational relatif à l'investissement. Nouveaux développements* (LGDJ 2006) 25, 38.

[61] Aron Broches, 'The Convention on the Settlement of Investment Disputes Between States and Nationals of Other States' (1972-II) 136 Recueil des Cours 331, 340, 351–52; C F Amerasinghe, 'Interpretation of Article 25(2)(b) of the ICSID Convention' in Richard B Lillich and Charles N Brower (eds), *International Arbitration in the 21st Century: Towards 'Judicialization' and Uniformity?* (Transnational Publishers, Inc 1993) 223, 231–32, 235; Georges R Delaume, 'ICSID Arbitration and the Courts' (1983) 77 American Journal of International Law 784, 794; M Sornarajah, *The International Law on Foreign Investment* (3rd edn, Cambridge University Press 2010) 330; C F Amerasinghe, 'Jurisdiction *Ratione Personae* Under the Convention on the Settlement of Investment Disputes Between States and Nationals of Other States' (1974-1975) 47 British Year Book of International Law 227, 229–30.

[62] *Salini Costruttori SpA and Italstrade SpA v Kingdom of Morocco*, ICSID Case No ARB/00/4, Decision on Jurisdiction, 31 July 2000, para 52; *Phoenix Action, Ltd v The Czech Republic*, ICSID Case No ARB/06/5, Award, 15 April 2009, para 96; *Malaysian Historical Salvors Sdn, Bhd v The Government of Malaysia*, ICSID Case No ARB/05/10, Award on Jurisdiction, 17 May 2007, paras 54–55; *Joy Mining Machinery Limited v Arab Republic of Egypt*, ICSID Case No ARB/03/11, Award on Jurisdiction, 6 August 2004, paras 49–50; *Société Générale de Surveillance SA (SGS) v Islamic Republic of Pakistan*, ICSID Case No ARB/01/13, Decision of the Tribunal on Objections to Jurisdiction, 6 August 2003, para 133, fn 153. Interestingly, the requirement of an 'inherent meaning' of the term 'investment' has been upheld by an UNCITRAL Tribunal, established under the Switzerland-Uzbekistan BIT (1993), cf *Romak SA (Switzerland) v The Republic of Uzbekistan*, UNCITRAL, PCA Case No AA280, Award, 26 November 2009, para 180, 207, quoting *Robert Azinian, Kenneth Davitian, & Ellen Baca v The United Mexican States*, ICSID Case No ARB(AF)/97/2, Award, 1 November 1999, para 90: 'labeling… is no substitute for analysis.'; *Alps Finance and Trade AG (AFT) v The Slovak Republic*, UNCITRAL, Award, 5 March 2011, para 243. See Anthony C Sinclair, 'ICSID's Nationality Requirements' (2008) 23 ICSID Review—Foreign Investment Law Journal 57, 63, who refers to 'the nationality requirements called for by the ICSID Convention and places these in the context of the criteria for protection found in investment treaties. These instruments form twin gateways through which investors must pass to bring a case to ICSID.' Then, he takes position on the issue of the relationship between the ICSID Convention and the relevant instrument of consent to arbitration by affirming that '[d]espite the unassailable position of consent as the "cornerstone" of ICSID jurisdiction, access to ICSID cannot be reduced simply to a matter of party autonomy'. Accord, Christoph Schreuer, with Loretta Malintoppi, August Reinisch, and Anthony Sinclair, *The ICSID Convention: A Commentary* (2nd edn, Cambridge University Press 2009) 83, para 6; C F Amerasinghe, *Jurisdiction of International Tribunals* (Kluwer Law International 2003) 658; Paul C Szasz, 'A Practical Guide to the Convention on Settlement of Investment Disputes' (1968) 1 Cornell Journal of International Law 1, 14.

not otherwise be attributable, but should not contract out cases of attribution provided by customary international law. Accordingly, a scholar has stated that States can definitely enlarge the operation of attribution mechanisms.[63] This may occur with particular regard to the attributability of conduct of non-state actors. Some treaty provisions establish the attribution to the State of activities of private individuals irrespective of an otherwise relevant link with a government.[64] However, it may be questioned whether this is an issue concerning the rules of attribution proper, rather than one of specific primary rules intended to create a regime of objective responsibility of the State. In addition, such provisions usually refer to times of crisis (revolutions, civil strife, or mob violence), in a context of evanescence in the divide between attribution rules and primary rules codifying a duty to prevent damage or to ensure compliance with given standards by any person involved in a certain activity, including parastatal entities.[65] James Crawford has recognized States' freedom to contract 'entirely new' secondary rules of attribution, by referring to Article 139(2) of the United Nations Convention on the Law of the Sea (UNCLOS).[66] This rule provides for the responsibility of States for exploration and exploitation activities undertaken by private entities (State enterprises or natural or juridical persons which possess the nationality of States Parties or are effectively controlled by them or their nationals) for which they stand as sponsors, provided that a Party has not taken 'all necessary and appropriate measures to secure effective compliance'.[67] The argument that this provision specifies a due diligence rule, rather than a test of attribution, may be reiterated, but it is also relevant to underline that in any case the rule entails a wider, not narrower, scope of attributability in comparison to ARSIWA Article 8. Another theoretical example of the extension of attribution mechanisms would be express stipulations in IIAs

[63] Yves Nouvel, 'Les entités paraétatiques dans la jurisprudence du CIRDI' in Charles Leben (ed), *Le contentieux arbitral transnational relatif à l'investissement. Nouveaux développements* (LGDJ 2006) 25, 38, referring to the former French Model BIT, whose Article 2 established attribution to a contracting party of the acts and omissions of any entity under its tutelage (*tutelle*).

[64] US–Zaire BIT (1984), Article IV(1) (*Compensation for Damages Due to War and Similar Events*):

> Nationals or companies of either Party whose investments in the territory of the other Party suffer: (a) damages due to war or other armed conflict between such other Party and a third country, or (b) damages due to revolution, state of national emergency, revolt, insurrection, riot or act of violence in the territory of such other Party, shall be accorded treatment no less favorable than that which such other Party accords to its own nationals or companies or to nationals or companies of any third country, whichever is the most favorable treatment, when making restitution, indemnification, compensation or any other settlement with respect to such damages.

See also *Cornelia J Pringle*, et al, *(Santa Isabel Claims) (USA) v United Mexican States*, 26 April 1926, 4 RIAA 783, 785, with regard to Article III(b) of the Convention of September 10, 1923, providing for the settlement and amicable adjustment of claims arising from losses or damages suffered by American citizens through revolutionary acts within the period from 20 November 1910 to 31 May 1920; *Kummerow, Otto Redler and Co, Fulda, Fischbach, and Friedericy Cases*, 1903, 10 RIAA 369, 370, with regard to Article III of the Germany–Venezuela protocol of 13 February 1903.

[65] See section 5.2 of this chapter.

[66] James Crawford, *State Responsibility. The General Part* (Cambridge University Press 2013) 114.

[67] UNCLOS Articles 139(2) and 153(2)(b).

that contractual breaches committed by State instrumentalities are attributable to their establishing State as being the latter's own acts. This rule of attribution would be broader than the functional test of ARSIWA Article 5, in that it would establish attributability to the State of *acta jure gestionis* of parastatals, beyond the subjective limits of application of conventional umbrella clauses.[68] In addition, such an attribution rule would also be broader that the factual test of instructions, or direction, or control under ARSIWA Article 8.

It is normatively submitted that IIAs may extend, but should not restrict the scope of attribution rules dictated by customary international law, provided that *de lege lata* States are at liberty to stipulate narrower tests for attributability of conduct to a Party. Attribution rules constitute a peculiar category of norms, in that they are preliminary in application to the other secondary rules (*trans-substantive* rules). By dispensing structural, technical, mechanical, and logical principles in order to build the bridge between given persons and the juridical entity of the State, they objectively mark the boundary of the international arena of State responsibility and create its codes of organization and functioning. There is indeed a logically indefeasible *noyeau dur* of rules of attribution that corresponds to the content of customary international law (a minimum *one-size-fits-all model*).[69] Derogation *ad minus* of rules of attribution of internationally wrongful acts would entail an indirect erosion or eventual circumvention of the relevant international primary rules.[70] This is not desirable, since such agreements *inter se* would be inconsistent

[68] See section 2.2 of this chapter.

[69] Luigi Condorelli, 'L'imputation à l'État d'un fait internationalement illicite: solutions classiques et nouvelles tendances' (1984) 189 Recueil des Cours 9, 166: '*On doit d'ailleurs admettre sans la moindre réticence que le critère clé à suivre lorsqu'il s'agit de déterminer les bases normatives du raisonnement relatif à l'imputation peut être synthétisé ainsi: l'applicabilité des principes "communs" doit être sans autre présumée, tant que l'existence d'un principe dérogatoire (conventionnel ou coutumier) à préférer en l'espèce n'est pas positivement démontrée.*'; Yves Nouvel, 'Les entités paraétatiques dans la jurisprudence du CIRDI' in Charles Leben (ed), *Le contentieux arbitral transnational relatif à l'investissement. Nouveaux développements* (LGDJ 2006) 25, 41: '*il y a peu de mécanismes d'imputation propres au droit des investissements.*'

[70] See, with regard to the entirety of secondary rules, Bruno Simma, 'Self-contained Regimes' (1985) 16 Netherlands Yearbook of International Law 111, 135: 'the exclusion or modification through a "self-contained regime" of "normal" secondary rules which leads to a "softening" of the legal consequences of wrongful acts should not be easily presumed.' See also Alfred Verdross, '*Jus Dispositivum* and *Jus Cogens* in International Law' (1966) 60 American Journal of International Law 55, 59: 'a state cannot waive the rights necessary for it to fulfill its international obligations.' Moreover, the stipulation by States of narrower tests for the attribution of conduct may entail the result of a *clause d'irresponsabilité réciproque*, namely the renunciation to invoke the international responsibility of another Party. See Institut de Droit International, 'Règlement sur la responsabilité des Etats à raison des dommages soufferts par des étrangers en cas d'émeute, d'insurrection ou de guerre civile', Résolution du 10 septembre 1900, Session de Neuchâtel, in *Résolutions de l'Institut de droit international. 1873-1956* (Editions Juridiques et Sociologiques 1957) 141–42:

Vœux

> L'Institut de Droit international exprime le vœu que les Etats évitent d'insérer dans les traités des clauses d'irresponsabilité réciproque. Il estime que ces clauses ont le tort de dispenser les Etats de l'accomplissement de leur devoir de protection sur leurs nationaux à l'étranger et de leur devoir de protection des étrangers sur leur territoire.

with the basic structure of the customary international law on State responsibility. On the contrary, there is neither legal rule nor policy preventing States from undertaking obligations in respect of conduct that would not otherwise be attributable.[71] This conclusion applies to IIAs, the primary norms of which usually establish substantive standards of protection of foreign investments, such as fair and equitable treatment (FET) and full protection and security(FPS). Instead, where the applicable primary rules are peremptory norms of general international law (*jus cogens*), the limitation of their effects through the stipulation of secondary rules of attribution of conduct to the States that are narrower than the tests under customary international law is prevented.

1.3 The Example of International Trade Law

In order to corroborate our conclusions with regard to the application of attribution rules by investment tribunals, it seems appropriate to provide a brief excursus of the solutions rendered on the same issues within the WTO dispute settlement system.[72] This analysis is suggested in light of the enhanced interdependence and even possible cross-fertilization between the regimes of international trade law and international investment law.[73]

The WTO-covered agreements contain provisions that entail issues of attribution *lato sensu*. This is the case for the General Agreement on Tariffs and Trade 1994 (GATT 1994) Articles III:8(a) (as to 'governmental agencies') and Article XVII:1 (as to 'state trading enterprises'), General Agreeement on Trade in Services (GATS)

[71] Georgios Petrochilos, 'Attribution' in Katia Yannaca-Small (ed), *Arbitration under International Investment Agreements: A Guide to the Key Issues* (Oxford University Press 2010) 287, 288.

[72] Graham Cook, *A Digest of WTO Jurisprudence on Public International Law Concepts and Principles* (Cambridge University Press 2015) 31–43; Joanna Gomula, 'Responsibility and the World Trade Organization' in James Crawford, Alain Pellet, and Simon Olleson (eds), *The Law of International Responsibility* (Oxford University Press 2010) 791, 795–97; Santiago M Villalpando, 'Attribution of Conduct to the State: How the Rules of State Responsibility May be Applied within the WTO Dispute Settlement System' (2002) 5 Journal of International Economic Law 393.

[73] *Continental Casualty Company v The Argentine Republic*, ICSID Case No ARB/03/9, Award, 5 September 2008, paras 192–95, using Appellate Body Report, *Korea—Measures Affecting Imports of Fresh, Chilled and Frozen Beef (Korea—Various Measures on Beef)*, WT/DS161/AB/R, WT/DS169/AB/R, 11 December 2000, para 161. See Giorgio Sacerdoti, 'The Application of BITs in Time of Economic Crisis: Limits to Their Coverage, Necessity and the Relevance of WTO Law' in Giorgio Sacerdoti et al, *General Interests of Host States in International Investment Law* (Cambridge University Press 2014) 3, 17; Tomer Broude, 'Investment and Trade: The "Lottie and Lisa" of International Economic Law?' in Roberto Echandi and Pierre Sauvé (eds), *Prospects in International Investment Law and Policy. World Trade Forum* (Cambridge University Press 2013) 139: 'they are in fact identical twins, separated at a very young age following an unfortunate divorce, each of them subsequently been raised by one of their parents, and developing different characters'.

Article I:3(b)–(c) (as to 'governmental authority'), Article VIII (as to 'monopolies and exclusive service suppliers'), and Article XIII:1 (as to 'governmental agencies'), Agreement on Subsidies and Countervailing Measures (SCM Agreement) Article 1.1(a)(1) (as to the definition of 'public body'), and Agreement on Agriculture Article 9.1(a) (as to 'governments or their agencies'). This notwithstanding, WTO panels and the Appellate Body have determined problems of attribution of conduct to the State by interpreting the provisions dictated by the applicable covered agreement as identical or consistent with the rules established by customary international law ('there is no major *lex specialis* on attribution in international trade law').[74] This judicial attitude may be suggested by the obligation to provide 'security and predictability to the multilateral trading system' pursuant to the Dispute Settlement Understanding (DSU) Article 3.2, which is an express networking device between general international law and special international trade law, so that the latter is not interpreted in 'clinical isolation' from the former.[75] Accordingly, WTO panels and the Appellate Body reiterated the principle of irrelevance of the separation of powers in order to identify a 'measure' as attributable to a Member,[76] as well as of the internal allocation of competences between the central government and territorial entities,[77] and the principle of responsibility of the State for acts of minor officials.[78] In general, WTO case law has found there to be attributability of acts and omissions

[74] Santiago M Villalpando, 'Attribution of Conduct to the State: How the Rules of State Responsibility May be Applied within the WTO Dispute Settlement System' (2002) 5 Journal of International Economic Law 393, 395.

[75] James Bacchus, 'Not in Clinical Isolation' in Gabrielle Marceau (ed), *A History of Law and Lawyers in the GATT/WTO. The Development of the Rule of Law in the Multilateral Trading System* (Cambridge University Press 2015) 507. cf Appellate Body Report, *United States—Standards for Reformulated and Conventional Gasoline (US—Gasoline)*, WT/DS2/AB/R, 29 April 1996, 17; Appellate Body Report, *United States—Import Prohibition of Certain Shrimp and Shrimp Products (US—Shrimp)*, WT/DS58/AB/R, 12 October 1998, paras 154–58.

[76] Appellate Body Report, *United States—Standards for Reformulated and Conventional Gasoline (US—Gasoline)*, WT/DS2/AB/R, 29 April 1996, 28-29; Appellate Body Report, *United States—Import Prohibition of Certain Shrimp and Shrimp Products (US—Shrimp)*, WT/DS58/AB/R, 12 October 1998, para 173; Appellate Body Report, *United States—Measures Relating to Zeroing and Sunset Reviews (Recourse to Article 21.5 of the DSU by Japan) (US—Zeroing (Japan))*, WT/DS322/AB/RW, 18 August 2009, para 182.

[77] Panel Report, *Australia—Measures Affecting Importation of Salmon (Recourse to Article 21.5 by Canada) (Australia—Salmon)*, WT/DS18/RW, 18 February 2000, para 7.12: 'we are of the view that the Tasmanian ban is to be regarded as a measure taken by Australia, in the sense that it is a measure for which Australia, under both general international law and relevant WTO provisions, is responsible.'; Panel Report, *Brazil—Measures Affecting Imports of Retreaded Tyres (Brazil—Retreaded Tyres)*, WT/DS332/R, 12 June 2007, para 7.400: 'We consider that the measures of Rio Grande do Sul, a state of the Federative Republic of Brazil, are attributable to Brazil as a WTO Member and therefore should be considered as "measures" for the purposes of Article 3.3 of the DSU.'; Panel Reports, *Canada—Certain Measures Affecting the Renewable Energy Generation Sector (Canada—Renewable Energy) and Measures Relating to the Feed-in Tariff Program (Canada—Feed-In Tariff Program)*, WT/DS412/R, WT/DS426/R, 19 December 2012, para 7.6, fn 37: 'It is not disputed that, under public international law, Canada is responsible for the actions of the Government of the Province of Ontario ("Government of Ontario").'

[78] Panel Report, *Korea—Measures Affecting Government Procurement (Korea—Procurement)*, WT/DS163/R, 1 May 2000, para 6.5.

to the State, based on the conduct of the legislature,[79] of the executive branch,[80] and of the judiciary.[81] Besides, the meaning of 'public body' pursuant to the SCM Agreement Article 1.1(a)(1) has been defined by the Appellate Body as 'an entity that possesses, exercises or is vested with governmental authority', in relevant consistency with the rule of ARSIWA Article 5.[82] Finally, both panels and the Appellate Body have rendered findings related to circumstances of instructions, direction, or control between a Member and 'private parties'.[83] Notably, the Appellate Body provided further elucidation on the tests dictated by ARSIWA Article 8 through its analysis of the situations of 'entrustment' and 'direction' by a government to a private body to carry out given functions, pursuant to the SCM Agreement Article 1.1(a)(1).[84]

It follows from the foregoing that no significant deviation from public international law is recorded in the WTO dispute settlement system with regard to issues of attribution. Rather, WTO case law has provided more accuracy and specificity where demanded by the covered agreements, functional to a demand of enhanced adjustment to international trade matters and with a view to offering solutions

[79] Appellate Body Report, *United States—Standards for Reformulated and Conventional Gasoline (US—Gasoline)*, WT/DS2/AB/R, 29 April 1996, 28.

[80] *United States—Sunset Review of Anti-Dumping Duties on Corrosion-Resistant Carbon Steel Flat Products from Japan (US—Corrosion-Resistant Steel Sunset Review)*, WT/DS244/AB/R, 15 December 2003, para 81: 'The acts or omissions that are so attributable are, in the usual case, the acts or omissions of the organs of the state, including those of the executive branch'.

[81] Appellate Body Report, *United States—Import Prohibition of Certain Shrimp and Shrimp Products (US—Shrimp)*, WT/DS58/AB/R, 12 October 1998, para 173: 'The United States, like all other Members of the WTO and of the general community of states, bears responsibility for acts of all its departments of government, including its judiciary.'; Appellate Body Report, *United States—Measures Relating to Zeroing and Sunset Reviews (Recourse to Article 21.5 of the DSU by Japan) (US—Zeroing (Japan))*, WT/DS322/AB/RW, 18 August 2009, para 182: 'Thus, the United States cannot seek to avoid the obligation to comply with the DSB's recommendations and rulings within the reasonable period of time, by relying on the timing of liquidation being "controlled by the independent judiciary".'; Panel Report, *Brazil—Measures Affecting Imports of Retreaded Tyres (Brazil—Retreaded Tyres)*, WT/DS332/R, 12 June 2007, para 7.305.

[82] Appellate Body Report, *United States—Definitive Anti-Dumping and Countervailing Duties on Certain Products from China (US—Anti-Dumping and Countervailing Duties (China))*, WT/DS379/AB/R, 11 March 2011, para 317: 'A public body within the meaning of Article 1.1.(a)(1) of the *SCM Agreement* must be an entity that possesses, exercises or is vested with governmental authority. Yet, just as no two governments are exactly alike, the precise contours and characteristics of a public body are bound to differ from entity to entity, State to State, and case to case.' Accord, Appellate Body Report, *United States—Countervailing Measures on Certain Hot-Rolled Carbon Steel Flat Products from India (US—Carbon Steel (India))*, WT/DS436/AB/R, 8 December 2014, para 4.37. See also Panel Report, *Canada—Measures Affecting the Importation of Milk and the Exportation of Dairy Products (Canada—Dairy)*, WT/DS103/R, WT/DS113/R, 17 May 1999, para 7.77 (provincial marketing boards).

[83] Panel Report, *Japan—Measures Affecting Consumer Photographic Film and Paper (Japan—Film)*, WT/DS44/R, 31 March 1998, para 10.52.

[84] *United States—Countervailing Duty Investigation on Dynamic Random Access Memory Semiconductors (DRAMS) from Korea (US—Countervailing Duty Investigation on DRAMs)*, WT/DS296/AB/R, 27 June 2005, para 116: 'In sum, we are of the view that, pursuant to paragraph (iv), "entrustment" occurs where a government gives responsibility to a private body, and "direction" refers to situations where the government exercises its authority over a private body. In both instances, the government uses a private body as proxy to effectuate one of the types of financial contributions listed in paragraphs (i) through (iii).'

'adapted to the realities of international economic law' ('*répondant à la diversité des besoins qui se manifestent dans le milieu social international*'), but ultimately in line with the core of the law of nations on attribution of acts and omissions to States.[85]

2. A Critique of the Application of Attribution Rules by International Investment Tribunals

From a comprehensive review of international investment cases, various problems emerge with regard to the application of attribution rules to the conduct or measures that represent the subject matter of an investment dispute. In this respect, it has been stated that arbitrators appear to be at the 'formative stage' in relation to their use and application of general categories of attributability under customary international law.[86] Although investment tribunals have usually provided reasoned analysis, in that they have comprehensively articulated and identified the spectrum of attribution rules,[87] others have not demonstrated the same methodological accuracy.[88] The most significant problems relate to the individual, independent, and autonomous application of each single test of attributability under ARSIWA Article 4, 5, or 8. Sometimes, tribunals have practically resorted to a

[85] The English quote is from *Bayindir Insaat Turizm Ticaret Ve Sanayi AS v Islamic Republic of Pakistan*, ICSID Case No ARB/03/29, Award, 27 August 2009, para 130. The French quote is from Luigi Condorelli, 'L'imputation à l'État d'un fait internationalement illicite: solutions classiques et nouvelles tendances' (1984) 189 Recueil des Cours 9, 166.

[86] Kaj Hobér, 'State Responsibility and Attribution' in Peter Muchlinski, Federico Ortino, and Christoph Schreuer (eds), *The Oxford Handbook of International Investment Law* (Oxford University Press 2008) 550, 582.

[87] *Saipem SpA v People's Republic of Bangladesh*, ICSID Case No ARB/05/07, Decision on Jurisdiction and Recommendation on Provisional Measures, 21 March 2007, para 148; *Noble Ventures, Inc v Romania*, ICSID Case No ARB/01/11, Award, 12 October 2005, para 69; *EDF (Services) Limited v Romania*, ICSID Case No ARB/05/13, Award, 8 October 2009, para 187; *Eureko BV v Republic of Poland*, Ad Hoc Arbitration, Partial Award, 19 August 2005, para 132; *Gustav F W Hamester GmbH & Co KG v Republic of Ghana*, ICSID Case No ARB/07/24, Award, 18 June 2010, para 172; *Alpha Projektholding GmbH v Ukraine*, ICSID Case No ARB/07/16, Award, 8 November 2010, para 400; *Bayindir Insaat Turizm Ticaret Ve Sanayi AS v Islamic Republic of Pakistan*, ICSID Case No ARB/03/29, Award, 27 August 2009, para 117.

[88] *EnCana Corporation v Republic of Ecuador*, LCIA Case No UN3481, UNCITRAL, Award, 3 February 2006, para 154: 'It does not matter for this purpose whether this result flows from the principle stated in Article 5 of the ILC's Articles on Responsibility of States for Intemationally Wrongful Acts or that stated in Article 8. *The result is the same.*' (emphasis added); *Eureko BV v Republic of Poland*, Ad Hoc Arbitration, Partial Award, 19 August 2005, para 134: 'whatever may be the status of the State Treasury'; *Waste Management, Inc v United Mexican States (Waste Management II)*, ICSID Case No ARB(AF)/00/3, Award, 30 April 2004, para 75: 'For the purposes of the present Award, however, it will be assumed that one way or another the conduct of Banobras was attributable to Mexico for NAFTA purposes.'; *Toto Costruzioni Generali SpA v The Republic of Lebanon*, ICSID Case No ARB/07/12, Decision on Jurisdiction, 11 September 2009, para 44: 'The *principal rule* (sic) of international law on attribution are presently reflected in Articles 4 and 5 of the International Law Commission's ("ILC") Draft Articles on Responsibility of States for Internationally Wrongful Acts, 2001 ("Draft Articles").' (emphasis added); *United Parcel Service of America Inc (UPS) v Government of Canada*, UNCITRAL, Award on the Merits, 24 May 2007, para 76: 'It will be recalled that UPS also contends, as an alternative to the argument based on the rules of customary international law reflected in article 4 of the ILC text, that the proposition reflected in its article 5 apply to make Canada directly responsible for actions of Canada Post. That

'super-test' of attribution, based on the arbitrary combination of elements of different tests upon the justification of the same operative conclusion, ie 'attribution' or 'non-attribution', as if ARSIWA dedicated only the provision under Article 2 to attribution. In addition, the application of attribution rules in connection with an umbrella clause (*clause de couverture*) has created legal uncertainty, especially with regard to contract claims based on the activities of State instrumentalities. Finally, the qualification of attribution as a question of merits vis-à-vis jurisdiction has not always been clear-cut in the arbitrators' analysis, especially in non-bifurcated proceedings or in connection with the special mechanism of designation of constituent subdivisions or agencies pursuant to Article 25(1)–(3) of the ICSID Convention.

From a more general perspective, some arbitrators have appeared parsimonious or even reluctant with regard to the application of principles and rules of customary international law.[89] This begets perfunctory analysis of the applicable rules of attribution, which nevertheless represent a threshold condition for State responsibility, especially where the parties agree on those issues in their submissions.[90] Such an approach reflects the tendency to exclusively apply the relevant investment treaty, thus emphasizing the self-containment of international investment law, notably in non-ICSID disputes.[91] Even the basic principle of the supremacy of international law vis-à-vis municipal law has not always been enforced in a full-fledged manner in investment litigation. In *EDF v Romania*, the tribunal asserted that '[a]s stated by ILC Article 4 (2), the State internal law determines whether an entity is a State organ'.[92] As mentioned in previous chapters, ARSIWA rather dictate an independent meaning of 'State organ' that also encompasses *de facto* agents.[93] While

provision (set out in paragraph 48 above) is concerned with the conduct of non-State entities. ... It is convenient at this point to return to article 5 of the ILC's State responsibility text and in particular to its commentary, quoted earlier (paragraph 48). That provision, it will be recalled, attributes to the State the conduct of non-State organs "empowered by the law of that State to exercise elements of the governmental authority" when it acts in that capacity.'

---

[89] Pierre-Marie Dupuy, 'Les émanations engagent-elles la responsabilité des Etats? Etude de droit international des investissements' (2006) EUI Working Paper LAW No 2006/7, 9: '*Cet emprunt de plus en plus fréquent et délibéré aux règles de droit international public en particulier pour identifier l'"émanation" de l'Etat a de quoi frapper. Il manifeste à n'en pas douter non pas seulement une utilisation occasionnelle du droit international public mais, bel et bien, une reconnaissance de moins en moins réticente du fait que, dans un grand nombre de cas, le droit reconnu comme applicable est bien le droit international, y compris la coutume.*'

[90] *Biwater Gauff (Tanzania) Ltd v United Republic of Tanzania*, ICSID Case No ARB/05/22, Award, 24 July 2008, para 479: 'The parties agree as to the general principles governing State responsibility and the attribution of acts and omissions to the State, as they have been restated in the ILC Articles, and in particular Articles 2, 4, 5, 12 and 13.'

[91] Chiefly, *United Parcel Service of America Inc (UPS) v Government of Canada*, UNCITRAL, Award on the Merits, 24 May 2007, paras 59–65.

[92] *EDF (Services) Limited v Romania*, ICSID Case No ARB/05/13, Award, 8 October 2009, para 188. Similarly, in *Impregilo SpA v Islamic Republic of Pakistan*, ICSID Case No ARB/03/3, Decision on Jurisdiction, 22 April 2005, para 199: 'The status of WAPDA as a party to the Contracts is a matter for the law of Pakistan, being both the law by which WAPDA was established and exists, and also the law governing the Contracts.'

[93] See Chapter I, section 2; Chapter II, sections 1.2 and 3.

it is established that the status of organs, agencies, or instrumentalities under domestic law remains a central element,[94] a finding of attribution pursuant to international law is decisively rooted within its own independent categories, as also widely approved in investment cases.[95]

The foregoing may display the circumstance that at least a part of the epistemic community of international investment law and arbitration regards ARSIWA as *external norms*, when applied or used in the context of treaty-based arbitration.[96] The progress in clarity and methodological rigour in the resolution of issues of attributability (and State responsibility in general) in investment arbitration hinges on the arbitrators' position on their dialectics with customary international law. Only a more inclusive perspective and an enhanced account of the public international law dimension of investment disputes can trigger an evolution from the formative to the learned stage.

2.1 Independent Application of the Tests of Attribution

The rules of attribution under ARSIWA Articles 4, 5, and 8 deserve a differentiated and separate application. Each test of attributability corresponds to a different link with the State, namely institutional (organic), functional, and factual. Moreover, the application of a given rule of attribution (either for State organs, State instrumentalities, or private individuals) also entails different consequences, first and

[94] For an example, see *Eureko BV v Republic of Poland*, Ad Hoc Arbitration, Partial Award, 19 August 2005, para 122, referring to Articles 33 and 34 of the Polish Civil Code within the analysis of the status of the State Treasury of the Republic of Poland.

[95] *F-W Oil Interests, Inc v The Republic of Trinidad and Tobago*, ICSID Case No ARB/01/14, Award, 3 March 2006, para 203: 'The internal law of the State will be the starting point, but not the end point'; *Emilio Agustín Maffezini v The Kingdom of Spain*, ICSID Case No ARB/97/7, Decision on Jurisdiction, 25 January 2000, para 82: 'The Tribunal is also of the view that a domestic determination, be it legal, judicial or administrative, as to the juridical structure of an entity undertaking functions which may be classified as governmental, while it is to be given considerable weight, is not necessarily binding on an international arbitral tribunal. Whether an entity is to be regarded as an organ of the State and whether this might ultimately engage its responsibility, is a question of fact and law to be determined under the applicable principles of international law.' The same dialectics between international and national law is contemplated with regard to the determination of the objective element of the internationally wrongful act. See *Continental Casualty Company v The Argentine Republic*, ICSID Case No ARB/03/9, Decision on Jurisdiction, 22 February 2006, para 88, quoting *Elettronica Sicula SpA (ELSI) (United States of America v Italy)*, Judgment, 20 July 1989, para 73, ICJ Reports 1989, 15: 'Compliance with municipal law and compliance with the provisions of a treaty are different questions. What is a breach of treaty may be lawful in municipal law and what is unlawful in the municipal law may be fully innocent of violation of a treaty provision.'

[96] Jürgen Kurtz, 'The Paradoxical Treatment of the ILC Articles on State Responsibility in Investor-State Arbitration' (2010) 25 ICSID Review—Foreign Investment Law Journal 200, 201: 'there is often remarkably little substantive analysis of the conditions under which those norms can and should penetrate the investment treaty under adjudication. … Investment treaty arbitrators repeatedly fail to consider not only the formal justification for their use of an external norm but also the systemic and normative implications of a given choice.'

foremost the attributability of *ultra vires* acts pursuant to ARSIWA Article 7, which operates in relation to the former cases, but not to the latter. Accordingly, attribution rules are cumulative, but remain reciprocally independent and should not be treated in conjunction and merged by way of holistic interpretations by arbitrators.[97] However, this is what has usually occurred in the practice of international investment tribunals:

> In strict theory, the presence of any one of the possible criteria (status as state organ, governmental function, control) would suffice to establish attribution. In practice, tribunals have not followed the strict separation of those categories but have typically looked at them in conjunction.[98]

This practice frequently consists in the combined application of the attribution tests dictated for State organs (ARSIWA Article 4) *and/or* State entities (ARSIWA Article 5),[99] and of the criteria established for State entities (ARSIWA Article 5) *and/or* private individuals (ARSIWA Article 8).[100] In the first instance, tribunals have mainly reasoned on the basis of the commonality relating to the exercise

[97] *Eureko BV v Republic of Poland*, Ad Hoc Arbitration, Partial Award, 19 August 2005, para 132: 'The principles of attribution are cumulative so as to embrace not only the conduct of any State organ but the conduct of a person or entity which is not an organ of the State but which is empowered by the law of that State to exercise elements of governmental authority. It embraces as well the conduct of a person or group of persons if he or it is in fact acting on the instructions of, or under the direction or control of, that State.'

[98] Rudolf Dolzer and Christoph Schreuer, *Principles of International Investment Law* (2nd edn, Oxford University Press 2012) 225.

[99] *Toto Costruzioni Generali SpA v The Republic of Lebanon*, ICSID Case No ARB/07/12, Decision on Jurisdiction, 11 September 2009, para 60: 'Based on the foregoing, the Tribunal's view is that the CEGP and thereafter the CDR are exercising in the context of the Contract the governmental authority of the Republic of Lebanon, Therefore their acts are acts of the State of Lebanon, *as also confirmed by Article 5 of the ILC Draft*. Lebanon may be internationally liable for the acts of the CEGP and thereafter the CDR.' (emphasis added); *Iurii Bogdanov, Agurdino-Invest Ltd and Agurdino-Chimia JSC v Republic of Moldova*, SCC, Arbitral Award, 22 September 2005, 2.2.2: 'The Department of Privatization is, therefore, a central Governmental body of the Republic of Moldova, delegated by Governmental regulations to carry out state functions, and the effects of its conducts may be attributed to the State. It is generally recognised, in international law, that States are responsible for acts of their bodies or agencies that carry out State functions'; *Sergei Paushok, CJSC Golden East Company and CJSC Vostokneftegaz Company v The Government of Mongolia*, UNCITRAL, Award on Jurisdiction and Liability, 28 April 2011, para 592: 'The Tribunal therefore has no hesitation in concluding that MongolBank acted *de jure imperii*, if not in entering into the SCSA, at least when it exported GEM's gold for refining and deposited it or its value in an unallocated account in England "with the purposes of increasing the country's reserves." Those actions were *de jure imperii* and went beyond a mere contractual relationship. Therefore, even if MongolBank were not to be considered an organ of the State but merely an entity exercising elements of governmental authority, Claimants would be entitled to pursue their claim against Respondent in connection with the actions mentioned above.'; *Alex Genin, Eastern Credit Limited, Inc and AS Baltoil v The Republic of Estonia*, ICSID Case No ARB/99/2, Award, 25 June 2001, para 327; *Emilio Agustín Maffezini v The Kingdom of Spain*, ICSID Case No ARB/97/7, Decision on Jurisdiction, 25 January 2000, paras 79-80; *Noble Ventures, Inc v Romania*, ICSID Case No ARB/01/11, Award, 12 October 2005, para 83.

[100] *Limited Liability Company Amto v Ukraine*, SCC Case No 080/2005, Final Award, 26 March 2008, para 102: 'In these circumstances the Arbitral Tribunal considers that the conduct of Energoatom is attributable to the Ukraine, in accordance with established principles of international law, where it is shown that Energoatom was exercising *puissance publique* (governmental authority) or acted on the instructions of, or under the direction or control of, the State in carrying out the conduct.'

of governmental authority and functions. While a treaty claim is usually based on measures embodying *acta jure imperii*, conduct of a private nature (*acta jure gestionis*) can be attributed to a State by virtue of ARSIWA Article 4, which dispenses a rule of plenitude encompassing both governmental and commercial acts, but not under Article 5.[101] Moreover, while a formal empowerment by law of *puissance publique* is required under ARSIWA Article 5, under Article 4 attribution of conduct may be found upon application of the theory of *de facto* agents, which has been envisaged in the practice of investment tribunals.[102] In the second instance, tribunals generally emphasize the common element of a delegation pattern, namely public agency vis-à-vis private agency. However, attribution of the conduct of private individuals usually concerns tasks of a private nature, while it is necessarily triggered by the execution of *acta jure imperii* in the case of State instrumentalities under ARSIWA Article 5. Moreover, as stated above, the attribution of *ultra vires* conduct operates only with regard to the latter, never to the former, which is not a trivial difference.

This attitude to 'multi-qualified' (but eventually unqualified) attribution is meant either to corroborate the same operative result based on alternative grounds or to counterbalance the insufficiency of mandatory requirements established by each single attributability rule.[103] Instead, it is submitted that tribunals should address the tests of attribution individually in order to preserve the functioning and legal consequences of each attributability rule.

2.2 Umbrella Clauses

International investment tribunals conventionally adjudicate treaty claims as contrasted to contract claims.[104] However, a treaty claim may certainly be substantiated

[101] Georgios Petrochilos, 'Attribution' in Katia Yannaca-Small (ed), *Arbitration under International Investment Agreements: A Guide to the Key Issues* (Oxford University Press 2010) 287, 289.

[102] See *Flemingo DutyFree Shop Private Limited v the Republic of Poland*, UNCITRAL, Award, 12 August 2016, para 435; *Deutsche Bank AG v Democratic Socialist Republic of Sri Lanka*, ICSID Case No ARB/09/2, Award, 31 October 2012, para 405(f); *Saipem SpA v People's Republic of Bangladesh*, ICSID Case No ARB/05/07, Decision on Jurisdiction and Recommendation on Provisional Measures, 21 March 2007, para 149; *Saipem SpA v People's Republic of Bangladesh*, ICSID Case No ARB/05/07, Decision on Jurisdiction and Recommendation on Provisional Measures, 21 March 2007, para 149; *F-W Oil Interests, Inc v The Republic of Trinidad and Tobago*, ICSID Case No ARB/01/14, Award, 3 March 2006, para 203; *Emilio Agustín Maffezini v The Kingdom of Spain*, ICSID Case No ARB/97/7, Decision on Jurisdiction, 25 January 2000, paras 79–80, 89; *Gustav F W Hamester GmbH & Co KG v Republic of Ghana*, ICSID Case No ARB/07/24, Award, 18 June 2010, para 186 et seq.

[103] Luca Schicho, 'Attribution and State Entities: Diverging Approaches in Investment Arbitration' (2011) 12 Journal of World Investment & Trade 283–88: 'Finally, tribunals should not compensate a lack of evidence for one ground of attribution by relying on facts relevant for another ground of attribution that is also not sufficiently substantiated: a miss is a miss, no matter the distance, and two misses do not make a hit - should an entity seem both "almost empowered" to exercise governmental authority and "almost controlled", its conduct remains, nonetheless, non-attributable'.

[104] *Société Générale de Surveillance SA (SGS) v Islamic Republic of Pakistan*, ICSID Case No ARB/01/13, Decision of the Tribunal on Objections to Jurisdiction, 6 August 2003, paras 166–67; *Waste*

on the ground of sovereign conduct affecting the performance of a contract stipulated between a State and foreign investors.[105] In this respect, it should also be demonstrated that the transaction concerned is part of an economic operation that may qualify as investment for the purposes of jurisdiction *ratione materiae*.[106] In addition, States—as Parties to IIAs—are at liberty to contract treaty provisions obliging them to observe any obligation they have entered into with a foreign investor (*umbrella clause, clause of observance of obligations or undertakings, clause de couverture, clause de respect des engagements, clause parapluie*).[107] Such clauses

Management, Inc v United Mexican States (Waste Mangement II), ICSID Case No ARB(AF)/00/3, Award, 30 April 2004, para 160; *Joy Mining Machinery Limited v The Arab Republic of Egypt*, ICSID Case No ARB/03/11, Award on Jurisdiction, 6 August 2004, para 72; *Impregilo SpA v Islamic Republic of Pakistan*, ICSID Case No ARB/03/3, Decision on Jurisdiction, 22 April 2005, paras 210, 214, 216, 260; *Consortium RFCC v Kingdom of Morocco*, ICSID Case No ARB/00/6, Decision on Jurisdiction, 16 July 2001, para 68; *Consortium RFCC v Kingdom of Morocco*, ICSID Case No ARB/00/6, Award, 22 December 2003, para 38: '*Le Tribunal considère qu'il n'existe pas de principe d'assimilation nécessaire des violations contractuelles aux violations d'un traité bilatéral d'investissement.*'; *Cable Television of Nevis v Federation of St Kitts and Nevis*, ICSID Case No ARB/95/2, Award, 13 January 1997, para 2.22; *Azurix Corp v The Argentine Republic*, ICSID Case No ARB/01/12, Award, 14 July 2006, para 315; *Bayindir Insaat Turizm Ticaret Ve Sanayi AS v Islamic Republic of Pakistan*, ICSID Case No ARB/03/29, Award, 27 August 2009, para 135, 180; *Noble Ventures, Inc v Romania*, ICSID Case No ARB/01/11, Award, 12 October 2005, paras 53, 85; *Robert Azinian, Kenneth Davitian, & Ellen Baca v The United Mexican States*, ICSID Case No ARB (AF)/97/2, Award, 1 November 1999, para 87; *Duke Energy Electroquil Partners & Electroquil SA v Republic of Ecuador*, ICSID Case No ARB/04/19, Award, 18 August 2008, para 342; *Gustav F W Hamester GmbH & Co KG v Republic of Ghana*, ICSID Case No ARB/07/24, Award, 18 June 2010, para 292: 'The starting premise is that only the State as a sovereign can be in violation of its international obligations.'; *Toto Costruzioni Generali SpA v The Republic of Lebanon*, ICSID Case No ARB/07/12, Decision on Jurisdiction, 11 September 2009, para 103.

---

[105] *Eureko BV v Republic of Poland*, Ad Hoc Arbitration, Partial Award, 19 June 2005, para 241: 'There is an amplitude of authority for the proposition that when a State deprives an investor of the benefit of its contractual rights, directly or indirectly, it may be tantamount to a deprivation in violation of the type of provision contained in Article 5 of the Treaty. The deprivation of contractual rights may be expropriatory in substance and in effect.', quoting *Metalclad Corporation v The United Mexican States*, ICSID Case No ARB(AF)/97/1, Award, 30 August 2000, paras 74–101; *CME Czech Republic BV v The Czech Republic*, UNCITRAL, Partial Award, 13 September 2001, paras 154–64. See also *Compañiá de Aguas del Aconquija SA and Vivendi Universal SA v Argentine Republic* (formerly *Compañía de Aguas del Aconquija, SA and Compagnie Générale des Eaux v Argentine Republic*) (*Vivendi I*), ICSID Case No ARB/97/3, Decision on Annulment, 3 July 2003, para 110: '*the passage appears to imply that conduct of Tucumán carried out in the purported exercise of its rights as a party to the Concession Contract could not,* a priori, *have breached the BIT. However, there is no basis for such an assumption: whether particular conduct involves a breach of a treaty is not determined by asking whether the conduct purportedly involves an exercise of contractual rights*'.

[106] *Eureko BV v Republic of Poland*, Ad Hoc Arbitration, Partial Award, 19 June 2005, para 144: 'The Tribunal has a measure of hesitation in finding that Eureko's corporate governance rights under the SPA, standing alone, qualify as an investment under the Treaty. On balance, however, it finds that those rights, critical as they were to the conclusion of the SPA and hence to the making of Eureko's very large investment, do so qualify'.

[107] Gérard Cahin, 'La clause de couverture (dite *umbrella clause*)' (2015) 119 Revue Générale de Droit International Public 103; Yves Nouvel, 'La compétence matérielle: contrat, traité et clauses parapluie' in Charles Leben (ed), *La procédure arbitrale relative aux investissements internationaux. Aspects récents* (LGDJ 2010) 13; James Crawford, 'Treaty and Contract in Investment Arbitration' (2008) 24 Arbitration International 351; Thomas W Wälde, 'The "Umbrella" Clause in Investment Arbitration: a Comment on Original Intentions and Recent Cases' (2005) 6 Journal of World Investment & Trade 183; Christoph H Schreuer, 'Travelling the BIT Route—Of Waiting Periods, Umbrella Clauses and Forks in the Road' (2004) 5 Journal of World Investment & Trade 231; Walid Ben Hamida, 'La clause relative

are generally drafted through recourse to mandatory language, as found in ECT Article 10.1, where it is established that 'Each Contracting Party shall observe any obligations it has entered into with an Investor or an Investment of an Investor of any other Contracting Party'.[108] Umbrella clauses may also adopt a less peremptory wording: 'Either Contracting Party shall constantly guarantee the observance of the commitments it has entered into with respect to the investments of the investors of the other Contracting Party.'[109] Under the applicability of a clause of observance of obligations, it is worth emphasizing that treaty and contract claims always maintain their analytical distinction even if brought about by the very same conduct of the State.[110] This is a corollary of the two principles of supremacy of international law, on the one hand, and privity of contract, on the other.

au respect des engagements dans les traités d'investissement' in Charles Leben (ed), *Le contentieux arbitral transnational relatif à l'investissement. Nouveaux développements* (LGDJ 2006) 53; Yuval Shany, 'Contract Claims vs. Treaty Claims: Mapping Conflicts Between ICSID Decisions on Multisourced Investment Claims' (2005) 99 American Journal of International Law 835; Stephan W Schill, 'Enabling Private Ordering: Function, Scope and Effect of Umbrella Clauses in International Investment Treaties' (2009) 18 Minnesota Journal of International Law 1; Anthony C Sinclair, 'The Origins of the Umbrella Clause in the International Law of Investment Protection' (2004) 20 Arbitration International 411; Nick Gallus, 'An Umbrella Just for Two? BIT Obligations Observance Clauses and the Parties to a Contract' (2008) 24 Arbitration International 157; Stanimir A Alexandrov, 'Breaches of Contract and Breaches of Treaty' (2004) 5 Journal of World Investment & Trade 555; Michael Feit, 'Attribution and the Umbrella Clause: Is there a Way out of the Deadlock?' (2012) 21 Minnesota Journal of International Law 21; Michael Feit, 'Responsibility of the State Under International Law for the Breach of Contract Committed by a State-Owned Entity' (2010) 28 Berkeley Journal of International Law 142; Katia Yannaca-Small, 'What about this "Umbrella Clause"?' in Katia Yannaca-Small (ed), *Arbitration under International Investment Agreements: A Guide to the Key Issues* (Oxford University Press 2010) 479.

[108] ECT Article 10(1). See also UK–Argentina BIT (1990), Article 2(2); Lebanon–Italy BIT (1997), Article 9(2); Germany–Ghana BIT (1995), Article 9(2); US–Romania BIT (1992), Article II(2)(c); Philippines–Switzerland BIT (1997), Article X(2); Netherlands–Poland BIT (1992), Article 3.5; Netherlands–Venezuela BIT (1991), Article 3(4); UK–Peru BIT (1993), Article 3(1).

[109] Pakistan–Switzerland BIT (1995), Article 11. See, in addition, Italy–Jordan BIT (1996), Article 2(4).

[110] *Compañiá de Aguas del Aconquija SA and Vivendi Universal SA v Argentine Republic* (formerly *Compañía de Aguas del Aconquija, SA and Compagnie Générale des Eaux v Argentine Republic*) *(Vivendi I)*, ICSID Case No ARB/97/3, Decision on Annulment, 3 July 2003, para 96: 'whether there has been a breach of the BIT and whether there has been a breach of contract are different questions. Each of these claims will be determined by reference to its own proper or applicable law in the case of the BIT, by international law; in the case of the Concession Contract, by the proper law of the contract.'; *Consortium RFCC v Kingdom of Morocco*, ICSID Case No ARB/00/6, Award, 22 December 2003, para 48: '*Une telle violation peut certes résulter d'une violation du contrat, mais sans qu'une éventuelle violation du contrat ne constitue, ipso jure et en elle-même, une violation du Traité, comme le Tribunal l'a rappelé ci-dessus*'; *Duke Energy Electroquil Partners & Electroquil SA v Republic of Ecuador*, ICSID Case No ARB/04/19, Award, 18 August 2008, para 342; *Impregilo SpA v Islamic Republic of Pakistan*, ICSID Case No ARB/03/3, Decision on Jurisdiction, 22 April 2005, para 258: 'the fact that a breach may give rise to a contract claim does not mean that it cannot also—and separately—give rise to a treaty claim. Even if the two perfectly coincide, they remain analytically distinct, and necessarily require different enquiries.'; *Bayindir Insaat Turizm Ticaret Ve Sanayi AS v Islamic Republic of Pakistan*, ICSID Case No ARB/03/29, Decision on Jurisdiction, 14 November 2005, para 148. See Bernardo M Cremades, 'Litigating Annulment Proceedings. The *Vivendi* Matter: Contract and Treaty Claims' in Emmanuel Gaillard and Yas Banifatemi (eds), *Annulment of ICSID Awards* (Juris Publishing, Inc 2004) 87, 93.

Whether the effect of an umbrella clause is the 'internationalization' of an otherwise ordinary contractual claim has been debated.[111] Some tribunals have tended to side in favour of the transformation of the claim from contractual to 'international'.[112] For instance, the *Noble Ventures v Romania* tribunal held:

> An umbrella clause is usually seen as transforming municipal law obligations into obligations directly cognizable in international law. ... In other words, two States may include in a bilateral investment treaty a provision to the effect that, in the interest of achieving the objects and goals of the treaty, the host State may incur international responsibility by reason of a breach of its contractual obligations towards the private investor of the other Party, the breach of contract being thus 'internationalized', i.e. assimilated to a breach of the treaty. In such a case, an international tribunal will be bound to seek to give useful effect to the provision that the parties have adopted.[113]

However, a complete assimilation of breaches of contractual arrangements, although being linked to a foreign investment, to breaches of an international investment treaty is hardly tenable. There is always a 'double step' to be taken into consideration. Only the proper law of contract should govern contractual obligations (including *ultra vires* issues), determined upon application of the choice-of-law rules of the relevant system of private international law. Accordingly, the law applicable to a contract may be a national law (for instance, the law of the host State) or other laws, including general principles of international law, identified through the conflict-of-laws or *voie directe* method. Once a breach of contract has been found pursuant to the proper law, then the umbrella clause may intervene to allow an investor to transpose a contract claim and its legal consequences from the municipal law arena to the 'forum' provided by international law, consistent with a justification of efficiency and concentration of remedies (umbrella clauses

[111] As to the *querelle* on the application of the principle *pacta sunt servanda* to contractual matters, cf Giorgio Sacerdoti, *I contratti tra Stati e stranieri nel diritto internazionale* (Giuffrè 1972) 325–28, 358–59, quoting Hans Wehberg, 'Pacta Sunt Servanda' (1959) 53 American Journal of International Law 775, 786; Paul de Visscher, 'Les aspects juridiques fondamentaux de la question de Suez' (1958) 62 Revue Générale de Droit International Public 400, 436–37; Philip C Jessup, 'Responsibility of States for Injuries to Individuals' (1946) 46 Columbia Law Review 903, 913; Clyde Eagleton, *The Responsibility of States in International Law* (New York University Press 1928) 167–68. For a certain support in early arbitral practice, see *Affaire relative à la concession des phares de l'Empire ottoman (Lighthouses Arbitration) (France v Greece)*, 24 July 1956, 12 RIAA 155, 198–99.

[112] *SGS Société Générale de Surveillance SA v Republic of the Philippines*, ICSID Case No ARB/02/6, Decision of the Tribunal on Objections to Jurisdiction, 29 January 2004, paras 115–18, 127; *Eureko BV v Republic of Poland*, Ad Hoc Arbitration, Partial Award, 19 June 2005, para 250; *Noble Ventures, Inc v Romania*, ICSID Case No ARB/01/11, Award, 12 October 2005, para 54; *Petrobart Limited v The Kyrgyz Republic*, SCC Case No 126/2003, Arbitral Award, 29 March 2005, paras 27–28; *Fedax NV v The Republic of Venezuela*, ICSID Case No ARB/96/3, Award, 9 March 1998, para 29.

[113] *Noble Ventures, Inc v Romania*, ICSID Case No ARB/01/11, Award, 12 October 2005, paras 53–54.

as dispute resolution agreements). Indeed, the umbrella clause functions as a lift to international investment law, but does not change the inner nature of a contract claim.[114] This explains how the international law of State responsibility, including attribution rules, does not apply to determine the subjective and objective elements of contractual breaches.[115] As James Crawford has warned:

> there has also been some confusion particularly between the law of attribution and issues of contractual responsibility or liability. . . . The rules of attribution have nothing to do with questions of contractual responsibility.[116]

This elucidation allows for an examination of the issue of the coverage of umbrella clauses in relation to contractual breaches of State instrumentalities or parastatal entities (the so-called 'it problem').[117] The question is whether a foreign investor may file before an ISDS tribunal a contract claim based on its arrangements with a State entity. The preponderant majority of investment tribunals answers in the negative, notably emphasizing that the separate juristic personality of parastatal entities precludes their inclusion in the 'it' of the umbrella clause.[118]

[114] *Toto Costruzioni Generali SpA v The Republic of Lebanon*, ICSID Case No ARB/07/12, Decision on Jurisdiction, 11 September 2009, para 202: 'Although Article 9.2 of the Treaty may be used as a mechanism for the enforcement of claims, it does not elevate pure contractual claims into treaty claims. The contractual claims remain based upon the contract; they are governed by the law of the contract and may be affected by the other provisions of the contract.'; *CMS Gas Transmission Company v The Republic of Argentina*, ICSID Case No ARB/01/8, Decision of the ad hoc Committee on the Application for Annulment of the Argentine Republic, 25 September 2007, para 95.

[115] Zachary Douglas, 'Other Specific Regimes of Responsibility: Investment Treaty Arbitration and ICSID' in James Crawford, Alain Pellet, and Simon Olleson (eds), *The Law of International Responsibility* (Oxford University Press 2010) 815, 819, fn 14.

[116] James Crawford, 'Investment Arbitration and the ILC Articles on State Responsibility' (2010) 25 ICSID Review—Foreign Investment Law Journal 127, 134.

[117] Gérard Cahin, 'La clause de couverture (dite *umbrella clause*)' (2015) 119 Revue Générale de Droit International Public 103, 133–35; Kaj Hobér, 'State Responsibility and Attribution' in Peter Muchlinski, Federico Ortino, and Christoph Schreuer (eds), *The Oxford Handbook of International Investment Law* (Oxford University Press 2008) 550, 575–82; Michael Feit, 'Responsibility of the State Under International Law for the Breach of Contract Committed by a State-Owned Entity' (2010) 28 Berkeley Journal of International Law 142, 161.

[118] *Salini Costruttori SpA and Italstrade SpA v Kingdom of Morocco*, ICSID Case No ARB/00/4, Decision on Jurisdiction, 31 July 2000, para 60: 'However, the Tribunal considers that its scope of application regarding the nature of disputes is limited as to the persons concerned. In the case where the State has organised a sector of activity through a distinct legal entity, be it a State entity, it does not necessarily follow that the State has accepted *a priori* that the jurisdiction offer contained in Article 8 should bind it with respect to contractual breaches committed by this entity.'; *Impregilo SpA v Islamic Republic of Pakistan*, ICSID Case No ARB/03/3, Decision on Jurisdiction, 22 April 2005, para 223: 'the Contracts were concluded by a separate and distinct entity'; *Limited Liability Company Amto v Ukraine*, SCC Case No 080/2005, Final Award, 26 March 2008, para 110: 'However, in the present case the contractual obligations have been undertaken by a separate legal entity, and so the umbrella clause has no direct application.'; *William Nagel v The Czech Republic*, SCC Case No 049/2002, Final Award, 9 September 2003, paras 162–63: 'When engaged in commercial activities, the State enterprise could not and did not act as an agent or instrumentality of the Government, and the Government did not assume any of the obligations or liabilities of the State enterprise's activities. Under the State Enterprise Act, a State enterprise could not bind the Government and the Government was not bound by a State enterprise's contractual obligations.'; *CMS Gas Transmission Company v The Republic of Argentina*, ICSID Case No ARB/01/8,

While it is recognized that attribution rules under public international law do not intervene with regard to an umbrella clause,[119] at the same time nothing prevents the proper law of contract from dispensing theories, such as representation or agency, on the extension of substantive liability to the State in connection with the undertakings of its parastatals (*imputation de la volonté* vis-à-vis *imputation du comportement*).[120] The factual findings for the application of such theories certainly may include elements of governmental (corporate) control and direction, or instructions specifically received from the State by a SOE, similarly to the requirements for a finding demanded by the structural test under ARSIWA Article 5 or the factual test under ARSIWA Article 8.[121] In addition, the consideration of the economic unity of the contractual dealings stipulated in relation to a foreign investment either by a State or its parastatals may support the extension of the

Decision of the ad hoc Committee on the Application for Annulment of the Argentine Republic, 25 September 2007, para 95; *Salini Costruttori SpA and Italstrade SpA v The Hashemite Kingdom of Jordan*, ICSID Case No ARB/02/13, Decision on Jurisdiction, 9 November 2004, paras 100–01: 'Indeed, the contract at issue was entered into between the Claimants and the Jordan Valley Authority, which under the laws of Jordan governing the contract, has a legal personality distinct from that of the Jordanian State.'; *EDF (Services) Limited v Romania*, ICSID Case No ARB/05/13, Award, 8 October 2009, paras 317–19: 'There is in principle no responsibility by the State for such breach in the instant case since the State, not being a party to the contract, has not directly assumed the contractual obligations the breach of which is invoked. ... Attribution does not change the extent and content of the obligations arising under the ASRO Contract and the SKY Contract, that remain contractual, nor does it make Romania party to such contracts.'; *Bayindir Insaat Turizm Ticaret Ve Sanayi AS v Islamic Republic of Pakistan*, ICSID Case No ARB/03/29, Award, 27 August 2009, para 113: 'From a contractual standpoint, these actions were those of NHA and not of the Government of Pakistan.'

[119] This conclusion does not receive unanimous consensus, see *Société Générale de Surveillance SA (SGS) v Islamic Republic of Pakistan*, ICSID Case No ARB/01/13, Decision of the Tribunal on Objections to Jurisdiction, 6 August 2003, para 167; *Eureko BV v Republic of Poland*, Ad Hoc Arbitration, Partial Award, 19 June 2005, para 121. For a doctrinal position advocating for the application of attribution rules to contract claims, see Kaj Hobér, 'State Responsibility and Attribution' in Peter Muchlinski, Federico Ortino, and Christoph Schreuer (eds), *The Oxford Handbook of International Investment Law* (Oxford University Press 2008) 550, 582: 'if the "it" problem were to be solved by applying only municipal law—and not the rules of attribution of international law—it would seem that this would allow states to do precisely what the rules of state responsibility were intended to prevent, namely, to avoid responsibility by delegating responsibilities, to allow states to 'contract out' of state responsibility.'; Michael Feit, 'Responsibility of the State Under International Law for the Breach of Contract Committed by a State-Owned Entity' (2010) 28 Berkeley Journal of International Law 142, 163.

[120] Yves Nouvel, 'Les entités paraétatiques dans la jurisprudence du CIRDI' in Charles Leben (ed), *Le contentieux arbitral transnational relatif à l'investissement. Nouveaux développements* (LGDJ 2006) 25, 50. See *SGS Société Générale de Surveillance SA v Republic of the Philippines*, ICSID Case No ARB/02/6, Decision of the Tribunal on Objections to Jurisdiction, 29 January 2004, para 117; *Impregilo SpA v Islamic Republic of Pakistan*, ICSID Case No ARB/03/3, Decision on Jurisdiction, 22 April 2005, para 167.

[121] Pierre-Marie Dupuy, 'Les émanations engagent-elles la responsabilité des Etats? Etude de droit international des investissements' (2006) EUI Working Paper LAW No 2006/7, 7-8: '*l'unification sous l'égide du droit international des solutions retenues en matière de responsabilité encourue par l'Etat pour les faits illicites de ses émanations n'est encore que partielle. Dans bien des cas, on doit relever la persistance, pas toujours aisément justifiable au regard du droit international classique, de solutions particulières. Révèlent elles le maintient d'une réticence chez certains arbitres ou la démonstration d'une spécificité de la matière, liée notamment à la dualité des types de requêtes soumises à l'arbitrage*'.

contractual obligations (*engagement substantiel*), corresponding to the extension of the subjective scope of the arbitration agreement (*engagement juridictionnel*), which is also found in early ICSID arbitration based on investment contracts.[122] The resulting 'attribution of liability' may be then elevated to the public international law dimension so as to allow investors to bring a contract claim in investment arbitration based on their transactions involving SOEs.[123]

Beyond the ordinary functioning of the proper law governing contractual arrangements, States may expressly stipulate umbrella clauses where they establish that the 'it' also includes State instrumentalities (or also territorial sub-state entities). Upon closer inspection, this clause, which is nearly absent in State practice, would create an effect of *ex post* 'ratification' of conduct, consistent with the traditional position applied to umbrella clauses.[124] Finally, as above mentioned, States may also create duties for their organs to ensure or monitor performance of contracts concluded between their instrumentalities or monopolies and foreign investors, as in ECT Article 22, which operates at the level of primary rules and does not affect the attribution of the conduct of parastatal entities.[125]

2.3 Merits versus Jurisdiction

Once the jurisdiction of an international tribunal is established, attribution issues receive preliminary analysis in comparison to the other secondary rules and to the applicable primary rules. Thus, the attribution of conduct to a State for the purposes of its international responsibility is to be considered as a question of merits, not of jurisdiction, in that it represents the 'subjective' element of an internationally wrongful act.[126] In the realm of ISDS, attribution of acts and omissions to a State should be alleged by the claimant investor and, accordingly, established. Therefore, it is appropriate to provide a brief account of the evidentiary standards required in investment arbitration in the jurisdictional vis-à-vis merits phase.

[122] *Holiday Inns v Morocco*, ICSID Case No ARB/72/1, Decision on Jurisdiction, 1 July 1973, unpublished, in Pierre Lalive, 'The First "World Bank" Arbitration (*Holiday Inns v. Morocco*) - Some Legal Problems' (1980) 51 British Year Book of International Law 123, 159; *Klöckner Industrie Anlagen GmbH v Republic of Cameroon*, ICSID Case No ARB/81/2, Award, 21 October 1983, 2 ICSID Reports 3, 69; *SARL Benvenuti & Bonfant v People's Republic of the Congo*, ICSID Case No ARB/77/2, Award, 8 August 1980, para 4.40, 1 ICSID Reports 354.

[123] Shotaro Hamamoto, 'Parties to the "Obligations" in the Obligations Observance ("Umbrella") Clause' in (2015) 30 ICSID Review—Foreign Investment Law 449, 463.

[124] See *supra* in this paragraph.

[125] *Nykomb Synergetics Technology Holding AB v The Republic of Latvia*, SCC, Arbitral Award, 16 December 2003, para 4.2.

[126] Christian Tomuschat, 'Attribution of International Responsibility: Direction and Control' in Malcolm Evans and Panos Koutrakos (eds), *The International Responsibility of the European Union: European and International Perspectives* (Hart Publishing 2013) 7, 33.

Based on a general principle of international law, each party to the process has to prove the facts on which its allegations are grounded (*onus probandi incumbit ei qui dicit, non ei qui negat*).[127] International courts and tribunals have methodologically distinguished the intensity of the burden of proof in the jurisdictional and merits phases.[128] In her Separate Opinion to the Preliminary Objection decision in the *Oil Platform* case, Judge Higgins addressed the various solutions rendered by the PCIJ and ICJ in relation to the evidentiary burden at the jurisdictional stage.[129] In this historic review, she emphasized the interpretative contrast between the requirement of a sufficient prima facie case (a 'provisional conclusion') for jurisdiction,[130] and the alternative view that a conclusive connection between the subject matter of the claim and the asserted basis for jurisdiction must be thoroughly assessed *in limine litis*.[131] She concluded that the decision whether an international court is vested of jurisdiction should be definitive and should be based on the *pro tempore* finding that the facts, as alleged by the claimant, if established, could result in a breach of the applicable international obligations.[132]

[127] *Military and Paramilitary Activities in and against Nicaragua (Nicaragua v United States of America)*, Jurisdiction and Admissibility, Judgment, 26 November 1984, para 101, ICJ Reports 1984, 392, 437: 'it is the litigant seeking to establish a fact who bears the burden of proving it'; *Avena and Other Mexican Nationals (Mexico v United States of America)*, Judgment, 31 March 2004, para 55, ICJ Reports 2004, 12, 41. In the ISDS context, see *Waguih Elie George Siag and Clorinda Vecchi v The Arab Republic of Egypt*, ICSID Case No ARB/05/15, Award, 1 June 2009, para 315: 'As to the burden of proof, the general rule, well established in international arbitrations, is that the Claimant bears the burden of proof with respect to the facts it alleges and the Respondent carries the burden of proof with respect to its defences.'; *Chevron Corporation (USA) and Texaco Petroleum Company (USA) v The Republic of Ecuador*, UNCITRAL, PCA Case No 34877, Interim Award, 1 December 2008, para 138. See Bin Cheng, *General Principles of Law as Applied by International Courts and Tribunals* (reprinted Cambridge University Press 2006, first published Stevens & Sons, Ltd 1953) 326 et seq.

[128] The ICJ has not invariably adopted the qualification of jurisdictional issues as matters of fact, susceptible to be proven by the parties. See *Fisheries Jurisdiction (Spain v Canada)*, Jurisdiction of the Court, Judgment, 4 December 1998, paras 37–38, ICJ Reports 1998, 432, 450–51: 'the establishment or otherwise of jurisdiction is not a matter for the parties but for the Court itself. ... the establishment of the Court's jurisdiction ... is a "question of law to be resolved in the light of the relevant facts." ... That being so, there is no burden of proof to be discharged in the matter of jurisdiction', quoting *Border and Transborder Armed Actions (Nicaragua v Honduras)*, Jurisdiction and Admissibility, Judgment, 20 December 1988, para 16, ICJ Reports 1988, 69, 76; and *The Factory at Chorzów*, Jurisdiction, Judgment No 8, 26 July 1927, PCIJ Reports 1927, Series A, No 9, 32.

[129] *Oil Platform (Islamic Republic of Iran v United States of America)*, Preliminary Objection, Judgment, Separate Opinion of Judge Higgins, 12 December 1996, paras 9–26, ICJ Reports 1996, 803, 847. See also *Oil Platform (Islamic Republic of Iran v United States of America)*, Judgment, Separate Opinion of Judge Higgins, 6 November 2003, para 33, ICJ Reports 2003, 161, 234: '[t]he principal judicial organ of the United Nations should likewise make clear what standards of proof it requires to establish what sorts of facts.'

[130] *Nationality Decrees Issued in Tunis and Morocco (French Zone) on November 8th, 1921*, Advisory Opinion, 7 February 1923, PCIJ Reports 1923, Series B, No 4, 26; *Ambatielos (Greece v United Kingdom)*, Merits: Obligation to Arbitrate, Judgment, 19 May 1953, ICJ Reports 1953, 10, 18: 'a sufficiently plausible character to warrant a conclusion that the claim is based on the Treaty'; *Interhandel (Switzerland v United States of America)*, Preliminary Objections, Judgment, 21 March 1959, ICJ Reports 1959, 6, 24.

[131] *Mavrommatis Palestine Concessions (Greece v United Kingdom)*, Judgment No 2, 30 August 1924, PCIJ Reports 1924, Series A, No 2, 15-17, 24.

[132] *Oil Platform (Islamic Republic of Iran v United States of America)*, Preliminary Objection, Judgment, Separate Opinion of Judge Higgins, 12 December 1996, paras 31–32, 34, ICJ Reports 1996, 803.

Investment tribunals have comprehensively applied the evidentiary standard proposed by Judge Higgins. Accordingly, at the jurisdictional phase, arbitrators retain competence on the claim in case the facts or contentions presented by the investor, if proven, would establish a case of violation of the relevant investment treaty.[133] At the same time, in case jurisdiction is necessarily dependent on the existence of given facts, tribunals require them to be finally proven in the jurisdictional phase upon fulfilment of a higher standard of evidence than the prima facie test.[134] Indeed, the distinction between facts establishing a breach of the applicable treaty and facts representing requirements for the tribunal's competence is of

[133] *Ambiente Ufficio SpA et al v Argentine Republic* (formerly *Giordano Alpi et al v Argentine Republic*), ICSID Case No ARB/08/9, Decision on Jurisdiction and Admissibility, 8 February 2013, paras 535–40; *Abaclat et al v Argentine Republic* (formerly *Giovanna Beccara et al v The Argentine Republic*), ICSID Case No ARB/07/5, Decision on Jurisdiction and Admissibility, 4 August 2011, para 303, 311, 314–15; *Saipem SpA v People's Republic of Bangladesh*, ICSID Case No ARB/05/07, Decision on Jurisdiction and Recommendation on Provisional Measures, 21 March 2007, paras 84–91; *Pac Rim Cayman LLC v Republic of El Salvador*, ICSID Case No ARB/09/12, Decision on the Respondent's Jurisdictional Objections, 1 June 2012, para 2.5; *Phoenix Action, Ltd v The Czech Republic*, ICSID Case No ARB/06/5, Award, 15 April 2009, para 61; *Gustav F W Hamester GmbH & Co KG v Republic of Ghana*, ICSID Case No ARB/07/24, Award, 18 June 2010, para 143: 'If jurisdiction rests on the existence of certain facts, they have to be proven at the jurisdictional stage. However, if facts are alleged in order to establish a violation of the relevant BIT, they have to be accepted as such at the jurisdictional stage, until their existence is ascertained (or not) at the merits stage.'; *Bayindir Insaat Turizm Ticaret Ve Sanayi AS v Islamic Republic of Pakistan*, ICSID Case No ARB/03/29, Decision on Jurisdiction, 14 November 2005, paras 196–97; *Impregilo SpA v Islamic Republic of Pakistan*, ICSID Case No ARB/03/3, Decision on Jurisdiction, 22 April 2005, para 237 et seq, 254; *Plama Consortium Limited v Republic of Bulgaria*, ICSID Case No ARB/03/24, Decision on Jurisdiction, 8 February 2005, paras 118–19, 128, 132; *Salini Costruttori SpA and Italstrade SpA v The Hashemite Kingdom of Jordan*, ICSID Case No ARB/02/13, Decision on Jurisdiction, 9 November 2004, para 137 et seq, 151: 'The Tribunal is in full agreement with this jurisprudence. It reflects the balance to be struck between two opposing preoccupations: to ensure that courts and tribunals are not flooded with claims which have no chance of success and sometimes are even of an abusive nature; but to ensure equally that, in considering issues of jurisdiction, courts and tribunals do not go into the merits of cases without sufficient prior debate.'; *Siemens AG v The Argentine Republic*, ICSID Case No ARB/02/8, Decision on Jurisdiction, 3 August 2004, para 180; *Société Générale de Surveillance SA (SGS) v Republic of the Philippines*, ICSID Case No ARB/02/6, Decision of the Tribunal on Objections to Jurisdiction, 29 January 2004, para 26, 157: 'Provided the facts as alleged by the Claimant and as appearing from the initial pleadings fairly raise questions of breach of one or more provisions of the BIT, the Tribunal has jurisdiction to determine the claim.'; *Société Générale de Surveillance SA (SGS) v Islamic Republic of Pakistan*, ICSID Case No ARB/01/13, Decision of the Tribunal on Objections to Jurisdiction, 6 August 2003, para 145; *United Parcel Service of America Inc (UPS) v Government of Canada*, UNCITRAL, Award on Jurisdiction, 22 November 2002, para 36; *Wena Hotels Limited v Arab Republic of Egypt*, ICSID Case No ARB/98/4, Decision on Jurisdiction, 29 June 1999, 41 ILM 881, 890-891; *Amco Asia Corporation, Pan American Development Limited and PT Amco Indonesia v Republic of Indonesia*, ICSID Case No ARB/81/1, Decision on Jurisdiction, 25 September 1983, para 38, 1 ICSID Reports 389; *Methanex Corporation v United States of America*, UNCITRAL, Partial Award, 7 August 2002, para 116 et seq, 121.

[134] *Pac Rim Cayman LLC v Republic of El Salvador*, ICSID Case No ARB/09/12, Decision on the Respondent's Jurisdictional Objections, 1 June 2012, paras 2.8–2.11; *Phoenix Action, Ltd v The Czech Republic*, ICSID Case No ARB/06/5, Award, 15 April 2009, paras 61–64; *Inceysa Vallisoletana, SL v Republic of El Salvador*, ICSID Case No ARB/03/26, Award, 2 August 2006, para 155; *Industria Nacional de Alimentos, SA and Indalsa Perú, SA v The Republic of Peru* (formerly *Empresas Lucchetti, SA and Lucchetti Peru, SA v The Republic of Peru*), ICSID Case No ARB/03/4, Decision on Annulment, 5 September 2007, paras 118–19; *Gustav F W Hamester GmbH & Co KG v Republic of Ghana*, ICSID Case No ARB/07/24, Award, 18 June 2010, para 143; *National Gas SAE v Arab Republic of Egypt*, ICSID Case No ARB/11/7, Award, 3 April 2014, para 118.

threshold importance and reasonably supports a different standard of the burden of proof at the stage of jurisdiction:

> In sum, the Tribunal considers that as a general approach, it is correct that factual matters should provisionally be accepted at face value, since the proper time to prove or disprove such facts is during the merits phase. But when a particular circumstance constitutes a critical element for the establishment of the jurisdiction itself, such fact must be proven, and the Tribunal must take a decision thereon when ruling on its jurisdiction. In our case, this means that the Tribunal must ascertain that the prerequisites for its jurisdiction are fulfilled, and that the facts on which its jurisdiction can be based are proven.[135]

Factual issues pertaining to the attribution of conduct should be completely demonstrated in the merits phase of an investment case.[136] Indeed, attributability might not be crystal clear at a preliminary phase of the international process, in that issues of attribution may hinge on factual or substantive elements to be ascertained in the course of the merits phase.[137] Accordingly, factual issues of attributability are subject to the prima facie ('at first sight') scrutiny applicable to merits claims at the stage of jurisdiction (*pro tem* conclusion that the facts alleged by the claimant, if established, can meet the requirements demanded by the rules of attribution).[138]

[135] *Phoenix Action, Ltd v The Czech Republic*, ICSID Case No ARB/06/5, Award, 15 April 2009, para 64.

[136] *Saipem SpA v People's Republic of Bangladesh*, ICSID Case No ARB/05/07, Decision on Jurisdiction and Recommendation on Provisional Measures, 21 March 2007, para 144: 'it is not for the Tribunal at the jurisdictional stage to examine whether the acts complained of give rise to the State's responsibility, except if it were manifest that the entity involved had no link whatsoever with the State. This is plainly not the case in the present dispute.'; *Jan de Nul NV and Dredging International NV v Arab Republic of Egypt*, ICSID Case No ARB/04/13, Decision on Jurisdiction, 16 June 2006, para 89: 'When assessing the merits of the dispute, the Tribunal will rule on the issue of attribution under international law.' But see *Teinver SA, Transportes de Cercanías SA and Autobuses Urbanos del Sur SA v The Argentine Republic*, ICSID Case No ARB/09/1, Decision on Jurisdiction, 21 December 2012, para 271: 'While Respondent asserts that substantial case law supports its position that the question of attribution is jurisdictional in nature, this case law also recognizes that not all questions of attribution are identical or involve an identical context.'; *Gustav F W Hamester GmbH & Co KG v Republic of Ghana*, ICSID Case No ARB/07/24, Award, 18 June 2010, para 140: 'The question whether the issue of attribution is, in a given case, one of jurisdiction or of merits is not, in the Tribunal's *view, susceptible of a clear-cut answer*'.

[137] *Gustav F W Hamester GmbH & Co KG v Republic of Ghana*, ICSID Case No ARB/07/24, Award, 18 June 2010, paras 142–43: 'Not all issues, however, are so discrete or easily answered. Many—as is the case with attribution—entail more complex considerations, which could be characterized both as jurisdictional and relevant to the merits (and so to be considered only if the Tribunal has jurisdiction). Moreover, each of the alleged acts is closely connected to the question of whether Respondent has committed substantive violations of the BIT. ... The question of "attribution" does not, itself, dictate whether there has been a violation of international law. Rather, it is only a means to ascertain whether the State is involved. As such, the question of attribution looks more like a jurisdictional question. But in many instances, questions of attribution and questions of legality are closely intermingled, and it is difficult to deal with the question of attribution without a full enquiry into the merits.' Accord, *Tulip Real Estate and Development Netherlands BV v Republic of Turkey*, ICSID Case No ARB/11/28, Award, 10 March 2014, para 276.

[138] *Impregilo SpA v Islamic Republic of Pakistan*, ICSID Case No ARB/03/3, Decision on Jurisdiction, 22 April 2005, para 266(a)-(b); *Saipem SpA v People's Republic of Bangladesh*, ICSID Case No ARB/

When the proceedings of an international investment dispute are bifurcated, the distinction between the evidentiary standards applicable at the jurisdictional and merits phases is more palpable. However, this reasoning is generally cursory in the arbitral decisions on jurisdiction. This is understood in light of the claimants' strategy invariably to plead attribution of the measures at issue to State organs. Accordingly, a plausible contention of governmental actions pursuant to ARSIWA Article 4 would be sufficient to meet the prima facie test with regard to attribution, it being unnecessary to further investigate attributability under ARSIWA Articles 5 or 8.[139]

States also retain the prerogative to widen the scope of the jurisdiction *ratione personae* of an ICSID tribunal pursuant to ICSID Convention Article 25(1)–(3).[140] Such provisions allow States to unilaterally designate constituent subdivisions

05/07, Decision on Jurisdiction and Recommendation on Provisional Measures, 21 March 2007, para 145: 'In fact, at first sight at least, Petrobangla appears to be part of the State under Bangladeshi law.'; *Emilio Agustín Maffezini v The Kingdom of Spain*, ICSID Case No ARB/97/7, Decision on Jurisdiction, 25 January 2000, para 89: 'the Tribunal concludes that the Claimant has made out a *prima facie* case that SODIGA is a State entity acting on behalf of the Kingdom of Spain.'

[139] *Mr Franck Charles Arif v Republic of Moldova*, ICSID Case No ARB/11/23, Award, 8 April 2013, para 344; *Salini Costruttori SpA and Italstrade SpA v Kingdom of Morocco*, ICSID Case No ARB/00/4, Decision on Jurisdiction, 31 July 2000, para 30: 'Since the claims of the Italian companies are being directed against the State and are founded on the violation of the Bilateral Treaty, it is not necessary, in order to determine whether the Tribunal has jurisdiction, to know whether ADM is a State entity'; *Consortium RFCC v Kingdom of Morocco*, ICSID Case No ARB/00/6, Decision on Jurisdiction, 16 July 2001, para 34: '*Les demandes du Consortium étant dirigées contre l'Etat et fondées sur la violation de l'Accord bilatéral, il n'est pas nécessaire, pour la détermination de la compétence du Tribunal, de savoir si ADM est une émanation de l'Etat.*'; *Helnan International Hotels A/S v Arab Republic of Egypt*, ICSID Case No ARB/05/19, Decision on Jurisdiction, 17 October 2006, para 91: 'The Arbitral Tribunal does not need to decide on the status of EGOTH in order to assess its jurisdiction in this case. It has already found that the Claimant has established the existence of a *prima facie* dispute directly arising out of an investment and involving EGYPT and that the dispute falls within the temporal scope of the Treaty. However, since the parties have thoroughly discussed this point, it considers *ex abundanti cautela* that it is its duty to solve this disputed issue in this Decision.'; *Salini Costruttori SpA and Italstrade SpA v The Hashemite Kingdom of Jordan*, ICSID Case No ARB/02/13, Decision on Jurisdiction, 9 November 2004, para 64; *Romak SA (Switzerland) v The Republic of Uzbekistan*, UNCITRAL, PCA Case No AA280, Award, 26 November 2009, para 161. In a different vein, cf *Aguas del Tunari, SA v Republic of Bolivia*, ICSID Case No ARB/02/3, Decision on Respondent's Objections to Jurisdiction, 21 October 2005, para 137: 'The Parties raise a number of issues which require more extensive findings based on additional evidence. At this jurisdictional phase of the proceedings, the Tribunal need not determine the questions of (1) attribution and State responsibility under the BIT, or (2) the precise relationship between the Republic of Bolivia and the Water Superintendency. These questions will be determined later, as needed, at the merits phase of the Tribunal's proceedings.'

[140] Christoph Schreuer, with Loretta Malintoppi, August Reinisch, and Anthony Sinclair, *The ICSID Convention: A Commentary* (2nd edn, Cambridge University Press 2009) 152, para 237: 'Therefore, designations of constituent subdivisions or agencies serve procedural convenience but do not affect questions of State responsibility. The State entity's party status is independent of the issue of the attribution of its actions to the State. In some instances the State entity may be the only potential respondent under the rules of State responsibility. In other cases, where attribution can be established, the State is an alternative or additional respondent despite the designation.'; Yves Nouvel, 'Les entités paraétatiques dans la jurisprudence du CIRDI' in Charles Leben (ed), *Le contentieux arbitral transnational relatif à l'investissement. Nouveaux développements* (LGDJ 2006) 25, 28; Clifford Larsen, 'ICSID Jurisdiction: the Relationship of Contracting States to Sub-states Entities' in Norbert Horn (ed), *Arbitrating Foreign Investment Disputes* (Kluwer Law International 2004) 353, 358–59.

or agencies of a contracting State, thus creating a special jurisdictional mechanism enabling such entities to be party to ICSID arbitration *eo nomine*.[141] The Convention does not expressly mention State instrumentalities or enterprises, but a functional reading may subsume them under the provision of ICSID Convention Article 25(1).[142]

In connection with this special mechanism, the status of designated entity pursuant to ICSID Convention Article 25(1) embodies a factual element that is determinative of the jurisdiction *ratione personae* of the tribunal and, accordingly, should be proven upon fulfilment of a complete evidentiary standard.[143] To this extent, the investor would be required to file evidence with regard to the specific involvement of the entity in the dispute, its designation by the host State, or the latter's approval or notification pursuant to ICSID Convention Article 25(3) in

[141] *Repsol YPF Ecuador, SA and others v Republic of Ecuador and Empresa Estatal Petróleos del Ecuador (PetroEcuador)*, ICSID Case No ARB/01/10, Award, 20 February 2004, para 120; *Repsol YPF Ecuador, SA et al v Republic of Ecuador and Empresa Estatal Petróleos del Ecuador (PetroEcuador)*, ICSID Case No ARB/08/10, Procedural Order No 1, 17 June 2009; *Perenco Ecuador Ltd v The Republic of Ecuador and Empresa Estatal Petróleos del Ecuador (Petroecuador)*, ICSID Case No ARB/08/6, Decision on Jurisdiction, 30 June 2011, paras 6–9; *Scimitar Exploration Limited v Bangladesh and Bangladesh Oil, Gas and Mineral Corporation*, ICSID Case No ARB/92/2, Award, 4 May 1994; *City Oriente Ltd v Republic of Ecuador and Petroecuador*, ICSID Case No ARB/06/21, Decision on Provisional Measures, 19 November 2007; *Burlington Resources Inc v Republic of Ecuador* (formerly *Burlington Resources Inc and others v Republic of Ecuador and Empresa Estatal Petróleos del Ecuador (PetroEcuador)*), ICSID Case No ARB/08/5, Decision on Jurisdiction, 2 June 2010; *Manufacturers Hanover Trust v Arab Republic of Egypt General Authority for Investment and Free Zones*, ICSID No ARB/89/1, Order Taking Note of the Discontinuance, 24 June 1993; *Government of the Province of East Kalimantan v PT Kaltim Prima Coal and others*, ICSID Case No ARB/07/3, Award, 28 December 2009; *Noble Energy, Inc and Machalapower Cia Ltda v The Republic of Ecuador and Consejo Nacional de Electricidad (CONELEC)*, ICSID Case No ARB/05/12, Decision on Jurisdiction, 5 March 2008, para 63; *Cable Television of Nevis Ltd and Cable Television of Nevis Holdings, Ltd v The Federation of St Christopher (St Kitts) and Nevis*, ICSID Case No ARB/95/2, Award, 13 January 1997, para 2.28; *Tanzania Electric Supply Company Limited v Independent Power Tanzania Limited (IPTL)*, ICSID Case No ARB/98/8, Final Award, 12 July 2001, para 13.

[142] *Cable Television of Nevis Ltd and Cable Television of Nevis Holdings, Ltd v The Federation of St Christopher (St Kitts) and Nevis*, ICSID Case No ARB/95/2, Award, 13 January 1997, para 2.28: 'a government statutory corporation or a company incorporated under national/local legislation in which the Government has some interest or shareholding.' See Christoph Schreuer, with Loretta Malintoppi, August Reinisch, and Anthony Sinclair, *The ICSID Convention: A Commentary* (2nd edn, Cambridge University Press 2009) 153, para 243: 'The concept of "agency" should be read not in structural terms but functionally. This means that whether the "agency" is a corporation, whether and to what extent it is government-owned and whether it has separate legal personality are of secondary importance. What matters is that it performs public functions on behalf of the Contracting State or one of its constituent subdivisions.'; C F Amerasinghe, 'Jurisdiction *Ratione Personae* Under the Convention on the Settlement of Investment Disputes Between States and Nationals of Other States' (1974-1975) 47 British Year Book of International Law 227, 233–34; C F Amerasinghe, 'The Jurisdiction of the International Centre for the Settlement of Investment Disputes' (1979) 19 Indian Journal of International Law 166, 185–86.

[143] *Teinver SA, Transportes de Cercanías SA and Autobuses Urbanos del Sur SA v The Argentine Republic*, ICSID Case No ARB/09/1, Decision on Jurisdiction, 21 December 2012, para 272: 'Case law on this subject *does* support the conclusion that matters of state attribution should be adjudicated at the jurisdictional stage when they represent a fairly cut-and-dry issue that will determine whether there is jurisdiction.'

relation to the consent to arbitration formulated by the entity itself in the investment contract.[144]

3. State Organs

In line with the *Gestalt* of the international law of State responsibility, the municipal constitutional principle of the separation of State powers is not of particular relevance to the application of attribution rules.[145] Accordingly, international investment tribunals do not emphasize distinctions based on the position of a State organ in relation to a given branch or level of government, but rather they comprehensively analyse whether an exercise of authority by a sovereign power has occurred,[146] so as to identify a measure of a Party, by way of act or omission,[147] to be subsumed under the relevant IIA.[148] In the context of the international protection of foreign direct investment (FDI), various forms of the phenomenology of the

[144] 'Designations by Contracting States Regarding Constituent Subdivisions or Agencies (Art. 25(1) and (3) of the Convention)', ICSID/8-C (May 2015).

[145] Ian Brownlie, *System of the Law of Nations. State Responsibility. Part I* (Clarendon Press 1983) 133, 136, 142, 150.

[146] Argentina-Spain BIT (1991) Article V (*Nationalization and Expropriation*): 'Nationalization, expropriation or any other measure having similar characteristics or effects that might be adopted by the authorities of one Party (*autoridades de una Parte*) against investments made in its territory by investors of the other Party.' See *Emilio Agustín Maffezini v The Kingdom of Spain*, ICSID Case No ARB/97/7, Decision on Jurisdiction, 25 January 2000, para 74.

[147] *Eureko BV v Republic of Poland*, Ad Hoc Arbitration, Partial Award, 19 June 2005, para 185 et seq.

[148] *Rumeli Telekom AS and Telsim Mobil Telekomunikasyon Hizmetleri AS v Republic of Kazakhstan*, ICSID Case No ARB/05/16, Award, 29 July 2008, para 338; *CMS Gas Transmission Company v The Republic of Argentina*, ICSID Case No ARB/01/8, Decision of the Tribunal on Objections to Jurisdiction, 17 July 2003, para 108: 'In so far as the international liability of Argentina under the Treaty is concerned, it also does not matter whether some actions were taken by the judiciary and others by an administrative agency, the executive or the legislative branch of the State. Article 4 of the Articles on State Responsibility adopted by the International Law Commission is abundantly clear on this point.'; *Loewen Group, Inc and Raymond L Loewen v United States of America*, ICSID Case No ARB(AF)/98/3, Decision on Hearing of Respondent's Objection to Competence and Jurisdiction, 5 January 2001, para 70: 'The modern view is that conduct of an organ of the State shall be considered as an act of the State under international law, whether the organ be legislative, executive or judicial, whatever position it holds in the organisation of the State.'; *Eureko BV v Republic of Poland*, Ad Hoc Arbitration, Partial Award, 19 June 2005, para 127: 'In the perspective of international law, it is now a well settled rule that the conduct of any State organ is considered an act of that State and that an organ includes any person or entity which has that status in accordance with the internal law of that State.'; *Noble Ventures, Inc v Romania*, ICSID Case No ARB/01/11, Award, 12 October 2005, para 69: 'Art. 4 2001 ILC Draft lays down the well-established rule that the conduct of any State organ, being understood as including any person or entity which has that status in accordance with the internal law of the State, shall be considered an act of that State under international law.'; *MCI Power Group LC and New Turbine, Inc v Republic of Ecuador*, ICSID Case No ARB/03/6, Award, 31 July 2007, para 225, fn 24; *CMS Gas Transmission Company v The Republic of Argentina*, ICSID Case No ARB/01/8, Decision of the Tribunal on Objections to Jurisdiction, 17 July 2003, para 108: 'In so far as the international liability of Argentina under the Treaty is concerned, it also does not matter whether some actions were taken by the judiciary and others by an administrative agency, the executive or the legislative branch of the State. Article 4 of the Articles on State Responsibility adopted by the International Law Commission is abundantly clear on this point.'

authority (for instance an administrative practice) may adversely affect the value of the investment and, as a consequence, enlarge the traditional set of State conducts susceptible to being scrutinized by an international tribunal according to ARSIWA Article 4.[149] This might also be the case with regard to press conferences, declarations, or speeches, even of an informal nature, delivered by heads of State, local governments, or ministries of the host State, announcing the introduction of normative measures generally or specifically affecting a foreign investment, endorsing certain conduct by citizens, or suggesting the termination of a concession contract by the government or one of its SOEs.[150]

3.1 Organs of the Central Government

Investment tribunals have recognized as attributable to the State (pursuant to ARSIWA Article 4) the conduct of the legislative,[151] executive,[152] and judicial power,[153] as well as 'any other functions'.[154] The most 'populated' category is, by a large majority, represented by acts and omissions being ascribed to the executive branch, such as those of political authorities (government and ministries),[155]

[149] *Ethyl Corp v The Government of Canada*, UNCITRAL, Award on Jurisdiction, 24 June 1998, para 66: 'Clearly something other than a "law", even something in the nature of a "practice", which may not even amount to a legal stricture, may qualify.'

[150] *Biwater Gauff (Tanzania) Ltd v United Republic of Tanzania*, ICSID Case No ARB/05/22, Award, 24 July 2008, para 497: 'On 13 May 2005, against the backdrop of forthcoming elections in Tanzania in which Minister Lowassa was running for the office of Prime Minister, the Tanzanian Government issued a press release in which Minister Lowassa announced the termination of the Lease Contract. This was followed by a similar declaration on television.' Contra, *Tradex Hellas SA v Republic of Albania*, ICSID Case No ARB/94/2, Award, 29 April 1999, para 156: 'But the Berisha speech was neither a legislative or executive act nor did it change the situation found above in Section e) created by Decision 452.'

[151] *EDF (Services) Limited v Romania*, ICSID Case No ARB/05/13, Award, 8 October 2009, para 186; *EnCana Corporation v Republic of Ecuador*, LCIA Case No UN3481, UNCITRAL, Award, 3 February 2006, para 157(a); *William Nagel v The Czech Republic*, SCC Case No 049/2002, Final Award, 9 September 2003, para 109.

[152] *Ex multis, Eureko BV v Republic of Poland*, Ad Hoc Arbitration, Partial Award, 19 June 2005, para 129.

[153] *Ex multis, Loewen Group, Inc and Raymond L Loewen v United States of America*, ICSID Case No ARB(AF)/98/3, Decision on Hearing of Respondent's Objection to Competence and Jurisdiction, 5 January 2001, para 70 et seq.

[154] *Alex Genin, Eastern Credit Limited, Inc and AS Baltoil v The Republic of Estonia*, ICSID Case No ARB/99/2, Award, 25 June 2001, para 327.

[155] *Impregilo SpA v Islamic Republic of Pakistan*, ICSID Case No ARB/03/3, Decision on Jurisdiction, 22 April 2005, para 227 (Ministry of Commerce, Ministry of Finance and Ministry of Water and Power); *Jan de Nul NV and Dredging International NV v Arab Republic of Egypt*, ICSID Case No ARB/04/13, Award, 6 November 2008, para 175 (Prime Minister of Egypt); *Eureko BV v Republic of Poland*, Ad Hoc Arbitration, Partial Award, 19 June 2005, para 129 (Minister of the State Treasury of Poland); *Mohammad Ammar Al-Bahloul v The Republic of Tajikistan*, SCC Case No V (064/2008), Partial Award on Jurisdiction and Liability, 2 September 2009, para 169 (Ministry of Energy of the Republic of Tajikistan); *Gustav F W Hamester GmbH & Co KG v Republic of Ghana*, ICSID Case No ARB/07/24, Award, 18 June 2010, para 293 (Ministry of Finance of Ghana); *Helnan International Hotels A/S v Arab Republic of Egypt*, ICSID Case No ARB/05/19, Award, 3 July 2008, para 56; *Tradex Hellas SA v Republic of Albania*, ICSID Case No ARB/94/2, Award, 29 April 1999,

military and armed forces,[156] ordinary police officials or financial guards,[157] customs authorities,[158] tax agencies,[159] environmental agencies,[160] and administrative offices in general.[161] Various investment cases have addressed the conduct of domestic courts, as such clearly covered by the cloak of attributability.[162] While this rule also encompasses quasi-judicial organs,[163] tribunals have not abstained from

para 142; *Eastern Sugar BV (Netherlands) v The Czech Republic*, SCC Case No 088/2004, Partial Award, 27 March 2007, para 200 (Government in general); *Joseph Charles Lemire v Ukraine*, ICSID Case No ARB/06/18, Decision on Jurisdiction and Liability, 14 January 2010, para 37 (President, Prime Minister and Ministry of Defence of Ukraine).

[156] *Impregilo SpA v Islamic Republic of Pakistan*, ICSID Case No ARB/03/3, Decision on Jurisdiction, 22 April 2005, para 264 (failure to ensure access to the Kamra Military base); *Asian Agricultural Products Ltd (AAPL) v Republic of Sri Lanka*, ICSID Case No ARB/87/3, Final Award, 27 June 1990, para 44; *Amco Asia Corporation, Pan American Development Limited and PT Amco Indonesia v Republic of Indonesia*, ICSID Case No ARB/81/1, Award, 20 November 1984, 1 ICSID Reports 413, 431, 438.

[157] *Gustav F W Hamester GmbH & Co KG v Republic of Ghana*, ICSID Case No ARB/07/24, Award, 18 June 2010, para 292: 'The police force is clearly a State organ and the acts performed during a police investigation are therefore attributable to the State.'; *Wena Hotels Limited v Arab Republic of Egypt*, ICSID Case No ARB/98/4, Award, 8 December 2000, para 109, 41 ILM 896; *Amco Asia Corporation, Pan American Development Limited and PT Amco Indonesia v Republic of Indonesia*, ICSID Case No ARB/81/1, Award, 20 November 1984, 1 ICSID Reports 413, 431, 438; *EDF (Services) Limited v Romania*, ICSID Case No ARB/05/13, Award, 8 October 2009, para 186.

[158] *Impregilo SpA v Islamic Republic of Pakistan*, ICSID Case No ARB/03/3, Decision on Jurisdiction, 22 April 2005, para 264 (failure to facilitate importation of equipment through the port of Karachi); *Gustav F W Hamester GmbH & Co KG v Republic of Ghana*, ICSID Case No ARB/07/24, Award, 18 June 2010, para 295 (suspension of any shipment by the investor).

[159] *Yukos Universal Limited (Isle of Man) v The Russian Federation*, UNCITRAL, PCA Case No AA 227, Final Award, 18 July 2014, para 1478 (tax authorities); *EnCana Corporation v Republic of Ecuador*, LCIA Case No UN3481, UNCITRAL, Award, 3 February 2006, para 157(a) (Servicio de Rentas Internas or SRI); *Jan Oostergetel and Theodora Laurentius v The Slovak Republic*, UNCITRAL, Final Award, 23 April 2012, para 153 (tax authorities).

[160] *Técnicas Medioambientales Tecmed, SA v The United Mexican States*, ICSID Case No ARB (AF)/00/2, Award, 29 May 2003, para 151 (Hazardous Materials, Waste and Activities Division of the National Ecology Institute of Mexico or INE).

[161] *Telenor Mobile Communications AS v The Republic of Hungary*, ICSID Case No ARB/04/15, Award, 13 September 2006, para 71.

[162] *Waguih Elie George Siag and Clorinda Vecchi v The Arab Republic of Egypt*, ICSID Case No ARB/05/15, Award, 1 June 2009, para 192; *Saipem SpA v People's Republic of Bangladesh*, ICSID Case No ARB/05/07, Decision on Jurisdiction and Recommendation on Provisional Measures, 21 March 2007, para 143; *Saipem SpA v People's Republic of Bangladesh*, ICSID Case No ARB/05/07, Award, 30 June 2009, para 190: 'It is self-evident and Bangladesh does not dispute that the courts are "part of the State", i.e., an organ of the State in the meaning of Article 4 of the ILC Articles.'; *Jan de Nul NV and Dredging International NV v Arab Republic of Egypt*, ICSID Case No ARB/04/13, Award, 6 November 2008, para 175: '*There is no doubt either that the Administrative Court of Ismaïlia qualifies as an organ of the State within the meaning of Article 4 of the ILC Articles, as acknowledged by the Respondent's expert.*'; *Toto Costruzioni Generali SpA v The Republic of Lebanon*, ICSID Case No ARB/07/12, Decision on Jurisdiction, 11 September 2009, para 152 et seq; *RosInvestCo UK Ltd v The Russian Federation*, SCC Case No V079/2005, Final Award, 12 September 2010, para 603; *Loewen Group, Inc and Raymond L Loewen v United States of America*, ICSID Case No ARB(AF)/98/3, Decision on Hearing of Respondent's Objection to Competence and Jurisdiction, 5 January 2001, para 70; *Robert Azinian, Kenneth Davitian, & Ellen Baca v The United Mexican States*, ICSID Case No ARB (AF)/97/2, Award, 1 November 1999, paras 97–103.

[163] *William Ralph Clayton, William Richard Clayton, Douglas Clayton, Daniel Clayton and Bilcon of Delaware Inc v Government of Canada*, UNCITRAL, PCA Case No 2009-04, 17 March 2015, paras 305–20 (Joint Review Panel or JRP); *Jan de Nul NV and Dredging International NV v Arab Republic of Egypt*,

remarking on the irrelevance of the constitutional prerogative of the independence of the judiciary, where applicable, for the sake of attribution of conduct to a State.[164] These cases usually consist of claims of 'denial of justice', both substantive and procedural, falling under the umbrella of the fair and equitable treatment standard of protection and as such entailing a gross or shocking departure by national judges from the international standards of due process and fair trial.[165] A finding of denial of justice necessarily requires the exhaustion of local remedies as an element of the merits of the claim, not of its admissibility, as it is instead the case in relation to so-called *Calvo clauses* or (*rectius*) *soft Calvo clauses* (for instance, eighteen–months-litigation provisions) provided by the relevant IIA in conformity with ICSID Convention Article 26.[166]

ICSID Case No ARB/04/13, Award, 6 November 2008, para 175 (Second Panel of Experts; Committee for Settling the Complaints of Foreign Investors).

[164] *Robert Azinian, Kenneth Davitian, & Ellen Baca v The United Mexican States*, ICSID Case No ARB (AF)/97/2, Award, 1 November 1999, para 98, quoting Eduardo Jiménez de Aréchaga, 'International Law in the Past Third of a Century' (1978-I) 159 Recueil des Cours 1, 278: 'the judgment given by a judicial authority emanates from an organ of the State in just the same way as a law promulgated by the legislature or a decision taken by the executive'.

[165] *Loewen Group, Inc and Raymond L Loewen v United States of America*, ICSID Case No ARB(AF)/98/3, Award, 26 June 2003, paras 54, 87, 95, 119, 122, 132, 135, 224, 242, where the domestic proceedings have been variously addressed with the expressions 'miscarriage of justice', 'manifest injustice', judicial 'mystery', 'disgrace', 'nefarious practice', and 'lack of due process' towards the foreign investor; *Robert Azinian, Kenneth Davitian, & Ellen Baca v The United Mexican States*, ICSID Case No ARB (AF)/97/2, Award, 1 November 1999, paras 102–03; *Waste Management, Inc v United Mexican States (Waste Management II)*, ICSID Case No ARB(AF)/00/3, Award, 30 April 2004, para 130; *Mondev International Ltd v United States of America*, ICSID Case No ARB(AF)/99/2, Award, 11 October 2002, para 127: 'In the end the question is whether, at an international level and having regard to generally accepted standards of the administration of justice, a tribunal can conclude in the light of all the available facts that the impugned decision was clearly improper and discreditable, with the result that the investment has been subjected to unfair and inequitable treatment.'; *ADF Group Inc v United States of America*, ICSID Case No ARB (AF)/00/1, Award, 9 January 2003, para 190; *Chevron Corporation (USA) and Texaco Petroleum Company (USA) v The Republic of Ecuador*, UNCITRAL, PCA Case No 34877, Partial Award on the Merits, 30 March 2010, paras 389 et seq; *Toto Costruzioni Generali SpA v The Republic of Lebanon*, ICSID Case No ARB/07/12, Decision on Jurisdiction, 11 September 2009, para 156; *Jan de Nul NV and Dredging International NV v Arab Republic of Egypt*, ICSID Case No ARB/04/13, Award, 6 November 2008, paras 184 et seq.; *Waste Management, Inc v United Mexican States (Waste Management II)*, ICSID Case No ARB(AF)/00/3, Award, 30 April 2004, para 98; *Compañiá de Aguas del Aconquija SA and Vivendi Universal SA v Argentine Republic* (formerly *Compañía de Aguas del Aconquija, SA and Compagnie Générale des Eaux v Argentine Republic*) (*Vivendi II*), ICSID Case No ARB/97/3, Award, 20 August 2007, para 7.4.11.

[166] Jan Paulsson, *Denial of Justice in International Law* (Cambridge University Press 2007) 245–46: 'States are held to an obligation to provide a fair and efficient system of justice, not to an undertaking that there will never be an instance of judicial misconduct. National responsibility for denial of justice occurs only when the system as a whole has been tested and the initial delict has remained uncorrected ... The very definition of denial of justice encompasses the notion of exhaustion of local remedies. There can be no denial of justice before exhaustion'. See *Loewen Group, Inc and Raymond L Loewen v United States of America*, ICSID Case No ARB(AF)/98/3, Decision on Hearing of Respondent's Objection to Competence and Jurisdiction, 5 January 2001, para 71: 'Viewed in this light, the rule of judicial finality is no different from the local remedies rule. Its purpose is to ensure that the State where the violation occurred should have an opportunity to redress it by its own means, within the framework of its own domestic legal system'; *Mr Franck Charles Arif v Republic of Moldova*, ICSID Case No ARB/11/23, Award, 8 April 2013, paras 345–46.

ISDS cases also provide innovative findings on organs of the State exercising 'any other functions' outside Montesquieu's separation of powers, thus contributing to the evolution of customary international law on the issue. The open-ended formula of ARSIWA Article 4 notably comprises independent public law bodies and agencies chiefly entrusted with regulatory, monitoring, and administrative functions in connection with services of general public interest. Upon analysis of the status of the central bank of Estonia, the *Alex Genin v Estonia* tribunal, established under the US–Estonia BIT (1994), concluded:

> The Bank of Estonia is an agency of a Contracting State. The Estonian central bank is a 'state agency', as defined by the BIT, which stipulates in Article II 2(b) that 'Each Party shall ensure that any state enterprise that it maintains or establishes acts in a manner that is not inconsistent with the Party's obligations under this Treaty wherever such enterprise exercises any regulatory, administrative or other governmental authority that the Party has delegated to it, such as the power to expropriate, grant licenses ... '. The Republic of Estonia is therefore the appropriate Respondent to a complaint relating to the conduct of the Bank of Estonia.[167]

The circumstance of a public entity benefiting from separate juristic personality under domestic law does not necessarily preclude a finding of *de jure* organ.[168] In this respect, the separate legal personality is usually *of public law* (for instance,

[167] *Alex Genin, Eastern Credit Limited, Inc and AS Baltoil v The Republic of Estonia*, ICSID Case No ARB/99/2, Award, 25 June 2001, para 327. On the attributability of conduct of central banks, see also *MNSS BV and Recupero Credito Acciaio NV v Montenegro*, ICSID Case No ARB(AF)/12/8, Award, 4 May 2016, para 297; *Bernhard von Pezold et al v Republic of Zimbabwe*, ICSID Case No ARB/10/15, Award, 28 July 2015, para 443; *Invesmart v Czech Republic*, UNCITRAL, Award, 26 June 2009, para 363; *Deutsche Bank AG v Democratic Socialist Republic of Sri Lanka*, ICSID Case No ARB/09/2, Award, 31 October 2012, para 402.

[168] *Eureko BV v Republic of Poland*, Ad Hoc Arbitration, Partial Award, 19 August 2005, para 120 (Polish State Treasury); *Toto Costruzioni Generali SpA v The Republic of Lebanon*, ICSID Case No ARB/07/12, Decision on Jurisdiction, 11 September 2009, para 46, 56: 'The circumstances in which the CEGP and/or the CDR would be considered separate entities pursuant to Lebanese law would be irrelevant in this context: a State cannot escape international responsibility by delegating its State functions to entities to which it gives separate. ... Moreover, the CDR acts as an agent of the State.'; *Joseph Charles Lemire v Ukraine*, ICSID Case No ARB/06/18, Decision on Jurisdiction and Liability, 14 January 2010, paras 287–92 (National Television and Radio Council of Ukraine, 'a "constitutional permanent collegiate agency". Its activities "shall be based upon the principles of legality, independence, impartiality, transparency..."'); *Empresa Eléctrica del Ecuador, Inc (EMELEC) v Republic of Ecuador*, ICSID Case No ARB/05/9, Award, 2 June 2009, para 41 (National Electricity Council—Consejo Nacional de Electricidad or CONELEC); *MCI Power Group LC and New Turbine, Inc v Republic of Ecuador*, ICSID Case No ARB/03/6, Award, 31 July 2007, para 225: 'The Tribunal finds that INECEL, in light of its institutional structure and composition as well as its functions, should be considered, in accordance with international law, as an organ of the Ecuadorian State.' (Instituto Ecuatoriano de Electrificación or INECEL); *Duke Energy Electroquil Partners & Electroquil SA v Republic of Ecuador*, ICSID Case No ARB/04/19, Award, 18 August 2008, para 10 (Instituto Ecuatoriano de Electrificación or INECEL); *Sergei Paushok, CJSC Golden East Company and CJSC Vostokneftegaz Company v The Government of Mongolia*, UNCITRAL, Award on Jurisdiction and Liability, 28 April 2011, para 582: 'the fact that the Mongolian Parliament has created it as an institution independent of the Government does not per se make it lose its status as an organ of the State. In fact, it fulfills a major State function and the list of its

personnes morales de droit public or *établissements publics administratifs*) established by national Constitution or statute.[169] The creation of separate legal entities of public law within the (internal) boundary of the State does not preclude a finding of a certain body being an organ of the State (acting *on its behalf*) pursuant to the *renvoi*, as defined in the previous chapter,[170] of international law to the internal law of that State.[171] Such agencies certainly exercise sovereign powers on an institutional basis.[172] Accordingly, the attribution of their acts and omissions is governed by ARSIWA Article 4, including commercial acts. On the contrary, separate juristic personality of private law generally (but there are exceptions) orients the interpreter not to treat the entity concerned, including a 'State entity', as a State organ under ARSIWA Article 4, but rather as a separate body whose conduct may be attributed to the State pursuant to ARSIWA Article 5 or 8, as discussed below.[173]

responsibilities clearly demonstrates that it fulfills a role that only a State can fulfill: exclusive right to issue currency, formulation and implementation of monetary policy, acting as the Government's financial intermediary; supervising activities of other banks; holding and managing the State's reserves of foreign currencies' (MongolBank); *Alpha Projektholding GmbH v Ukraine*, ICSID Case No ARB/07/16, Award, 8 November 2010, para 401 (State Administration Authority or SAA); *CME Czech Republic BV v The Czech Republic*, UNCITRAL, Final Award, 14 March 2003, para 8 (Czech Media Council); *Aguaytia Energy LLC v Republic of Peru*, ICSID Case No ARB/06/13, Award, 11 December 2008, para 40 (Organismo Supervisor de la Inversión en Energía or OSINERGO); *William Nagel v The Czech Republic*, SCC Case No 049/2002, Final Award, 9 September 2003, para 144 (Czech National Property Fund). For a different approach, see *Bayindir Insaat Turizm Ticaret Ve Sanayi AS v Islamic Republic of Pakistan*, ICSID Case No ARB/03/29, Award, 27 August 2009, para 119: 'Because of its separate legal status, the Tribunal discards the possibility of treating NHA as a State organ under Article 4 of the ILC Articles' (National Highway Authority or NHA); *Mr Kristian Almås and Mr Geir Almås v The Republic of Poland*, PCA Case No 2015-13, Award, 27 June 2016, para 209 (Polish Agricultural Property Agency or ANR); *Luigiterzo Bosca v Lithuania*, UNCITRAL, Award, 17 May 2013, para 127 (Lithuanian State Property Fund or SPF). Contra, Nick Gallus, 'State Enterprises as Organs of the State and BIT Claims' (2006) 7 Journal of World Investment & Trade 761, 777.

[169] See *Ampal-American Israel Corporation et al v Arab Republic of Egypt*, ICSID Case No ARB/12/11, Decision on Liability and Heads of Loss, 21 February 2017, para 138 (Egyptian General Petroleum Corporation or EGPC); *Toto Costruzioni Generali SpA v The Republic of Lebanon*, ICSID Case No ARB/07/12, Decision on Jurisdiction, 11 September 2009, para 52 (Conseil Exécutif des Grands Projets or CEPG, and Council for Development and Reconstruction or CDR); *Bosh International, Inc and B&P Ltd Foreign Investments Enterprise v Ukraine*, ICSID Case No ARB/08/11, Award, 25 October 2012, para 145 (Education Control Division of the General Control and Revision Office or CRO); *Renée Rose Levy de Levi v Republic of Peru*, ICSID Case No ARB/10/17, Award, 26 February 2014, paras 157–62 (Superintendency of Banking, Insurance, and Pension Fund Administration or SBS); *Mr Hassan Awdi, Enterprise Business Consultants, Inc and Alfa El Corporation v Romania*, ICSID Case No ARB/10/13, 2 March 2015, paras 322–23 (Authority for State Assets Recovery or AVAS).

[170] See Chapter II, section 1.2.

[171] Pierre-Marie Dupuy, 'Les émanations engagent-elles la responsabilité des Etats? Etude de droit international des investissements' (2006) EUI Working Paper LAW No 2006/7, 6: '*Dans les cas limites où l'arbitre se poserait des questions sur l'appartenance de l'organe considéré à la structure administrative de l'Etat, c'est le droit international qui lui fait alors obligation de consulter le droit interne de cet Etat pour se prononcer sur le statut exact de l'organe en cause. Le renvoi au droit interne comporte cependant des limites strictes. Il ne vise que la détermination de la qualité de l'organe en cas de doutes*'.

[172] cf Georgios Petrochilos, 'Attribution' in Katia Yannaca-Small (ed), *Arbitration under International Investment Agreements: A Guide to the Key Issues* (Oxford University Press 2010) 287, 294.

[173] See sections 4 and 5 of this chapter. See also *EDF (Services) Limited v Romania*, ICSID Case No ARB/05/13, Award, 8 October 2009, para 190; *Tulip Real Estate and Development Netherlands BV v*

To this extent, a decisive element is represented by the business orientation and the profit motive pursued by the entity, as in the case of the Suez Canal Authority (SCA) in *Jan de Nul v Egypt*.[174] The difference is not trivial, since the *acta jure gestionis* of a State organ would be attributable to the sovereign under ARSIWA Article 4 (plenary attribution), while those of a State instrumentality would not be so under ARSIWA Article 5 (functional test for attribution).[175] This notwithstanding, arbitral tribunals have not refrained from embarking on the application of the doctrine of *de facto* agents under ARSIWA Article 4.2 in order to qualify a SOE vested with separate legal personality as a parcel of the State, as discussed in the following paragraph.

3.2 *De Facto* Organs

While the public international law doctrine of *de facto* organs has been forged in relation to the activities of paramilitary groups, investment tribunals have contemplated it in the context of the promotion and protection of foreign investments by taking into consideration the different policies and nuances of international economic litigation.[176] This theory should be based on the demanding requirements illustrated by the ICJ in the *Bosnian Genocide* case, namely complete dependence and strict control.[177] Consequently, tribunals may qualify a SOE, formally

Republic of Turkey, ICSID Case No ARB/11/28, Award, 10 March 2014, para 287. But see *Saipem SpA v People's Republic of Bangladesh*, ICSID Case No ARB/05/07, Decision on Jurisdiction and Recommendation on Provisional Measures, 21 March 2007, para 146; *Nykomb Synergetics Technology Holding AB v The Republic of Latvia*, SCC, Arbitral Award, 16 December 2003, para 4.2.

---

[174] *Jan de Nul NV and Dredging International NV v Arab Republic of Egypt*, ICSID Case No ARB/04/13, Award, 6 November 2008, paras 158–62; *Sergei Paushok, CJSC Golden East Company and CJSC Vostokneftegaz Company v The Government of Mongolia*, UNCITRAL, Award on Jurisdiction and Liability, 28 April 2011, para 583: 'There is a huge difference to be found between public authorities established to operate and maintain a navigational canal or to construct and maintain highways and a central bank charged with the issuance of the currency and running the State's monetary policy'.

[175] *Noble Ventures, Inc v Romania*, ICSID Case No ARB/01/11, Award, 12 October 2005, para 82: 'With regard to the argument of the Respondent that a distinction has to be drawn between attribution of governmental and commercial conduct, the latter not being attributable, the following has to be said. The distinction plays an important role in the field of sovereign immunity when one comes to the question of whether a State can claim immunity before the courts of another State. However, in the context of responsibility, it is difficult to see why commercial acts, so called *acta iure gestionis*, should by definition not be attributable while governmental acts, so called *acta iure imperii*, should be attributable. The ILC-Draft does not maintain or support such a distinction'.

[176] *F-W Oil Interests, Inc v The Republic of Trinidad and Tobago*, ICSID Case No ARB/01/14, Award, 3 March 2006, para 203; *Saipem SpA v People's Republic of Bangladesh*, ICSID Case No ARB/05/07, Decision on Jurisdiction and Recommendation on Provisional Measures, 21 March 2007, para 149; *Gustav F W Hamester GmbH & Co KG v Republic of Ghana*, ICSID Case No ARB/07/24, Award, 18 June 2010, para 186; *Deutsche Bank AG v Democratic Socialist Republic of Sri Lanka*, ICSID Case No ARB/09/2, Award, 31 October 2012, para 406(f) et seq.; *Flemingo DutyFree Shop Private Limited v the Republic of Poland*, UNCITRAL, Award, 12 August 2016, paras 418–35.

[177] *Application of the Convention on the Prevention and Punishment of the Crime of Genocide (Bosnia and Herzegovina v Serbia and Montenegro)*, Judgment, 26 February 2007, para 391, ICJ Reports 2007, 43, 201.

benefiting from the separate legal personality of private law, as a *de facto* agent of the State under ARSIWA Article 4.2, in connection with a finding of serious lack of independence, institutional and financial insufficiency, and overwhelming mandates by the State, so that the SOE appears as an arm of governmental functions, rather than a business actor.[178]

In *Almås v Poland*, the tribunal observed that 'internal status does not necessarily imply that an entity is not a State organ if other factors, such as the performance of core governmental functions, direct day-to-day subordination to central government, or lack of all operational autonomy, point the other way'.[179] This seems to be the rationale resorted to by the *Nykomb v Latvia* tribunal in relation to the conduct of Latvenergo, a SOE that was totally owned by the State and organized in the form of a joint-stock company. Indeed, the tribunal emphasized that the State company in question appeared as the 'instrument of the State' in the electricity market, since it did not have any commercial freedom in the negotiation of purchase prices for electric power that were fixed by the legislation and the regulatory bodies of the State:

> Latvenergo cannot be considered to be, or to have been, an independent commercial enterprise, but clearly a constituent part of the Republic's organization of the electricity market and a vehicle to implement the Republic's decisions concerning the price setting for electric power.[180]

In *Deutsche Bank v Sri Lanka*, the tribunal had to determine whether the Ceylon Petroleum Company (CPC) could be qualified as an organ of the State under ARSIWA Article 4, without prejudice to the attributability of conduct under ARSIWA Articles 5 or 8. The arbitrators notably benefited from the previous finding by the Supreme Court of Sri Lanka that CPC was '"a Government creation clothed with juristic personality so as to give it an aura of independence" with "deep and pervasive State control"'.[181] In addition, the tribunal found that CPC lacked any true independence, since it was subject to the State's pervasive control consisting inter alia in the mandatory directions of the Minister of Petroleum,

[178] Georgios Petrochilos, 'Attribution' in Katia Yannaca-Small (ed), *Arbitration under International Investment Agreements: A Guide to the Key Issues* (Oxford University Press 2010) 287, 296–99; Nick Gallus, 'State Enterprises as Organs of the State and BIT Claims' (2006) 7 Journal of World Investment & Trade 761, 778.

[179] *Mr Kristian Almås and Mr Geir Almås v The Republic of Poland*, PCA Case No 2015-13, Award, 27 June 2016, para 207.

[180] *Nykomb Synergetics Technology Holding AB v The Republic of Latvia*, SCC, Arbitral Award, 16 December 2003, para 4.2.

[181] *Deutsche Bank AG v Democratic Socialist Republic of Sri Lanka*, ICSID Case No ARB/09/2, Award, 31 October 2012, para 405(a).

'regardless of whether those directions are in the best interests of CPC'.[182] As a consequence the tribunal held that:

> While it may be unusual for a state enterprise to be considered an organ of the State, this is only the case where the state enterprise is genuinely independent—the fact that it takes the form of a separate legal entity is not decisive.[183]

The tribunal did not explicitly mention the doctrine of *de facto* organs (nor did the *Nykomb v Latvia* tribunal), but nevertheless stated that 'CPC's actions would be attributable to the State, either because CPC is an organ of the State under ILC Article 4 or because CPC lacked separate legal existence, and/or acted under the instruction of the State'.[184]

The *Flemingo v Poland* tribunal expressly resorted to the theory of *de facto* organs in its analysis on attribution of the conduct of the Polish Airports State Enterprise (PPL). PPL was wholly owned by the Polish State Treasury, was subject to the close, structural, and substantial control and supervision of the Ministry of Transport and, according to the State itself, performed strategic functions for the existence of the latter. Moreover, the tribunal was not constrained by the requirements of independence, self-governance, and financial autonomy that were established in the statute that regulated PPL: 'compared to the many restrictions and forms of government control and interference, the above expressions of quasi-independence and quasi-autonomy do not tip the scales'.[185] In their reasoning, the arbitrators referred to ARSIWA Article 4.2, which is the legal basis of the doctrine of *de facto* agents:

> Article 4(2) of the ILC Articles, however, only provides that entities, which in accordance with the internal law of a State are qualified as State-organs, are State organs for purpose of State responsibility; it does not *per se* exclude entities which are not qualified as State organs under domestic law. In other words, although under Article 4(2), an entity is a State organ when it has such status attributed to it under domestic law, the circumstance that an entity is not considered a State organ under domestic law does not prevent that entity from being considered as such under international law for State responsibility purposes.[186]

182 ibid, para 405(b).
183 ibid, para 405(a).
184 ibid, para 405(f).
185 *Flemingo DutyFree Shop Private Limited v the Republic of Poland*, UNCITRAL, Award, 12 August 2016, para 432.
186 ibid, para 433.

The tribunal in particular emphasized that, according to government officials' declarations, PPL functioned 'within' the structure of the Ministry of Transport,[187] which prompted the conclusion that PPL could be qualified as a State organ, notwithstanding its corporate separateness under domestic law.[188]

3.3 Territorial Units

The international principle of the unity of the State is recognized by investment arbitrators so as to attribute to the State the conduct of its constituent units or political subdivisions entailing a treaty claim: 'under public international law (ie as will apply to an alleged breach of treaty), a State may be held responsible for the acts of local public authorities or public institutions under its authority'.[189] The principle is also formulated under NAFTA Article 105, providing for a Party's obligation to ensure the observance of the treaty by 'state and provincial governments'.[190] Similar provisions are found in ECT Article 23(1),[191] as well as

[187] ibid, para 434.

[188] ibid, para 435.

[189] *Impregilo SpA v Islamic Republic of Pakistan*, ICSID Case No ARB/03/3, Decision on Jurisdiction, 22 April 2005, para 262; *Gustav F W Hamester GmbH & Co KG v Republic of Ghana*, ICSID Case No ARB/07/24, Award, 18 June 2010, para 182: 'An organ is part of the structure of the State itself, whether its central organisation (i.e. its legislative, executive or judicial structures), or decentralised organisation. (e.g. territorial entities such as federated States; provinces; municipalities; etc.).'; *Enron Corporation and Ponderosa Assets, LP v Argentine Republic* (also known as *Enron Creditors Recovery Corp and Ponderosa Assets, LP v The Argentine Republic*), ICSID Case No ARB/01/3, Decision on Jurisdiction, 14 January 2004, para 32: 'The Tribunal is mindful in this respect that under international law the State incurs international responsibility and liability for unlawful acts of its various agencies and subdivisions. The same holds true under Article XIII of the Bilateral Investment Treaty when providing that this "...Treaty shall apply to the political subdivisions of the Parties"'; *Compañiá de Aguas del Aconquija SA and Vivendi Universal SA v Argentine Republic* (formerly *Compañía de Aguas del Aconquija, SA and Compagnie Générale des Eaux v Argentine Republic*) (*Vivendi I*), ICSID Case No ARB/97/3, Award, 21 November 2000, para 49: 'Under international law, and for purposes of jurisdiction of this Tribunal, it is well established that actions of a political subdivision of federal state, such as the Province of Tucumán in the federal state of the Argentine Republic, are attributable to the central government.'; *ADF Group Inc v United States of America*, ICSID Case No ARB (AF)/00/1, Award, 9 January 2003, para 166: 'The view taken above by the Tribunal is in line with the established rule of customary international law that acts of all its governmental organs and entities and territorial units are attributable to the State and that that State as a subject of international law is, accordingly, responsible for the acts of all its organs and territorial units'; *Grand River Enterprises Six Nations, Ltd, et al v United States of America*, UNCITRAL, Decision on Objections to Jurisdiction, 20 July 2006, para 1: 'While the specific actions complained of are taken by various states of the United States, the United States acknowledges that it is internationally responsible under NAFTA for their actions'.

[190] NAFTA Article 105:

Extent of Obligations

> The Parties shall ensure that all necessary measures are taken in order to give effect to the provisions of this Agreement, including their observance, except as otherwise provided in this Agreement, by state and provincial governments.

[191] ECT Article 23:

Observance by Sub-National Authorities

> (1) Each Contracting Party is fully responsible under this Treaty for the observance of all provisions of the Treaty, and shall take such reasonable measures as may be available to it to ensure such observance by regional and local governments and authorities within its Area.

in BITs.[192] The French Model BIT of 2006 dictates the attributability of the conduct of territorial units on the basis of political control (*tutelle*), by establishing that 'the Contracting Parties are responsible for the actions or omission of their sub-sovereign entities, including though not exclusively their federal states, regions, local governments or any other entity over which the Contracting Party exercises the control, the representation or the responsibility of its international affairs, or its sovereignty consistent with its internal legislation'.[193] The Final 2015 Indian Model BIT seems to deviate in fact from the principle of the unity of the State by excluding measures of local governments from the substantive scope of investment protection.[194] The entry into force of similar or comparable provisions would embody a departure from the principles of customary international law, which instead impose attributability of conduct of every political subdivision, such as federated states,[195] provinces,[196] or municipalities.[197]

The *Vivendi v Argentina I* Annulment Committee remarked that the attribution of conduct of political subdivisions is characterized by the very same legal mechanism pertaining to the attributability rules applicable to State organs, by criticizing the unfortunate distinction between 'federal claims' and '*Tucumán claims*' adopted in the award:

> The terminology employed by the Tribunal in this regard is not entirely happy. All international claims against a state are based on attribution, whether the

[192] See US–Argentina BIT (1991):

Article XIII

This Treaty shall apply to the political subdivisions of the Parties.

[193] France Model BIT (2006) Article 1.7.

[194] See section 1.2 of this chapter.

[195] *Waste Management, Inc v United Mexican States (Waste Management II)*, ICSID Case No ARB(AF)/00/3, Award 30 April 2004, paras 40, 75; *Mondev International Ltd v United States of America*, ICSID Case No ARB(AF)/99/2, Award, 11 October 2002, para 67; *Mytilineos Holdings SA v The State Union of Serbia and Montenegro and Republic of Serbia*, UNCITRAL, Partial Award on Jurisdiction, 8 September 2006, para 175; *Methanex Corporation v United States of America*, UNCITRAL, Final Award of the Tribunal on Jurisdiction and Merits, 3 August 2005, para 1 (State of California's ban on the sale and use of the gasoline additive); *Grand River Enterprises Six Nations, Ltd, et al v United States of America*, NAFTA/UNCITRAL Arbitration, Decision on Objections to Jurisdiction, 20 July 2006, para 1, fn 1.

[196] *Enron Corporation and Ponderosa Assets, LP v Argentine Republic*, ICSID Case No ARB/01/3 (also known as *Enron Creditors Recovery Corp and Ponderosa Assets, LP v The Argentine Republic*), Decision on Jurisdiction, 14 January 2004, para 32; *Azurix Corp v The Argentine Republic*, ICSID Case No ARB/01/12, Award, 14 July 2006, para 52.

[197] *Waste Management, Inc v United Mexican States (Waste Management II)*, ICSID Case No ARB(AF)/00/3, Award 30 April 2004, paras 40, 75; *Biloune and Marine Drive Complex Ltd v Ghana Investments Centre and the Government of Ghana*, Ad Hoc Tribunal, UNCITRAL, Award on Jurisdiction and Liability, 27 October 1989, 95 ILR 184, 191, 208; *Metalclad Corporation v The United Mexican States*, ICSID Case No ARB(AF)/97/1, Award, 30 August 2000, para 73; *Tokios Tokelės v Ukraine*, ICSID Case No ARB/02/18, Decision on Jurisdiction, 29 April 2004, para 102, fn 113; *Generation Ukraine, Inc v Ukraine*, ICSID Case No ARB/00/9, Award, 16 September 2003, paras 8.12, 10.2; *Mondev International Ltd v United States of America*, ICSID Case No ARB(AF)/99/2, Award, 11 October 2002, para 67, fn 12; *Parkerings-Compagniet AS v Republic of Lithuania*, ICSID Case No ARB/05/8, Award, 11 September 2007, para 258; *UAB E Energija v Latvia*, ICSID Case No ARB/12/33, Award, 22 December 2017, paras 796–801.

conduct in question is that of a central or provincial government or other subdivision.[198]

The rule of the unity of the State has been recognized by investment tribunals as a counterbalance to the unlimited freedom of self-organization of sovereigns as to internal matters.[199]

In case the applicable IIA contains an umbrella clause, a foreign investors' contract claims against a political subdivisions are not attributable to their State, at least as far as public international law is concerned. As mentioned above,[200] a contractual relationship, even if transposed by an umbrella clause at the international level, is governed by its proper law only, including *ultra vires* issues. In principle, the State is not liable for the contractual obligations concluded by its territorial units, 'there being, in general, no conception of the unity of the State in domestic law'.[201] However, nothing prevents the proper law of contract from providing a theory that establishes the joint liability of the State, based on its involvement in the economic operation formally concluded between a local government and an investor, consistent with the principle of privity of contract.[202]

[198] *Compañiá de Aguas del Aconquija SA and Vivendi Universal SA v Argentine Republic* (formerly *Compañía de Aguas del Aconquija, SA and Compagnie Générale des Eaux v Argentine Republic) (Vivendi I)*, ICSID Case No ARB/97/3, Decision on Annulment, 3 July 2003, para 16, fn 17.

[199] *Compañiá de Aguas del Aconquija SA and Vivendi Universal SA v Argentine Republic* (formerly *Compañía de Aguas del Aconquija, SA and Compagnie Générale des Eaux v Argentine Republic*) (*Vivendi I*), ICSID Case No ARB/97/3, Award, 21 November 2000, para 49: 'It is equally clear that the internal constitutional structure of a country can not alter these obligations.'; *Swembalt AB, Sweden v The Republic of Latvia*, UNCITRAL, Decision by the Court of Arbitration, 23 October 2000, para 37: 'In such a case, the subdivisions of the state and the way in which each state chooses to divide the work between such subdivisions is without relevance. If the state delegates certain work to lower levels of government, be they federal, regional or municipal, it must be an obligation of the state under international law to ensure that its obligations under international law, whether general or treaty law, are fulfilled by such subdivisions.'; *Autopista Concesionada de Venezuela (Aucoven) v Bolivarian Republic of Venezuela*, ICSID Case No ARB/00/5, Award, 23 September 2003, para 127: 'The fact that "the Venezuelan Constitution ascribes separate legal identity to the federal, state and municipal governments, and that the actions of one may not be attributed to another" ... may be accurate, but is irrelevant for the present purposes.'

[200] See para 2.2 of this chapter.

[201] James Crawford, 'Investment Arbitration and the ILC Articles on State Responsibility' (2010) 25 ICSID Review—Foreign Investment Law Journal 127, 134. See Harvard Law School (Manley O Hudson, Director), 'Research in International Law (Nationality, Responsibility of States, Territorial Waters). Drafts of Conventions Prepared in Anticipation of the First Conference on the Codification of International Law, The Hague, 1930', 1 April 1929, Part II, 'Responsibility of States' (Edwin M Borchard, Rapporteur), Article 8(a), (1929) 23 Special Number American Journal of International Law Special Supplement 133: 'A State is not responsible if an injury to an alien results from the non-performance of a contractual obligation which its political subdivision owes to an alien, apart from responsibility because of a denial of justice.' Accord, *La Guaira Electric Light and Power Company Case (US v Venezuela)*, 1903-1905, 9 RIAA 240, 243.

[202] *Azurix Corp v The Argentine Republic*, ICSID Case No ARB/01/12, Award, 14 July 2006, para 51 et seq.

3.4 *Ultra Vires* Conduct

Ultra vires conduct of State organs are recognized as attributable by investment tribunals in application of the rule of ARSIWA Article 7.[203] As a NAFTA tribunal has reiterated in the case of *ADF v USA*:

> An unauthorized or *ultra vires* act of a governmental entity of course remains, in international law, the act of the State of which the acting entity is part, if that entity acted in its official capacity.[204]

The act *ultra vires* should retain a sufficient homogeneity with the office entrusted to the agent concerned, or at least should not appear as manifestly outside the actual or apparent authority of the organ.[205] As already underlined, the practice of investment tribunals generally reproduces the customary interpretation of the *ultra vires* rule, with unprecedented applications with regard to the activities of State instrumentalities under ARSIWA Article 5, which nevertheless confirm the content of the conventional rule.[206]

Ultra vires issues related to contract claims are not regulated by customary international law, as reflected by ARSIWA Article 7, but by the law governing the substance of the domestic law obligations at issue, namely its proper law. Accordingly, the contractual obligation stipulated by a State official outside of its competences

[203] *Waguih Elie George Siag and Clorinda Vecchi v The Arab Republic of Egypt*, ICSID Case No ARB/05/15, Award, 1 June 2009, para 195; *ADF Group Inc v United States of America*, ICSID Case No ARB (AF)/00/1, Award, 9 January 2003, para 190; *Noble Ventures, Inc v Romania*, ICSID Case No ARB/01/11, Award, 12 October 2005, para 81: 'Even if one were to regard some of the acts of SOF or APAPS as being *ultra vires*, the result would be the same. This is because of the generally recognized rule recorded in Art. 7 2001 ILC Draft according to which the conduct of an organ of a State or of a person or entity empowered to exercise elements of governmental authority shall be considered an act of the State under international law if the organ, person or entity acts in that capacity, even if it exceeds its authority or contravenes instructions. Since, from the Claimant's perspective, SOF and APAPS always acted as if they were entities entitled by the Respondent to do so, their acts would still have to be attributed to the Respondent, even if an excess of competence had been shown.'; *Ioannis Kardassopoulos v The Republic of Georgia*, ICSID Case No ARB/05/18, Decision on Jurisdiction, 6 July 2007, para 190: 'The principle of attribution, in principle, applies to Georgia by virtue of its status as a sovereign State and is not contingent on the timing of its adherence to a treaty. It is also immaterial whether or not SakNavtobi and Transneft were authorized to grant the rights contemplated by the JVA and the Concession or whether or not they otherwise acted beyond their authority under Georgian law. Article 7 of the *Articles on State Responsibility* provides that even in cases where an entity empowered to exercise governmental authority acts ultra vires of it, the conduct in question is nevertheless attributable to the State.'

[204] *ADF Group Inc v United States of America*, ICSID Case No ARB (AF)/00/1, Award, 9 January 2003, para 190.

[205] *Ioannis Kardassopoulos v The Republic of Georgia*, ICSID Case No ARB/05/18, Decision on Jurisdiction, 6 July 2007, paras 190–92: 'the fact remains that these two agreements were "cloaked with the mantle of Governmental authority".'

[206] *Noble Ventures, Inc v Romania*, ICSID Case No ARB/01/11, Award, 12 October 2005, para 81; *Ioannis Kardassopoulos v The Republic of Georgia*, ICSID Case No ARB/05/18, Decision on Jurisdiction, 6 July 2007, para 190.

might be declared as invalid pursuant to its applicable law.[207] For instance, the reference of the *Eureko* tribunal to the 'clear authority' of the Minister of the State Treasury of Poland to conclude a Share Purchase Agreement (SPA) for the placement of shares of a parastatal entity under a process of privatization should be interpreted as referring to domestic law, and not to the *ultra vires* rule of ARSIWA Article 7, which does not necessarily require actual authority.[208] This determination does not preclude a finding of a treaty breach (or a breach of customary international law) in connection with or even based on the very same facts on which a contractual claim is rooted. As mentioned above, the two questions retain their analytical distinction.[209] Investment tribunals have notably applied this legal scheme to the issue of representations or assurances rendered by State organs or State entities pursuant to ARSIWA Article 5, even if *ultra vires*, in relation to the performance of a public contract or concession agreement with foreign investors. In such cases, the protection of investors' legitimate expectations may beget a treaty claim against the host State for breach of the FET standard. On the same line of argument, a respondent State may be held to be estopped from reliance on the illegality of the investment pursuant to its domestic law (for the sake of an objection to the jurisdiction *ratione materiae* or to the admissibility of the claim),[210] on the ground of its previous assurances on the same point.[211] This principle of law had already been established by an ICSID tribunal in the early case of *SPP v Egypt*:

> Whether legal under Egyptian law or not, the acts in question were the acts of Egyptian authorities, including the highest executive authority of the Government. These acts, which are now alleged to have been in violation of the Egyptian municipal legal system, created expectations protected by established principles of international law. A determination that these acts are null and void under municipal law would not resolve the ultimate question of liability for damages suffered by the victim who relied on the acts. If the municipal law does

[207] But see the early case of *Trumbull*, in Moore, IV (GPO 1898) 3569–71, where it was held that a diplomatic agent had 'authority' to conclude a professional contract with an intermediary counsel and that the act could be attributed to the sending State, even if *ultra vires*.

[208] *Eureko BV v Republic of Poland*, Ad Hoc Arbitration, Partial Award, 19 August 2005, para 129.

[209] See section 2.2 of this chapter.

[210] *Phoenix Action, Ltd v The Czech Republic*, ICSID Case No ARB/06/5, Award, 15 April 2009, para 114.

[211] *Kardassopoulos v The Republic of Georgia*, ICSID Case No ARB/05/18, Decision on Jurisdiction, 6 July 2007, para 193; *Oko Pankki Oyj, VTB Bank (Deutschland) AG and Sampo Bank Plc v The Republic of Estonia*, ICSID Case No ARB/04/6 (formerly *OKO Osuuspankkien Keskuspankki Oyj et al v Republic of Estonia*), Award, 19 November 2007, para 274: 'The Respondent also submitted that the [redacted] Letter was illegal, even patently illegal under Article 65 of the Respondent's Constitution. This submission is not accepted by the Tribunal. Under the applicable BITs, it is the obligation of the host State to deal with covered investments in accordance with the FET standard. If legitimate expectations are raised by the Respondent with a specific foreign investor that his investment will be treated fairly and equitably, such expectations must be honoured as a matter of international law. The fact that, according to the law of the host country, its officials or minister(s) may need certain internal approvals cannot later be held against that investor so as to defeat those expectations'.

not provide a remedy, the denial of any remedy whatsoever cannot be the final answer.[212]

Since the question of treaty breaches based on the violation of FET is governed by public international law, the *ultra vires* rule of ARSIWA Article 7 may intervene to this extent only, so as to render attributable to the State the conduct of representation and assurance performed by its agents or by its parastatals for the purposes of State responsibility for internationally wrongful acts.

4. Parastatals

4.1 Parastatals in the Context of Foreign Direct Investment

The practice of ISDS tribunals displays the preponderant majority of cases of application of the customary rule of attribution codified by ARSIWA Article 5 having regard to international law disputes in general. It may provide for elucidation of customary international law and further enhance its development, directly affecting its content, rather than being constrained by a *lex specialis* argument, at least on attribution issues. Therefore, ISDS represents one of the most relevant fields for the study and clarification of attributability matters involving the plethora of economic operators revolving around the State (*émanations de l'État*).[213] Investment tribunals have addressed the treatment of SOEs operating in strategic sectors, such as infrastructure,[214] energy and commodities,[215]

[212] *Southern Pacific Properties (Middle East) Limited v Arab Republic of Egypt*, ICSID Case No ARB/84/3, Award on the Merits, 20 May 1992, para 83.

[213] Yves Nouvel, 'Les entités paraétatiques dans la jurisprudence du CIRDI' in Charles Leben (ed), *Le contentieux arbitral transnational relatif à l'investissement. Nouveaux développements* (LGDJ 2006) 25. See also Roberto Ago, Third Report on State Responsibility, by Mr Roberto Ago, Special Rapporteur, 'The internationally wrongful act of the State, source of international responsibility', 5 March, 7 April, 28 April, and 18 May 1971, para 164, document A/CN.4/246 and Add.1-3, Yearbook of the International Law Commission, 1971, Volume II (Part One), 199, 254, document A/CN.4/SER.A/1971/Add.1 (Part 1).

[214] *Consortium RFCC v Kingdom of Morocco*, ICSID Case No ARB/00/6, Decision on Jurisdiction, 16 July 2001, para 34 et seq (Société Nationale des Autoroutes du Maroc or ADM); *Salini Costruttori SpA and Italstrade SpA v Kingdom of Morocco*, ICSID Case No ARB/00/4, Decision on Jurisdiction, 31 July 2000, para 2 (Société Nationale des Autoroutes du Maroc or ADM); *Toto Costruzioni Generali SpA v The Republic of Lebanon*, ICSID Case No ARB/07/12, Decision on Jurisdiction, 11 September 2009, para 17 (Council for Development and Reconstruction or CDR); *Bayindir Insaat Turizm Ticaret Ve Sanayi AS v Islamic Republic of Pakistan*, ICSID Case No ARB/03/29, Award, 27 August 2009, para 119 (National Highway Authority or NHA); *United Parcel Service of America Inc (UPS) v Government of Canada*, UNCITRAL, Award on the Merits, 24 May 2007, para 10, 45 (Canada Post); *EDF (Services) Limited v Romania*, ICSID Case No ARB/05/13, Award, 8 October 2009, para 185 et seq (CN Bucarest Aeroport Otopeni or AIBO, and Compania de Transportationuri Aeriene Romane Tarom SA or TAROM).

[215] *Deutsche Bank AG v Democratic Socialist Republic of Sri Lanka*, ICSID Case No ARB/09/2, Award, 31 October 2012, para 401 et seq (Ceylon Petroleum Company or CPC); *EnCana Corporation v Republic of Ecuador*, LCIA Case No UN3481, UNCITRAL, Award, 3 February 2006, para 154 et seq

mining,[216] water and irrigation management,[217] banking and insurance services,[218] telecommunications,[219] and tourism.[220] Parastatal entities may also have a non-sectoral mandate, for instance national or local development agencies or privatization agencies having corporate form and participating in economic operations involving foreign investment in their country.[221] In the latter case, the distinction from the category of public bodies having the status of State organ fades, but such entities still tend to be subsumed into the category of 'persons … empowered by the law of that State to exercise elements of the governmental authority' pursuant to ARSIWA Article 5.[222]

(Petroecuador); *Repsol YPF Ecuador, SA and others v Republic of Ecuador and Empresa Estatal Petróleos del Ecuador (PetroEcuador)*, ICSID Case No ARB/08/10, Procedural Order No 1, 17 June 2009, para 3; *Wintershall AG, et al v Government of Qatar*, Ad Hoc Arbitration, Partial Award on Liability, 5 February 1988, 28 ILM 795, 811-812 (Qatar General Petroleum Corporation or QGPC) in R Doak Bishop, James Crawford, and W Michael Reisman, *Foreign Investment Disputes. Cases, Materials and Commentary* (2nd edn, Kluwer Law International 2014) 558–59; *Saipem SpA v People's Republic of Bangladesh*, ICSID Case No ARB/05/07, Decision on Jurisdiction and Recommendation on Provisional Measures, 21 March 2007, para 6 (Bangladesh Oil Gas and Mineral Corporation or Petrobangla); *Limited Liability Company Amto v Ukraine*, SCC Case No 080/2005, Final Award, 26 March 2008, para 101 (Energoatom); *F-W Oil Interests, Inc v The Republic of Trinidad and Tobago*, ICSID Case No ARB/01/14, Award, 3 March 2006, para 200 (Trinmar and Petrotrin).

[216] *Adel A Hamadi Al Tamimi v Sultanate of Oman*, ICSID Case No ARB/11/33, Award, 3 November 2015, paras 314–44 (Oman Mining Company LLC or OMCO); *Crystallex International Corporation v Bolivarian Republic of Venezuela*, ICSID Case No ARB(AF)/11/2, Award, 4 April 2016, para 700 (Corporación Venezolana de Guyana or CVG).

[217] *Impregilo SpA v Islamic Republic of Pakistan*, ICSID Case No ARB/03/3, Decision on Jurisdiction, 22 April 2005, para 13 (Pakistani Water and Power Development Authority or WAPDA); *Consortium Groupement LESI—DIPENTA v République algérienne démocratique et populaire*, ICSID Case No ARB/03/08, Award, 10 January 2005, para 3 (Agence nationale des barrages or ANB); *Salini Costruttori SpA and Italstrade SpA v The Hashemite Kingdom of Jordan*, ICSID Case No ARB/02/13, Decision on Jurisdiction, 9 November 2004, para 80 et seq (Jordan Valley Authority or JVA).

[218] *Eureko BV v Republic of Poland*, Ad Hoc Arbitration, Partial Award, 19 August 2005, paras 36–38 (Powszechny laklad Ubezpieczen SA or PZU); *Waste Management, Inc v United Mexican States (Waste Management II)*, ICSID Case No ARB(AF)/00/3, Award, 30 April 2004, para 75 (Banco Nacional de Obras y Servicios Públicos or Banobras).

[219] *William Nagel v The Czech Republic*, SCC Case No 049/2002, Final Award, 9 September 2003, para 136 (České Radiokomunikace a.s. or ČRa).

[220] *Biloune and Marine Drive Complex Ltd v Ghana Investments Centre and the Government of Ghana*, Ad Hoc Tribunal, UNCITRAL, Award on Jurisdiction and Liability, 27 October 1989, 95 ILR 184, 191 (Ghana Tourist Development Company or GTDC); *Helnan International Hotels A/S v Arab Republic of Egypt*, ICSID Case No ARB/05/19, Decision on Jurisdiction, 17 October 2006, para 91 et seq (Egyptian Organization for Tourism and Hotels or EGOTH).

[221] *Biloune and Marine Drive Complex Ltd v Ghana Investments Centre and the Government of Ghana*, Ad Hoc Tribunal, UNCITRAL, Award on Jurisdiction and Liability, 27 October 1989, 95 ILR 184, 187 (Ghana Investment Centre or GIC); *Emilio Agustín Maffezini v The Kingdom of Spain*, ICSID Case No ARB/97/7, Decision on Jurisdiction, 25 January 2000, para 71 et seq (Sociedad por el Desarrollo Industrial de Galicia or SODIGA); *Noble Ventures, Inc v Romania*, ICSID Case No ARB/01/11, Award, 12 October 2005, para 79 (Authority for Privatization and Management of the State Ownership or APAPS, and State Ownership Fund or SOF).

[222] *Emilio Agustín Maffezini v The Kingdom of Spain*, ICSID Case No ARB/97/7, Decision on Jurisdiction, 25 January 2000, paras 79–80, 87; *Emilio Agustín Maffezini v The Kingdom of Spain*, ICSID Case No ARB/97/7, Award, 13 November 2000, para 48: 'But even if the structural test is applied, it is clear that financial companies such as SODIGA could not at the period relevant to the present dispute be held to fall entirely outside the overall scheme of public administration.'; *Noble Ventures, Inc v*

In the context of foreign direct investment, the creation by a State of instrumentalities acting in a specific economic sector is meant to signal to foreign investors a more attractive sociopolitical and economic environment for the establishment of their business, based on their alleged market orientation and their technical expertise.[223] Therefore, investors may have a selective preference to conclude investment agreements directly with SOEs, instead of conducting negotiations with the organs (ministries) of the host State. A typical vehicle for the investment is a Joint Venture Agreement (JVA), or more complex corporate engineering, between the investor(s) and a SOE establishing a mixed consortium of enterprises or Public–Private Partnership (PPP) for the performance of the economic operation.[224] Thus, the creation of economic parastatals corresponds to a strategic policy of capital-importing countries to enhance the attraction of FDI, at the same time interposing between them and foreign investors the corporate veil of a formally independent, separate, and business-oriented economic actor.[225]

Separate juristic personality of private law generally represents a threshold element for the identification of a 'State entity' pursuant to ARSIWA Article 5. However, as mentioned above, a decisive account is bestowed on the profit motive and to the circumstance of the enterprise pursuing an economic method of management, for the purposes of the qualification of the entity either as forming a parcel of the State machinery or as being a parastatal entity.[226] However, tribunals

Romania, ICSID Case No ARB/01/11, Award, 12 October 2005, para 83. Both tribunals confuse the tests under ARSIWA Article 4 and Article 5.

[223] Wolfgang G Friedmann and Jean-Pierre Béguin, *Joint International Business Ventures in Developing Countries. Case Studies and Analysis of Recent Trends* (Columbia University Press 1971) 4–10.

[224] *EDF (Services) Limited v Romania*, ICSID Case No ARB/05/13, Award, 8 October 2009, para 46 et seq; *Gustav F W Hamester GmbH & Co KG v Republic of Ghana*, ICSID Case No ARB/07/24, Award, 18 June 2010, para 22 et seq; *Emilio Agustín Maffezini v The Kingdom of Spain*, ICSID Case No ARB/97/7, Award, 13 November 2000, para 39. See also *Joint Venture Yashlar (Turkmenistan) and Bridas SAPIC (Argentina) v Government of Turkmenistan (or Turkmenistan or the State of Turkmenistan and/or the Ministry of Oil of Turkmenistan) (Turkmenistan)*, ICC Case No 9151, Interim Award, 8 June 1999, para 58. See also, more generally, Emmanuel Gaillard, 'Effectiveness of Arbitral Awards, State Immunity from Execution and Autonomy of State Entities. Three Incompatible Principles' in Emmanuel Gaillard and Jennifer Younan (eds), *State Entities In International Arbitration*, IAI Series on International Arbitration, No 4 (Juris Publishing, Inc 2008) 179; Eduardo Silva Romero, 'Some Remarks on the Contribution of ICC Arbitrators to the Development of International Commercial Arbitration Involving States and State Entities' in Andrea Carlevaris, Laurent Lévy, Alexis Mourre, Eric A Schwartz (eds), *International Arbitration Under Review. Essays in Honour of John Beechey* (ICC Publishing 2015) 401.

[225] *First National City Bank v Banco Para el Comercio Exterior de Cuba (BANCEC)*, 462 US 611, 624–25 (1983): 'These distinctive features permit government instrumentalities to manage their operations on an enterprise basis while granting them a greater degree of flexibility and independence from close political control than is generally enjoyed by government agencies. These same features frequently prompt governments in developing countries to establish separate juridical entities as the vehicles through which to obtain the financial resources needed to make large-scale national investments.'

[226] See section 3.1 of this chapter. See *Limited Liability Company Amto v Ukraine*, SCC Case No 080/2005, Final Award, 26 March 2008, para 101: 'Energoatom is a separate legal entity owned by the Respondent. It is not an ordinary private company, but a specific juridical person known as a state company.'; *Jan de Nul NV and Dredging International NV v Arab Republic of Egypt*, ICSID Case No ARB/04/13, Award, 6 November 2008, para 160: 'Article 2 of Law No. 30/1975, embodying the Suez Canal

have also found that a State enterprise or entity not having the separate juristic personality of private law, but being classified as a public body, may be categorized as a State instrumentality, therefore falling outside the mechanism of attributability enshrined in ARSIWA Article 4.[227] Conversely, State instrumentalities with separate legal personality under private law may be exceptionally qualified as State organs upon application of the doctrine of *de facto* agency.[228] This scenario is certainly contemplated, as stated by the *F-W Oil Interests v Trinidad and Tobago* tribunal:

> where the operation of a State enterprise is at the core of an international dispute, it is theoretically possible that the enterprise's conduct (acts or omissions) may engage the responsibility of the State either as an organ of the State; or as a body exercising elements of the governmental authority of the State; or as a body which is in fact acting on the instructions of the State, or under its direction or control (ILC draft Articles 4-8). There is in other words a whole gamut of possibilities, whose application to particular situations depends upon an amalgam of questions of law and questions of fact which will vary from case to case according to the circumstances.[229]

4.2 Test for Attribution: A Functional Test Applied on the Basis of a Structural Finding

In international investment arbitration, and in international economic litigation in general, the application of the attribution rule of ARSIWA Article 5 is inevitably associated with the complexity of the various forms of the intervention of the State into the economic system.[230] Since most SOEs adopt the corporate form, further

Authority Statutes (Exh. C-9), states that "Suez Canal Authority is a Public Authority" and that SCA "enjoys an independent juristic personality." '

[227] *Limited Liability Company Amto v Ukraine*, SCC Case No 080/2005, Final Award, 26 March 2008, para 101: 'Energoatom is a separate legal entity owned by the Respondent. It is not an ordinary private company, but a specific juridical person known as a state company.'; *Jan de Nul NV and Dredging International NV v Arab Republic of Egypt*, ICSID Case No ARB/04/13, Award, 6 November 2008, para 160: 'Article 2 of Law No. 30/1975, embodying the Suez Canal Authority Statutes (Exh. C-9), states that "Suez Canal Authority is a Public Authority" and that SCA "enjoys an independent juristic personality." '

[228] See Nick Gallus, 'State Enterprises as Organs of the State and BIT Claims' (2006) 7 Journal of World Investment & Trade 761, 777–79.

[229] *F-W Oil Interests, Inc v The Republic of Trinidad and Tobago*, ICSID Case No ARB/01/14, Award, 3 March 2006, para 203.

[230] *Salini Costruttori SpA and Italstrade SpA v Kingdom of Morocco*, ICSID Case No ARB/00/4, Decision on Jurisdiction, 31 July 2000, para 35: 'the Tribunal notes that the fact that a State may act through the medium of a company having its own legal personality is no longer unusual if one considers the extraordinary expansion of public authority activity. In order to perform its obligations, and at the same time take into account the sometimes diverging interests that the private economy protects, the State uses a varied spectrum of modes of organisation, among which are in particular semi-public

peculiar issues arise with regard to the combination of principles of public international law and municipal corporate law. The *Maffezini v Spain* tribunal has depicted this scenario as follows:

> the Tribunal may look to the applicable rules of international law in deciding whether a particular entity is a state body. These standards have evolved and been applied in the context of the law of State responsibility. Here, the test that has been developed looks to various factors, such as ownership, control, the nature, purposes and objectives of the entity whose actions are under scrutiny, and to the character of the actions taken. The relevance of these standards is clearer when there is a direct State operation and control, such as by a section or division of a Ministry, but less so when the State chooses to act through a private sector mechanism, such as a corporation (*sociedad anonima*) or some other corporate structure.[231]

In ISDS proceedings, the attribution of conduct of parastatal entities, usually of an economic nature, is operated on the basis of customary international law, which provides for a sequence of a preliminary structural analysis, followed by the application of a functional test, provided that the State instrumentality in question is formally empowered by law to exercise elements of the governmental authority. Indeed, this normative operation consists in the two steps of *identification* of the parastatal entity as being such (*structural* test) and *attribution* of the specific act or omission based on the exercise of sovereign authority (*functional* test).[232]

4.2.1 Structural Test

The application of the structural test for the identification of a State instrumentality is based on factual findings. In the absence of a ritual or orthodox formula of 'parastatal entity', certain characteristic elements thereof are definitely recurring, but no particular one is necessary or decisive for a conclusion that a certain 'person'

companies, similar to ADM, a company mostly held by the State which, considering the size of its participation (over 80%), directs and manages it. All these factors resolutely imprint a public nature on the said company.' In French, 'semi-public companies' is translated as '*sociétés d'économie mixte*'. See *Consortium RFCC v Kingdom of Morocco*, ICSID Case No ARB/00/6, Decision on Jurisdiction, 16 July 2001, para 39.

---

[231] *Emilio Agustín Maffezini v The Kingdom of Spain*, ICSID Case No ARB/97/7, Decision on Jurisdiction, 25 January 2000, paras 76–78. See Abby Cohen Smutny, 'State Responsibility and Attribution When is a State Responsible for the Acts of State Enterprises? *Emilio Agustín Maffezini v. The Kingdom of Spain*' in Todd Weiler (ed), *International Investment Law and Arbitration: Leading Cases from the ICSID, NAFTA, Bilateral Treaties and Customary International Law* (Cameron May 2005) 17.

[232] Pierre-Marie Dupuy, 'Les émanations engagent-elles la responsabilité des Etats? Etude de droit international des investissements' (2006) EUI Working Paper LAW No 2006/7, 11–12.

falls under the scope of ARSIWA Article 5. Hence, the methodology resorted to by the interpreter is inevitably inductive, while being oriented or informed by a 'typologic' model of what a parastatal is or may be. All the indexes or symptoms of the status of a 'State entity' under ARSIWA Article 5, which have been listed in the preceding chapter, are applicable in the context of international economic litigation.[233] Nevertheless, it here seems appropriate to provide another enumeration of the symptoms of the status of (economic) parastatal, more suited to the peculiarities of international investment cases. While the factual elements illustrated with regard to general international law chiefly reflect the practice of the Iran–US Claims Tribunal, the following list is based on a comprehensive review of the relevant decisions of international investment tribunals. While an affirmative conclusion as to the fulfilment of the structural test is not as such determinative of attribution under ARSIWA Article 5, the elements involved in the structural test may nevertheless be relevant for the application of the factual prong for attribution of the conduct of 'private' individuals under ARSIWA Article 8, based on 'instructions, or direction or control'. Accordingly, a finding of a legal entity as being a State-controlled company does not automatically end in attribution based on ARSIWA Article 5, but may nevertheless represent an applicable basis for attribution under Article 8.

The following (non-exhaustive) list of 'symptomatic' elements describes the elements that have usually revealed, in investment arbitration, the status of 'parastatal entity', so as to meet the structural test required under ARSIWA Article 5:

a) establishment by statutory act or decree[234] (including privatization laws);[235]

[233] See Chapter II, section 4.3.

[234] *Waste Management, Inc v United Mexican States (Waste Management II)*, ICSID Case No ARB(AF)/00/3, Award 30 April 2004, para 75; *Impregilo SpA v Islamic Republic of Pakistan*, ICSID Case No ARB/03/3, Decision on Jurisdiction, 22 April 2005, para 200; *Saipem SpA v People's Republic of Bangladesh*, ICSID Case No ARB/05/07, Decision on Jurisdiction and Recommendation on Provisional Measures, 21 March 2007, para 6; *Bayindir Insaat Turizm Ticaret Ve Sanayi AS v Islamic Republic of Pakistan*, ICSID Case No ARB/03/29, Decision on Jurisdiction, 14 November 2005, para 10; *Noble Ventures, Inc v Romania*, ICSID Case No ARB/01/11, Award, 12 October 2005, para 71; *EDF (Services) Limited v Romania*, ICSID Case No ARB/05/13, Award, 8 October 2009, para 204; *Jan de Nul NV and Dredging International NV v Arab Republic of Egypt*, ICSID Case No ARB/04/13, Award, 6 November 2008, paras 45, 160; *United Parcel Service of America Inc (UPS) v Government of Canada*, UNCITRAL, Award on the Merits, 24 May 2007, para 9; *Toto Costruzioni Generali SpA v The Republic of Lebanon*, ICSID Case No ARB/07/12, Decision on Jurisdiction, 11 September 2009, paras 51, 54; *William Nagel v The Czech Republic*, SCC Case No 049/2002, Final Award, 9 September 2003, paras 144, 162; *Salini Costruttori SpA and Italstrade SpA v The Hashemite Kingdom of Jordan*, ICSID Case No ARB/02/13, Decision on Jurisdiction, 9 November 2004, para 81; *United Parcel Service of America Inc (UPS) v Government of Canada*, UNCITRAL, Award on the Merits, 24 May 2007, para 9; *Gustav F W Hamester GmbH & Co KG v Republic of Ghana*, ICSID Case No ARB/07/24, Award, 18 June 2010, para 22; *Emilio Agustín Maffezini v The Kingdom of Spain*, ICSID Case No ARB/97/7, Decision on Jurisdiction, 25 January 2000, para 83.

[235] *Eureko BV v Republic of Poland*, Ad Hoc Arbitration, Partial Award, 19 June 2005, para 38; *Nykomb Synergetics Technology Holding AB v The Republic of Latvia*, SCC, Arbitral Award, 16 December 2003, para 1.1.

b) mission to provide a public service or to pursue a public purpose;[236]
c) entitlement to acquire, hold, and dispose of property;[237]
d) management of State-owned property;[238]
e) capacity to sue and to be sued;[239]
f) autonomous budget;[240]
g) funds deposited in a special account or accounts at the central bank of the establishing State;[241]
h) subsidization by the government;[242]
i) exercise of a delegated monopoly (including the power to set prices);[243]
j) board of directors appointed (and revoked) by the government or political power;[244]
k) ministers sitting as president or members of the board of directors;[245]

[236] *Bosh International, Inc and B&P Ltd Foreign Investments Enterprise v Ukraine*, ICSID Case No ARB/08/11, Award, 25 October 2012, para 173; *Salini Costruttori SpA and Italstrade SpA v Kingdom of Morocco*, ICSID Case No ARB/00/4, Decision on Jurisdiction, 31 July 2000, para 32; *Salini Costruttori SpA and Italstrade SpA v The Hashemite Kingdom of Jordan*, ICSID Case No ARB/02/13, Decision on Jurisdiction, 9 November 2004, para 81; *Waste Management, Inc v United Mexican States (Waste Management II)*, ICSID Case No ARB(AF)/00/3, Award, 30 April 2004, para 75; *Jan de Nul NV and Dredging International NV v Arab Republic of Egypt*, ICSID Case No ARB/04/13, Award, 6 November 2008, para 45; *Gustav F W Hamester GmbH & Co KG v Republic of Ghana*, ICSID Case No ARB/07/24, Award, 18 June 2010, para 184, 189; *Helnan International Hotels A/S v Arab Republic of Egypt*, ICSID Case No ARB/05/19, Decision on Jurisdiction, 17 October 2006, para 92; *Emilio Agustín Maffezini v The Kingdom of Spain*, ICSID Case No ARB/97/7, Decision on Jurisdiction, 25 January 2000, para 86; *Bayindir Insaat Turizm Ticaret Ve Sanayi AS v Islamic Republic of Pakistan*, ICSID Case No ARB/03/29, Decision on Jurisdiction, 14 November 2005, para 10.

[237] *Bayindir Insaat Turizm Ticaret Ve Sanayi AS v Islamic Republic of Pakistan*, ICSID Case No ARB/03/29, Award, 27 August 2009, para 119; *Jan de Nul NV and Dredging International NV v Arab Republic of Egypt*, ICSID Case No ARB/04/13, Award, 6 November 2008, para 149(iv); *Salini Costruttori SpA and Italstrade SpA v The Hashemite Kingdom of Jordan*, ICSID Case No ARB/02/13, Decision on Jurisdiction, 9 November 2004, para 81; *Impregilo SpA v Islamic Republic of Pakistan*, ICSID Case No ARB/03/3, Decision on Jurisdiction, 22 April 2005, para 205; *Gustav F W Hamester GmbH & Co KG v Republic of Ghana*, ICSID Case No ARB/07/24, Award, 18 June 2010, para 185.

[238] *Bosh International, Inc and B&P Ltd Foreign Investments Enterprise v Ukraine*, ICSID Case No ARB/08/11, Award, 25 October 2012, para 173.

[239] *Impregilo SpA v Islamic Republic of Pakistan*, ICSID Case No ARB/03/3, Decision on Jurisdiction, 22 April 2005, para 200; *Gustav F W Hamester GmbH & Co KG v Republic of Ghana*, ICSID Case No ARB/07/24, Award, 18 June 2010, para 184; *Bayindir Insaat Turizm Ticaret Ve Sanayi AS v Islamic Republic of Pakistan*, ICSID Case No ARB/03/29, Decision on Jurisdiction, 14 November 2005, para 10.

[240] *Jan de Nul NV and Dredging International NV v Arab Republic of Egypt*, ICSID Case No ARB/04/13, Award, 6 November 2008, para 161; *Toto Costruzioni Generali SpA v The Republic of Lebanon*, ICSID Case No ARB/07/12, Decision on Jurisdiction, 11 September 2009, para 51, 55.

[241] *Salini Costruttori SpA and Italstrade SpA v The Hashemite Kingdom of Jordan*, ICSID Case No ARB/02/13, Decision on Jurisdiction, 9 November 2004, para 82.

[242] *United Parcel Service of America Inc (UPS) v Government of Canada*, UNCITRAL, Award on the Merits, 24 May 2007, para 45.

[243] *United Parcel Service of America Inc (UPS) v Government of Canada*, UNCITRAL, Award on the Merits, 24 May 2007, para 9.

[244] *Noble Ventures, Inc v Romania*, ICSID Case No ARB/01/11, Award, 12 October 2005, para 76; *Impregilo SpA v Islamic Republic of Pakistan*, ICSID Case No ARB/03/3, Decision on Jurisdiction, 22 April 2005, para 201; *William Nagel v The Czech Republic*, SCC Case No 049/2002, Final Award, 9 September 2003, para 164; *Wintershall AG, et al v Government of Qatar*, Partial Award on Liability, 5 February 1988, 28 ILM 795, 811–12.

[245] *Consortium RFCC v Kingdom of Morocco*, ICSID Case No ARB/00/6, Decision on Jurisdiction, 16 July 2001, para 19, 36; *Helnan International Hotels A/S v Arab Republic of Egypt*, ICSID Case No ARB/

l) applicability to employees of the labour regime governing public servants;[246]
m) registration on the Treasury's accounts of the charges collected and revenues received by the parastatal;[247]
n) auditing of accounts and balance sheets by the General Auditor of the State;[248]
o) palpable governmental oversight (also through a *Conseil d'État*), mandatory approval of resolutions and operations, and mandates;[249]
p) jurisdiction of administrative courts over the activities of the parastatal entity;[250]
q) applicability of the administrative regulation for public contracts (including concessions and procurements);[251]
r) general and broad power to issue regulations to implement a parastatal's mandate;[252]

05/19, Decision on Jurisdiction, 17 October 2006, para 92; *Salini Costruttori SpA and Italstrade SpA v The Hashemite Kingdom of Jordan*, ICSID Case No ARB/02/13, Decision on Jurisdiction, 9 November 2004, para 83; *Salini Costruttori SpA and Italstrade SpA v Kingdom of Morocco*, ICSID Case No ARB/00/4, Decision on Jurisdiction, 31 July 2000, para 32.

[246] *Impregilo SpA v Islamic Republic of Pakistan*, ICSID Case No ARB/03/3, Decision on Jurisdiction, 22 April 2005, para 203; *Salini Costruttori SpA and Italstrade SpA v The Hashemite Kingdom of Jordan*, ICSID Case No ARB/02/13, Decision on Jurisdiction, 9 November 2004, para 82.

[247] *Helnan International Hotels A/S v Arab Republic of Egypt*, ICSID Case No ARB/05/19, Decision on Jurisdiction, 17 October 2006, para 92.

[248] *Impregilo SpA v Islamic Republic of Pakistan*, ICSID Case No ARB/03/3, Decision on Jurisdiction, 22 April 2005, para 207.

[249] *Nykomb Synergetics Technology Holding AB v The Republic of Latvia*, SCC, Arbitral Award, 16 December 2003, para 4.2; *Helnan International Hotels A/S v Arab Republic of Egypt*, ICSID Case No ARB/05/19, Decision on Jurisdiction, 17 October 2006, para 92; *EnCana Corporation v Republic of Ecuador*, LCIA Case No UN3481, UNCITRAL, Award, 3 February 2006, para 154; *Toto Costruzioni Generali SpA v The Republic of Lebanon*, ICSID Case No ARB/07/12, Decision on Jurisdiction, 11 September 2009, para 51; *Impregilo SpA v Islamic Republic of Pakistan*, ICSID Case No ARB/03/3, Decision on Jurisdiction, 22 April 2005, para 204, 209; *Bayindir Insaat Turizm Ticaret Ve Sanayi AS v Islamic Republic of Pakistan*, ICSID Case No ARB/03/29, Award, 27 August 2009, para 118; *Noble Ventures, Inc v Romania*, ICSID Case No ARB/01/11, Award, 12 October 2005, para 77; *EDF (Services) Limited v Romania*, ICSID Case No ARB/05/13, Award, 8 October 2009, para 205; *William Nagel v The Czech Republic*, SCC Case No 049/2002, Final Award, 9 September 2003, para 164 (decisions on winding up the State enterprise; decisions on merger with another State enterprise); *Waste Management, Inc v United Mexican States (Waste Management II)*, ICSID Case No ARB(AF)/00/3, Award, 30 April 2004, para 75; *Salini Costruttori SpA and Italstrade SpA v Kingdom of Morocco*, ICSID Case No ARB/00/4, Decision on Jurisdiction, 31 July 2000, para 32; *EnCana Corporation v Republic of Ecuador*, LCIA Case No UN3481, UNCITRAL, Award, 3 February 2006, para 154.

[250] *Jan de Nul NV and Dredging International NV v Arab Republic of Egypt*, ICSID Case No ARB/04/13, Award, 6 November 2008, para 146(vi).

[251] *United Parcel Service of America Inc (UPS) v Government of Canada*, UNCITRAL, Award on the Merits, 24 May 2007, para 51; *Consortium RFCC v Kingdom of Morocco*, ICSID Case No ARB/00/6, Decision on Jurisdiction, 16 July 2001, para 38; *Salini Costruttori SpA and Italstrade SpA v Kingdom of Morocco*, ICSID Case No ARB/00/4, Decision on Jurisdiction, 31 July 2000, para 34; *Emilio Agustín Maffezini v The Kingdom of Spain*, ICSID Case No ARB/97/7, Award, 13 November 2000, para 49.

[252] *Adel A Hamadi Al Tamimi v Sultanate of Oman*, ICSID Case No ARB/11/33, Award, 3 November 2015, para 327; *United Parcel Service of America Inc (UPS) v Government of Canada*, UNCITRAL, Award on the Merits, 24 May 2007, para 9; *Gustav F W Hamester GmbH & Co KG v Republic of Ghana*, ICSID Case No ARB/07/24, Award, 18 June 2010, para 190: '[t]he Board of Directors may, *by legislative instrument*, make such regulations as it may see fit for the purpose of giving effect to the provisions of this Law.'; *Impregilo SpA v Islamic Republic of Pakistan*, ICSID Case No ARB/03/3, Decision on Jurisdiction, 22 April 2005, para 208.

s) empowerment to impose coercive measures, such as charges, fines, and penalties;[253]
t) protection of immunity from suit.[254]

In certain cases, the element of the mission of a SOE to provide a public service or to pursue a public purpose has been confused with the functional test of the exercise of governmental authority, so that a finding of the 'public aim' of the entity has been considered as a sufficient basis to establish the attribution of conduct. This seems to have occurred in *Salini v Morocco*, where the tribunal held:

> it is clear that ADM's main object is to accomplish tasks that are under State control (building, managing and operating of assets falling under the province of the public utilities responding to the structural needs of the Kingdom of Morocco with regard to infrastructure and efficient communication networks).[255]

However, ascertaining the public dimension of the corporate objective (*object social*) of a State enterprise does not conclusively solve the issue of attribution, since it just remains an element falling under the structural analysis in ARSIWA Article 5, which additionally requires the application of the functional test for attributability proper.[256] As observed by the *Jan de Nul v Egypt* tribunal, 'the fact that the subject matter of the Contract related to the core functions of the SCA, i.e., the maintenance and improvement of the Suez Canal, is irrelevant. … What matters is not the "service public" element, but the use of "*prérogatives de puissance publique*" or governmental authority.'[257] Accordingly, the public purpose or nationwide strategic role of the concerned State entity (for instance, 'to contribute to the development of national economy',[258] 'the general nature of the activity in question',[259] 'an essential

[253] *Jan de Nul NV and Dredging International NV v Arab Republic of Egypt*, ICSID Case No ARB/04/13, Award, 6 November 2008, para 166; *Gustav F W Hamester GmbH & Co KG v Republic of Ghana*, ICSID Case No ARB/07/24, Award, 18 June 2010, para 190; *Bayindir Insaat Turizm Ticaret Ve Sanayi AS v Islamic Republic of Pakistan*, ICSID Case No ARB/03/29, Award, 27 August 2009, para 121.

[254] *Deutsche Bank AG v Democratic Socialist Republic of Sri Lanka*, ICSID Case No ARB/09/2, Award, 31 October 2012, para 405(b).

[255] *Salini Costruttori SpA and Italstrade SpA v Kingdom of Morocco*, ICSID Case No ARB/00/4, Decision on Jurisdiction, 31 July 2000, para 33. Accord, *Consortium RFCC v Kingdom of Morocco*, ICSID Case No ARB/00/6, Decision on Jurisdiction, 16 July 2001, para 37: '*Il est ainsi clair que le but social d'ADM poursuit la réalisation de tâches de nature étatique (construction, gestion et exploitation de biens relevant du service public répondant aux besoins structurels du Royaume du Maroc en matière d'infrastructures et de réseaux de communications efficaces)*'. See also *Flemingo DutyFree Shop Private Limited v the Republic of Poland*, UNCITRAL, Award, 12 August 2016, para 442.

[256] *Bosh International, Inc and B&P Ltd Foreign Investments Enterprise v Ukraine*, ICSID Case No ARB/08/11, Award, 25 October 2012, paras 175–78.

[257] *Jan de Nul NV and Dredging International NV v Arab Republic of Egypt*, ICSID Case No ARB/04/13, Award, 6 November 2008, paras 169–70.

[258] *Helnan International Hotels A/S v Arab Republic of Egypt*, ICSID Case No ARB/05/19, Decision on Jurisdiction, 17 October 2006, para 92.

[259] *F-W Oil Interests, Inc v The Republic of Trinidad and Tobago*, ICSID Case No ARB/01/14, Award, 3 March 2006, para 204.

role in the economic, social and cultural life' of a State,[260] 'an instrument of State action',[261] 'to promote and finance activities carried out by the Federal, State, and Municipal Governments of the Country',[262] 'an institution of public interest')[263] is not determinative as such of a result whereby its acts and omissions are attributed to its establishing State, since this entails a normative operation that cannot neglect the actual exercise of sovereign authority in connection with the specific act at issue.[264]

4.2.2 Functional Test

The structural test 'in itself clearly does not resolve the issue of attribution'.[265] Indeed, a tribunal should subsequently resort to the functional test of the actual exercise of elements of the governmental authority pursuant to ARSIWA Article 5. This test basically corresponds with the nature test under the law of State immunity from adjudication, which is grounded on the dichotomy between *acta jure imperii* and *acta jure gestionis*.[266] Indeed, this approach is not unknown to the practice of investment tribunals, as found in *Maffezini v Spain*:

> the Tribunal must again rely on the functional test, that is, it must establish whether specific acts or omissions are essentially commercial rather than governmental in nature or, conversely, whether their nature is essentially governmental rather than commercial. Commercial acts cannot be attributed to the Spanish State, while governmental acts should be so attributed.[267]

The formalistic argument that the requirement of the *exercise of elements of the governmental authority* pursuant to ARSIWA Article 5 provides for a larger

[260] *United Parcel Service of America Inc (UPS) v Government of Canada*, UNCITRAL, Award on the Merits, 24 May 2007, para 57.

[261] *Emilio Agustín Maffezini v The Kingdom of Spain*, ICSID Case No ARB/97/7, Decision on Jurisdiction, 25 January 2000, para 86.

[262] *Waste Management, Inc v United Mexican States (Waste Management II)*, ICSID Case No ARB(AF)/00/3, Award, 30 April 2004, para 75.

[263] *Noble Ventures, Inc v Romania*, ICSID Case No ARB/01/11, Award, 12 October 2005, para 76 (this references is kept in so far as the tribunal confuses the tests of attribution under ARSIWA Article 4 and 5).

[264] *Gustav F W Hamester GmbH & Co KG v Republic of Ghana*, ICSID Case No ARB/07/24, Award, 18 June 2010, para 202: 'It is not enough for an act of a public entity to have been performed in the general fulfilment of some general interest, mission or purpose to qualify as an attributable act'.

[265] *Gustav F W Hamester GmbH & Co KG v Republic of Ghana*, ICSID Case No ARB/07/24, Award, 18 June 2010, para 193.

[266] See Chapter I, section 6, and Chapter II, section 4.2.

[267] *Emilio Agustín Maffezini v The Kingdom of Spain*, ICSID Case No ARB/97/7, Award, 13 November 2000, para 52, 57; *Gustav F W Hamester GmbH & Co KG v Republic of Ghana*, ICSID Case No ARB/07/24, Award, 18 June 2010, para 201(i): 'Under Article 5 of the ILC Articles, if the acts of Cocobod which are the subject of complaint were performed in the exercise of governmental power, they will be attributed to the State. If they were performed in the fulfilment of commercial relations, they will not be attributable on that basis to the State'.; *Bosh International, Inc and B&P Ltd Foreign Investments Enterprise v Ukraine*, ICSID Case No ARB/08/11, Award, 25 October 2012, paras 175–78.

category than the requirement of the *exercise of sovereign authority of the State* under UNCSI Article 2.1(b)(iii) does not seem persuasive. Instead, the use of the nature test, elaborated in relation to the theory of restrictive immunity from adjudication in the context of attribution of conduct under ARSIWA Article 5, is meant to foster consistency within these two areas of public international law.[268]In addition, the very same distinction between *acta jure imperii* and *acta jure gestionis* is used for jurisdictional purposes to establish whether a SOE may retain *jus standi* as a 'national of another Contracting State', ie in the position of claimant investor, pursuant to ICSID Convention Article 25(1). Accordingly, standing is granted in so far as the subject matter of the dispute involves the activity *jure privatorum* of the SOE.[269] Otherwise, the involvement of the discharge of essentially governmental functions by the State entity would transform an investor–State dispute into interstate litigation, which is not contemplated by the jurisdiction of the Centre.[270]

With regard to the definition of 'governmental authority', the general point of departure is the acknowledgement of the absence of conclusive guidance in ARSIWA Article 5 and in the Commentaries:[271]

> In short, the notion is intended to be a flexible one, not amenable to general definition in advance; and the elements that would go in its definition in particular cases would be a mixture of fact, law and practice.[272]

IIAs do not usually provide definitions of 'governmental authority', but may provide a specification thereof. For instance, NAFTA Article 1502(3)(a) refers to 'any regulatory, administrative or other governmental authority ... such as the power to grant import or export licenses, approve commercial transactions or impose

[268] See Chapter II, section 4.2.

[269] *Masdar Solar & Wind Cooperatief UA v Kingdom of Spain*, ICSID Case No ARB/14/1, Award, 16 May 2018, paras. 166–73; *Ceskoslovenska Obchodni Banka, AS (CSOB) v The Slovak Republic,* ICSID Case No ARB/97/4, Decision on Jurisdiction, 24 May 1999, para 16; *CDC Group plc v Republic of Seychelles*, ICSID Case No ARB/02/14, Award, 17 December 2003, para 17; *Rumeli Telekom AS and Telsim Mobil Telekomunikasyon Hizmetleri AS v Republic of Kazakhstan*, ICSID Case No ARB/05/16, Award, 29 July 2008, paras 324–29; *Emilio Agustín Maffezini v The Kingdom of Spain*, ICSID Case No ARB/97/7, Decision on Jurisdiction, 25 January 2000, para 80; *Flughafen Zürich AG and Gestión e Ingenería IDC SA v Bolivarian Republic of Venezuela*, ICSID Case No ARB/10/19, Laudo, 18 November 2014, paras 279–86; *Beijing Urban Construction Group Co Ltd v Republic of Yemen*, ICSID Case No ARB/14/30, Decision on Jurisdiction, 17 May 2017, paras 31 et seq. See Mark Feldman, 'State-Owned Enterprises as Claimants in International Investment Arbitration' (2016) 31 ICSID Review—Foreign Investment Law Journal 24.

[270] Aaron Broches, 'The Convention on the Settlement of Investment Disputes Between States and Nationals of Other States' (1972-II) 136 Recueil des Cours 331, 340, 355: 'a mixed economy company or government-owned corporation should not be disqualified as a "national of another Contracting State" unless it is acting as an agent for the government or is discharging an essentially governmental function'.

[271] Kaj Hobér, 'State Responsibility and Attribution' in Peter Muchlinski, Federico Ortino, and Christoph Schreuer (eds), *The Oxford Handbook of International Investment Law* (Oxford University Press 2008) 550, 556, 560.

[272] *F-W Oil Interests, Inc v The Republic of Trinidad and Tobago*, ICSID Case No ARB/01/14, Award, 3 March 2006, para 203.

quotas, fees or other charges'. However, a definition of 'governmental authority' is not (nor does it necessarily have to be) dispensed by IIAs. Therefore, it is appropriate, in the first place, to proceed from a casuistic review of arbitral resolutions on the distinction between *acta jure imperii* and *acta jure gestionis*, and, in the second place, to embark on a doctrinal attempt at definition.

International investment tribunals have found the following activities, of either a general or a specific application, to embody an exercise of governmental authority (*puissance publique*): the issue of decrees or regulations of a normative nature,[273] the imposition and collection of charges,[274] the infliction of sanctions or penalties,[275] the ejection of unauthorized persons,[276] the grant of subsidies,[277] marketing and export regulations,[278] land inspections,[279] site expropriations,[280] official certification of products,[281] the handling and moving of financial accounts without the consent of the account holder,[282] and the unilateral rescission of a mining concession based on the SOE's power of *autotutela*.[283] Instead, arbitrators have categorized as commercial, and as such not attributable to States, the following acts of parastatal entities: the default on settlement of contractual debts owed to a service provider,[284] the failure to pay the amounts owing under an hedging agreement,[285]

[273] *Impregilo SpA v Islamic Republic of Pakistan*, ICSID Case No ARB/03/3, Decision on Jurisdiction, 22 April 2005, para 208; *Jan de Nul NV and Dredging International NV v Arab Republic of Egypt*, ICSID Case No ARB/04/13, Award, 6 November 2008, para 149; *Bayindir Insaat Turizm Ticaret Ve Sanayi AS v Islamic Republic of Pakistan*, ICSID Case No ARB/03/29, Award, 27 August 2009, para 121; *United Parcel Service of America Inc (UPS) v Government of Canada*, UNCITRAL, Award on the Merits, 24 May 2007, para 9; *Gustav F W Hamester GmbH & Co KG v Republic of Ghana*, ICSID Case No ARB/07/24, Award, 18 June 2010, para 190.

[274] *Jan de Nul NV and Dredging International NV v Arab Republic of Egypt*, ICSID Case No ARB/04/13, Award, 6 November 2008, para 149; *Bayindir Insaat Turizm Ticaret Ve Sanayi AS v Islamic Republic of Pakistan*, ICSID Case No ARB/03/29, Award, 27 August 2009, para 121.

[275] *Gustav F W Hamester GmbH & Co KG v Republic of Ghana*, ICSID Case No ARB/07/24, Award, 18 June 2010, para 190.

[276] *Bayindir Insaat Turizm Ticaret Ve Sanayi AS v Islamic Republic of Pakistan*, ICSID Case No ARB/03/29, Award, 27 August 2009, para 121.

[277] *Emilio Agustín Maffezini v The Kingdom of Spain*, ICSID Case No ARB/97/7, Decision on Jurisdiction, 25 January 2000, para 86.

[278] *Gustav F W Hamester GmbH & Co KG v Republic of Ghana*, ICSID Case No ARB/07/24, Award, 18 June 2010, para 189.

[279] *Bayindir Insaat Turizm Ticaret Ve Sanayi AS v Islamic Republic of Pakistan*, ICSID Case No ARB/03/29, Award, 27 August 2009, para 121.

[280] *Toto Costruzioni Generali SpA v The Republic of Lebanon*, ICSID Case No ARB/07/12, Decision on Jurisdiction, 11 September 2009, para 102.

[281] *Gustav F W Hamester GmbH & Co KG v Republic of Ghana*, ICSID Case No ARB/07/24, Award, 18 June 2010, para 189.

[282] *Emilio Agustín Maffezini v The Kingdom of Spain*, ICSID Case No ARB/97/7, Award, 13 November 2000, para 78.

[283] *Crystallex International Corporation v Bolivarian Republic of Venezuela*, ICSID Case No ARB(AF)/11/2, Award, 4 April 2016, para 700.

[284] *Limited Liability Company Amto v Ukraine*, SCC Case No 080/2005, Final Award, 26 March 2008, para 107.

[285] *Deutsche Bank AG v Democratic Socialist Republic of Sri Lanka*, ICSID Case No ARB/09/2, Award, 31 October 2012, para 405(f).

the undertaking of business with an assumption of reasonable commercial risk,[286] the exercise of shareholders' rights,[287] advising and providing information to businesses, accounting services, and technical assistance,[288] the organization of auctions of commercial spaces,[289] and the refusal to grant an extension of time in the context of a tender process.[290] The determinations of national courts with regard to State immunity from adjudication may complete this review in light of the application of the same distinction between *acta jure imperii* and *acta jure gestionis*.[291]

From the foregoing analysis, it is possible to isolate the thresholds for the definition of acts in exercise of elements of governmental authority, as contrasted to commercial acts. Arbitrators (like national judges) apply a 'private contractor' test recognizing as 'sovereign' such activities in which a private party may not engage, or, conversely, as 'commercial' such activities that a private party may perform.[292] The profit motive of the act executed by the parastatal retains a central role in this analysis.[293] Moreover, the power or prerogative exercised by the State instrumentality in relation to a given foreign investment should not go beyond, and as such actually override, the ordinary schemes of private law.[294] As observed with regard

[286] *William Nagel v The Czech Republic*, SCC Case No 049/2002, Final Award, 9 September 2003, para 163.

[287] *EDF (Services) Limited v Romania*, ICSID Case No ARB/05/13, Award, 8 October 2009, para 194.

[288] *Emilio Agustín Maffezini v The Kingdom of Spain*, ICSID Case No ARB/97/7, Award, 13 November 2000, paras 61–62; *Emilio Agustín Maffezini v The Kingdom of Spain*, ICSID Case No ARB/97/7, Decision on Jurisdiction, 25 January 2000, para 85.

[289] *EDF (Services) Limited v Romania*, ICSID Case No ARB/05/13, Award, 8 October 2009, para 196: 'They were not acts performed in the exercise of delegated governmental authority, but rather were acts aiming at the better exploitation by AIBO of commercial spaces, which were part of its private property, and the conduct of its own duty-free business, subject only to its corporate bodies' determinations.'

[290] *Jan de Nul NV and Dredging International NV v Arab Republic of Egypt*, ICSID Case No ARB/04/13, Award, 6 November 2008, paras 169–70.

[291] *Ex multis*, Court of Appeal of The Hague, 28 November 1968, *NV Cabolent v National Iranian Oil Company (NIOC)*, 47 ILR 138; Cour d'Appel de Rouen, 13 November 1984, *Société européenne d'études et d'entreprises (SEEE) v Yugoslavia*, (1985) 112 Journal du Droit International (Clunet) 473, (1986) 90 Revue Générale de Droit International Public 707; High Court of West Pakistan, 2 November 1970, *Secretary of State of the United States of America v Gammon-Layton*, 64 ILR 587.

[292] *Jan de Nul NV and Dredging International NV v Arab Republic of Egypt*, ICSID Case No ARB/04/13, Award, 6 November 2008, para 169–70: 'In its dealing with the Claimants during the tender process, the SCA acted *like any contractor* trying to achieve the best price for the services it was seeking. It did not act as a State entity. The same applies to the SCA's conduct in the course of the performance of the Contract. … *Any private contract partner could have acted in a similar manner*.' (emphasis added); *United Parcel Service of America Inc (UPS) v Government of Canada*, UNCITRAL, Award on the Merits, 24 May 2007, para 74: 'That contrast with commercial activities emphasizes the particular character of the limiting phrase. The monopoly or enterprise is exercising a "*governmental* authority" delegated to it by the State Party. To be contrasted with the exercise of that authority is the use by a monopoly or State enterprise of those rights and powers which it *shares* (emphasis added) with other businesses competing in the relevant market and undertaking commercial activities.'; *Gustav F W Hamester GmbH & Co KG v Republic of Ghana*, ICSID Case No ARB/07/24, Award, 18 June 2010, para 202: 'In considering the application of Article 5 of the ILC Articles, the Tribunal has carefully assessed whether, in its dealings with Hamester in relation to the JVA, Cocobod *acted like any contractor/shareholder*, or rather as a State entity enforcing regulatory powers.' (emphasis added); *InterTrade Holding GmbH v The Czech Republic*, UNCITRAL, PCA Case No 2009-12, Final Award, 29 May 2012, para 183.

[293] *EDF (Services) Limited v Romania*, ICSID Case No ARB/05/13, Award, 8 October 2009, para 197.

[294] *Impregilo SpA v Islamic Republic of Pakistan*, ICSID Case No ARB/03/3, Decision on Jurisdiction, 22 April 2005, para 260, 266(b): 'In fact, the State or its emanation, may have behaved as an ordinary

to the *Maffezini v Spain* award, '*une telle irrégularité ne pouvait se réaliser sans les pouvoirs exorbitants du droit commun dont était investie l'entité paraétatique*'.[295] The connection between UNCSI Article 2.2 and ARSIWA Article 5 suggests the adoption of a comprehensive nature test in order to functionally categorize the acts of SOEs.[296] This test should be applied upon reference to a context-based analysis taking into consideration all the elements and circumstances surrounding a given act or transaction, so that the resulting threshold be thicker than the traditional 'private contractor' test under the law of sovereign immunity.[297] In addition, competitive neutrality considerations may certainly be inserted in such context-based reasoning, including the various competitive advantages benefiting parastatals under domestic law.[298]

The principle of the competitive neutrality of SOEs has been elaborated and developed under the aegis of the OECD (Organization for Economic Cooperation and Development), which adopted its 'Guidelines on Corporate Governance of State-Owned Enterprises' in 2005. Section III of these guidelines is dedicated to the activities of SOEs in the marketplace, where it is provided that: '[c]onsistent with the rationale for state ownership, the legal and regulatory framework for SOEs should ensure a level playing field and fair competition in the marketplace

contracting party having a difference of approach, in fact or in law, with the investor. In order that the alleged breach of contract may constitute a violation of the BIT, it must be the result of behaviour going beyond that which an ordinary contracting party could adopt.'; *Emilio Agustín Maffezini v The Kingdom of Spain*, ICSID Case No ARB/97/7, Award, 13 November 2000, para 62; *Siemens AG v The Argentine Republic*, ICSID Case No ARB/02/8, Award, 19 January 2007, para 248; *Consortium RFCC v Kingdom of Morocco*, ICSID Case No ARB/00/6, Award, 22 December 2003, para 65.

[295] Yves Nouvel, 'Les entités paraétatiques dans la jurisprudence du CIRDI' in Charles Leben (ed), *Le contentieux arbitral transnational relatif à l'investissement. Nouveaux développements* (LGDJ 2006) 25, 38.

[296] *Gustav F W Hamester GmbH & Co KG v Republic of Ghana*, ICSID Case No ARB/07/24, Award, 18 June 2010, para 197.

[297] UNCSI Article 10. See Lord Wilberforce in *I Congreso del Partido* [1983] 1 AC 244, 278: 'The conclusion which emerges is that in considering, under the "restrictive" theory whether state immunity should be granted or not, the court must consider the whole context in which the claim against the state is made, with a view to deciding whether the relevant act(s) upon which the claim is based, should, in that context, be considered as fairly within an area of activity, trading or commercial, or otherwise of a private law character, in which the state has chosen to engage, or whether the relevant act(s) should be considered as having been done outside that area, and within the sphere of governmental or sovereign activity.'

[298] See Chapter II, section 4.2. cf Antonio Capobianco and Hans Christiansen, *Competitive Neutrality and State-Owned Enterprises: Challenges and Policy Options*, OECD Corporate Governance Working Papers, No 1 (OECD Publishing 2011) 5–7; Sébastien Miroudot and Alexandros Ragoussis, 'Actors in the International Investment Scenario: Objectives, Performance and Advantages of Affiliates of State-Owned Enterprises and Sovereign Wealth Funds' in Roberto Echandi and Pierre Sauvé (eds), *Prospects in International Investment Law and Policy: World Trade Forum* (Cambridge University Press 2013) 51, 61; Anne van Aaken, 'Blurring Boundaries between Sovereign Acts and Commercial Activities: A Functional View on Regulatory Immunity and Immunity from Execution' in Anne Peters, Evelyne Lagrange, Stefan Oeter, and Christian Tomuschat (eds), *Immunities in the Age of Global Constitutionalism* (Brill 2015) 131, 173.

when SOEs undertake economic activities.'[299] This is the conceptual basis of the principle of competitive neutrality of SOEs, which posits that the public ownership of a given economic undertaking should not affect its competitiveness on the market arena. SOEs, unlike their privately owned competitors, benefit from various competitive advantages under the domestic law of the country where they are established based purely on total or partial public ownership: outright subsidization from the government; concessionary financing and guarantees from the government or State-controlled financial institutions; exemption from compliance with disclosure requirements, antitrust enforcement, or building permit, zoning, or public procurement regulations; monopolies and advantages of incumbency; captive equity; exemption from bankruptcy rules; preferential tax treatment; and, information advantages (asymmetries).[300] Consequently, the principle of competitive neutrality compels States and international organizations to enact policies and legal frameworks that aim to prevent market distortions in the economic sectors where SOEs and privately owned undertakings compete. An express reference in IIAs to the principle of competitive neutrality of SOEs may represent an indication of the intention of States to pursue such policies.

In *Maffezini v Spain*, the tribunal had to determine whether the act of handling the bank accounts of a PPP (EAMSA) without the holder's authorization by the public shareholder, which was a SOE of the regional level of government of Galicia (SODIGA), could be attributed to the Kingdom of Spain. The arbitrators held that:

> Handling the accounts of EAMSA as a participating company, managing its payments and finances and generally intervening on its behalf before the Spanish authorities without being paid for these services, are all elements that responded to SODIGA's public nature and responsibility. Moreover, the manner in which the private banks conducted themselves in this case with regard to the loan, can be explained in large measure only because of their recognition that SODIGA's orders and instructions were entitled to be honored because of the public functions it performed in Galicia.[301]

299 *OECD Guidelines on Corporate Governance of State-Owned Enterprises. 2015 edition* (OECD Publishing 2015), Section III.

300 Antonio Capobianco and Hans Christiansen, *Competitive Neutrality and State-Owned Enterprises: Challenges and Policy Options*, OECD Corporate Governance Working Papers, No 1 (OECD Publishing 2011). See also Ming Du, 'China's State Capitalism and World Trade Law' (2014) 63 International & Comparative Law Quarterly 409, 422, who proposes the following classification of SOEs' competitive advantages: (i) financial (including tax reductions and exemptions, direct subsidization, low-cost capital from state-controlled banks), (ii) regulatory (including exemptions from antitrust enforcement and bankruptcy rules, preferential access to raw materials, favourable dividend policies, and preference in government procurement); and, (iii) other forms of advantages.

301 *Emilio Agustín Maffezini v The Kingdom of Spain*, ICSID Case No ARB/97/7, Award, 13 November 2000, para 78.

More recently, in *Crystallex v Venezuela*, the tribunal decided that the unilateral rescission of a mining administrative concession by the Corporación Venezolana de Guyana (CVG) based on its power of *autotutela* represented an 'exercise of sovereign authority', even though the agreement was terminated for alleged contractual reasons. Interestingly, the tribunal added that: 'the evidence on the record clearly shows that the MOC was terminated [by CVG] to give effect to the superior policy decisions dictated by the higher governmental spheres.'[302]

These decisions seem to suggest that in order to qualify an act of a parastatal entity as attributable to the State it is not necessary to demonstrate that it was exercised strictly out of governmental authority (*imperium*), but it may also be taken into consideration that said act was 'growing out' of the public functions of the State instrumentality.[303] Thus, by virtue of a qualified redolence of governmental authority (*allure étatique*), an activity may be attributed to the State, in light of the casuistic finding that a SOE could not have performed it on a rational basis, like any other private competitor in the market arena, without availing itself of its status.[304] Accordingly, the acts of SOEs that lie outside the ordinary schemes of private law and, as such, are executed or may be executed only because of State ownership (and backing) may be held to be attributable. Therefore, the application of the principle of competitive neutrality may strengthen the scope of attribution of conduct under ARSIWA Article 5. This result may be normatively advocated in furtherance of the general policy to level the playing field in domestic markets receiving FDI and is

[302] *Crystallex International Corporation v Bolivarian Republic of Venezuela*, ICSID Case No ARB(AF)/11/2, Award, 4 April 2016, para 701. See also *Vigotop Limited v Hungary*, ICSID Case No ARB/11/22, Award, 1 October 2014, paras 328 and: 'the Tribunal will first examine whether, as alleged by Claimant, Respondent had "a hidden political agenda," which was the true reason for its termination of the Concession Contract, meaning that Respondent in fact took this decision in order to give effect to a change in government policy, and thus in its sovereign capacity'; *Luigiterzo Bosca v Lithuania*, UNCITRAL, Award, 17 May 2013, para 128: 'Regardless of whether the Tribunal considers the SPF to have acted in a sovereign capacity, the SPF's actions were vetted and in this case approved by higher authorities that clearly acted in sovereign capacities. The Privatization Regulations make clear that the Privatization Commission and, in the case of its refusal, the Government itself could be called upon by the SPF to make a final decision on a proposed SPA; the stamp of sovereign involvement could not be clearer. The Tribunal considers that this administrative evaluation further reflects the governmental endorsement of the process. Here, the Government acted at multiple steps, projecting its sovereign authority'; *Ampal-American Israel Corporation et al v Arab Republic of Egypt*, ICSID Case No ARB/12/11, Decision on Liability and Heads of Loss, 21 February 2017, para 146: 'The Tribunal finds that there is overwhelming evidence that the decisions of EGPC and EGAS to conclude and terminate the GSPA were all taken with the blessing of the highest levels of the Egyptian Government' (concerning attribution under ARSIWA Article 8).

[303] *Emilio Agustín Maffezini v The Kingdom of Spain*, ICSID Case No ARB/97/7, Award, 13 November 2000, para 49, 79: 'It was not until the adoption of Law 6/ 1997 of April 14, 1997 that state commercial corporations were clearly forbidden to "perform functions that imply the exercise of public authority."' This explains that SODIGA was even prohibited by law to exercise governmental activities.

[304] Georgios Petrochilos, 'Attribution' in Katia Yannaca-Small (ed), *Arbitration under International Investment Agreements: A Guide to the Key Issues* (Oxford University Press 2010) 287, 322: 'It is irrelevant whether the act so taken is generically of a kind that in some circumstances a private person could take: the question is, rather, whether the act was in fact taken on a legal basis available specifically to the entity concerned, as a complement of its governmental functions.'

consistent with the initiative of host States to attract foreign investors by creating specialized State instrumentalities. As a caveat, international tribunals should not overturn the requirement that attribution be based on specific conduct executed by SOEs 'in the particular instance' at issue, as required by ARSIWA Article 5.

4.3 Empowerment by Law

Parastatal entities are generally empowered by statutory law to exercise 'elements of governmental authority' such as regulatory, coercive, and fiscal powers.[305] As mentioned in the previous chapter, a contractual arrangement may be sufficient to meet the formal requirement of ARSIWA Article 5, including the charter or the articles of association of a State enterprise.[306] The delegation of governmental authority by the State should be express, as such providing for a specific enumeration of powers. An illustrative example is represented by the Pakistani National Highway Authority Act of 1991, analysed by the *Bayindir v Pakistan* tribunal:

> It is not disputed that NHA is generally empowered to exercise elements of governmental authority. Section 10 of the NHA Act vests broad authority in NHA to take 'such measures and exercise such powers it considers necessary or expedient for carrying out the purposes of this Act,' including to 'levy, collect or cause to be collected tolls on National Highways, strategic roads and such other roads as may be entrusted to it and bridges thereon.' Other relevant provisions of the NHA Act are section 12 on 'Powers to eject unauthorized occupants' and section 29 on the NHA's 'Power to enter' upon lands and premises to make inspections.[307]

In the case of *Helnan v Egypt*, the tribunal decided that '[e]ven if EGOTH has not been officially empowered by law to exercise elements of the governmental authority, its actions within the privatisation process are attributable to the Egyptian State.'[308] Rather than finding attribution under ARSIWA Article 5, the *Helnan v*

[305] *Jan de Nul NV and Dredging International NV v Arab Republic of Egypt*, ICSID Case No ARB/04/13, Award, 6 November 2008, para 166 (Egyptian Law No 30/1975); *United Parcel Service of America Inc (UPS) v Government of Canada*, UNCITRAL, Award on the Merits, 24 May 2007, para 9 (Canada Post Corporation Act 1981); *Impregilo SpA v Islamic Republic of Pakistan*, ICSID Case No ARB/03/3, Decision on Jurisdiction, 22 April 2005, para 208 (Pakistan Water and Power Development Authority Act of 1958); *Gustav F W Hamester GmbH & Co KG v Republic of Ghana*, ICSID Case No ARB/07/24, Award, 18 June 2010, para 190 (Ghana Cocoa Board Law of 3 May 1984, amended in 1991); *Bayindir Insaat Turizm Ticaret Ve Sanayi AS v Islamic Republic of Pakistan*, ICSID Case No ARB/03/29, Award, 27 August 2009, para 121 (Pakistani National Highway Authority Act of 1991).

[306] See Chapter II, section 4.4.

[307] *Bayindir Insaat Turizm Ticaret Ve Sanayi AS v Islamic Republic of Pakistan*, ICSID Case No ARB/03/29, Award, 27 August 2009, para 121.

[308] *Helnan International Hotels A/S v Arab Republic of Egypt*, ICSID Case No ARB/05/19, Decision on Jurisdiction, 17 October 2006, para 93.

Egypt tribunal seems to have resorted to the attribution of conduct of 'private' individuals based on instructions, or direction or control, pursuant to ARSIWA Article 8.

4.4 Collusive Interference of State Organs in the Commercial Operations of State-Owned Enterprises

The previous chapter has already addressed the issue of the collusive interference of the State, through its organs, in the business of its parastatal entities, as illustrated by the Iran–US Claims Tribunal in *Int'l Technical Products v Iran*.[309] This problem has been resolved in a similar fashion in ISDS cases:

> if organs of Government choose to intervene in the operations of its para-statal entities (or if the State, for whatever reason, interferes in what would otherwise be purely commercial operations), an international tribunal ought to be ready to infer that by doing so they have engaged the international responsibility of the State for effects that, in substance, amounts to breaches of the standards expressly accepted by the State by treaty. The Tribunal considers that this conclusion is moreover in harmony with a series of arbitral decisions establishing that interference by the State with the operation of a private contract is capable of constituting a breach of treaty.[310]

As mentioned above, such conduct is subject to attribution pursuant to ARSIWA Article 4 only, without resorting to ARSIWA Article 5. State practice may enforce in a more predictable way the responsibility of the State for such kinds of actions by establishing the primary obligations of the State to ensure or surveil on the observance of investment treaties by its State instrumentalities, including in connection with their contractual undertakings, as provided by NAFTA Articles 1502(3) and 1503(2), and by ECT Article 22. Where State officials interfere in the conduct of business by State enterprises, the arbitral award rendered against the State may even be enforced against the assets of the SOE, in light of its collusive involvement in the dispute (*reverse attribution*, or *reverse piercing*, or *umgekehrter Durchriff*).[311]

[309] *International Technical Products Corporation and ITP Export Corporation, its wholly-owned subsidiary, v The Government of the Islamic Republic of Iran and its agencies, The Islamic Republic Iranian Air Force and the Ministry of National Defense, acting for the Civil Aviation Organization*, Case No 302, 24 October 1985, Award No 196-302-3, 9 IRAN-US CTR 206, 239 (1985-II). See Chapter II, section 4.2.

[310] *F-W Oil Interests, Inc v The Republic of Trinidad and Tobago*, ICSID Case No ARB/01/14, Award, 3 March 2006, para 206.

[311] This issue has been phrased as follows: 'Can a party benefiting from an award rendered against a State enforce the award against an instrumentality of such State?'. See Emmanuel Gaillard and Jennifer Younan (eds), *State Entities in International Arbitration* (Juris Publishing, Inc 2008) 97–178, with contributions from Charles Poncet, Eric Teynier, Judith Gill, Eugene Gulland, and Sigvard Jarvin.

To this extent, a sufficient link or relationship pertaining to the dispute should be established between the State and a given SOE for the purposes of execution proceedings, since the latter does not usually stands as formal party in the arbitral process.[312]

5. Individuals

5.1 General Rule of Non-Attribution of Conduct of 'Private' Individuals

In line with the liberal political philosophy of the international law of State responsibility,[313] investor–State tribunals have applied the general rule of the State not being responsible for the acts and omissions of private individuals, unless those individuals are instructed, or directed or controlled, by organs of the State itself.[314] Thus, in *AAPL v Sri Lanka*, the tribunal deliberated:

> It is a generally accepted rule of International Law, clearly stated in international arbitral awards and in the writings of the doctrinal authorities, that ... [a] State on whose territory an insurrection occurs is not responsible for loss or damage sustained by foreign investors unless it can be shown that the Government of that state failed to provide the standard of protection required, either by treaty, or under general customary law, as the case may be.[315]

The traditional rule clearly denies attributability to the State of the conduct of private individuals, while recognizing attribution to the State of the acts and omissions

[312] This principle is also established in UNCSI Article 19(c): 'post-judgment measures of constraint may only be taken against the property that has a connection with the entity against which the proceeding was directed'. See Draft Articles on Jurisdictional Immunities of States and Their Property, with commentaries, in Report of the International Law Commission on the Work of its Forty-Third Session, 29 April–19 July 1991, document A/46/10, Yearbook of the International Law Commission, 1991, Volume II (Part Two), 13, 57, para 7, document A/CN.4/SER.A/1991/Add.1 (Part 2). This test has been famously established by Cour de Cassation, 14 March 1984, *République Islamique d'Iran et al v Société Eurodif et al*, (1984) 111 Journal du Droit International (Clunet) 598, (1984) 73 Revue Critique de Droit International Privé 644. See Hervé Synvet, 'Quelques réflexions sur l'immunité d'exécution de l'Etat étranger' (1985) 112 Journal du Droit International (Clunet) 865–87.

[313] See Chapter II, section 5.1.

[314] *Asian Agricultural Products Ltd (AAPL) v Republic of Sri Lanka*, ICSID Case No ARB/87/3, Final Award, 27 June 1990, para 72; *Tradex Hellas SA v Republic of Albania*, ICSID Case No ARB/94/2, Award, 29 April 1999, para 165; *Bayindir Insaat Turizm Ticaret Ve Sanayi AS v Islamic Republic of Pakistan*, ICSID Case No ARB/03/29, Award, 27 August 2009, para 124.

[315] *Asian Agricultural Products Ltd (AAPL) v Republic of Sri Lanka*, ICSID Case No ARB/87/3, Final Award, 27 June 1990, para 72(i) et seq, quoting *Affaire des biens britanniques au Maroc espagnol (Espagne contre Royaume-Uni) (Spanish Zone of Morocco)*, 1 May 1925, 2 RIAA 615; *Sambiaggio Case (of a general nature)*, 1903, 10 RIAA 499; *Kummerow, Otto Redler and Co, Fulda, Fischbach, and Friedericy Cases*, 1903, 10 RIAA 369; *The Home Insurance Co (USA) v United Mexican States*, 31 March 1926, 4 RIAA 48.

of State organs (or, in principle, also State entities) in relation to the substantive standards of protection owed to foreign investors. As confirmed by an ICSID tribunal in *von Pezold v Zimbabwe*:

> indirect liability for the acts of others can also occur under Article 4—for example, the failure to stop someone doing something that violated an obligation. It does not matter that a third party actually undertook the action, if a State organ (such as the police) was aware of it and did nothing to prevent it. The Tribunal finds, on the evidence before it, that this is the case here, as regards police inaction in the face of Settlers/War Veterans coming on to the Zimbabwean Properties. (…) With respect to attributing acts of non-State organs to the Respondent, the acts of the Settlers/War Veterans do not appear to fall within the scope of Article 8 of the ILC Articles. While there is ample evidence of Government involvement and encouragement, the Tribunal is not persuaded that the acts of the invaders were based on a direct order or under the direct control of the Government when they initially invaded the Claimants' properties. Rather, the Government appears to have encouraged (and endorsed) the action once it had begun. Encouragement would not meet the test set out in Article 8. However, the Tribunal agrees with the Claimants that the State action of encouragement and facilitation, etc. should be considered separately when it comes to treaty violations (this includes the inaction of the police). The actions of the invaders themselves need not be considered.[316]

Finally, the old theory of implied State complicity is not applied, not even considered, by arbitrators, who usually dismiss it in so far as sporadic allegations of 'conspiracy' are raised by investors.[317] Even a general declaration of the political powers calling for or encouraging particular actions by civilians does not result in the attribution of such actions to the State. This issue has been analysed by the *Tradex v Albania* tribunal, which accordingly observed:

> Subsidiarily, even if the villagers felt encouraged to such occupations by Decision 452 and the Berisha speech, that would not be a sufficient basis to attribute such occupations to the State of Albania, and no other evidence has been provided as a basis for such an attributability.[318]

[316] *Bernhard von Pezold et al v Republic of Zimbabwe*, ICSID Case No ARB/10/15, Award, 28 July 2015, paras 445–48.

[317] *Waste Management, Inc v United Mexican States (Waste Management II)*, ICSID Case No ARB(AF)/00/3, Award, 30 April 2004, paras 137–38: 'a deliberate conspiracy—that is to say, a conscious combination of various agencies of government without justification to defeat the purposes of an investment agreement–'; *Saipem SpA v People's Republic of Bangladesh*, ICSID Case No ARB/05/07, Award, 30 June 2009, para 148: 'the Tribunal is not satisfied that the Bangladeshi courts acted in collusion or conspired with Petrobangla.'; *Bayindir Insaat Turizm Ticaret Ve Sanayi AS v Islamic Republic of Pakistan*, ICSID Case No ARB/03/29, Award, 27 August 2009, para 258.

[318] *Tradex Hellas SA v Republic of Albania*, ICSID Case No ARB/94/2, Award, 29 April 1999, para 165.

5.2 Fair and Equitable Treatment, Full Protection and Security, and Compensation for Loss

Under international investment law, the primary obligation of due diligence incumbent on the State and its organs under customary international law is usually complemented and strengthened through the codification in IIAs of higher standards of protection, such as fair and equitable treatment or full protection and security.[319] The two standards are distinguishable:

> The FET standard consists mainly of an obligation on the host State's part to desist from behaviour that is unfair and inequitable. By contrast, by assuming the obligation of full protection and security the host State promises to provide a factual and legal framework that grants security and to take the measures necessary to protect the investment against adverse action by private persons as well as State organs.[320]

Both standards posit a model of responsibility based on negligence (fault theory), but States may nevertheless provide for rules of strict or objective liability for damage incurred by foreign investors, traditionally in times of social, political, and civil unrest (international conflicts, revolutionary upheavals, civil wars),

[319] *Jan de Nul NV and Dredging International NV v Arab Republic of Egypt*, ICSID Case No ARB/04/13, Award, 6 November 2008, para 262 et seq, 269: 'The notion of continuous protection and security is to be distinguished here from the fair and equitable standard since they are placed in two different provisions of the BIT, even if the two guarantees can overlap. As put forward by the Claimants, this concept relates to the exercise of due diligence by the State.'; *Parkerings-Compagniet AS v Republic of Lithuania*, ICSID Case No ARB/05/8, Award, 11 September 2007, para 354 et seq; *Eureko BV v Republic of Poland*, Ad Hoc Arbitration, Partial Award, 19 August 2005, para 237: 'However, in any event, there is no clear evidence before the Tribunal that the RoP was the author or instigator of the actions in question. If such actions were to be repeated and sustained, it may be that the responsibility of the Government of Poland would be incurred by a failure to prevent them.'; *Nykomb Synergetics Technology Holding AB v The Republic of Latvia*, SCC, Arbitral Award, 16 December 2003, paras 4.2–4.3; *American Manufacturing & Trading, Inc (AMT) v Republic of Zaire*, ICSID Case No ARB/93/1, Award, 21 February 1997, paras 6.05–6.11; *Noble Ventures, Inc v Romania*, ICSID Case No ARB/01/11, Award, 12 October 2005, para 166; *Toto Costruzioni Generali SpA v The Republic of Lebanon*, ICSID Case No ARB/07/12, Award, 7 June 2012, paras 226–30; *Tradex Hellas SA v Republic of Albania*, ICSID Case No ARB/94/2, Award, 29 April 1999, para 146: 'Tradex has also not shown that it contacted the authorities after these alleged invasions so that a failure to act by the authorities could be considered under the aspect of attributability to the State.'; *Asian Agricultural Products Ltd (AAPL) v Republic of Sri Lanka*, ICSID Case No ARB/87/3, Final Award, 27 June 1990, para 49: 'Consequently, both the oldest reported arbitral precedent and the latest I.C.J. ruling confirms that the language imposing on the host State an obligation to provide "protection and security" or "full protection and security required by international law" (the other expression included in the same Article V) could not be construed according to the natural and ordinary sense of the words as creating a "strict liability".'

[320] Christoph H Schreuer, 'Full Protection and Security' (2010) Journal of International Dispute Settlement 1, 14.

irrespective of their involvement by way of act or omission in the relevant events.[321] As decided in *American Manufacturing & Trading v Zaire*:

> Such is the case without the Tribunal enquiring as to the identity of the author of the acts of violence committed on the Zairian territory. It is of little or no consequence whether it be a member of the Zairian armed forces or any burglar whatsoever.[322]

The stipulation of such clauses—which apply irrespective not only of State fault, but also of State conduct—is very limited in investment treaties and practice.[323] Moreover, as mentioned above,[324] such provisions do not establish rules of attribution proper, but operate at the level of the creation of primary obligations establishing for the benefit of foreign investors a more favourable treatment than that established by the customary standard of due diligence. In this scenario, States are in a practical way prompted to prevent the occurrence of damage or loss to aliens, which would otherwise have been outside the ordinary coverage of State responsibility for internationally wrongful acts:[325]

> Even if not (i.e., even if the applicable secondary rules of State responsibility remain unaffected), the fact that the treaty is a BIT opens up a further possibility at the level of primary obligation, specifically that the broad scope mutually agreed by the Contracting Parties for encouraging as well as protecting the investments of one in the territory of the other may have the effect of requiring (sc. as a matter

[321] US–Zaire BIT (1984), Article IV(1) (*Compensation for Damages Due to War and Similar Events*): 'Nationals or companies of either Party whose investments in the territory of the other Party suffer: (a) damages due to war or other armed conflict between such other Party and a third country, or (b) damages due to revolution, state of national emergency, revolt, insurrection, riot or act of violence in the territory of such other Party, shall be accorded treatment no less favorable than that which such other Party accords to its own nationals or companies or to nationals or companies of any third country, whichever is the most favorable treatment, when making restitution, indemnification, compensation or any other settlement with respect to such damages.'. See also *Cornelia J Pringle, et al, (Santa Isabel Claims) (USA) v United Mexican States*, 26 April 1926, 4 RIAA 783, 785, with regard to Article III(b) of the Convention of September 10, 1923, providing for the settlement and amicable adjustment of claims arising from losses or damages suffered by American citizens through revolutionary acts within the period from 20 November 1910 to 31 May 1920; *Kummerow, Otto Redler and Co, Fulda, Fischbach, and Friedericy Cases*, 1903, 10 RIAA 369, 370, with regard to Article III of the Germany–Venezuela protocol of 13 February 1903.

[322] *American Manufacturing & Trading, Inc (AMT) v Republic of Zaire*, ICSID Case No ARB/93/1, Award, 21 February 1997, para 6.13.

[323] Yves Nouvel, 'Les entités paraétatiques dans la jurisprudence du CIRDI' in Charles Leben (ed), *Le contentieux arbitral transnational relatif à l'investissement. Nouveaux développements* (LGDJ 2006) 25, 41: '*Il est vrai que la responsabilité du plein droit ainsi mise en place tend à constituer un véritable mécanisme de garantie. Or, tel n'est pas l'objet des conventions bilatérales d'investissement. C'est pourquoi ces stipulations forment une pratique conventionnelle extrêmement marginale.*'

[324] See section 1.2 of this chapter.

[325] Luca Schicho, 'Attribution and State Entities: Diverging Approaches in Investment Arbitration' (2011) 12 Journal of World Investment & Trade 283, 293.

of treaty obligation) the Government to adopt patterns of conduct in respect of its State organs and para-statal entities different from those that would ordinarily be required under general international law or treaty law.[326]

5.3 State-Owned Enterprises

As already mentioned, the conduct *jure gestionis* of a SOE, for instance a State enterprise, may fall under the scope of attribution of ARSIWA Article 8.[327] This possibility is contemplated in so far as the requirements dictated by ARSIWA Article 5 are not met, which occurs in the absence of a formal delegation of powers or where the exercise of elements of governmental authority is lacking in the actual case at issue. Accordingly, symptomatic elements displaying the status of a para-statal entity (pursuant to the structural test applied under ARSIWA Article 5) may nonetheless function as the basis for attribution pursuant to ARSIWA Article 8, in so far as they embody evidence of instructions, or direction or control, by State organs.[328] This conclusion may be reached upon the finding of palpable governmental oversight, previous approval of resolutions and operations, and mandates from the State to the SOE, and upon consideration of corporate governance provisions envisaging the governmental appointment of its managers, consistently with the case law of the Iran–US Claims Tribunal.[329] The *F-W Oil Interests v Trinidad and Tobago* tribunal adopted the following logical sequence in its analysis of attribution relating to the activities of SOEs:

> Moreover—and the point is of some importance—it is not the case that the same answer would necessarily emerge on every occasion; in some of its activities a State

[326] *F-W Oil Interests, Inc v The Republic of Trinidad and Tobago*, ICSID Case No ARB/01/14, Award, 3 March 2006, para 206.

[327] See Chapter II, section 5.3.2.

[328] See section 4.2.1 of this chapter.

[329] *RayGo Warner Equipment Company v Star Line Iran Company*, Case No 17, 15 December 1982, 1 IRAN-US CTR 411, 413 (1982); *Kimberley-Clark Corporation v Bank Markazi Iran, Novzohour Paper Industries, Government of the Islamic Republic of Iran*, Case No 57, Award No 46-57-2, 25 May 1983, 2 IRAN-US CTR 334, 338 (1983-I); *Cal-Maine Foods, Inc v The Government of the Islamic Republic of Iran and Sherkat Seamourgh Company, Inc*, Case No 340, 31 May 1984, Award No 133-340-3, 6 IRAN-US CTR 52, 58-59 (1984-II); *Rexnord, Inc v The Islamic Republic of Iran, Tchacosh Company and Iran Siporex Industrial and Manufacturing Works, Limited*, Case No 132, 10 January 1983, Award No 21-132-3, 2 IRAN-US CTR 6 (1983-I); *Sedco, Inc v National Iranian Oil Company and The Islamic Republic of Iran*, Case No 129, 24 October 1985, Award No ITL 55-29-3, 9 IRAN-US CTR 248, 277 (1985-III); *SeaCo, Inc v The Islamic Republic of Iran, The Iranian Meat Organization, Iran Express Lines, and Star Line Co*, 11 IRAN-US CTR 210, 215 (1986-II); *McLaughlin Enterprises, Ltd v The Government of the Islamic Republic of Iran, Information System Iran*, Case No 289, 16 September 1986, Award No 253-289-1, 12 IRAN-US CTR 146, 149 (1986-III); *Emanuel Too v Greater Modesto Insurance Associates and The United States of America*, Case No 880, 29 December 1989, Award No 460-880-2, 23 IRAN-US CTR 378, 384 (1989-III); *Kaysons International Corporation v The Government of the Islamic Republic of Iran, The Ministry of Industries and Mines, The Alborz Investment Corporation, The Tolid Daru Company, The Payegozar, The Pakhs Alborz Company, and The KBC Company*, Case No 367, 28 June 1993, Award No

> enterprise might fall on one side of the line, in others on the other. Considerations of a very similar kind would apply to the case lying on the outer edge of the spectrum of possibilities described above, that in which the State enterprise was not exercising 'governmental authority' as such, but has to be regarded as acting in fact on State instructions, or under State direction, or under State control.[330]

In general terms, this further elucidates the absence of any requirement for official or governmental authority, for the purposes of attribution pursuant to ARSIWA Article 8. Instead, a factual link of instructions, or direction or control, between State organs and non-state actors shall be established.[331]

5.4 Test for Attribution

Investment tribunals confirm that attribution under ARSIWA Article 8 is to be regarded as an exceptional mechanism, which requires a high threshold based on the two alternative prongs of instructions or authorization, on the one hand, and direction or control, on the other.[332] Tribunals have also upheld that control by a State organ on the activities of private individuals is required to be effective, as is

548-367-2, 29 IRAN-US CTR 222, 229 (1993); *Schering Corporation v The Islamic Republic of Iran*, Case No 38, 13 April 1984, Award No 122-38-3, 5 IRAN-US CTR 361, 370 (1984-I).

[330] *F-W Oil Interests, Inc v The Republic of Trinidad and Tobago*, ICSID Case No ARB/01/14, Award, 3 March 2006, para 203.

[331] *Bayindir Insaat Turizm Ticaret Ve Sanayi AS v Islamic Republic of Pakistan*, ICSID Case No ARB/03/29, Award, 27 August 2009, para 129: 'The Tribunal also notes that attribution under Article 8 is without prejudice to the characterization of the conduct under consideration as either sovereign or commercial in nature. For the sake of attribution under this rule, it does not matter that the acts are commercial, jure gestionis, or contractual. . . . In other words, a finding of attribution does not necessarily entail that the acts under review qualify as sovereign acts'; *Noble Ventures, Inc v Romania*, ICSID Case No ARB/01/11, Award, 12 October 2005, para 82: 'in principle, a certain factual link between the State and the actor is required in order to attribute to the State acts of that actor.'; *Limited Liability Company Amto v Ukraine*, SCC Case No 080/2005, Final Award, 26 March 2008, para 31: 'It follows from Article 8 of the ILC Articles that any act, which is in fact carried out on the instructions of, or under the direction or control of the State, is attributable to it'.

[332] *White Industries Australia Limited v The Republic of India*, UNCITRAL, Final Award, 30 November 2011, para 8.1.4, 8.1.10: 'As foreshadowed by the wording of Article 8, the test under public international law for whether a state "controls" or "directs" the acts and omissions of a person or group of persons involves a high threshold.'; *EDF (Services) Limited v Romania*, ICSID Case No ARB/05/13, Award, 8 October 2009, para 200; *Tradex Hellas SA v Republic of Albania*, ICSID Case No ARB/94/2, Award, 29 April 1999, paras 169–70; *EnCana Corporation v Republic of Ecuador*, LCIA Case No UN3481, UNCITRAL, Award, 3 February 2006, para 154; *Waste Management, Inc v United Mexican States (Waste Management II)*, ICSID Case No ARB(AF)/00/3, Award, 30 April 2004, para 75; *Plama Consortium Limited v Republic of Bulgaria*, ICSID Case No ARB/03/24, Award, 27 August 2008, para 297; *Limited Liability Company Amto v Ukraine*, SCC Case No 080/2005, Final Award, 26 March 2008, para 102; *Fireman's Fund Insurance Company v The United Mexican States*, ICSID Case No ARB(AF)/02/1, Award, 17 July 2006, paras 148–55; *Saint-Gobain Performance Plastics Europe v Bolivarian Republic of Venezuela*, ICSID Case No ARB/12/13, Decision on Liability and the Principles of Quantum, 30 December 2016, para 450.

consistent with customary international law.[333] With regard to the attribution of the conduct of SOEs, notably private or privatized State enterprises organized in corporate form, the analysis of the arbitrators has been influenced by municipal law tenets of corporate law pertaining to the doctrine of 'piercing of the corporate veil'. This is also generally spelled out in the ARSIWA Commentaries, which make explicit reference to the ICJ judgment in *Barcelona Traction* by stating that 'international law acknowledges the general separateness of corporate entities at the national level, except in those cases where the "corporate veil" is a mere device or a vehicle for fraud or evasion'.[334]

In *EDF v Romania*, the tribunal found that the Ministry of Transportation of Romania had issued instructions and directions to C.N. Bucarest Aeroport Otopeni (AIBO) and Compania de Transportationuri Aeriene Romane Tarom S.A. (TAROM), Romania's national airline company, in relation to their conduct in the exercise of their rights as shareholders of a PPP with the foreign investor and with regard to other activities *jure gestionis*, such as the organization of auctions of commercial spaces at Bucharest's airport. The attribution of conduct to Romania pursuant to ARSIWA Article 8 was established upon the finding of an articulated system of mandates through which the government had issued compelling directives to the two SOEs. This was manifestly demonstrated by the adoption by AIBO's general assembly of the shareholders of a resolution conforming verbatim to said instructions.[335] In addition, the tribunal held that:

> the evidence before the Tribunal indicates that the Romanian State was using its ownership interest in or control of corporations (AIBO and TAROM) specifically 'in order to achieve a particular result' within the meaning of the ILC Commentary above. The particular result in this case was bringing to an end, or not extending, the contractual arrangements with EDF and ASRO and instituting a system of auctions.[336]

The application of the 'particular result' theory is plainly consistent with the position found in the ARSIWA Commentaries, which state that: 'where there was evidence ... that the State was using its ownership interest in or control of

[333] *Ex multis, Jan de Nul NV and Dredging International NV v Arab Republic of Egypt*, ICSID Case No ARB/04/13, Award, 6 November 2008, para 173; *White Industries Australia Limited v The Republic of India*, UNCITRAL, Final Award, 30 November 2011, paras 8.1.10-8.1.18; *Gustav F W Hamester GmbH & Co KG v Republic of Ghana*, ICSID Case No ARB/07/24, Award, 18 June 2010, para 179.

[334] ARSIWA Commentaries 48, para 6, quoting *Barcelona Traction Light and Power Company, Limited (Belgium v Spain)*, Second Phase, Judgment, 5 February 1970, paras 56-58, ICJ Reports 1970, 3, 38-39.

[335] *EDF (Services) Limited v Romania*, ICSID Case No ARB/05/13, Award, 8 October 2009, paras 204–08.

[336] *EDF (Services) Limited v Romania*, ICSID Case No ARB/05/13, Award, 8 October 2009, paras 201. Accord, *Tulip Real Estate and Development Netherlands BV v Republic of Turkey*, ICSID Case No ARB/11/28, Award, 10 March 2014, para 306.

a corporation specifically in order to achieve a particular result, the conduct in question has to be attributed to the State.'[337] However, the *EDF v Romania* tribunal seems to equate the 'particular result' test to the demonstration that a State mandated its SOEs to undertake specific actions, against the subjective interest of the latter.[338] According to the arbitrators, the management of AIBO and TAROM perceived that the extension of the contract with the foreign investor for a second term of ten years and the additional acquisition of shares in the PPP corresponded to the business interest of the two SOEs. However, following the change of government in 2000, the new Minister of Transportation of Romania did not approve the SOEs' previous decisions, as required under domestic law, thus preventing the aforesaid business operations from coming into effect.[339]

In *Tulip v Turkey*, the tribunal had to determine whether the Housing Development Organization (TOKI), a State organ of the Republic of Turkey, exercised effective control over Emlak, a real estate investment trust that was owned and controlled by TOKI itself, in relation to the SOE's administration and termination of the construction contract stipulated with the foreign investor. Pursuant to Emlak's articles of association, TOKI held 'dominancy in management' in Emlak, which meant that the State could exercise 'sovereign control' over the SOE in order to implement 'elements of a particular state purpose'.[340] This notwithstanding, the majority of the tribunal did not conclude in favour of the attribution of conduct pursuant to ARSIWA Article 8, since it established that Emlak terminated the contract independently in the pursuit of its best commercial interest:

> An analysis of the content and nature of key decisions taken by Emlak's Board with respect to the Contract, including minutes and agenda papers, does not lead to the conclusion that Emlak acted under the governmental control, direction or instructions of TOKI with a view to achieving a certain State purpose. Rather, the evidence confirms that Emlak acted in each relevant instance to pursue what it perceived to be its best commercial interest within the framework of the Contract.[341]

[337] ARSIWA Commentaries 48, para 6, quoting *Foremost Tehran, Inc v Iran*, Cases Nos 37 and 231, 10 April 1986, Award No 220-37/231-1, 10 IRAN-US CTR 228 (1986-I); *American Bell International, Inc v The Islamic Republic of Iran, The Ministry of Defense of the Islamic Republic of Iran, The Ministry of Post, Telegraph and Telephone of the Islamic Republic of Iran, and The Telecommunications Company of Iran*, Case No 48, 19 September 1986, Award No 255-48-3, 12 IRAN-US CTR 170 (1986-III).

[338] *EDF (Services) Limited v Romania*, ICSID Case No ARB/05/13, Award, 8 October 2009, para 210: 'The test, as it has to be, is subjective, not objective, under the "particular result" formulation of the Commentary to Article 8, if for no other reason than neither this Tribunal nor any tribunal is generally in a position to make a judgment as to what is objectively in the best interests of a company for purposes of State attribution'.

[339] ibid, paras 211–12.

[340] *Tulip Real Estate and Development Netherlands BV v Republic of Turkey*, ICSID Case No ARB/11/28, Award, 10 March 2014, paras 307–08.

[341] ibid, para 311.

In this respect, the analysis of the *Tulip v Turkey* tribunal is largely consistent with the interpretation of the 'particular result' test offered in *EDF v Romania*, which requires that the interest of the State (controller) prevails to the antithetical subjective interest of the SOE (controlled) in relation to the performance of a given act or omission.[342] Arbitrator Jaffe rendered a separate opinion on the question of attribution under ARSIWA Article 8, stating that the evidence before the tribunal credibly showed that Emlak terminated the contract under the direction and control of TOKI.[343] He did not express any position on the application of the 'particular result' test by the majority of the tribunal. The *Tulip v Turkey* award later resisted the investor's application for annulment.[344]

Other investment tribunals did not rely on the 'particular result' test in the same manner as *EDF v Romania* and *Tulip v Turkey*.[345] The *Bayindir v Pakistan* tribunal found that the termination of a contract by a parastatal was attributable to the State under ARSIWA Article 8 by virtue of the 'express clearance' from the government.[346] In *Ampal-American Israel Corporation v Egypt*, the tribunal addressed the conduct of termination of a contract of supply and purchase of gas by the Egyptian Gas Holding Company (EGAS), a public sector holding company wholly owned by the Egyptian General Petroleum Corporation (EGPC), a State organ. The arbitrators decided that the confirmation of the termination of the contract by EGPC's board of directors, which comprised the Minister of Petroleum and other ministers of the Republic of Egypt, constituted sufficient grounds to substantiate attribution under ARSIWA Article 8.[347] In this respect, the tribunal held that:

> The Tribunal finds that there is overwhelming evidence that the decisions of EGPC and EGAS to conclude and terminate the GSPA were all taken with the blessing of the highest levels of the Egyptian Government. Such acts are attributable to the Respondent pursuant to Article 8 of the ILC Draft Articles on State Responsibility as EGPC and EGAS were '*in fact acting on the instructions of, or*

[342] *EDF (Services) Limited v Romania*, ICSID Case No ARB/05/13, Award, 8 October 2009, paras 210 et seq.

[343] *Tulip Real Estate and Development Netherlands BV v Republic of Turkey*, ICSID Case No ARB/11/28, Separate Opinion of Michael Evan Jaffe, 7 April 2014, para 11.

[344] *Tulip Real Estate and Development Netherlands BV v Republic of Turkey*, ICSID Case No ARB/11/28, Decision on Annulment, 30 December 2015.

[345] As to earlier investment cases, see *Consortium Groupement LESI—DIPENTA v République algérienne démocratique et populaire*, ICSID Case No ARB/03/08, Award, 10 January 2005, para 19 (ii): '*La jurisprudence admet toutefois que la responsabilité de l'Etat peut être engagée dans des contrats pourtant passés par des entreprises de droit public distinctes de lui lorsque son influence n'en reste pas moins importante voire prédominante.*'; *LESI SpA and ASTALDI SpA v République Algérienne Démocratique et Populaire*, ICSID Case No ARB/05/3, Decision, 12 July 2006, para 78(ii). cf Pierre-Marie Dupuy, 'Les émanations engagent-elles la responsabilité des Etats? Etude de droit international des investissements' (2006) EUI Working Paper LAW No 2006/7, 6-7: '*c'était en réalité l'Etat qui "tirait les ficelles"*'.

[346] *Bayindir Insaat Turizm Ticaret Ve Sanayi AS v Islamic Republic of Pakistan*, ICSID Case No ARB/03/29, Award, 27 August 2009, para 125.

[347] *Ampal-American Israel Corporation et al v Arab Republic of Egypt*, ICSID Case No ARB/12/11, Decision on Liability and Heads of Loss, 21 February 2017, para 144.

under the direction or control of the Respondent in relation to the particular conduct.[348]

Moreover, the tribunal also found that State organs had subsequently ratified the contract termination, which embodied an acknowledgement and adoption of conduct pursuant to ARSIWA Article 11.[349] In *Karkey v Pakistan*, the tribunal decided that the conduct of Lakhra Power Generation Company Ltd (Lakhra) and Pakistan Electric Power Company Limited (PEPCO) relating to the performance of a contract was the result of 'direct and explicit instructions' and mandates by the government and, therefore, was attributable to the Republic of Pakistan.[350] Finally, in *UAB v Latvia*, the arbitrators had to determine whether the bringing of civil actions resulting in a freezing order against the investor by two companies wholly owned by a Latvian municipality could be attributed to the State under ARSIWA Article 8. The tribunal held that the 'body of circumstantial evidence' before it suggested that the municipality orchestrated the legal claims using the two companies as an instrument to implement its public policies in the sector of the local supply of heating.[351] This permitted it to infer that the municipality instructed and directed the conduct of the two companies.[352]

In conclusion, arbitral tribunals consistently hold that majority ownership or shareholding by the State of a corporate entity is insufficient for the purposes of attribution pursuant to ARSIWA Article 8.[353] Instead, it is questionable whether the establishment of a conflict of interests between the State and a SOE (the former prevailing over the latter) should be decisive for the purposes of attribution of conduct. This restrictive requirement seems to derive from the municipal law doctrines of the 'piercing of the corporate veil', which are based on the abuse of the corporate form by the parent company in order to further its own, rather than the subsidiary company's, interests. However, the interests of the State and its SOEs are usually coincident.[354] Moreover, an act may be executed by a SOE in its own

[348] ibid, para 146.

[349] ibid.

[350] *Karkey Karadeniz Elektrik Uretim AS v Islamic Republic of Pakistan*, ICSID Case No. ARB/13/1, Award, 22 August 2017, paras 573, 590, 595.

[351] *UAB E Energija v Latvia*, ICSID Case No ARB/12/33, Award, 22 December 2017, paras 827–29.

[352] ibid, para 830.

[353] *Ex multis*, *EDF (Services) Limited v Romania*, ICSID Case No ARB/05/13, Award, 8 October 2009, para 210; *Tulip Real Estate and Development Netherlands BV v Republic of Turkey*, ICSID Case No ARB/11/28, Award, 10 March 2014, para 289; *UAB E Energija v Latvia*, ICSID Case No ARB/12/33, Award, 22 December 2017, para 825.

[354] The *EDF v Romania* tribunal established a conflict between the subjective business interest of the two SOEs in question in relation to the extension of the relevant contract and the additional acquisition of shares in the PPP formed with the foreign investor and the interest of the State, which—after the change in government in Romania—prevented the coming into effect of such business operations by failing to issue its mandatory approval. However, the tribunal itself noted that, after the change of policy by the new government, the policy of the two SOEs came to coincide with the position of the new Ministry: 'AIBO and TAROM then changed their position to coincide with the new policy of the Ministry'. See *EDF (Services) Limited v Romania*, ICSID Case No ARB/05/13, Award, 8 October 2009, para 212.

interest and at the same time upon implementation of instructions and mandates from the State. Therefore, the unity of interest between the State and its SOEs may render the doctrine of 'veil piercing'—which has traditionally been elaborated and applied in relation to business-to-business corporate relations—inadequate in the context of attribution of conduct to the sovereign pursuant to ARSIWA Article 8.[355]

6. Concluding Remarks

IIAs do not normally contain attribution rules, or, where such rules are provided, significant deviations from customary international law, as codified by ARSIWA Articles 4, 5, and 8, are not found ('*il y a peu de mécanismes d'imputation propres au droit des investissements*').[356] Accordingly, international investment law offers interesting analysis of the contemporary functioning of the ordinary mechanisms of attributability with a view to contributing to their understanding and progressive development. However, this chapter has also addressed critical problems that are found in the reasoning of investment tribunals.[357] Such problems relate to the attitude of some tribunals to treat customary international law in general and ARSIWA in particular as a set of norms that are external to their self-contained mandate.[358] The resulting cursory treatment of the legal theory tenets underlying the function and nature of the international rules of attribution of conduct to States has engendered their application through a holistic combination of different tests of attributability,[359] which instead should remain as distinct and independent, and has led to confusion with aspects of contractual liability, governed as such by the proper law of contract, in relation to the operation of umbrella clauses.[360]

[355] See Jane Chalmers, 'State Responsibility for Acts of Parastatals Organized in Corporate Form' (1990) 84 American Society of International Law Procedings 60, 63: 'What I am suggesting is that the presumption against piercing the corporate veil in the public sector need not be the same as in private sector analysis. The corporate veil concept may not need the diligent protection in the public sphere that it needs in the private sector . . . wholesale importation of the limited liability/corporate veil metaphor is not appropriate'.

[356] Yves Nouvel, 'Les entités paraétatiques dans la jurisprudence du CIRDI' in Charles Leben (ed), *Le contentieux arbitral transnational relatif à l'investissement. Nouveaux développements* (LGDJ 2006) 25, 41.

[357] Kaj Hobér, 'State Responsibility and Attribution' in Peter Muchlinski, Federico Ortino, and Christoph Schreuer (eds), *The Oxford Handbook of International Investment Law* (Oxford University Press 2008) 550, 582.

[358] Jürgen Kurtz, 'The Paradoxical Treatment of the ILC Articles on State Responsibility in Investor-State Arbitration' (2010) 25 ICSID Review—Foreign Investment Law Journal 200, 201; Pierre-Marie Dupuy, 'Les émanations engagent-elles la responsabilité des Etats? Etude de droit international des investissements' (2006) EUI Working Paper LAW No 2006/7, 11: '*Toutefois, en l'absence de précisions conventionnelles de cet ordre, les arbitres sont en quelque sorte laissés à eux-mêmes pour appliquer le droit international général. Ils le font alors, parfois, selon des raisonnements et des méthodes aboutissant à des solutions partiellement hétérodoxes*'.

[359] Luca Schicho, 'Attribution and State Entities: Diverging Approaches in Investment Arbitration' (2011) 12 Journal of World Investment & Trade 283–88.

[360] James Crawford, 'Investment Arbitration and the ILC Articles on State Responsibility' (2010) 25 ICSID Review—Foreign Investment Law Journal 127, 134.

With regard to ARSIWA Article 4, tribunals have provided important analysis on the attribution of acts and omissions of State organs exercising 'any other functions', for instance central banks and independent administrative bodies such as competition authorities and market regulators. Tribunals have generally established *de jure* agency, notwithstanding their separate juristic personality (of public law). Otherwise, the independent juristic personality of private law would usually trigger the attraction of SOEs within the orbit of the attributability mechanism devised for parastatal entities under ARSIWA Article 5. Arbitrators have also embarked on the application of the doctrine of *de facto* organs under ARSIWA Article 4.2, which has been elaborated under different branches of public international law in relation to the activities of paramilitary groups, so as to qualify a SOE, formally benefiting from separate legal personality under private law, as an agent of the State in connection with its lack of true independence, its institutional and financial insufficiency, and its subjection to overwhelming mandates by the State.[361]

With regard to ARSIWA Article 5, tribunals have applied the functional test of the exercising of elements of governmental authority, as is consistent with the distinction between *acta jure imperii* and *acta jure gestionis*, pursuant to the restrictive doctrine of State immunity from jurisdiction. This test is based on the nature and the context of the relevant State conduct. In this respect, the traditional 'private contractor' test may be strengthened by taking into consideration the principle of competitive neutrality of SOEs. Accordingly, a SOE's conduct may be attributed to the State, based on the casuistic finding that the SOE could not have performed it on a rational basis, like any other private competitor in the market, without the benefit of State ownership.

With regard to ARSIWA Article 8, tribunals have rendered insightful solutions for the attribution to States of the conduct *jure privatorum* undertaken by their SOEs, which has traditionally been influenced by corporate law doctrines under municipal legal systems. In this respect, the more recent arbitral practice reveals the independent application of the international tests of attributability under ARSIWA Article 8, particularly in light of the peculiar features of governmental control as contrasted with private control within corporate relations.

Progress in the resolution of attribution issues in investment arbitration hinges on the arbitrators' position on their dialectics with customary international law. Only the arbitrators' inclusive perspective and account of the public international law dimension of investment disputes can foster their beneficial contribution to the evolution and modernization of public international law in relation to attribution rules.

[361] Georgios Petrochilos, 'Attribution' in Katia Yannaca-Small (ed), *Arbitration under International Investment Agreements: A Guide to the Key Issues* (Oxford University Press 2010) 287, 296–99; Nick Gallus, 'State Enterprises as Organs of the State and BIT Claims' (2006) 7 Journal of World Investment & Trade 761, 778.

Conclusion

The Pedagogic Role of Attribution Principles

Each single rule of attributability of conduct provided by customary international law, as codified by ARSIWA, for State organs, 'State entities', and 'private' individuals is respectively vested with its own specificity and independence, which is supported by the difference in the nature of the relevant link whence they proceed (institutional, functional, and factual). Indeed, the analytical distinction between the various tests of attribution is of threshold importance in order to determine the precise regime of attributability and the reach of the effects of their application. The main consequences affect the possibility of attribution of the conduct of a private nature (*acta jure gestionis*), which operates for State organs only (plenary attribution), and of the *ultra vires* conduct executed by a given 'person', which is excluded with regard to 'private' individuals. In relation to the thresholds of control of the State on its organs (both *de jure* and *de facto*) for the purposes of attribution, this study has concluded that it should not necessarily be effective, which was instead upheld in early arbitration practice (for instance, in the *Zafiro* case) and by the ICJ in the *Nicaragua* case. This is confirmed by the customary rule of attribution of *ultra vires* conduct of State officials and 'State entities', which represents a corollary of the cardinal principles of supremacy of international law and of institutional unity and continuity of the State. Indeed, the institutional link of the status of organ (even if exceptionally established *ex post facto*) normatively supplements the absence of an official empowerment (authority or superior instructions) to execute a particular act. This principle is also fully applicable in the case of *de facto* organs, which, once the establishment of *de facto* agency has been completed, are to be treated exactly as if they were *de jure* organs as to the relevant regime of attribution. The conduct of 'State entities', namely non-organs of the State, including SOEs having corporate separateness, is attributable to the State in so far as it embodies the exercise of governmental authority, which is to be interpreted consistently with the dichotomy between *acta jure imperii* and *acta jure gestionis* as elaborated under the restrictive theory of sovereign immunity. Especially in international economic litigation, the traditional 'private contractor' test may also be strengthened by taking into consideration the principle of competitive neutrality of SOEs. Finally, the element of official or governmental authority is not required for the purposes of attribution to the State of the conduct of 'private' individuals, including SOEs. To this extent, the act or omission at issue should have occurred on the instructions or

Attribution in International Law and Arbitration. Carlo de Stefano, Oxford University Press (2020).

DOI: 10.1093/law-oso/9780198844648.001.0001

under the direction or effective control of a State organ. As a general remark, attribution mechanisms under public international law are independent and preeminent in relation to attribution principles under municipal laws.

Public international law provides well-settled customary rules for the treatment of State acts that establish specific tests for the purposes of attribution of conduct to the sovereign. Concerning the dichotomy between *acta jure imperii* and *acta jure gestionis*, such tests are convergent with the criteria elaborated under the theory of restrictive immunity from jurisdiction, as applied by domestic courts. This convergence is desirable in so far as it contributes to building a coherent concept of the State '*selon le droit international*'.[1] The ILC addressed the peculiar nature and function of the international rules of attribution as follows:

> As a normative operation, attribution must be clearly distinguished from the characterization of conduct as internationally wrongful. Its concern is to establish that there is an act of the State for the purposes of responsibility. To show that conduct is attributable to the State says nothing, as such, about the legality or otherwise of that conduct, and rules of attribution should not be formulated in terms which imply otherwise.[2]

This reveals the trait of 'neutrality' of attribution rules with respect to the law applicable to the objective element of liability or responsibility and, moreover, to the structure and design of a given dispute settlement system. Logical, technical, and 'objective' features of the rules of attribution, as codified by ARSIWA, prompt them to be taken into consideration by adjudicators also outside the realm of public international law dispute settlement to further a consistent treatment of the 'State' (ie, its organs, instrumentalities, and 'private' agents). This is confirmed by the practice of domestic courts and international commercial arbitrators when confronted with international business litigation involving States and SOEs.[3]

[1] Mathias Forteau, 'L'État selon le droit international: une figure à géométrie variable?' (2007) 111 Revue Générale de Droit International Public 737.

[2] ARSIWA Commentaries 39, para 4. See J G Starke, 'Imputability in International Delinquencies' (1938) 19 British Year Book of International Law 104, 106: 'Responsibility only begins where imputability ends.' See also *Compañiá de Aguas del Aconquija SA and Vivendi Universal SA v Argentine Republic* (formerly *Compañía de Aguas del Aconquija, SA and Compagnie Générale des Eaux v Argentine Republic*) (*Vivendi I*), ICSID Case No ARB/97/3, Decision on Annulment, 3 July 2003, para 16, fn 17: 'Attribution has nothing to do with the standard of liability or responsibility.'

[3] As to domestic courts, see *La Générale des Carrières et des Mines v FG Hemisphere Associates LLC*, 17 July 2012, Privy Council Appeal No 6/2011 [2012] UKPC 27 (Judicial Committee of the Privy Council), paras 15–19 (referring to ARSIWA Articles 4 and 5); *Compagnie Noga d'Importation et d'Exportation SA v The Russian Federation*, 361 F.3d 676, 688-689 (2004) (referring to ARSIWA Article 4). As to international commercial arbitrators, see *Salini Costruttori SpA v Ethiopia and Addis Ababa Water and Sewerage Authority*, ICC Case No 10623, Award Regarding the Suspension of the Proceedings and Jurisdiction, 7 December 2001, paras 169–70, 173–74, (2003) 21 ASA Bulletin 82: 'From the perspective of an international arbitral tribunal in this context, the state must be regarded as one entity. . . . This conclusion is supported by reference to public international law, which treats the organs of a state as

A complete privatization (for all purposes) of the *statut personnel* of the State as merchant (*État commerçant*) and of its SOEs engaging in *acta jure gestionis* is not tenable in light of the sociopolitical phenomena of the intervention of the State in the economic system. The pedagogic role and influence of the international rules of attribution may instil the development of consistent practices for the scrutiny of State activities in trans-boundary situations.[4] The customary rules of attribution of conduct to States phrase the narrative of the phenomenology of the State authority that proceeds from the physiology of the State itself, its apparatus, and ramifications in society.[5]

the state itself for the purposes of determining state responsibility, irrespective of whether or not those organs are independent or separate for the purposes of a state's internal law. This principle is frequently declared in the context of determining state responsibility for wrongful (in the general sense of tortious) acts. The International Law Commission has recently adopted new draft articles approving this principle in this context. See the draft articles regarding the 'Responsibility of States for Internationally Wrongful Acts', Article 4 ... For the same reason, the Respondent, as a state entity, must be considered part and parcel of the state itself for the purposes of addressing the present question. ... The principle that equates the organs of a state with the state itself reinforces our conclusion that we should proceed with our own duties to determine whether or not we have jurisdiction in this case.'

---

[4] Kaj Hobér, 'State Responsibility and Attribution' in Peter Muchlinski, Federico Ortino, and Christoph Schreuer (eds), *The Oxford Handbook of International Investment Law* (Oxford University Press 2008) 550, 554: 'the ILC Articles are widely accepted as guidelines for purposes of attribution in situations where the activities of state organs are being reviewed.'

[5] The ILC made reference to the 'colour of authority'. cf ARSIWA Commentaries 42, para 13. See also Daniel Cohen, 'Sur l'émanation d'État' in Louis d'Avout, Dominique Bureau, and Horatia Muir Watt (eds), *Mélanges en l'honneur du Professeur Bernard Audit. Les relations privées internationales* (LGDJ 2014) 233, 233–34: *'l'émanation d'Etat ... "sent" effectivement l'Etat, elle en a l'odeur et en partage les effluves, elle provient bien de lui, à l'origine de sa création.'* As to the doctrine of *narrative norms*, see Erik Jayme, 'Narrative Norms in Private International Law—The Example of Art Law' (2014) 375 Recueil des Cours 9, 49: 'They help to find solutions in international situations, particularly in cases where the domestic law has to be adapted in order to resolve transboundary fact situations.'

Bibliography

A

Accioly, H, 'Principes généraux de la responsabilité internationale d'après la doctrine et la jurisprudence' (1959) 96 Recueil des Cours 349.
Ago, R, 'Le délit international' (1939) 68 Recueil des Cours 415.
Ago, R, 'Nouvelles réflexions sur la codification du droit international' (1988) 92 Revue Générale du Droit International Public 539.
Alexandrov, S A, 'Breaches of Contract and Breaches of Treaty' (2004) 5 Journal of World Investment & Trade 555.
Allen, E W, *The Position of Foreign States Before National Courts, Chiefly in Continental Europe* (The Macmillan Company 1933).
Amadio, M, *Le contentieux international de l'investissement privé et la Convention de la Banque Mondial du 18 mars 1965* (LGDJ 1967).
Amerasinghe, C F, 'Imputability in the Law of State Responsibility for Injuries to Aliens' (1966) 22 Revue Égyptienne de Droit International 91.
Amerasinghe, C F, 'Jurisdiction *Ratione Personae* Under the Convention on the Settlement of Investment Disputes Between States and Nationals of Other States' (1974-1975) 47 British Year Book of International Law 227.
Amerasinghe, C F, 'The Jurisdiction of the International Centre for the Settlement of Investment Disputes' (1979) 19 Indian Journal of International Law 166.
Amerasinghe, C F, 'Interpretation of Article 25(2)(b) of the ICSID Convention' in Richard B Lillich and Charles N Brower (eds), *International Arbitration in the 21st Century: Towards 'Judicialization' and Uniformity?* (Transnational Publishers, Inc 1993) 223.
Amerasinghe, C F, *Jurisdiction of International Tribunals* (Kluwer Law International 2003).
Anzilotti, D, 'La responsabilité internationale des États a raison des dommages soufferts par des étrangers' (1906) 13 Revue Générale de Droit International Public 5.
Anzilotti, D, 'L'esenzione degli stati stranieri dalla giurisdizione (Saggio di critica e di ricostruzione)' (1910) 5 Rivista di Diritto Internazionale 477.
Anzilotti, D, *Corso di diritto internazionale, Volume Primo: Introduzione—Teorie generali* (3rd edn, Athenaeum 1928).
Arangio-Ruiz, G, 'State Fault and the Forms and Degrees of International Responsibility: Questions of Attribution and Relevance' in *Le droit international au service de la paix, de la justice et du développement. Mélanges Michel Virally* (Éditions A Pedone 1991) 25.
Arangio-Ruiz, G, 'State Responsibility Revisited: The Factual Nature of the Attribution of Conduct to the State' (2017) 100 (Supplement to Issue No. 1) Rivista di Diritto Internazionale 1.
Arcari, M, 'Le juge et la codification du droit de la responsabilité: quelques remarques concernant l'application judiciaire des articles de la CDI sur la responsabilité de l'État pour fait internationalement illicite' in Nerina Boschiero et al (eds), *International Courts*

and the Development of International Law: Essays in Honour of Tullio Treves (TMC Asser Press 2013) 19.

Arsanjani, M H, and Reisman, W M, 'Interpreting Treaties for the Benefit of Third Parties: The "Salvors' Doctrine" and the Use of Legislative History in Investment Treaties' (2010) 104 American Journal of International Law 597.

Audit, B, 'Le Tribunal de Différends Irano-Américains (1981-1984)' (1985) 112 Journal du Droit International (Clunet) 791.

Aust, H P, 'Through the Prism of Diversity: the Articles on State Responsibility in the Light of the ILC Fragmentation Report' (2006) 49 German Yearbook of International Law 165.

B

Bacchus, J, 'Not in Clinical Isolation' in Gabrielle Marceau (ed), *A History of Law and Lawyers in the GATT/WTO. The Development of the Rule of Law in the Multilateral Trading System* (Cambridge University Press 2015) 507.

Badia, A, *Piercing the Veil of State Enterprises in International Arbitration* (Kluwer Law International 2014).

Badia, A, 'Attribution of Conducts of State-Owned Enterprises Based on Control by the State' in Crina Baltag (ed), *ICSID Convention after 50 Years: Unsettled Issues* (Kluwer Law International 2016) 189.

Badr, G M, *State Immunity: An Analytical and Prognostic View* (Martinus Nijhoff Publishers 1984).

Bastid, S, 'L'affaire Nottebohm devant la C.I.J.' (1956) 45 Revue Critique de Droit International Privé 607.

Ben Hamida, W, 'La clause relative au respect des engagements dans les traités d'investissement' in Charles Leben (ed), *Le contentieux arbitral transnational relatif à l'investissement. Nouveaux développements* (LGDJ 2006) 53.

Bianchi, A, 'Gazing at the Crystal Ball (again): State Immunity and *Jus Cogens* beyond *Germany v Italy*' (2013) 4 Journal of International Dispute Settlement 457.

Bjorklund, A K, 'The Emerging Civilization of Investment Arbitration' (2009) 113 Penn State Law Review 1269.

Böckstiegel, K-H, *Arbitration and State Enterprises. A Survey on the National and International State of Law and Practice* (Kluwer Law and Taxation Publishers 1984).

Borchard, E M, *The Diplomatic Protection of Citizens Abroad or The Law of International Claims* (The Banks Law Publishing Co 1915).

Borchard, E M, '"Responsibility of States" at the Hague Codification Conference' (1930) 24 American Journal of International Law 517.

Bouchez, L J, 'The Nature and Scope of State Immunity from Jurisdiction and Execution' (1979) 10 Netherlands Yearbook of International Law 1.

Brierly, J L, 'The Theory of Implied State Complicity in International Claims' (1928) 9 British Year Book of International Law 42.

Broches, A, 'The Convention on the Settlement of Investment Disputes Between States and Nationals of Other States' (1972-II) 136 Recueil des Cours 331.

Broude, T, 'Investment and Trade: The "Lottie and Lisa" of International Economic Law?' in Roberto Echandi and Pierre Sauvé (eds), *Prospects in International Investment Law and Policy. World Trade Forum* (Cambridge University Press 2013) 139.

Brownlie, I, *System of the Law of Nations. State Responsibility. Part I* (Clarendon Press 1983).

Brownlie, I, 'State Responsibility and the International Court of Justice' in Malgosia Fitzmaurice and Dan Sarooshi (eds), *Issues of State Responsibility before International Judicial Institutions* (Hart Publishing 2004) 11.

C

Cahin, G, 'La clause de couverture (dite *umbrella clause*)' (2015) 119 Revue Générale de Droit International Public 103.

Calvo, C, 'De la non-responsabilité des États à raison des pertes et dommages éprouvés par des étrangers en temps de troubles intérieurs ou de guerres civiles' (1869) 1 Revue de Droit International et de Legislation Comparée 417.

Capobianco, A, and Christiansen, H, *Competitive Neutrality and State-Owned Enterprises: Challenges and Policy Options*, OECD Corporate Governance Working Papers, No 1 (OECD Publishing 2011).

Carabiber, C, 'De quelques aspects nouveaux de l'immunité de juridiction des Ètats' (1938) 33 Revue Critique de Droit International 369.

Caron, D D, 'The Basis of Responsibility: Attribution and Other Trans-substantive Rules of State Responsibility' in Richard B Lillich and Daniel B Magraw (eds), *The Iran-United States Claims Tribunal: Its Contribution to the Law of State Responsibility* (Transnational Publishers, Inc 1998) 109.

Caron, D D, 'The ILC Articles on State Responsibility: the Paradoxical Relationship Between Form and Authority' (2002) 96 American Journal of International Law 857.

Cassese, A, *International Law* (2nd edn, Oxford University Press 2005).

Cassese, A, 'The *Nicaragua* and *Tadić* Tests Revisited in Light of the ICJ Judgement on Genocide in Bosnia' (2007) 18 European Journal of International Law 649.

Cavaré, L, 'L'immunité de juridiction des États étrangers' (1954) 58 Revue Générale de Droit International Public 177.

Chalmers, J, 'State Responsibility for Acts of Parastatals Organized in Corporate Form' (1990) 84 American Society of International Law Proceedings 60.

Cheng, B, *General Principles of Law as Applied by International Courts and Tribunals* (reprinted Cambridge University Press 2006, first published Stevens & Sons, Ltd 1953).

Chinkin, C, 'A Critique of the Public/Private Dimension' (1999) 10 European Journal of International Law 387.

Christenson, G A, 'The Doctrine of Attribution in State Responsibility' in Richard B Lillich (ed), *International Law of State Responsibility for Injuries to Aliens* (University Press of Virginia 1983) 321.

Christenson, G A, 'Attributing Conduct to the State: Is Anything New?' (1990) 84 American Society of International Law Proceedings 51.

Christenson, G A, 'Attributing Acts of Omission to the State' (1990-1991) 12 Michigan Journal of International Law 312.

Cohen, D, 'Sur l'émanation d'État' in Louis d'Avout, Dominique Bureau, and Horatia Muir Watt (eds), *Mélanges en l'honneur du Professeur Bernard Audit. Les relations privées internationales* (LGDJ 2014) 233.

Cohen Smutny, A, 'State Responsibility and Attribution When is a State Responsible for the Acts of State Enterprises? *Emilio Agustín Maffezini v. The Kingdom of Spain*' in Todd Weiler (ed), *International Investment Law and Arbitration: Leading Cases from the ICSID, NAFTA, Bilateral Treaties and Customary International Law* (Cameron May 2005) 17.

Combacau, J, and Alland, D, '"Primary" and "Secondary" Rules in the Law of State Responsibility: Categorizing International Obligations' (1985) 16 Netherlands Yearbook of International Law 81.

Combacau, J, 'Le droit international: bric-à-brac ou système?' (1986) 31 Archives de Philosophie du Droit 85.

Conforti, B, *Diritto internazionale* (9th edn, Editoriale Scientifica 2013).

Conforti, B, 'La Cour constitutionnelle italienne et le droits de l'homme méconnus sur le plan international' (2015) 119 Revue Générale de Droit International Public 353.

Condorelli, L, 'L'imputation à l'État d'un fait internationalement illicite: solutions classiques et nouvelles tendances' (1984) 189 Recueil des Cours 9.

Condorelli, L, and Kress, C, 'The Rules of Attribution: General Considerations' in James Crawford, Alain Pellet, and Simon Olleson (eds), *The Law of International Responsibility* (Oxford University Press 2010) 237.

Constant, B, *De la liberté des Anciens comparée à celle des Modernes* (Athénée Royal de Paris 1819).

Cook, G, *A Digest of WTO Jurisprudence on Public International Law Concepts and Principles* (Cambridge University Press 2015).

Cosnard, M, *La soumission des États aux tribunaux internes. Face à la théorie des immunités des États* (Éditions A Pedone 1996) 226.

Crawford, J, 'The Criteria for Statehood in International Law' (1976-1977) 48 British Year Book of International Law 93.

Crawford, J, 'Execution of Judgments and Foreign Immunity' (1981) 75 American Journal of International Law 820.

Crawford, J, 'International Law and Foreign Sovereigns: Distinguishing Immune Transactions' (1983) 54 British Year Book of International Law 75.

Crawford, J, 'Revising the Draft Articles on State Responsibility' (1999) 10 European Journal of International Law 435.

Crawford, J, Peel, J, and Olleson, S, 'The ILC's Articles on Responsibility of States for Internationally Wrongful Acts: Completion of the Second Reading' (2001) 12 European Journal of International Law 963.

Crawford, J, *The International Law Commission's Articles on State Responsibility. Introduction, Text and Commentaries* (Cambridge University Press 2002).

Crawford, J, 'The ILC's Articles on Responsibility of States for Internationally Wrongful Acts: A Retrospect' (2002) 96 American Journal of International Law 874.

Crawford, J, and Olleson, S, 'The Continuing Debate on a UN Convention on State Responsibility' (2005) 54 International & Comparative Law Quarterly 959.

Crawford, J, 'Treaty and Contract in Investment Arbitration' (2008) 24 Arbitration International 351.

Crawford, J, Grant, T, and Messineo, F, 'Towards An International Law of Responsibility: Early Doctrine' in Laurence Boisson de Chazournes and Marcelo Kohen (eds), *International Law and the Quest for its Implementation. Liber Amicorum Vera Gowlland-Debbas* (Brill 2010) 377.

Crawford, J, 'Investment Arbitration and the ILC Articles on State Responsibility' (2010) 25 ICSID Review—Foreign Investment Law Journal 127.

Crawford, J, *State Responsibility. The General Part* (Cambridge University Press 2013).

Crawford, J, 'The International Court of Justice and the Law of State Responsibility' in Christian J Tams and James Sloan, *The Development of International Law by the International Court of Justice* (Oxford University Press 2013) 85.

Crawford, J, and Mertensktter, P, 'The Use of the ILC's Attribution Rules in Investment Arbitration' in Meg N Kinnear, Geraldine R Fischer, Jara Mínguez Almeida, Luisa Fernanda Torres, and Mairée Uran Bidegain (eds), *Building International Investment Law. The First 50 Years of ICSID* (Kluwer Law International 2015) 27.

Cremades, B M, 'Litigating Annulment Proceedings. The *Vivendi* Matter: Contract and Treaty Claims' in Emmanuel Gaillard and Yas Banifatemi (eds), *Annulment of ICSID Awards* (Juris Publishing, Inc 2004) 87.

D

De Brabandere, E, *Investment Treaty Arbitration as Public International Law. Procedural Aspects and Implications* (Cambridge University Press 2014).

de Frouville, O, 'Attribution of Conduct to the State: Private Individuals' in James Crawford, Alain Pellet, and Simon Olleson (eds), *The Law of International Responsibility* (Oxford University Press 2010) 257.

de Hoogh, André J J, 'Articles 4 and 8 of the 2001 ILC Articles on State Responsibility, the *Tadić* Case and Attribution of Acts of Bosnian Serb Authorities to the Federal Republic of Yugoslavia' (2001) 72 British Year Book of International Law 255.

de Stefano, C, 'Arbitration Agreements as Waivers to Sovereign Immunity' (2014) 30 Arbitration International 59.

de Stefano, C, 'Adel A Hamadi Al Tamimi v Sultanate of Oman. Attributing to Sovereigns the Conduct of State-Owned Enterprises: Towards Circumvention of the Accountability of States under International Investment Law' (2017) 32(2) ICSID Review—Foreign Investment Law Journal 267.

de Visscher, C, 'La responsabilité internationale des États' in *Bibliotheca Visseriana*, vol II (Brill 1924) 89.

de Visscher, P, 'L'Affaire Nottebohm' (1956) 60 Revue Générale de Droit International Public 238.

de Visscher, P, 'Les aspects juridiques fondamentaux de la question de Suez' (1958) 62 Revue Générale de Droit International Public 400.

de Visscher, P, 'La Protection Diplomatique des Personnes Morales' (1961) 102 Recueil des Cours 395.

Del Mar, K, 'The Requirement of "Belonging" under International Humanitarian Law' (2010) 21 European Journal of International Law 105.

Delaume, G R, 'ICSID Arbitration and the Courts' (1983) 77 American Journal of International Law 784.

Delaume, G R, 'Enforcement of State Contract Awards: Jurisdictional Pitfalls and Remedies' (1993) 8 ICSID Review—Foreign Investment Law Journal 29.

Dickinson, A, Lindsay, R, and Loonam, J P, *State Immunity. Selected Materials and Commentary* (Oxford University Press 2004).

Dolzer, R, and Schreuer, C, *Principles of International Investment Law* (2nd edn, Oxford University Press 2012).

Domke, M, 'Act of State: Sabbatino in the Courts and in Congress' (1964) 3 Columbia Journal of Transnational Law 99.

Dopagne, F, 'La responsabilité de l'État du fait des particuliers: les causes d'imputation revisitées par les articles sur la responsabilité de l'État pour fait internationalement illicite' (2001) 34 Revue Belge du Droit International 492.

Douglas, Z, 'The Hybrid Foundations of Investment Treaty Arbitration' (2003) 74 British Year Book of International Law 151.

Douglas, Z, 'Other Specific Regimes of Responsibility: Investment Treaty Arbitration and ICSID' in James Crawford, Alain Pellet, and Simon Olleson (eds), *The Law of International Responsibility* (Oxford University Press 2010) 815.

Douglas, Z, 'International Responsibility for Domestic Adjudication: Denial of Justice Deconstructed' (2014) 63 International and Comparative Law Quarterly 867.

Du, M, 'China's State Capitalism and World Trade Law' (2014) 63 International & Comparative Law Quarterly 409.

Dunbar, N C H, 'Controversial Aspects of Sovereign Immunity in the Case Law of Some States' (1971) 132 Recueil des Cours 197.

Dupuy, P-M, 'Due Diligence in the International Law of State Responsibility' in *Legal Aspects of Transfrontier Pollution* (Organisation for Economic Co-operation and Development 1977) 369.

Dupuy, P-M, 'Attribution Issues in State Responsibility. Commentary' (1990) 84 American Society of International Law Proceedings 51.

Dupuy, P-M, 'Quarante ans de codification du droit de la responsabilité internationale des États: un bilan' (2003) 107 Revue Génerale de Droit International Public 305.

Dupuy, P-M, 'Les émanations engagent-elles la responsabilité des Etats? Etude de droit international des investissements' (2006) EUI Working Paper LAW No 2006/7.

Dupuy, P-M, 'Relations Between the International Law of Responsibility and Responsibility in Municipal Law' in James Crawford, Alain Pellet, and Simon Olleson (eds), *The Law of International Responsibility* (Oxford University Press 2010) 173.

E

Eagleton, C, *The Responsibility of States in International Law* (New York University Press 1928).

Eagleton, C, 'Denial of Justice in International Law' (1928) 22 American Journal of International Law 538.

El Sawah, S, *Les immunités des Etats et des organisations internationales. Immunités et procès équitable* (Larcier 2012).

Eustathiades, C T, *La responsabilité internationale de l'État pour les actes des organes judiciaires et le problème du déni de justice en droit international*, Tome II (Éditions A Pedone 1936).

Eustathiades, C T, 'Les sujets du droit international et la responsabilité internationale: nouvelles tendances' (1953) 84 Recueil des Cours 397.

F

Fairman, C, 'Some Disputed Applications of the Principle of State Immunity' (1928) 22 American Journal of International Law 566.

Falk, R A, *The Role of Domestic Court in the International Legal Order* (Syracuse University Press 1964) 139.

Fawcett, J E S, 'Legal Aspects of State Trading' (1948) 25 British Year Book of International Law 34.

Feit, M, 'Responsibility of the State Under International Law for the Breach of Contract Committed by a State-Owned Entity' (2010) 28 Berkeley Journal of International Law 142.

Feit, M, 'Attribution and the Umbrella Clause: is there a Way out of the Deadlock?' (2012) 21 Minnesota Journal of International Law 21.

Feldman, M, 'State-Owned Enterprises as Claimants in International Investment Arbitration' (2016) 31 ICSID Review—Foreign Investment Law Journal 24.

Fitzmaurice, G G, 'State Immunity from Proceedings in Foreign Courts' (1933) 14 British Year Book of International Law 101.

Forteau, M, 'L'État selon le droit international: une figure à géométrie variable?' (2007) 111 Revue Générale de Droit International Public 737.

Fox, H, 'Reexamining the Act of State Doctrine: An Integrated Conflicts Analysis' (1992) 33 Harvard International Law Journal 521.

Fox, H, 'The International Court of Justice's Treatment of Acts of the State and in Particular the Attribution of Acts of Individuals to the State' in Nisuke Ando, Edward McWhinney, and Rüdiger Wolfrum (eds), *Liber Amicorum Judge Shigeru Oda*, vol 1 (Kluwer Law International 2002) 147.

Fox, H, and Webb, P, *The Law of State Immunity* (3rd edn revised and updated, Oxford University Press 2013).

Freeman, A V, *The International Responsibility of States for Denial of Justice* (Longmans, Greenman and Company 1938).

Freeman, A V, *Responsibility of States for Unlawful Acts of their Armed Forces* (A W Sijthoff 1957).

Freyria, C, 'Les limites de l'immunité de juridiction et d'exécution des États étrangers' (1951) 40 Revue Critique de Droit International Privé 207.

Friedmann, W G, 'The Growth of State Control over the Individual, and its Effect upon the Rules of International State Responsibility' (1938) 19 British Year Book of International Law 118.

Friedmann, W G, 'Some Impacts of Social Organization on International Law' (1956) 50 American Journal of International Law 475.

Friedmann, W G, *The Changing Structure of International Law* (Stevens & Sons 1964).

Friedmann, W G, and Béguin, J-P, *Joint International Business Ventures in Developing Countries. Case Studies and Analysis of Recent Trends* (Columbia University Press 1971).

Friedmann, W G, *Law in a Changing Society* (2nd edn, Stevens & Sons 1972).

Friedmann, W G, 'Public and Private Enterprise in Mixed Economies: Some Comparative Observations' in Wolfgang G Friedmann (ed), *Public and Private Enterprise in Mixed Economies* (Stevens & Sons 1974) 359.

G

Gaeta, P, 'Génocide d'Etat et responsabilité pénale individuelle' (2007) 111 Revue Général de Droit International Public 273.

Gaillard, E, 'Effectivité des sentences arbitrales: immunité des Etats et autonomie des personnes morales dépendant d'eux' in Isabelle Pingel-Lenuzza (ed), *Droit des immunités et exigences du procès équitable. Actes du colloque du 30 avril 2004* (Éditions A Pedone 2004) 119.

Gaillard, E, and Younan, J, (eds), *State Entities in International Arbitration* (Juris Publishing, Inc 2008).

Gaja, G, 'Primary and Secondary Rules in the International Law on State Responsibility' (2014) 97 Rivista di Diritto Internazionale 981.

Gallus, N, 'State Enterprises as Organs of the State and BIT Claims' (2006) 7 Journal of World Investment & Trade 761.

Gallus, N, 'An Umbrella Just for Two? BIT Obligations Observance Clauses and the Parties to a Contract' (2008) 24 Arbitration International 157.

García-Amador, F V, 'State Responsibility: Some New Problems' (1958) 94 Recueil des Cours 365.

Gomula, J, 'Responsibility and the World Trade Organization' in James Crawford, Alain Pellet, and Simon Olleson (eds), *The Law of International Responsibility* (Oxford University Press 2010) 791.

Gradoni, L, Regime failure *nel diritto internazionale* (CEDAM 2009).

Griebel, J, and Plücken, M, 'New Developments Regarding the Rules of Attribution? The International Court of Justice's Decision in *Bosnia v. Serbia*' (2008) 21 Leiden Journal of International Law 601.

Grotius, H, *De Jure Belli ac Pacis Libri Tres* (Amsterdam 1646).

H

Hafner, G, and Köhler, G, 'The United Nations Convention on Jurisdictional Immunities of States and Their Property' (2004) 35 Netherlands Yearbook of International Law 3.

Hafner, G, and Lange, L, 'La Convention des Nations Unies sur les immunités juridictionnelles des Etats et de leurs biens' (2004) 50 Annuaire Français de Droit International 45.

Hamamoto, S, 'Parties to the "Obligations" in the Obligations Observance ("Umbrella") Clause' (2015) 30 ICSID Review—Foreign Investment Law 449.

Hamson, C J, 'Immunity of Foreign States: The Practice of the French Courts' (1950) 27 British Year Book of International Law 321.

Hanessian, G, and Duggal, K, 'The 2015 Indian Model BIT: Is This Change the World Wishes to See?' (2015) 30 ICSID Review—Foreign Investment Law Journal 729.

Hanessian, G, and Duggal, K, 'The Final 2015 Indian Model BIT: Is This the Change the World Wishes to See?' (2017) 32 ICSID Review—Foreign Investment Law Journal 216.

Hessbruegge, J A, 'The Historical Development of the Doctrines of Attribution and Due Diligence in International Law' (2003-2004) 36 New York University Journal of International Law and Politics 265.

Higgins, R, 'Aspects of the Case Concerning the Barcelona Traction, Light and Power Company, Ltd.' (1970-1971) 11 Virginia Journal of International Law 327.

Higgins, R, 'Certain Unresolved Aspects of the Law of State Immunity' (1982) 29 Netherlands International Law Review 265.

Higgins, R, 'The Concept of "The State": Variable Geometry and Dualist Perceptions' in Laurence Boisson de Chazournes and Vera Gowlland-Debbas (eds), *The International Legal System in Quest of Equity and Universality. Liber Amicorum Georges Abi-Saab* (Martinus Nijhoff Publishers 2001) 547.

Higgins, R, 'Issues of State Responsibility before the International Court of Justice' in Malgosia Fitzmaurice and Dan Sarooshi (eds), *Issues of State Responsibility before International Judicial Institutions* (Hart Publishing 2004) 1.

Hill, T H, 'Sovereign Immunity and Act of the State Doctrine. Theory and Policy in the United States' (1982) 46 Rabels Zeitschrift für Ausländisches und Internationales Privatrecht 118.

Hobér, K, 'State Responsibility and Attribution' in Peter Muchlinski, Federico Ortino, and Christoph Schreuer (eds), *The Oxford Handbook of International Investment Law* (Oxford University Press 2008) 550.

Howse, R, 'From Politics to Technocracy—and Back Again: The Fate of the Multilateral Trade Regime' (2002) 96 American Journal of International Law 94.

J

Jayme, E, 'Narrative Norms in Private International Law—The Example of Art Law' (2014) 375 Recueil des Cours 9.

Jessup, P C, 'Responsibility of States for Injuries to Individuals' (1946) 46 Columbia Law Review 903.

Jiménez de Aréchaga, E, 'International Law in the Past Third of a Century' (1978-I) 159 Recueil des Cours 1.

Jinks, D, 'State Responsibility for the Acts of Private Armed Groups' (2003) 4 Chicago Journal of International Law 83.

Jones, J M, 'The Nottebohm Case' (1956) 5 International & Comparative Law Quarterly 230.

K

Kelsen, H, *(The) Pure Theory of Law* (2nd edn, University of California Press 1960, translated 1967).

Kessedjan, C, and Schreuer, C H, 'Le projet d'articles de la Commission du Droit International sur les immunités des Etats' (1992) 96 Revue Générale de Droit International Public 299.

Kincaid, P J, 'Sovereign Immunity of Foreign State-Owned Corporations' (1976) 10 Journal of World Trade Law 110.

Kingsbury, H T, 'The "Act of State" Doctrine' (1910) 4 American Journal of International Law 359.

Koh, H H, 'International Business Transactions in United States Courts' (1996) 261 Recueil des Cours 9.

Kolb, R, 'La détermination du concept de "*jus cogens*"' (2014) 118 Revue Générale de Droit International Public 5.

Koskenniemi, M, 'The Future of Statehood' (1991) 32 Harvard International Law Journal 397.

Kovács, C, *Attribution in International Investment Law* (Kluwer Law International 2018).

Kress, C, 'L'organe de facto en droit international public' (2001) 105 Revue Générale de Droit International Public 93.

Kurtz, J, 'The Paradoxical Treatment of the ILC Articles on State Responsibility in Investor-State Arbitration' (2010) 25 ICSID Review—Foreign Investment Law Journal 200.

Kurtz, J, *The WTO and International Investment Law: Converging Systems* (Cambridge University Press 2016).

L

Lagarde, P, 'Une notion ambivalente: l'« émanation » de l'Etat nationalisant' in *Droits et libertés à la fin du XXe siècle—Etudes offertes à Claude-Albert Colliard* (Éditions A Pedone 1984) 539.

Lalive, J-F, 'L'immunité de juridiction des Etats et des organisations internationales' (1953) 84 Recueil des Cours 205.

Lalive, J-F, 'Contracts Between a State or a State Agency and a Foreign Company' (1964) 13 International & Comparative Law Quarterly 987.

Lalive, P, 'The First "World Bank" Arbitration (*Holiday Inns v. Morocco*) - Some Legal Problems' (1980) 51 British Year Book of International Law 123.

Larsen, C, 'ICSID Jurisdiction: the Relationship of Contracting States to Sub-states Entities' in Norbert Horn (ed), *Arbitrating Foreign Investment Disputes* (Kluwer Law International 2004) 353.

Lauterpacht, H, 'The Problem of Jurisdictional Immunities of Foreign States' (1951) 28 British Year Book of International Law 220.

Leben, C, 'La responsabilité internationale de l'Etat sur le fondement des traités de promotion et de protection des investissements' (2004) 50 Annuaire Français de Droit International 683.

Leboulanger, P, *Les contrats entre états et entreprises étrangères* (Economica 1985).

Lillich, R B, 'The Rigidity of Barcelona' (1971) 65 American Journal of International Law 522.

Luzzatto, R, *Stati stranieri e giurisdizione nazionale* (Giuffré 1972).

Luzzatto, R, 'La giurisdizione sugli Stati stranieri tra Convenzione di New York, norme internazionali generali e diritto interno' (2007) 23 Comunicazioni e Studi 1.

M

Mann, F A, 'The Sacrosanctity of Foreign Acts of State' (1943) 59 Law Quarterly Review 42.

Mann, F A, 'The Protection of Shareholders' Interests in the Light of the Barcelona Traction Case' (1973) 67 American Journal of International Law 259.

Marinoni, M, *La responsabilità degli stati per gli atti dei loro rappresentanti secondo il diritto internazionale* (Athenaeum 1913).

Meron, T, 'International Responsibility of States for Unauthorized Acts of Their Officials' (1957) 33 British Year Book of International Law 85.

Meron, T, 'Classification of Armed Conflict in the Former Yugoslavia: Nicaragua's Fallout' (1998) 92 American Journal of International Law 236.

Miroudot, S, and Ragoussis, A, 'Actors in the International Investment Scenario: Objectives, Performance and Advantages of Affiliates of State-Owned Enterprises and Sovereign Wealth Funds' in Roberto Echandi and Pierre Sauvé (eds), *Prospects in International Investment Law and Policy: World Trade Forum* (Cambridge University Press 2013) 51.

Momtaz, D, 'Attribution of Conduct to the State: State Organs and Entities Empowered to Exercise Elements of Governmental Authority' in James Crawford, Alain Pellet, and Simon Olleson (eds), *The Law of International Responsibility* (Oxford University Press 2010) 237.

Monaco, R, 'La responsabilità internazionale dello Stato per fatti degli individui' (1939) 18 Rivista di Diritto Internazionale 3, 193, 216.

Morelli, G, 'Limiti dell'ordinamento statuale e limiti della giurisdizione' (1933) 25 Rivista di Diritto Internazionale 382.

N

Niboyet, J-P, 'Les immunités des États étrangers engagés dans des transactions privées' (1936) 43 Revue Générale de Droit International Public 525
Niboyet, J-P, 'Immunité de juridiction et incompétence d'attribution' (1950) 39 Revue Critique de Droit International Privé 139.
Nouvel, Y, 'Les entités paraétatiques dans la jurisprudence du CIRDI' in Charles Leben (ed), *Le contentieux arbitral transnational relatif à l'investissement. Nouveaux développements* (LGDJ 2006) 25.
Nouvel, Y, 'La compétence matérielle: contrat, traité et clauses parapluie' in Charles Leben (ed), *La procédure arbitrale relative aux investissements internationaux. Aspects récents* (LGDJ 2010) 13.

O

Okany, N, and Constantinides, A, 'State Delegation of Public Functions to Private Entities: a Basis for Attribution under the Rules of State Responsibility' in Kalliopi Koufa (ed), *State Responsibility and the Individual: 2003 International Law Session* (Sakkoulas Publications 2006) 327.

P

Palchetti, P, 'Comportamento di organi di fatto e illecito internazionale nel progetto di articoli sulla responsabilità internazionale degli Stati' in Marina Spinedi, Alessandra Gianelli, and Maria Luisa Alaimo (eds), *La codificazione della responsabilità internazionale degli Stati alla prova dei fatti: problemi e spunti di riflessione* (Giuffrè 2006) 3.
Palchetti, P, *L'organo di fatto dello Stato nell'illecito internazionale* (Giuffrè 2007).
Paparinskis, M, 'Investment Treaty Arbitration and the New Law of State Responsibility' (2013) 24 European Journal of International Law 617.
Paulsson, J, 'Arbitration Without Privity' (1995) 10 ICSID Review—Foreign Investment Law Journal 232.
Paulsson, J, *Denial of Justice in International Law* (Cambridge University Press 2005).
Pauwelyn, J, *Conflict of Norms in Public International Law. How WTO Law Relates to Other Rules of International Law* (Cambridge University Press 2003).
Pellet, A, 'The ILC's Articles on State Responsibility for Internationally Wrongful Acts and Related Texts' in James Crawford, Alain Pellet, and Simon Olleson (eds), *The Law of International Responsibility* (Oxford University Press 2010) 75.
Pellet, A, 'Remarques sur la jurisprudence récente de la C.I.J. dans le domaine de la responsabilité internationale' in Marcelo Kohen, Robert Kolb, and Djacoba Liva Tehindrazanarivelo (eds), *Perspective of International Law in the 21st Century. Liber Amicorum Professor Christian Dominicé* (Martinus Nijhoff Publishers 2012) 321.
Perassi, T, *Lezioni di diritto internazionale*, Parte Prima (Edizioni Italiane 1942).

Perera, S M, 'State Responsibility: Ascertaining the Liability of States in Foreign Investment Disputes' (2005) 6 Journal of World Investment & Trade 499.

Peters, A, Lagrange, E, Oeter, S, and Tomuschat, C, (eds), *Immunities in the Age of Global Constitutionalism* (Brill 2015).

Petrochilos, G, 'Attribution' in Katia Yannaca-Small (ed), *Arbitration under International Investment Agreements: A Guide to the Key Issues* (Oxford University Press 2010) 287.

Phillimore, G G, 'Immunité des Ètats au point de vue de la juridiction ou de l'exécution forcée' (1925) 8 Recueil des Cours 413.

Pingel-Lenuzza, I, 'Observations sur la convention du 17 janvier 2005 sur les immunités juridictionnelles des Etats et de leurs biens' (2005) 122 Journal du Droit International (Clunet) 1045.

Pisillo Mazzeschi, R, *"Due diligence" e responsabilità internazionale degli Stati* (1989 Giuffrè).

Pisillo Mazzeschi, R, 'The Due Diligence Rule and the Nature of the International Responsibility of States' (1992) 35 German Yearbook of International Law 9.

Q

Quadri, R, *La giurisdizione sugli Stati stranieri* (Giuffrè 1941).

Quéneudec, J-P, *La responsabilité internationale de l'État pour les fautes personnelles de ses agents* (LGDJ 1966).

Quigley, J, *The Soviet Foreign Trade Monopoly. Institution and Laws* (Ohio State University Press 1974).

R

Reisman, W M, *Nullity and Revision. The Review and Enforcement of International Judgments and Awards* (Yale University Press 1971).

Reymond, J, *L'attribution de comportements d'organes* de facto *et d'agents de l'Etat en droit international. Etude sur la responsabilité internationale des Etats* (Schultess 2013).

Reuter, P, 'Trois observations sur la codification de la responsabilité internationale des États pour fait illicite' in *Le droit international au service de la paix, de la justice et du développement. Mélanges Michel Virally* (Éditions A Pedone 1991) 389.

Riad, F A M, 'L'entreprise publique ou semi-publique en droit international privé' (1963) 108 Recueil des Cours 561.

Roberts, A, 'Clash of Paradigms: Actors and Analogies Shaping the Investment Treaty System' (2013) 107 American Journal of International Law 45.

Ronzitti, N, and Venturini, G, *Le immunità giurisdizionali degli Stati e degli altri enti internazionali* (CEDAM 2008).

Rosenne, S, 'State Responsibility—*Festina Lente*' in Shabtai Rosenne, *Essays on International Law and Practice* (Martinus Nijhoff Publishers 2007) 533.

Rousseau, C, 'Compétence des tribunaux internes à l'égard des États étrangers' (1939) 46 Revue Générale de Droit International Public 427.

Ruiz Fabri, H, 'Genèse et disparition de l'État à l'époque contemporaine' (1992) 38 Annuaire Français de Droit International 153.

Ruiz Fabri, H, 'Enhancing the Rhetoric of *Jus Cogens*' (2012) 23 European Journal of International Law 1049.

S

Sacerdoti, G, 'La Convenzione di Washington del 1965 per la soluzione delle controversie tra Stati e nazionali di altri Stati in materia di investimenti' (1969) 5 Rivista di Diritto Internazionale Privato e Processuale 614.

Sacerdoti, G, *I contratti tra Stati e stranieri nel diritto internazionale* (Giuffrè 1972).

Sacerdoti, G, 'La Convenzione di Washington del 1965: bilancio di un ventennio dell'ICSID' (1987) 23 Rivista di Diritto Internazionale Privato e Processuale 13.

Sacerdoti, G, 'The Application of BITs in Time of Economic Crisis: Limits to Their Coverage, Necessity and the Relevance of WTO Law' in Giorgio Sacerdoti, with Pia Acconci, Mara Valenti, and Anna De Luca, *General Interests of Host States in International Investment Law* (Cambridge University Press 2014) 3.

Sassòli, M, 'La première décision de la chambre d'appel du Tribunal Pénal pour l'ex Yougoslavie: *Tadić* (Compétence)' (1996) 100 Révue Générale de Droit International Public 101.

Szasz, P C, 'A Practical Guide to the Convention on Settlement of Investment Disputes' (1968) 1 Cornell Journal of International Law 1.

Schicho, L, 'Attribution and State Entities: Diverging Approaches in Investment Arbitration' (2011) 12 Journal of World Investment & Trade 283.

Schicho, L, *State Entities in International Investment Law* (Nomos 2012).

Schill, S W, 'Enabling Private Ordering: Function, Scope and Effect of Umbrella Clauses in International Investment Treaties' (2009) 18 Minnesota Journal of International Law 1.

Schreuer, C H, *State Immunity: Some Recent Developments* (Cambridge University Press 1988).

Schreuer, C H, 'The Waning of the Sovereign State: Towards a New Paradigm for International Law?' (1993) 4 European Journal of International Law 447.

Schreuer, C H, 'Travelling the BIT Route—Of Waiting Periods, Umbrella Clauses and Forks in the Road' (2004) 5 Journal of World Investment & Trade 231.

Schreuer, C H, with Loretta Malintoppi, August Reinisch, and Anthony Sinclair, *The ICSID Convention: A Commentary* (2nd edn, Cambridge University Press 2009).

Schreuer, C H, 'Full Protection and Security' (2010) Journal of International Dispute Settlement 1.

Seidl-Hohenveldern, I, 'L'immunité de juridiction et d'exécution des États et d'organisations internationales' in Institut des Hautes Etudes Internationales de Paris, *Cours et Travaux* (Éditions A Pedone 1981).

Shany, Y, 'Contract Claims vs. Treaty Claims: Mapping Conflicts Between ICSID Decisions on Multisourced Investment Claims' (2005) 99 American Journal of International Law 835.

Silva Romero, E, 'Some Remarks on the Contribution of ICC Arbitrators to the Development of International Commercial Arbitration Involving States and State Entities' in Andrea Carlevaris, Laurent Lévy, Alexis Mourre, Eric A Schwartz (eds), *International Arbitration Under Review. Essays in Honour of John Beechey* (ICC Publishing 2015) 401.

Simma, B, 'Self-contained Regimes' (1985) 16 Netherlands Yearbook of International Law 111.

Simma, B, 'The Work of the International Law Commission and its Fifty-Third Session (2001)' (2002) 71 Nordic Journal of International Law 123.

Simma, B, and Pulkowski, D, 'Of Planets and the Universe: Self-contained Regimes in International Law' (2006) 17 European Journal of International Law 483.

Simma, B, and Pulkowski, D, '*Leges Speciales* and Self-contained Regimes' in James Crawford, Alain Pellet, and Simon Olleson (eds), *The Law of International Responsibility* (Oxford University Press 2010) 139.

Simma, B, and Pulkowski, D, 'Two Worlds, but not Apart: International Investment Law and General International Law' in Marc Bungenberg, Jörn Griebel, Stephan Hobe, and August Reinisch (eds), *International Investment Law* (CH Beck-Hart-Nomos 2015) 361.

Sinclair, A C, 'The Origins of the Umbrella Clause in the International Law of Investment Protection' (2004) 20 Arbitration International 411.

Sinclair, A C, 'ICSID's Nationality Requirements' (2008) 23 ICSID Review—Foreign Investment Law Journal 57.

Sinclair, I, 'The Law of Sovereign Immunity. Recent Developments' (1980) 167 Recueil des Cours 113.

Singer, M, 'The Act of State Doctrine of the United Kingdom: An Analysis with Comparisons to United States Practice' (1981) 75 American Journal of International Law 283.

Sloane, R D, 'Breaking the Genuine Link: The Contemporary International Legal Regulation of Nationality' (2009) 50 Harvard International Law Journal 1.

Sornarajah, M, 'Problems in Applying the Restrictive Theory of Sovereign Immunity' (1982) 31 International & Comparative Law Quarterly 661.

Sornarajah, M, *The International Law on Foreign Investment* (3rd edn, Cambridge University Press 2010).

Spinedi, M, 'La responsabilità dello Stato per comportamenti di *private contractors*' in Marina Spinedi, Alessandra Gianelli, and Maria Luisa Alaimo (eds), *La codificazione della responsabilità internazionale degli Stati alla prova dei fatti: problemi e spunti di riflessione* (Giuffrè 2006) 67.

Starke, J G, 'Imputability in International Delinquencies' (1938) 19 British Year Book of International Law 104.

Stern, B, 'Et si on utilisait la notion de préjudice juridique? Retour sur une notion délaissée à l'occasion de la fin des travaux de la C.D.I. sur la responsabilité des États' (2001) 47 Annuaire Français de Droit International 3.

Stern, B, 'The Elements of an Internationally Wrongful Act' in James Crawford, Alain Pellet, and Simon Olleson (eds), *The Law of International Responsibility* (Oxford University Press 2010) 193.

Stewart, D P, 'The UN Convention on Jurisdictional Immunities of States and Their Property' (2005) 99 American Journal of International Law 194.

Stiglitz, J E, et al, *The Economic Role of the State* (Arnold Heertje ed, Basil Blackwell in association with Bank Insinger de Beaufort NV 1989).

Stoupnitzky, A, *Statut international de l'U.R.S.S. État commerçant* (LGDJ 1936).

Sucharitkul, S, *State Immunities and Trading Activities in International Law* (Stevens & Sons 1959).

Sucharitkul, S, 'Immunities of Foreign States Before National Authorities' (1976) 149 Recueil des Cours 87.

Synvet, H, 'Quelques réflexions sur l'immunité d'exécution de l'Etat étranger' (1985) 112 Journal du Droit International (Clunet) 865.

T

Tams, C J, 'All's Well that Ends Well: Comments on the ILC's Articles on State Responsibility' (2002) 62 Zeitschrift für Ausländisches Öffentliches Recht und Völkerrecht 759.

Tomuschat, C, 'In the Twilight Zones of the State' in Isabelle Buffard, James Crawford, Alain Pellet, and Stephan Wittich (eds), *International Law Between Universalism and Fragmentation. Festschrift in Honour of Gerhard Hafner* (Martinus Nijhoff Publishers 2008) 479.

Tomuschat, C, 'Attribution of International Responsibility: Direction and Control' in Malcolm Evans and Panos Koutrakos (eds), *The International Responsibility of the European Union: European and International Perspectives* (Hart Publishing 2013) 7.

Toninelli, P A, 'The Rise and Fall of Public Enterprise. The Framework' in Pier Angelo Toninelli (ed), *The Rise and Fall of State-Owned Enterprise in the Western World* (Cambridge University Press 2000) 3.

Townsend, A, 'State Responsibility for Acts of De Facto Agents' (1997) 14 Arizona Journal of International & Comparative Law 635.

Trachtman, J P, 'L'Etat, C'est Nous: Sovereignty, Economic Integration and Subsidiarity' (1992) 33 Harvard International Law Journal 459.

Troboff, P D, 'Foreign State Immunity: Emerging Consensus on Principles' (1986) 200 Recueil des Cours 235.

V

van Aaken, A, 'Blurring Boundaries between Sovereign Acts and Commercial Activities: A Functional View on Regulatory Immunity and Immunity from Execution' in Anne Peters, Evelyne Lagrange, Stefan Oeter, and Christian Tomuschat (eds), *Immunities in the Age of Global Constitutionalism* (Brill 2015) 131.

van Houtte, H, and Concolino, B, 'The Iran-United States Claims Tribunal and its Contribution to International Law' in Geert De Baere and Jan Wouters (eds), *The Contribution of International and Supranational Courts to the Rule of Law* (Edward Elgar Publishing, Inc 2015) 303.

(de) Vattel, E, *Le droit des gens, ou principes de la loi naturelle, appliqués à la conduit et aux affaires des nations et des souverains* (Londres 1758).

Verdross, A, '*Jus Dispositivum* and *Jus Cogens* in International Law' (1966) 60 American Journal of International Law 55.

Verhoeven, J, (ed), *Le droit international des immunités: contestation ou consolidation?* (Larcier 2004).

Villalpando, S M, 'Attribution of Conduct to the State: How the Rules of State Responsibility May be Applied within the WTO Dispute Settlement System' (2002) 5 Journal of International Economic Law 393.

W

Wade, E C S, 'Act of State in English Law: Its Relation with International Law' (1934) 15 British Year Book of International Law 98.

Wälde, T W, and Wouters, P K, 'State Responsibilty and the Energy Charter Treaty: the Rules Regarding State Enterprises, Entities, and Subnational Authorities' (1997) 2 Hofstra Law and Policy Symposium 117.

Wälde, T W, 'The "Umbrella" Clause in Investment Arbitration: a Comment on Original Intentions and Recent Cases' (2005) 6 Journal of World Investment & Trade 183.

Wedderburn, K W, 'Sovereign Immunity of Foreign Public Corporations' (1957) 6 International & Comparative Law Quarterly 290.

Wehberg, H, 'Pacta Sunt Servanda' (1959) 53 American Journal of International Law 775.

Weiss, A, 'Compétence ou incompétence des tribunaux a l'égard des États étrangers' (1923) 1 Recueil des Cours 521.

Wengler, W, *Völkerrecht*, Bd 1 (Springer Verlag 1964).

Wittich, S, 'The International Law Commission's Articles on the Responsibility of States for Internationally Wrongful Acts Adopted on Second Reading' (2002) 15 Leiden Journal of International Law 891.

Woolsey, L H, 'The Arbitration of the Sabotage Claims Against Germany' (1939) 33 American Journal of International Law 737.

Wolfrum, R, 'State Responsibility for Private Actors: an Old Problem of Renewed Relevance' in Maurizio Ragazzi (ed), *International Responsibility Today. Essays in Memory of Oscar Schachter* (Martinus Nijhoff Publishers 2005) 423.

Y

Yannaca-Small, K, 'What about this "Umbrella Clause"?' in Katia Yannaca-Small (ed), *Arbitration under International Investment Agreements: A Guide to the Key Issues* (Oxford University Press 2010) 479.

Z

Karl Zemanek, 'Appropriate Instruments for Codification. Reflections on the ILC Draft on State Responsibility' in *Studi di diritto internazionale in onore di Gaetano Arangio-Ruiz,* Volume II (Editoriale Scientifica 2004) 897.

Index

Note: *For the benefit of digital users, indexed terms that span two pages (e.g., 52–53) may, on occasion, appear on only one of those pages.*